THE WHISKEY MERCHANT'S DIARY

JOSEPH J. MERSMAN

Edited by Linda A. Fisher

The WHISKEY MERCHANT'S Diary

An Urban Life in the Emerging Midwest

OHIO UNIVERSITY PRESS ATHENS

Ohio University Press, Athens, Ohio 45701
www.ohio.edu/oupress

Ohio University Press books are printed on acid-free paper ∞ ™

14 13 12 11 10 09 08 07 5 4 3 2 1

Library of Congress Cataloging-in-Publication Data

Mersman, Joseph J., 1824–1892.
The whiskey merchant's diary : an urban life in the emerging Midwest / Joseph J. Mersman ; edited by Linda A. Fisher.
p. cm.
Includes bibliographical references and index.
ISBN-13: 978-0-8214-1745-4 (hc : alk. paper)
ISBN-10: 0-8214-1745-2 (hc : alk. paper)
ISBN-13: 978-0-8214-1746-1 (pb : alk. paper)
ISBN-10: 0-8214-1746-0 (pb : alk. paper)
1. Mersman, Joseph J., 1824–1892—Diaries. 2. German Americans—Ohio—Cincinnati—19th century—Diaries. 3. German Americans—Missouri—Saint Louis—19th century—Diaries. 4. German Americans—Ohio—Cincinnati—Social conditions—19th century. 5. German Americans—Missouri—Saint Louis—Social conditions—19th century. 6. Cincinnati (Ohio)—History—19th century. 7. Saint Louis (Mo.)—History—19th century. 8. Liquor industry—Ohio—Cincinnati—History—19th century. 9. Liquor industry—Missouri—Saint Louis—History—19th century. I. Fisher, Linda A., 1947–2006. II. Title.
F499.C553M47 2007
305.8931077866090'34—dc22

2006037207

I have so incessantly applied myself and have become what I at present am, i.e. fully competent to Cope with the world, and fight my way with the permission and blessings of the Allmighty towards an easy Competence.

—Joseph J. Mersman, 31 January 1849

CONTENTS

ILLUSTRATIONS

MAPS

PREFACE

And this Song of the Vine,
This greeting of mine,
The winds and the birds shall deliver
To the Queen of the West,
In her garlands dressed,
On the banks of the Beautiful River.
—Longfellow, "Catawba Wine"[1]

When you begin reading a diary, you drop abruptly into someone else's life. In order to make sense of the people, places, and events—all familiar to the writer—you must master a vocabulary of names and locations. Joseph J. Mersman's journal, filled with thirty dozen people, fifteen dozen locations, and a vocabulary of words whose meanings have changed, reveals the activities of a German American bachelor who aspired to be a self-made man. He describes the bounties "[o]n the banks of the Beautiful River," for Mersman was a liquor merchant in Cincinnati, the city of Longfellow's poem, before he moved to St. Louis in 1849. Mersman's record tells how he faced the challenges of mid-nineteenth-century American frontier cities.

When I first discovered this diary in 1993, I was preparing a lecture about the 1849 cholera epidemic in St. Louis. I didn't relate to most of the entries, but I did comprehend Mersman's description of cholera and then syphilis. The symptoms of those diseases have remained constant despite progress in treatment, and medical school prepared me well to interpret that aspect of Mersman's life.

However, additional visits to the Missouri Historical Society stimulated my curiosity about the diary, and I began to search for information about the rest of Joseph Mersman's life: his circle of friends, his after-work activities, and his educational endeavors. I realized that thorough annotation would help any reader who was trying to make sense of Mersman's complex social network.

Studying the people, places, and events that filled Mersman's world has made details of nineteenth-century life become clearer to me. I learned about whiskey making, ballroom dancing, circus history, German immigration, theater history, card games, steamboat transportation, gender roles, Victorian etiquette, and much more. The research required about five years and took me to archives in twenty-five states, plus Germany. In the process, I stopped being just a physician and became a documentary editor. This volume compresses all that information and makes Mersman's complete record accessible, because you, too, may not be familiar with his era. The indexes and annotation provide succinct explanations that will help you decipher the significance of Mersman's remarks and focus on the aspects of importance to you. Whether you are a genealogist, a historian, or a student of American civilization, this diary contains details you will appreciate.

This is not just the story of a man who confronted serious disease. Longfellow's poem lauded a life in the antebellum West—and Joseph J. Mersman lived it.

Linda A. Fisher, MD
Annandale, Virginia

NOTES

1. At the time that Longfellow wrote, Ohio was the premier American wine region. In 1850, nearly one-quarter of the wine produced east of California originated in Hamilton County (Rorabaugh 104–6; Longfellow 107–9).

INTRODUCTION

> The historian can give you an orderly . . . account of major social practices and general events at particular times, but only a good diary can give you the fine detail and the wondrous confusions of daily life and the feelings and momentary reflections that reveal the living reality of the period.
>
> —William Matthews[1]

You hold in your hands the diary of a young man who lived first in Cincinnati, and then in St. Louis, during the heady days when the frontier of the United States began slightly west of the Mississippi River. His record gives us a bachelor's view of antebellum urban life, with all the power that a contemporaneous account can pack.

Joseph J. Mersman (1824–92), an immigrant from the Grand Duchy of Oldenburg (now part of the State of Lower Saxony in northwestern Germany), began writing in his notebook on 8 November 1847, at the age of twenty-three. Mersman reported his activities in a bound volume, small enough to fit into his coat pocket, which he called his "daily companion."[2] From time to time, Mersman mentioned current events of national importance, but mostly he wrote about his own activities. Making entries as he sat in his boardinghouse at bedtime, and also when he traveled, Mersman wrote nearly every day for fifteen months while living in Cincinnati, Ohio, before relocating to St. Louis, Missouri, in February 1849. For about two years after that he added notes once a week, and from June 1851 until September 1864 he made episodic entries. Unfortunately, his record was silent during the years of the Civil War, except for two brief entries. Although he wrote most of the diary in English, Mersman recorded some (less than 10 percent) of the entries in French and German, presented here with translation.

Mersman's diary, the record of a man transforming himself from an impoverished, unschooled newcomer into a successful, skilled merchant, provides a view of the path many took in the mid-nineteenth century. From 1833 to 1843, nearly 200,000 Germans entered the United States, primarily through the ports of Baltimore, New York, Philadelphia, and New Orleans.[3] Thousands traveled to Cincinnati, where the northeast quadrant of the city became an ethnic enclave. Because one reached that neighborhood by crossing the Miami and Erie Canal,[4]

Joseph J. Mersman (1824–93), c. 1850 (detail). Mersman was living in St. Louis by the time this photo was taken, and was preparing for his marriage. This is the picture of a young, successful businessman of the time. (Personal collection of Linda A. Fisher.)

which locals referred to as the "Rhine," the entire district became known as the "Over-the-Rhine" neighborhood. Encompassing nearly one hundred city blocks, the neighborhood included churches, schools, markets, beer gardens, and theaters as well as residences.[5] Gothic lettering on signage gave the streetscape a European look, and four German-language newspapers united the community. By the 1850 federal census, one-quarter of Cincinnati's population had been born in German states.[6]

Frontispiece of Mersman's diary. Mersman began his diary entries on November 8, 1847, although the frontispiece note begins it on November 10th. (Missouri Historical Society, St. Louis.)

Mersman's account—filled with work and play, eating and drinking, flirting and dancing—is an action-oriented journal with little introspection. However, several overarching themes unify the record:

Bachelor culture. Contemporaries referred to unmarried men in the nineteenth century as "rogue elephants," because they moved about in society unfettered by responsibility.[7] Mersman attended theater performances, patronized saloons, and danced until dawn. He documented boardinghouse experiences,

"The Soaplocks, or Bowery Boys." Newspaper and periodical articles of the times were sarcastic about urban bachelors, referring to them as "rogue elephants" and disparaging their lifestyle. (Nicolino Calyo, c. 1840, accession number 1980.33, Collection of the New York Historical Society.)

alcohol consumption, tobacco use, and membership in fraternal organizations. He described flirtation, courtship, and eventually marriage, providing insight into gender relations during his era.[8] The maps in this edition show the spatial relationships of residences, places of employment, and nightspots Mersman frequented.

Social networks. One-third of the residents of Mersman's hometown, some eighteen hundred individuals, immigrated to America during the 1830s, and many settled in Cincinnati.[9] German church services, philanthropies, singing societies (such as the *Liedertafel*), and other ethnic customs remained important to them, as the diarist notes. Mersman mentions dozens of individuals who were European transplants;[10] the Annotated List of Persons, Places, and Businesses identifies most of them and cites the sources of information.

Family relationships. The interactions of three families—the Mersmans, the Nulsens, and the Creuzbauers (the kinfolk of the diarist, his business partner, and his wife)—form the centerpiece of the diary. The relatives assumed multiple roles with respect to each other—friends, business partners, and in-laws—in a manner common in immigrant communities. Mersman's sister, Agnes Mersman Lake (1826–1907), wife of circus clown William Lake Thatcher (c. 1816–69) and later of James Butler "Wild Bill" Hickok (1837–76),[11] is just one of the many colorful relatives who appear on the pages. This diary documents Agnes Lake's early circus career, filling the gaps in the historical record, where Agnes herself provided misinformation. It also reveals how other family members aided Mersman's efforts to launch his wholesale tobacco and liquor business.

Business practices. Mersman was a whiskey rectifier.[12] He describes scrambling for capital, marketing his wares, and arranging transportation for his goods. To accomplish his business objectives, he uses steamboats, omnibuses, trains, and the telegraph. His story illustrates improvements in transportation and communication, puts a face on the growth of the American middle class, and reveals how merchants confronted the challenges that faced business development.

Language skills. Mersman's knowledge of English, French, and German appears throughout the diary and influences his choice of words. His idiosyncratic capitalization, spelling, and punctuation, reproduced in this volume, capture the diarist's language skills for further study by scholars.

Disease outbreaks. Mersman describes a community-wide cholera outbreak in 1849 and again in 1853. Unlike other residents who fled to the relative safety of the countryside, he remained in St. Louis and witnessed the epidemics' impact. Mersman also recorded the treatment for syphilis that he endured. His writing exemplifies the psychological stages that Elisabeth Kübler-Ross described in the twentieth century.[13] Mersman documents his denial, bargaining, anger, depression, and acceptance—profound emotions that resonate with the feelings patients experience today.

Personal finances. Partly an expense ledger and partly a social calendar, Mersman's diary details how he used his most precious resources—time and money. Repeatedly, he berates himself for wasting either. Paid an annual salary of seven hundred dollars (the equivalent of approximately $14,000 in 2005[14]) for his work as a store clerk, Mersman saved nearly 40 percent of his 1848 income so that he would have capital to start his own business the next year. By tallying Mersman's outlays for room, board, clothing, laundry, amusements, books, and other personal expenses, we see how much he valued various items. Despite his limited resources, he spent money on educational endeavors, such as flute lessons and French instruction.

Cultural assimilation. Throughout his account, Mersman reflects the national spirit of his day. Intensely patriotic, he celebrates the anniversary of the Battle of New Orleans, the end of the Mexican War, and the presidential election campaign of 1848. He notes the passing of John Quincy Adams and the visit of President-elect Zachary Taylor. Eventually, he becomes the founder and president of the Fourth National Bank of St. Louis. The enthusiasm of this German American immigrant for his new homeland demonstrates how one new arrival responded to American culture and politics.

Although Mersman had a keen sense of the dramatic, he never imagined that the secrets he entrusted to paper would someday appear in published form. Since he believed that he alone would read the entries during his lifetime, he recorded potentially embarrassing information such as drunkenness, prostitution, sexually transmitted disease, and marital discord. He envisioned an audience—a very small one—that might materialize only after he had gone to his grave.

On four occasions[15] Mersman wrote a last will and testament in his book, indicating that he thought his life was in peril and that he expected his relatives would read the journal after his death. However, Mersman's fears were unfounded: he died 26 March 1892, nearly twenty-seven years after making his final diary entry. By that time, he was sixty-seven years old, had been infirm for decades, and had been predeceased by his wife, Claudine; his brothers, Henry and Frank; and his older sister, Elizabeth. Of his siblings, only his younger sister, Agnes Lake, survived him.

Perhaps Mersman's heirs—his eight children—read the book, but eventually it came into the possession of John Henry Gundlach (1861–1926), a member of the Missouri Historical Society (MHS) who collected historical documents. In 1926, after Gundlach's death, his estate donated Mersman's diary to the MHS archives.[16] The book lay for nearly eighty years, carefully preserved in archival storage, but seldom opened. Now, more than a century after Mersman's demise, this edition makes his diary available to individuals outside of his family and outside of St. Louis. A case study of one man's experience in America's frontier cities, Mersman's record shows modern readers how American life has evolved in one hundred fifty years. Major gaps in the diary appear after 1851, but in this edition biographical information from other sources bridges the years when the author did not add to the record. By the conclusion of this record, Joseph J. Mersman, a self-made man, had established a thriving business, a growing family, and a responsible position in the community, offering his children opportunities found only in America.

NOTES

1. Arksey, ix.
2. JJM diary, 25 September 1864.
3. Wilcox, 1:404–11; Luebke, 100, 162.
4. Constructed in 1826, the canal remained in use until 1919. Now paved over, the route is known as Central Parkway (Wimberg, 4, 70).
5. Wimberg, 84.
6. Cist (2), 45, 47.
7. Chudacoff, 21.

8. Mersman wed Claudine Creuzbauer in January 1851. Only thirty-nine diary entries out of a total of 533 (about 7 percent) were made after that date.

9. Ostendorf, 164–95.

10. Schmaul has written that they were "transplanted but not uprooted"; whole villages emigrated and reassembled on American soil.

11. Laramie County Marriage Book B: 364–65, County Clerk's Office, Cheyenne, Wyoming.

12. Rectifying whiskey, the process of redistilling or reprocessing spirits to remove contaminants or increase the alcohol content, was a common practice in the pre–Civil War era (Carson, 66, 235–37; Monzert, 51–52, 64–68; Regan, 40–41).

13. Kübler-Ross, 38–137.

14. McCusker, 101–6.

15. JJM diary, 18 February 1849, 19 June 1849, 9 July 1851, and 28 July 1853.

16. "Accessions for July 1926," Minutes of the Missouri Historical Society, 18 November 1925–14 December 1927 (MHS Archives).

EDITORIAL NOTES

Joseph J. Mersman's diary, a single volume of unlined pale blue pages, measures 7½ inches by 9½ inches. The unlettered, half leather binding, with a mahogany spine and outer corners, features marbled boards. Hand-numbered pages, from 1 to 296, are covered on both sides with writing in ink that has faded to brown. The flyleaf, inscribed with Mersman's signature and rubric, is shown in the illustrations. Mersman wrote several undated notes on the front and back endleaves; they appear in the appendix.

This edition aims to convert Mersman's very legible text into typescript as literally as possible. The entire text, without omissions, has been preserved with Mersman's creative spelling, erratic capitalization, and imperfect grammar. Words struck out in the original are transcribed with a strike-out bar through them. Most of the journal was written in English, although some entries are entirely in French or German. Several editorial policies deserve elaboration:

Spelling reflects Mersman's pronunciation, his knowledge of foreign languages, and his association with an English-born grocer. At the time Mersman put pen to paper, orthography was not standardized. The many misspelled words on these pages, not marked with an editorial [*sic*], show exactly how the diarist wrote. A puzzled reader may discern the diarist's meaning by reading passages aloud. In this manner, "magasin's" can be identified as "magazines," "brot" as "brought," and "preciding" as "presiding." Mersman occasionally used common spellings of the day, now considered to be British spellings, for example, "labour," "parlour," and "behaviour." Some errors, such as "thing" for "think," "els" for "else," and "avery" for "every," suggest how Mersman spoke. In some instances, to facilitate comprehension, the correct spelling appears in brackets, [thus].

Mersman often used multiple spellings to refer to the same individual, and we retained such variations in the text. For example, Mersman wrote the surname of his roommate, "Delamater," also as "Delamettre," "Delamaitre," "DeLaMaître," and ten other ways. The Annotated List of Persons, Places, and Businesses lists Mersman's variations, with entries alphabetized according to the spelling found in city directories. Most of Mersman's friends have been identified with reasonable certainty; citations may help readers search further.

In a few instances, for example, "Mr. Bradley," research was inconclusive. Mr. Dow and Sarah Cook are among those unidentified because multiple individuals with similar names and ages resided in the same locale. Women were especially difficult to trace because of name changes that followed matrimony.

For geographical locations, English spellings are used, for example, Hanover (German, *Hannover*). Throughout the annotation and indices, "Oldenburg" refers to the Grand Duchy of Oldenburg; "Hanover" indicates the Kingdom of Hanover; and "Baden" indicates the Grand Duchy of Baden.

Capitalization in the source text is both inconsistent and uncertain. In many instances, Mersman's capitalization of letters such as "e," "c," "m," "o," "s," "t," and "w" becomes a matter of judgment. For example, he wrote the letter "s" at the beginning of words four different ways: one is clearly lowercase, one is definitely uppercase, and two are indeterminate. Mersman did not necessarily start sentences with capital letters, but he often capitalized nouns and important words. He did not capitalize the adjectival forms referring to foreign languages, such as "german" and "french." This approach to capitalization follows the grammatical rules of German. In this edition, modern usage appears when Mersman's intent, a capital or lowercase letter, was unclear.

Mersman's capitalized letters are reproduced with two notable exceptions. Mersman wrote the letter "K" almost always as a capital, even in the middle of a word. Similarly, he used a capital "V" whenever it was the first letter of a word. To facilitate reading, those letters now follow modern usage.

Punctuation appears generally as Mersman wrote it, but punctuation missing because of the gutter or edge of the page is silently supplied. Mersman did not use commas with appositives, parenthetical expressions, or compound sentences, so his sentences may require several readings to fully appreciate his meaning. He sometimes wrote terminal punctuation that looked like commas; but those appear here as periods. Terminal dashes remain as Mersman wrote them. Missing terminal punctuation is otherwise indicated by a longer space between sentences.

Mersman wrote abbreviations such as "i e" for "id est," "do" for "ditto," and honorifics ("Mr," "Mrs," and "Dr") without punctuation. He wrote contractions incorrectly—such as "did'nt," "had'nt," and "could'nt"—and used apostrophes to indicate plurals, e.g., "solo's," and "duette's." All these errors are reproduced. Words underlined for emphasis appear as Mersman wrote them. The names of books, plays, and steamboats are italicized and the quotation marks that Mersman sometimes put around them have been removed.

Mersman's most common **abbreviations** appear at the end of this summary. Text in square brackets, e.g., bdy [brandy], or annotation will help readers discern Mersman's meaning. Mersman often used initials for the names of individuals. In instances where the full name is known, the missing letters are supplied, e.g., M[oulinier]. If a name has been expanded in brackets, Mersman's punctuation has been removed. Mersman recorded his expenses, and routinely put dollar and cents signs *following* numbers, as did many other writers of his day. For example, he wrote "65$" for "sixty-five dollars" and "30c" or "30¢" for "thirty cents." Mersman's style of recording currency and his ampersands have been retained. Superscript letters and interlineations have been lowered.

French and German language words or phrases appear in italics and are translated in the annotation, with an identifying [Fr.] or [Ger.]. For example, "*Schwager*" is translated as "[Ger.] brother-in-law." Entries written entirely in French or German are transcribed with an English translation immediately following.

Line breaks, pagination, and spacing of the original are not replicated in this transcription, but paragraphs are indicated as Mersman wrote them. Obvious slips of the pen (for example, duplicate words) were removed and quotation marks were closed. Some missing words have been supplied in square brackets [thus] or indicated [?] when they could not be guessed. Mersman commonly omitted articles and wrote abrupt sentences. Crossed-out words or interlineations are rare in the original manuscript, suggesting that the diarist wrote a draft before copying some entries into his bound book. The few corrections Mersman indicated have been printed in the corrected form. Mersman added marginal notes in some instances, usually recording financial details that he had omitted earlier. Each note, identified with square brackets, is printed following the associated entry.

Annotation explains the text and clarifies many details of Mersman's world. Illustrations include maps, advertisements, and period portraits. The Annotated List of Persons, Places, and Businesses provides biographical information about individuals and details about locations as Mersman knew them.

We hope that this edition's fidelity to the original text will permit readers to appreciate Mersman's trilingual competence, enjoy his humor, and make discoveries of their own.

NOTES

1. Baptized "Maria Elisabeth Pohlschneider," JJM's older sister appears as the anglicized "Elizabeth" throughout his diary. Following a longstanding tradition, German immigrants commonly used the second or third baptized name as the given name.

ABBREVIATIONS USED BY JOSEPH J. MERSMAN

Amt	amount
bbls	barrels
Bdy	brandy
c, cts	cents
clk	clock
&c	et cetera
do	ditto
Exp	expenses
gls, gall	gallons
Hhd	hogshead
inst	instant, the present month
N. O.	New Orleans
Spt	spirits
ulto	ultimo, the previous month

EDITORIAL MARKS

[Margin note]	entries written in the diary margin, perpendicular to other text.
[missing]	missing word or letters known
[?]	missing word or letters unknown
crossout	crossed-out word
[Translation]	translation
[Fr.]	word or phrase translated from French
[Ger.]	word or phrase translated from German
[Lat.]	word or phrase translated from Latin
?	unknown
&	indicates a business partnership
b.	born
c.	circa, approximately
d.	died, death
fl.	flourished
JJM	Joseph J. Mersman
JCN	John Clemens Nulsen
N & M	Nulsen & Mersman
m.	married

CHRONOLOGY OF JOSEPH J. MERSMAN'S LIFE

17 July 1824	JJM is born in Borringhausen, a hamlet of Damme, in the Duchy of Oldenburg, the fourth of six surviving children of Catharina Maria Pohlschneider and Friedrich Messmann. He is baptized "Johann Joseph Jacob Pohlschneider."
1832	JJM's older sister Elisabeth (eighteen years old) and brother Friedrich (fifteen) emigrate to America.
27 February 1833	JJM's mother, Catharina Maria Pohlschneider, dies in Damme.
Spring 1833	JJM's father, Friedrich Messmann, sells the Pohlschneider farm and sails from Bremen to Baltimore with the four youngest children: Heinrich (twelve), Joseph (nine), Agnes (seven), and Franz (five). They anglicize their first names to Frederick, Henry, Joseph, Agnes, and Frank and use the surname Messmann.
1833	JJM's family settles in a German settlement in northwest Ohio called Stallotown (today, Minster).
1834	JJM's sister, Elizabeth Messmann, marries Arnd Kattenhorn, a Cincinnati grocer, and soon has two daughters, Sophia and Louisa Kattenhorn.
1836	JJM attends school taught by the village priest in Minster.
Summer 1837	JJM gets his first job, as a waterboy on the Miami and Ohio Canal.
18 January 1839	JJM begins an apprenticeship with Edmund Dexter, a Cincinnati merchant who teaches him how to rectify whiskey and keep business records.
1840	JJM, his father, and siblings appear in the 1840 federal census as the "Henry Messman" household in Cincinnati, Ohio.

1842	Henry Messman establishes a tobacco business in Cincinnati with an immigrant from Hanover, Anthony Nulsen, styled as Nulsen & Mersman. The family begins to use Mersman as their surname.
19 August 1845	Henry Mersman marries Adelaide Tebbelman, another immigrant from Oldenburg, in Cincinnati.
1 May 1846	JJM's younger sister, Agnes Mersman, marries a circus clown, William Lake Thatcher, and begins a life as a professional equestrian and rope-walker.
8 November 1847	JJM begins his diary and documents his activities in Cincinnati.
18 January 1849	JJM completes his apprenticeship with Edmund Dexter.
1 March 1849	JJM relocates to St. Louis, Missouri, and establishes a whiskey and tobacco business styled as Nulsen & Mersman with John Clemens Nulsen, Anthony Nulsen's younger brother.
March–July, 1849	A cholera epidemic decimates Cincinnati, St. Louis, and other American cities. JJM celebrates his survival.
9 December 1849	JJM reports symptoms of secondary syphilis and starts treatment with Dr. Ignatius Petri, a German doctor.
3 June 1850	JJM visits Cincinnati to seek a second opinion about treatment for syphilis from Dr. Franz Joseph Obendorf, a German doctor. JJM conducts business for Nulsen & Mersman as well.
June–November, 1850	JJM undergoes additional treatment for syphilis as directed by Drs. Obendorf and Petri.
December 1850	Dr. Petri pronounces JJM cured; JJM proposes marriage to Claudine Creuzbauer, his partner's sister-in-law.
30 January 1851	JJM marries Claudine Creuzbauer in St. Louis at a private residence.
31 March 1852	Birth of Joseph John Mersman Jr., JJM's first child.
2 February 1853	JJM joins Erwin Lodge # 121 of the Masonic Order and works to become a prominent St. Louis merchant.
13 March 1855	Birth of Frederick Clemens Mersman, JJM's second child.
28 September 1857	Birth of Clara Caroline Mersman, JJM's third child.

18 November 1859	Birth of Arthur Arnd Mersman, JJM's fourth child. Arnd and Elizabeth Kattenhorn are his godparents (4 June 1860).
12 April 1861	The Civil War begins. Nulsen & Mersman establish contracts with the U.S. government to provide whiskey to federal troops.
29 March 1862	Birth of Emma C. Mersman, JJM's fifth child. Claudine Mersman, her mother, is named her godparent (30 January 1876).
1 February 1864	JJM becomes president of the Fourth National Bank of St. Louis.
21 April 1864	JJM's father dies in Cincinnati.
18 September 1864	Birth of Otto Lewis Mersman, JJM's sixth child. Ottilie Creuzbauer Rhoades is named his godmother (28 January 1865). JJM makes his last diary entry.
12 October 1864	Henry Mersman dies in Cincinnati.
24 January 1865	JJM becomes a naturalized citizen in St. Louis.
9 April 1865	The Civil War ends.
Summer 1865	JJM develops eye problems. He resigns from the presidency of the Fourth National Bank of St. Louis.
11 January 1866	Frank Mersman dies in Cincinnati of "lung fever."
1867	Nulsen & Mersman is dissolved. Peper, Rassfield & Company continues the wholesale liquor business.
6 June 1868	Birth of Alice Albertine Mersman, JJM's seventh child. Albertine Nulsen and Clemens Nulsen are named godparents (17 July 1869).
25 February 1870	JJM resigns his membership in the Erwin Lodge.
1870	JJM provides capital for Charles F. Orthwein (JCN's son-in-law) to expand his St. Louis-based grain business. The firm Orthwein & Mersman prospers.
4 November 1871	Birth of Ella Claudine Mersman, JJM's eighth (and last) child.
30 July 1880	JJM retires. Orthwein & Mersman is dissolved. Orthwein continues with his brother, William D. Orthwein, and calls the business Orthwein Brothers.

10 December 1881	Elizabeth Mersman Kattenhorn, JJM's sister, dies in Cincinnati.
21 February 1890	Claudine Mersman dies in St. Louis of "senile gangrene."
26 March 1892	JJM dies of "paralysis" (probably complications of advanced syphilis) in St. Louis, leaving a large estate to be shared by his eight children. Two testamentary trusts manage the assets for decades.
1896	One dispute among the Mersman heirs reaches the Missouri Supreme Court. Other disagreements about the management of JJM's estate continue to erupt for decades.
22 August 1907	Agnes Mersman Lake, JJM's last surviving sibling, dies in Jersey City, New Jersey.
9 October 1953	The testamentary trusts established by JJM are terminated with the final distribution of funds to his heirs.

MAPS

Map 1. The valleys of the Ohio and Mississippi rivers, showing towns of significance to JJM. (NB: West Virginia was formed as a separate state in 1863.)

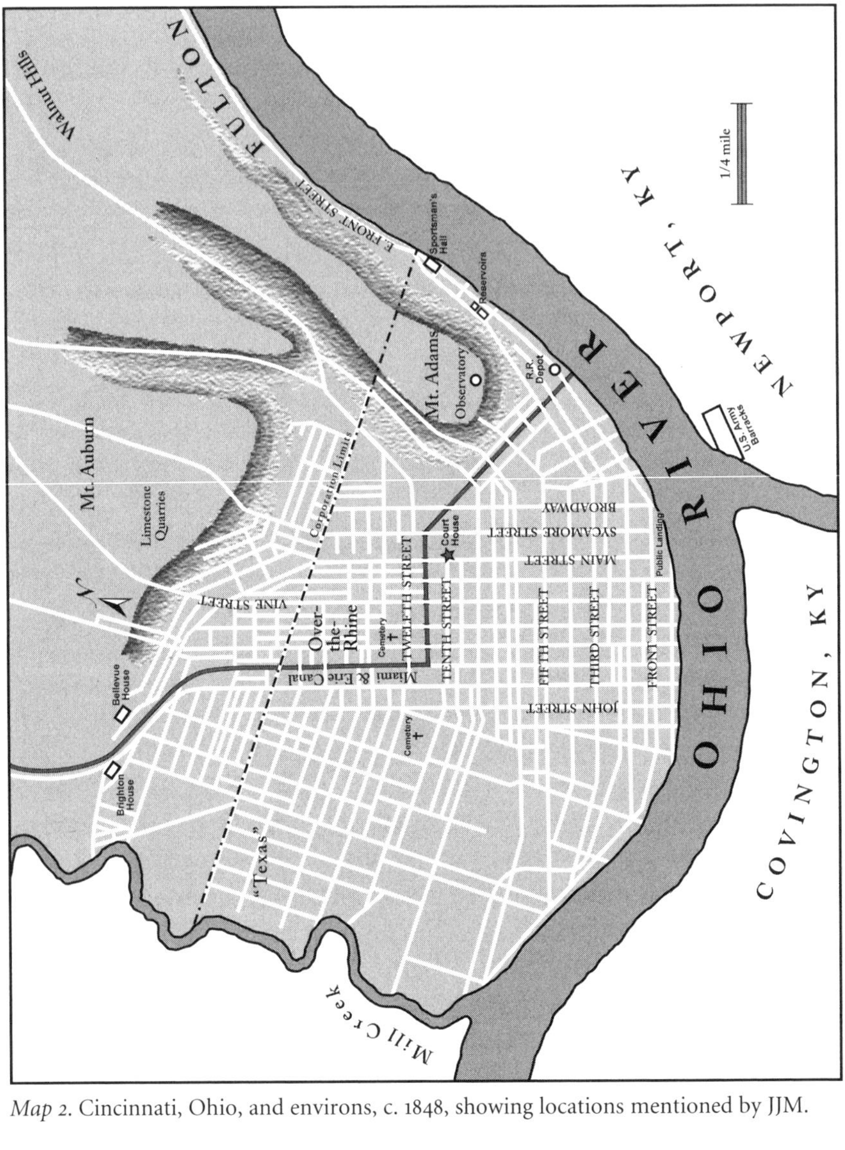

Map 2. Cincinnati, Ohio, and environs, c. 1848, showing locations mentioned by JJM.

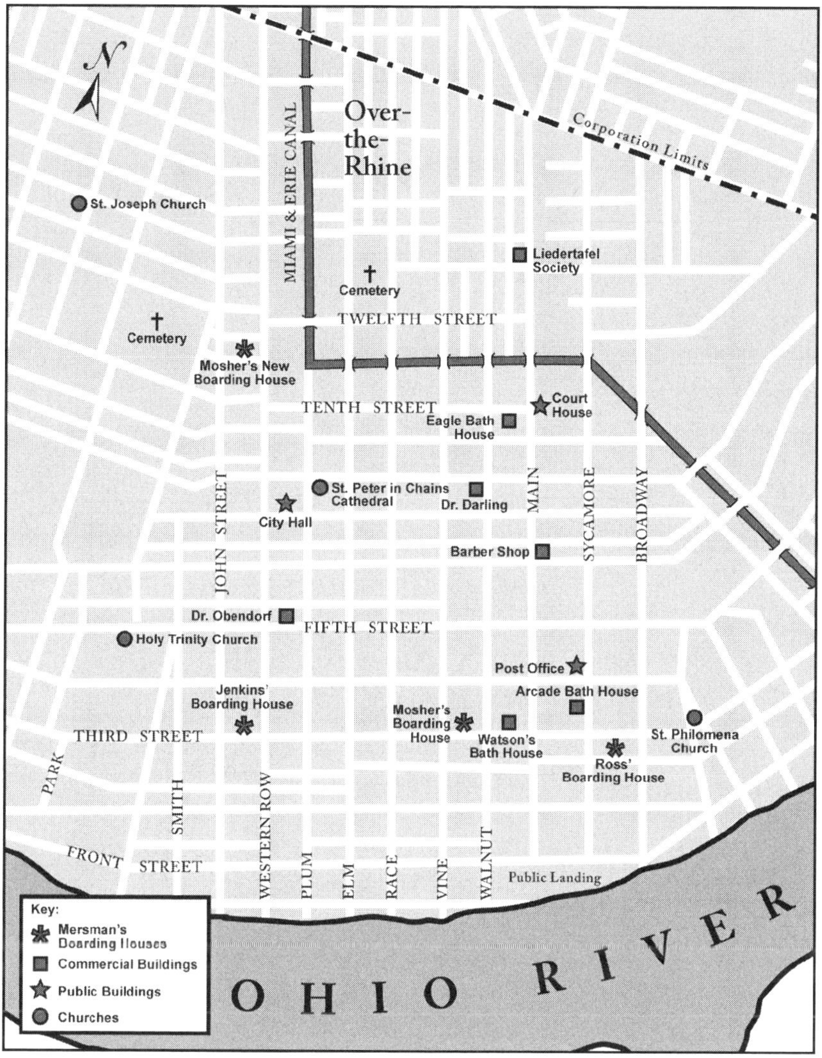

Map 3. Downtown Cincinnati, c. 1848, showing the location of boardinghouses, churches, and personal services used by JJM.

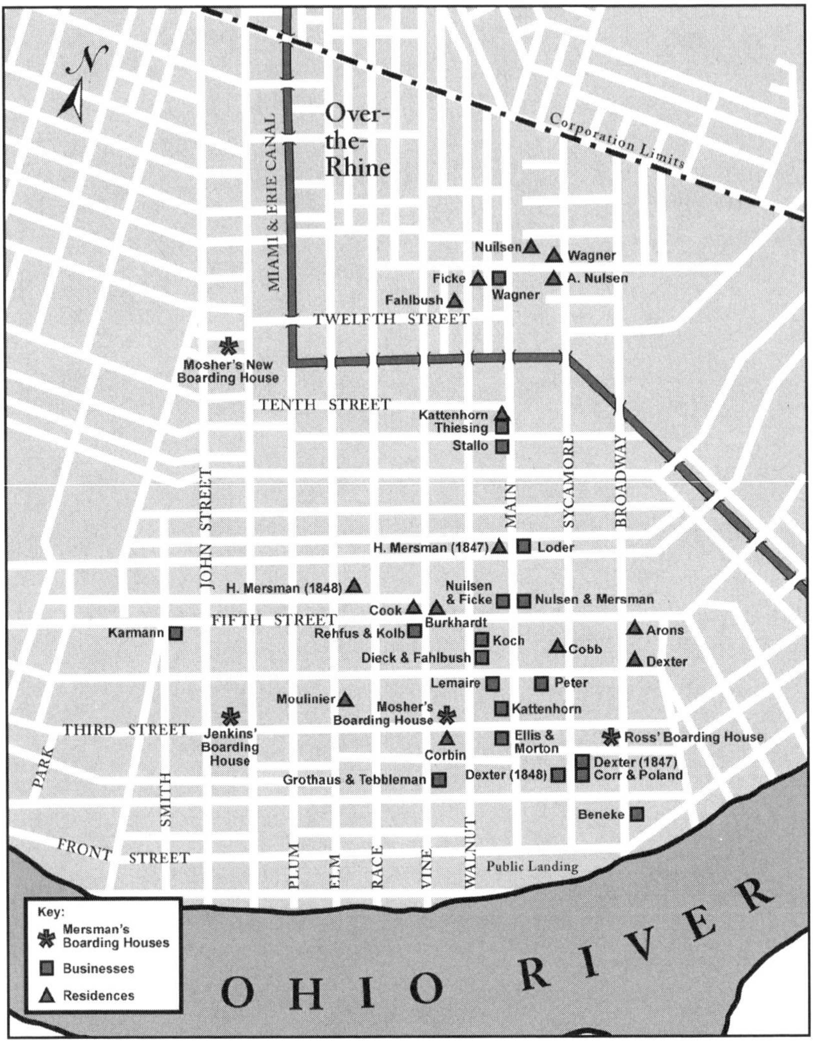

Map 4. Downtown Cincinnati, c. 1848, showing the location of the businesses and residences of JJM's family and friends.

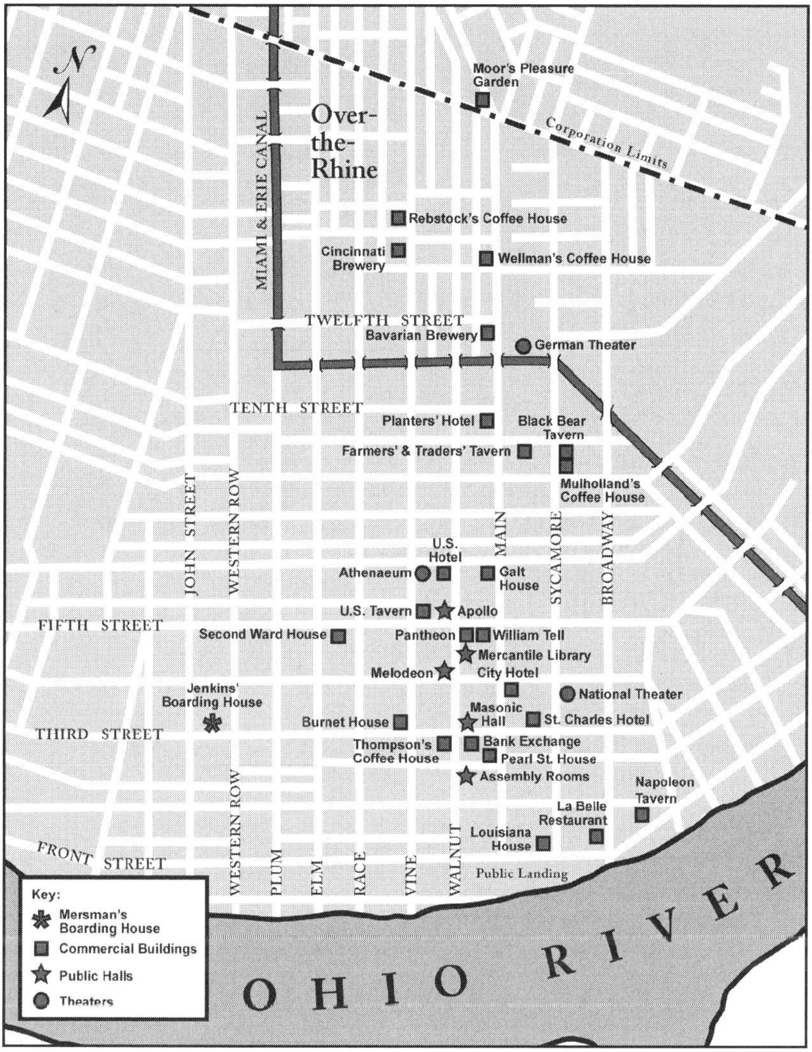

Map 5. Downtown Cincinnati, c. 1848, showing the location of the theaters, saloons, and restaurants frequented by JJM.

Map 6. The Miami and Erie Canal, c. 1848, showing towns mentioned in JJM's account of his canal boat travels.

Map 7. St. Louis County, Missouri, and environs, c. 1853, including Jefferson and Franklin counties.

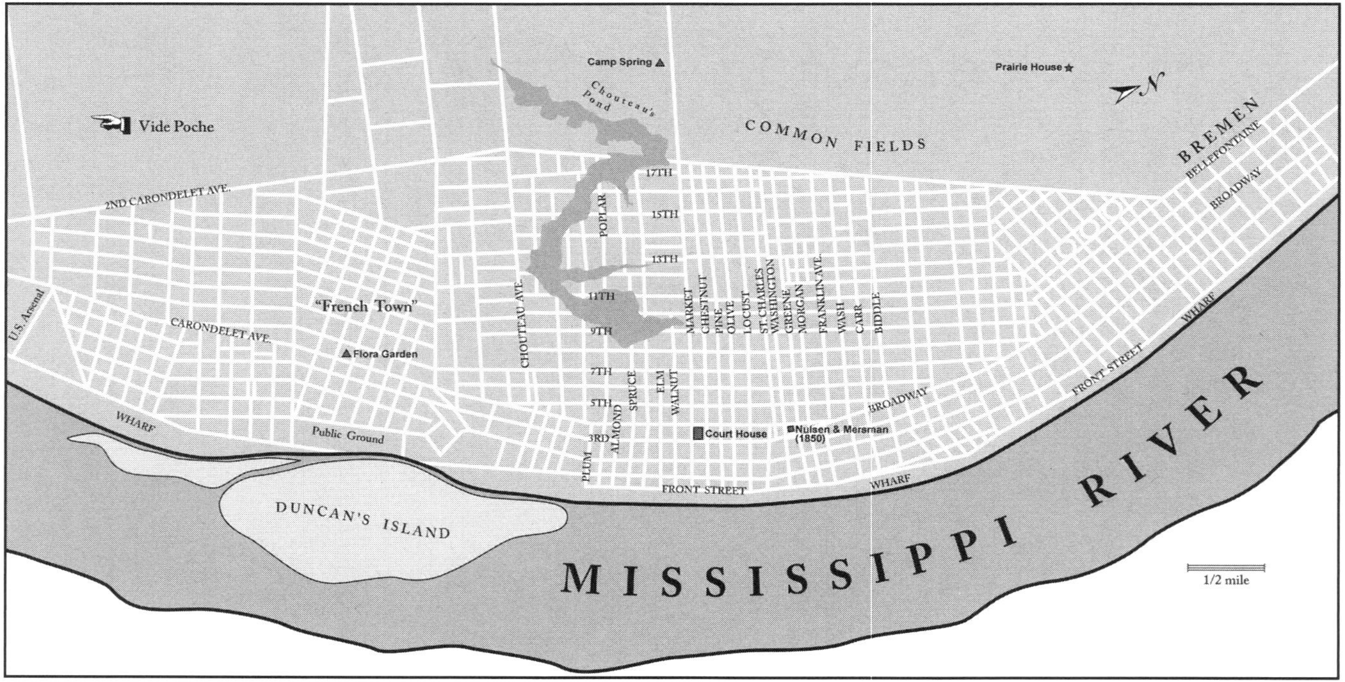

Map 8. City of St. Louis, c. 1849, showing locations mentioned by JJM.

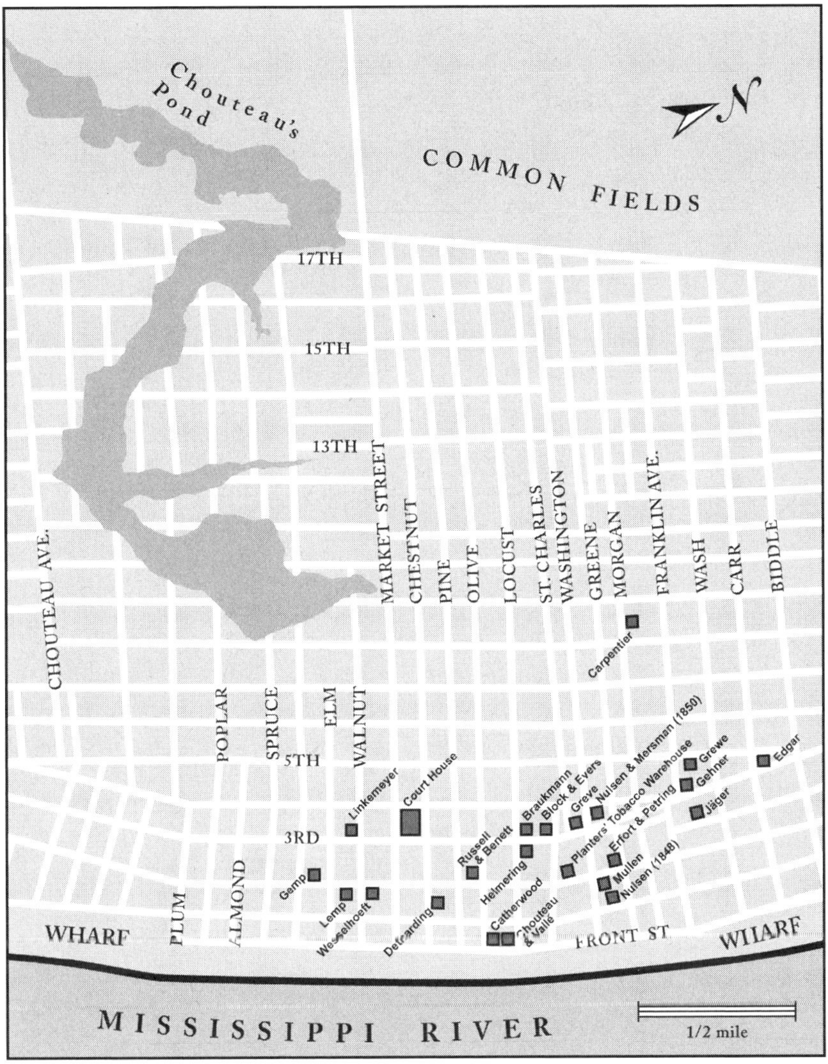

Map 9. Downtown St. Louis, c. 1849, showing the location of the businesses of JJM's friends and associates.

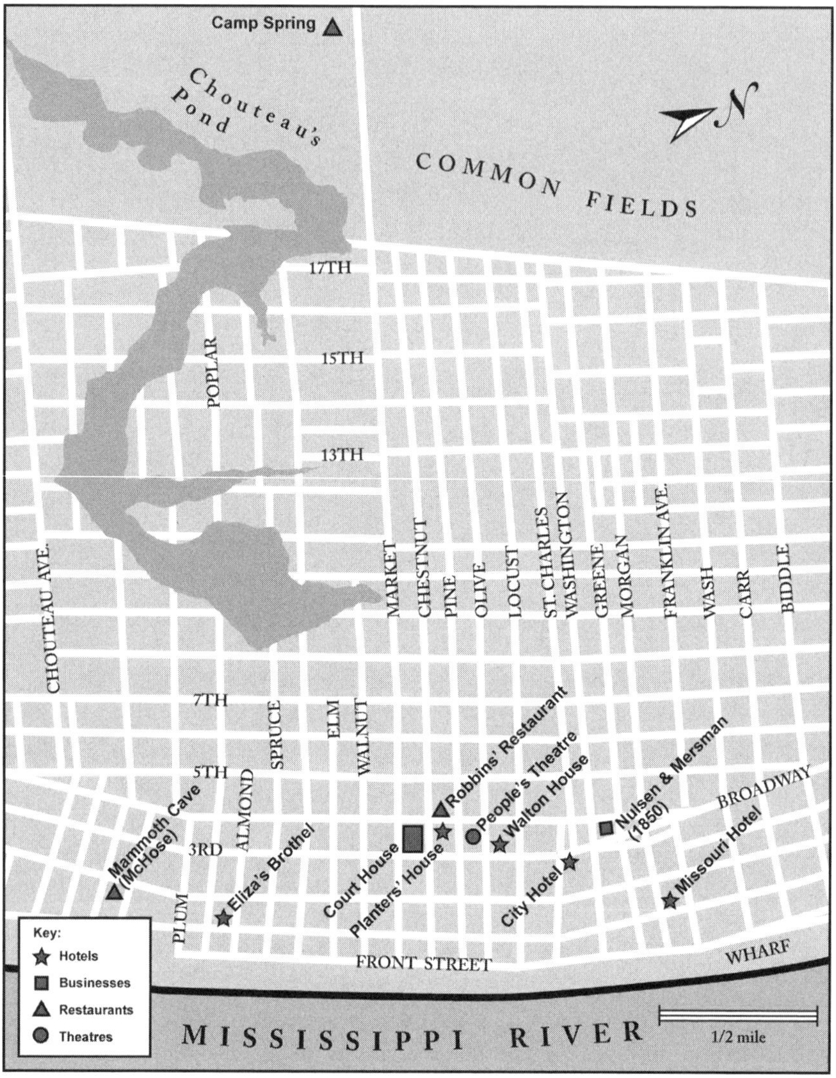

Map 10. Downtown St. Louis, c. 1849, showing the location of the theaters, hotels, and restaurants mentioned by JJM.

PEDIGREES

Mersman Family Tree

- Catharina Pohlschneider (1789–1833) m. 1811 Friedrich Messmann (1782–1864)
  - Elizabeth (1813–81) m. 1834 Arnd Kattenhorn (1810–87)
  - Frederick (1815–c. 1833)
  - Henry (1820–64) m. 1842 Mary Imsicke (c. 1825–c. 1844) m. 1845 Adelaide Tebbelman (1830–81)
  - Joseph (1824–92) m. 1851 Claudine Creuzbauer (1830–90)
    - Joseph John Jr. 31 March 1852–2 August 1925
    - Frederick Clemens 13 March 1855–14 December 1918
    - Clara Caroline 28 September 1857–1 September 1929
    - Arthur Arnd 18 November 1859–28 December 1904
    - Emma C. 29 March 1862–25 May 1942
    - Otto Lewis 18 September 1864–28 December 1940
    - Alice Albertine 6 June 1868–11 July 1943
    - Ella Claudine 4 November 1871–25 October 1952
  - Maria Agnes (1826–1907) m. 1846 William Lake Thatcher (1817–69) m. 1876 James Butler "Wild Bill" Hickock (1837–76) m. 1877 "Texas George" Carson (c. 1850–?)
  - Frank (1828–66)

Nulsen Family Tree*

- Phillippine Holstein (1790–1856) m. 1807 Franz Nülsen (1778–1843)
  - Francis Nuilsen** (1809–63) m. 1839 Dorothea Tice
  - Joseph (1811–57) m. 1843 Mary Pinger
  - Amalia (1814–89) m. 1840 Dr. Ludwig S. Jacoby (1813–74)
  - Philippina (1818–1908) m. 1842 Augustus Wagner (1818–86)
  - Anthony (1821–1907) m. 1845 Maria Risch (1828–1905)
  - John Clemens (1824–1906) m. 1848 Albertine Creuzbauer (1830–98)
  - Henry (1826–1911) m. 1849 Magdalena Reuter (?–1862) m. 1864 Rosalie Mueller (1832–1914)

- Caroline Phillipine, 5 March 1849–22 December 1908
- Anna Ottilla, 22 August 1852–14 July 1899
- Anthony Joseph, 10 June 1856–20 March 1938
- Maximillian A., 16 July 1858–16 September 1897
- Julia Estella, 23 July 1860–15 March 1924
- Maria Alice, 9 May 1862–28 January 1936
- Julia Clementine, 14 February 1865–1957
- Francis Edwin, 12 August 1867–12 August 1934
- Albert George, 1 February 1870–7 May 1942

*Does not include children who died.

** While the rest of the family adopted "Nulsen" as the spelling in America, Francis persisted with a slightly different surname.

Creuzbauer Family Tree

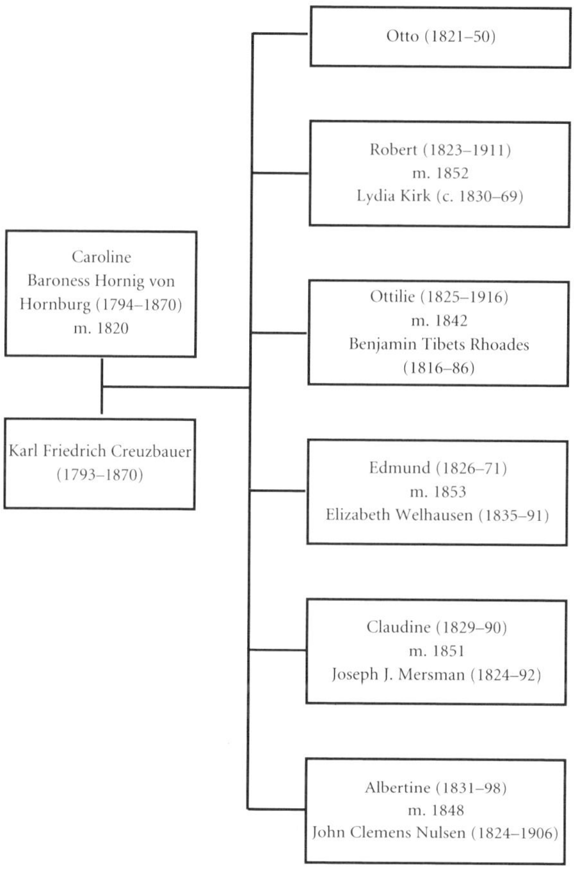

PROLOGUE

Two Immigrant Families and Their Start in America

Although the author of this diary inscribed his book with the signature "Joseph J. Mersman" and a rubric, that name is an American invention, not a birthright. To document the child's birth on 17 July 1824,[1] the village priest wrote "Johann Joseph Jacob Pohlschneider" in the church book of Saint Viktor's parish, in the village of Damme, the Grand Duchy of Oldenburg.

The seventh child of Friedrich Messmann and Catharina Maria Pohlschneider, Joseph was born on a farm originally owned by his maternal grandparents, approximately one hundred miles southwest of Bremen and directly east of the Netherlands, in what is now Lower Saxony. Following local custom, when Joseph's parents married in April 1811 and settled on the twelve acres that belonged to the bride's parents, they began using the farm name as their surname. The Pohlschneider farm became the home of a new Pohlschneider family, and Friedrich Messmann, once a hired hand, soon became a farm owner called Friedrich Pohlschneider.[2] By 1828, six of his children played in the yard: sons Friedrich, Heinrich, Joseph, and Franz, and daughters Elisabeth and Agnes. Three other little Pohlschneiders had died in early childhood.[3]

Joseph Pohlschneider's early life was typical of that community of subsistence farmers. Surrounded by bogs, the ground around Damme was perpetually so damp that families planted rye, not wheat, as the grain for bread.[4] The farmers cut peat moss from the moor to burn as fuel and used ditches instead of fences to divide the fields. The villagers wore winter clothing made from sheep's wool, and summer apparel made from linen. Chickens and hogs provided most of the animal protein in the diet. Dozens of men from Joseph's village migrated annually to work in hay fields in the Netherlands, bringing home cash that helped their families in Oldenburg, but Joseph's father found another way to earn talers:[5] he rolled cigars from American tobacco and had his children help by sorting the leaves and stacking molds.[6]

As Joseph grew older and the population in his homeland increased, economic conditions in his homeland became precarious. Farm families multiplied, but economic opportunities failed to materialize. Crop failures, a shrinking job market, and the sheer lack of available land forced many to leave.[7] In the 1830s, hundreds from Damme and neighboring villages emigrated to the United States, sailing from Bremerhaven to Baltimore.[8] Passage cost some thirty-five talers, took about six weeks, and was fraught with danger, but the promise of a better life made it a shrewd investment.[9]

In concert with friends and relatives, the Pohlschneider family made plans to leave their homeland. In 1832, the oldest children, teenagers Elisabeth and Friedrich, went ahead to Ohio, while the parents and younger children stayed behind to sell the farm and settle their affairs.[10] In February 1833, in the midst of the preparations, Frau Pohlschneider died,[11] but that tragic event only strengthened the widower's resolve to find a better place. By the end of June 1833, the family had arrived at Baltimore and anglicized their given names. Listed on the passenger manifest as the "Messmann" family, twelve-year-old Henry, nine-year-old Joseph, six-year-old Agnes, three-year-old Frank, and their fifty-one-year-old father, now called "Frederick," went on to Ohio.[12] They had left both the Pohlschneider farm and the surname far behind in Oldenburg and now used the father's original surname, spelled with one or two terminal Ns by various clerks who ignored the subtle details of spelling.[13]

For a few years, the renamed Messman family lived in rural Minster, Ohio, 100 miles north of Cincinnati, where many former inhabitants of Damme also settled.[14] Sometime in the early 1830s, the oldest son, Friedrich, apparently died.[15] By 1839, the Messmans moved to Cincinnati, where fourteen-year-old Joseph began a ten-year apprenticeship with Edmund Dexter, a wholesale liquor dealer and English immigrant. A member of the Unitarian Church, Dexter was a leading whiskey importer and rectifier.[16] He had been in America long enough, and had been financially successful enough, to have developed contacts all the way to Washington, DC.[17] Dexter's mansion on the corner of Fourth Street and Broadway was Cincinnati's premier showplace. He enjoyed sharing his wealth and knowledge and found Joseph an eager student.

The business which Joseph sought to master no longer exists in modern America. In the mid-nineteenth century, many farmers made alcohol from their surplus corn. Barrels of "white dog"[18] were easier to ship than grain, which was bulky and a target for mold and vermin. However, individual producers distilled only a few barrels, and the raw, colorless, liquid varied significantly in taste and alcohol content from one maker to the next.[19] Therefore, distillers sold their raw product to "rectifiers," who distilled it a second time, occasionally added other ingredients, converted it to a palatable beverage, and marketed it to the public. Most rectifiers were reputable wholesalers who bought whiskey from many distilleries and created a product they could call their own. What they produced might now be called blended whiskey, but the process was wide open to adulteration. Even highly regarded rectifiers considered it necessary to add colors and flavors. The opportunities to make huge profits abounded.[20] Eventually, the passage of the Pure Food Law in 1906 sounded the death knell for the rectifying business. Today, whiskey is carefully defined by the federal standards enforced by the Bureau of Alcohol, Tobacco and Firearms.[21]

However, in the days of Edmund Dexter, rectifiers played an important role in creating and distributing beverages. Dexter bought barrels of raw whiskey from many sources in Ohio and Kentucky, distilled it on the premises of his Cincinnati store, and then supplied groceries, taverns, restaurants, and other places that furnished liquid refreshment.[22] His customers, retailers as far away as St. Louis and New Orleans, sold whiskey as a thirst-quencher or as medicine.[23] Consumers were largely unaware of the origin of the beverages they drank, but Dexter enjoyed a positive reputation with the public. Long after Edmund Dexter's death, his son registered "Old Dexter" as a trademark name.[24] However, in 1847, aged domestic whiskey was unknown, and the use of charred barrels, which impart a characteristic brown color to the contents, was an innovation.[25] The whiskey Joseph handled was the color of vodka.

In the years before the Civil War, cheap whiskeys were commonly produced in this manner all over the United States. Joseph learned Dexter's techniques and subsequently launched his own business in St. Louis. The undated recipes in the appendix of this book illustrate the methods that rectifiers used to alter the color, aroma, and taste of their products. Joseph's diary reveals the ingredients that remained secret for one hundred and fifty years.

While Joseph learned the rectifying business, his brother Henry found a job in Cincinnati as a grocery clerk. Within a few years, Henry had changed his surname to "Mersman" (sometimes "Mersmann"), and other family members followed suit.[26] Perhaps an error in either typography or pronunciation led to that change: the use of "Mersman" was inconsistent at first. However, the 1840 Cincinnati city directory listed "Henry Mersmann" as a clerk, and the 1842 directory included a retail tobacco business styled as "Nuilsen & Mersmann," a partnership Henry formed with another German immigrant, Anthony Nulsen.[27]

John Clemens Nulsen (1824–1906), c. 1894. Nulsen and Mersman began a business partnership in 1849, which evolved into a lifelong friendship, including becoming brothers-in-law. Their lives remained intertwined for the next half century. (Special Collections, St. Louis Public Library.)

The Nulsen family—two parents, five boys, and two girls—had owned a cigar factory in Nörten, in the Kingdom of Hanover.[28] Devout Roman Catholics, they had been merchants for four generations. In the late 1830s, the oldest son, Francis Nuelsen, emigrated to Cincinnati and opened a retail tobacco shop on Main Street.[29] Francis encouraged his father, mother, and siblings to follow him

Agnes Mersman Lake (1826–1907), c. 1850. Agnes married a circus clown and spent much of her life on the road with various circus companies. When her husband was killed, she operated her own circus—the first woman to do so. She later married James Butler "Wild Bill" Hickok, shortly before he was shot in Deadwood, South Dakota, in 1876. (Kansas State Historical Society.)

to America. Other members of the Nulsen family arrived in 1839 and 1842 and lived in the same neighborhood as the Mersman family.[30] In 1842, Anthony

Arnd Kattenhorn (1810–87), c. 1872. Mersman's brother-in-law, a successful Cincinnati wholesale grocer, married Elizabeth Mersman, the eldest of Joseph's siblings, in 1834. Mersman spent many Sundays at the family's home, located on Seventh Street between Main and Walnut streets. (From M. Joblin, *Cincinnati Past and Present: Its Industrial History as Exhibited in the Life-Labors of Its Leading Men* [1872].)

Nulsen, the third son, partnered with Henry Mersman and opened a cigar store at 210 Main Street. The business sometimes employed the siblings of both owners, giving them mercantile experience in their new country. After a few years, two younger brothers, John Clemens Nulsen and Joseph Mersman, made plans to seek their fortune together farther west, in St. Louis, and that initiative is described in chapters 9 to 12 of this diary.

By 1847, the start of this record, both of Mersman's sisters had married. In 1834, Elizabeth, the elder, wed Arnd Kattenhorn, an emigrant from the Kingdom of Hanover who owned a Cincinnati grocery.[31] By 1840, the Kattenhorn family had two daughters, Louisa and Sophia, and Kattenhorn was investing in real estate.[32]

Agnes, Mersman's younger sister, eloped in 1846 with William Lake Thatcher, a clown appearing with Stone & McCollum's Great Western Circus.[33] The couple found a priest to marry them in New Orleans[34] and thereafter led a life on the road, traveling with tent shows. Their stage name, "Lake," appeared in newspaper advertisements and handbills throughout the Ohio and Mississippi river valleys. In 1847, they joined Rockwell & Company and remained with that company until it disbanded in 1849. Lake starred as clown and ringmaster, while

Agnes thrilled audiences as an equestrian and rope walker. During warmer months, they journeyed by riverboat to dozens of towns. Agnes often visited her family in Cincinnati, the winter quarters of Rockwell & Company.[35]

Following a German tradition, the entire Mersman clan in Cincinnati routinely gathered together on Sundays for a midday dinner. The patriarch, who never remarried, resided with his daughter Elizabeth Kattenhorn and her family, or at the home of his son Henry, who had a wife and one daughter by 1849. The youngest Mersman, Frank, never held a job for long and remained a bachelor. Working as a circus roustabout, a tobacconist, or a laborer, he found jobs in St. Louis, Louisville, and other places, but always made his way back to Cincinnati, where he could count on relatives to feed and house him when he wore out his welcome elsewhere.

Unmarried at the start of this diary, Joseph J. Mersman attended theater and concert performances as often as his limited time and budget would permit. His record reveals the lifestyle that single men enjoyed in America's cities during the antebellum years. He worked ten-hour days, six days a week, and also holidays. He filled his leisure hours with masculine camaraderie and lots of cigar smoking, alcohol drinking, and ballroom dancing. However, Mersman was committed to improving himself, and spent as much money on educational activities (such as French instruction, classic literature, and music lessons) as he spent on amusements.[36] He flirted with women, but did not have many sexual exploits, possibly because he was saving his money to start his own business. Determined to better his lot in life, Mersman used his diary to chart his progress.

In this edition, the diarist's words are presented as he wrote them: a sometimes misspelled account of his daily activities. A summary at the start of each chapter crystallizes the themes found on the pages that follow. We hope that this device helps the reader to see beyond the minutiae of daily life and identify the larger issues that Joseph J. Mersman confronted.

NOTES

1. Kirchenbuch, 1650–1875, Taufen, 1820–39, 144, Katholische Kirche, Damme, FHL Microfilm 909912.

2. Farm names remained constant, even when owners changed, and the owners therefore took their surnames from the farms (Schlumbohm, 506–8). Baptism records for each of his children note that Friedrich Pohlschneider was born Friedrich Messmann (Kirchenbuch, 1650–1875, Taufen 1801–20, 334, 417, 482, 558, Katholische Kirche, Damme, FHL Microfilm 90991; Taufen 1820–39, 57, 144, 227, 297, FHL Microfilm 909912). See also note 13 below.

3. Kirchenbuch, 1650–1875, Tote, 1811–19, 226, Katholische Kirche, Damme, FHL Microfilm 909911; Tote, 1819–29, 308, 387, FHL Microfilm 909912.

4. Hinrichs, 677.

5. The taler or thaler, the official currency in the German states of the Holy Roman Empire, was valued at approximately seventy-one American cents (Kamphoefner [1], 608).

6. Description of the development of this cottage industry is found in DTZ 32–37, 66. Frederic Mersmann was listed as a tobacconist in the CCD 1843, 239.

7. Ostendorf, 184; Walker, 42–69; Kamphoefner [2], 9–22.

8. See Lachs.

9. A description of conditions for transatlantic travelers appears in Moltmann 47; FDS, Nr. 5; Kamphoefner [2], 27–53.

10. Ostendorf, 256.

11. Kirchenbuch, 1650–1875, Tote, 1830–66, 74, Katholische Kirche, Damme, FHL Microfilm 909913.

12. JJM's diary uses only anglicized names: Elizabeth (for the German *Elisabeth*), Henry (*Heinrich*), Joseph, Frank (*Franz*), and Agnes. The ship manifest lists the children as "Henry, Joseph, Franz and Catrina," suggesting that Agnes had a nickname. (Entry for Fredk Meisman [*sic*] and family; Second Quarter 1833, 46, lines 30–34, in *Quarterly Abstracts of Passenger Lists of Vessels Arriving at Baltimore, 1820–1869;* NA Microfilm M596, roll 2.)

13. Documentation of this name change appears in Shelby County Deed Book, L:287, where a clerk noted: "Joseph Surmann in the year 1833 at the land office at the Town of Wapakonnetta in the state of Ohio . . . gave him the name of Frederick Pohlschneider which is not in name of the grantor (his name being Frederick Messmann) but is the name of a farm or place in Germany on which said grantor some years resided, and by which name he was sometimes called but never opined it as his last name."

14. Called Stallotown in 1832 after founder Joseph Stallo (1800–32), the village was incorporated as Minster in March 1839. Originally in Mercer County, Minster is now in Auglaize County, created in 1848 (Burke, 31). Accounts of the settling of Stallotown have been written by several authors (Williamson, 838; Lammers, 11; Hoying, 1–4, 13–17).

15. Friedrich died after he left Damme in 1832. Since there is no record of him in the United States, it appears that he perished en route to America or soon after arrival. In the 1830s, former Damme residents living in Minster referred to the family as the Pohlschneiders. The 1836 roster of the St. Augustine Parish listed Frederick Pohlschneider and four children; the priest assessed school tuition for two Pohlschneiders, possibly JJM and Frank. A Franz Pohlschneider died in Minster in 1839, but his exact identity is uncertain. In 1840, the federal census listed Henry Messman as the head of a Cincinnati household. JJM's diary never mentions Friedrich, suggesting he was dead by 1847 (Entry for Franz Pohlschneider, Death Records, St. Augustine Parish, unpaginated, arranged by date, HAC; Hoying 232; St. Augustine Parish Records, as transcribed by Rita and David Hoying, Minster, Ohio; USC 1840, M704, roll 399, page 235, line 27).

16. Herz, 8.

17. On 30 March 1850, the 31st Congress, 1st sess., passed HR 176, providing financial relief for Edmund Dexter, who had lost a shipment of brandy and was liable for warehouse charges in New Orleans. This episode may be related to the litigation JJM describes, *Dexter v. Phoenix* (JJM diary, 26 January 1849).

18. White dog (also called white lightning or moonshine) is so named because it is clear and it "bites" the drinker (WAS, 12 June 2002, p. C 1, col. 3–6). Whiskey, made primarily from corn and barley, may have other cereal grains added to the mash, which is fermented and then distilled (Monzert, 19–24; Getz, 23).

19. "Much of the whiskey distilled before the Civil War was . . . scarcely drinkable and indeed was never intended to reach the consumer" (Carson, 66). See also Regan, 19.

20. Regan, 40–41; Robins, 41.

21. 27 CFR 5.22.

22. A grocery store of that era always sold alcoholic beverages (Rorabaugh, 204–5).

23. One type of medication, bitters, which contained whiskey as its active ingredient, was enthusiastically marketed by Dexter & Sons (Carson, 65; Dexter [3], 20–25).

24. The "Old Dexter" brand was registered in 1879 by Edmund Dexter. Owen J. Carpenter of Covington, Kentucky, registered the name in 1906, and it subsequently made its appearance on bar glassware (http://www.pre-pro.com/midacore/view_glass.php?sid=PVV191).

25. Kroll, 26.

26. The 1840 federal census lists Henry as "Messman," while the 1840 Cincinnati city directory calls him "Mersman"; Henry's 1842 marriage license records his surname as "Mersman," as does the 1842 Cincinnati city directory. However, an 1843 church record lists Agnes's surname as "Messman" (when she witnessed an aunt's wedding) and when she married in 1846, the record listed her as "Messman" (Geise-Messman marriage, 23 May 1843, Holy Trinity Catholic Church Marriage Record, unpaginated, arranged by date, HAC; Hamilton County Marriage Book, 14:75).

27. The surname in German documents, which appears as "Nilsen," "Nülsen," "Nüllse," or "Nülse," became "Nulsen" or "Nelson" in America for most family members. However, son Francis consistently spelled his last name as "Nuelsen," "Neilsen," or "Nuilsen." So did son Henry. To avoid confusion here, "Nulsen" is used when discussing the family and "Nuelsen" appears as the surname of Francis and Henry. Quotations contain spellings as they appear in the documents cited (Hamilton County Probate Records, 31:417).

28. A description of his father's vocation is found in Johann Joseph Nuelsens Tagebuch, 1833–39, MHS; Stevens, 3:238–41.

29. Francis Nuelsen household (USC 1840, M704, roll 399, page 236, line 10; CCD 1842, 338).

30. Entry for Francis Nulsen family, *Ship Gustav* Passenger Manifest, 10 May 1842, p. 3, lines 59–65, *Passenger Lists of Vessels Arriving at Baltimore, 1820–69,* NA M255, roll 3; entries for Jos Nulsen, Anth Nulsen and Amalia Nulsen, Second Quarter 1839, p. 15, lines 26–28, *Quarterly Abstracts of Passenger Lists of Vessels Arriving at Baltimore, 1820–1869,* NA M596, roll 4.

31. CCD 1834, 96.

32. Landy, 181–82; Aaron Kattenhorn household, USC 1840, M704, roll 398, page 131, line 3.

33. Slout, 164–65; ENQ, 23 April 1846.

34. Thatcher-Messmann marriage license, May 1, 1846, Jefferson Parish, Louisiana, VCP 670M:279.

35. Rockwell & Company Circus advertisements appeared daily (COM, December 1846 through March 1847).

36. Augst and Chudacoff have written about the experiences of antebellum bachelors.

CHAPTER ONE

Jenkins's Boarding House
8 November 1847–31 December 1847

Boardinghouses provided the setting for nineteenth-century bachelor life; in 1850, Cincinnati had nearly two hundred such establishments.[1] *When JJM began his journal on 8 November 1847, he lived in Mrs. Jenkins's residence. The "Old Woman," as he called her, was the single mother of Fanny and Mary Jane Jenkins. Mrs. Jenkins was likely a widow, supporting her family in one of the few ways open to her.*[2] *Servants helped with domestic chores. The guests (at various times) included John Bradley and son; Charles Brown; Dr. Emerick G. and Mary Darling; Mr. Delamater; Mr. Dow; Mr. and Mrs. Granger; Mary Howe and children; Mr. Johnson; Mary Price; and Mr. Wardner.*

Located a few blocks from JJM's workplace, Edmund Dexter's store, Jenkins's was near other Third Street boardinghouses. A house of prostitution was on the next block.[3] *Mrs. Jenkins charged $3.00 weekly per person for lodging and meals. JJM and Brown shared a room with one double bed, a common sleeping arrangement. Boarders visited each other's rooms for small parties or socialized in the parlor. JJM supplemented the daily fare with special treats—cakes, oysters, and bottled beverages—from neighborhood shops. Every Sunday he dined at the home of his oldest sister, Elizabeth Kattenhorn, but the boardinghouse residents comprised his surrogate family.*

Although JJM mentions he had been keeping a record for several years, the earlier volume was apparently lost. Therefore, JJM's story begins abruptly, as 1847 is drawing to a close. JJM worked six ten-hour days per week, but he had many other activities.

Cincinnati Riverfront Landing, 1848. This plate is one of eight daguerrotype plates made in 1848, which show the entire length of the Cincinnati, Ohio, riverfront. It is the sight Mersman saw in his trips to and from Cincinnati. (From the Collection of the Public Library of Cincinnati and Hamilton County.)

Monday Novr 8th 1847

Cloudy and disagreable Weather. Business commenced very favorably for the Week.[4] The weather lately has been very changeable. at our last Ball I caught a severe cold of which I have been unable to rid myself as yet. the changes of weather and temperature are so Sudden. one Consolation (allthough a poor one) is that one half of the people of this good City seem to be in the same dilemma. I amused myself with my flute until nearly 8. then went to the *Liedertafel* singing meeting.[5] the attendance was poor so I did not overstrain myself with singing. from there some 4 or 5 of us went to Drachs old Establishment now termed "Mikes Headquarters"[6] Menzel Junr treated me to a good Cigar and unexceptionable Ale. from there direct home 11 oclock. ☞[7] I Borowed 10$ from A. Nulsen. ~ ~ ~Exp—00—
[Margin note] Paid 1.20 for this Book

November 9th.

Not much doing at the Store. had no difficulte in getting my french exercise ready for this Evening. I had my french exercise or rather lesson after supper.[8] did not go out afterwards. to Bed 10. Exp 10. ☞ Repaid Mr Nulsen 5$ Balance due him 5$.

Wednesday 10th.g

Towards Evening the Weather was beautifully Cold and Clear. The evening I passed with my Sister.[9] she noticed my severe cold, and with a Sisters kindness, immediatly had a footbath prepared for me. also gave me a fresh pair of Woolen Socks. nothing like a kind Sister. To Bed 10. Exp 10c.

Thursday November 11th 1847

The Weather allthough Cold, is really beautiful. I am Sorrry to add that Business is almost too dull.

I have determined to pass my Evenings at home, at least until I am rid of my cold which is really too anoying. I went to Mr Lange after supper. he has at present the honor to be my boot maker. left a pair of Boots with him to be repaired. then went to my Brothers Store,[10] took a box of principee Cigars[11] with me. I did not pay for them. returned home at 8 oclock. Amused myself with the little girls[12] there till 10 oclock, when in Company with Brown and a Mr DeLaMaître went to Billy Tell's,[13] indulged in a glass of Ale, which I shall not do again so late before going to Bed. it having the disagreable effect of making me a little too hot for Comfort. we returned home immediatly—To Bed ½ past 10. Exp 15c

Friday 12th.

Another change in Weather and Temperature. I am destined to keep my cold a little while longer. however I am taking all the Care of myself that it is possible for any young Man. The Evening I passed at home with the little girls. Went to Bed 10. Exp 5

Saturday 13th

Rained more or less throughout the whole day. About 6 oclock as I was going home, there was a very Severe Shower which drenched me Completely. remain'd home during the Evening. To Bed at 11. Expe 4.10.
[Margin note] August Ulrich paid 4.50. I paid N[ulsen] & M[ersman] 3.25 for Cigars, Lange & Co 75 cts repairing boots.

Sunday Novr 14th 1847.

Disagreable, Cloudy, Windy and Cold Weather. I arose suffisciently early to dress before breakfast. About 8 oclock, after the morning dampness had somewhat evaporated I walked slowly to my brothers. It was too Cold to go out dressed so I did not take any particular pains in dressing merely putting on a Clean shirt, and wrapping my Old Cloak about me. I felt in Condition to go any where and be seen by any body. Henry was unwell, so I could not get him to go out with me. I Amused myself with his Old Guitar until ½ past 10. then went down Called on Menzel[14] at his rooms. the young Man was busy drawing a plan for new kind of Canal lock. I kept him from his work for a ½ hour, then went home and wrote two pages french exercise to finish my lesson. Dinner Bell rung a few minutes after I had finished writing. After dinner Mr Moulinier Called to give me my lesson. As we were in no hurry we of Course took it easy. it was 4'clk when we were through. We Walked out to Tappe's for the purpose of inspecting some Guitars that he has made but he was not at home. Walked about for an hour or so, without any diffinite object. I went to my Sisters to get supper a little earlier than where I board, but they kept me at the Card Table till near 7 oclock. I then went Post haste to Julia's.[15] found the good girls in good health and apparently glad to see me. Apparantly is suffiscient for me. dont care whether they were or not. I received an invitation through them to a Wedding Ball. To Bed 11. Exp 5c

Monday 15th Novr 1847.

Beautiful and lovely Weather at present. Businiss opened very briskly this Morning and continued so throughout the day. The Evening I passed at home playing "not precisely Duetts" but Continually attempting to play with Fanny.[16] went out a little from 9 to ¼ past merely to smoke a Cigar. To Bed 10. Exp 5c
[Margin note] Bot a beautiful Edition of Milton[17] for 2.50—paid—

Tuesday 16th

Another beautiful day. Commerce is as good with us as desired. I had a hurried french Lesson this Evening. Went with Moulinier to Tappe's to look at some Guitars he has made. He had two finished they were both very good indeed. I have given him permission to make one for me, he offering to take mine in trade or exchange. We did'nt get home until 11 oclock. Expence 5c

Wednesday 17th.

Business very good. The Evening ~~beautifully~~ pleasantly mild and Automne like. bright moonshine. I was at Julia's a little before 8 oclock. We had a very pleasant [walk] down to the Assembly rooms.[18] The Company was large, but any thing except select. I underwent some hard jostlings. The best Amusement for me was to see the others enjoy themselves. The native Wine they had there was pretty good. I Showed my appreciation of by drinking a good deal of it. I danced quite as often as I intended. had to pay 75 cents for Supper. Went home at 3 oclock precisely. Total Exp 1.50¢—

Thursday Novr 18th 1847

Another change in the Weather, raining again. Business fortuneately is dull. I am a little dull also. 'Though I do not feel the effects as much as usually. Julia tried to make me Jealous last Evening. If she knew how hard and difficulte matter that is for any young Lady, she would safe herself the trouble. towards Evening it turned cold again. I did not leave the house after supper. played on my Guitar for an hour or so. then went down ~~stairs~~ in the parlor where the Ladies of the house were all assembled. Amused myself with them until 10 oclock then went to Bed. Exp 5c

Friday 19th

Quite cold this morning. Business slow. We are shipping very extensively which gives me plenty to do.[19] I have however as yet found time to do my french writings in the Store. I as usually devoted an hour or [so?] after Supper to my Guitar and Flute. then called on my sister Mrs Kattenhorn.[20] passed my time very agreably until 9 oclock. When I came home Fanny was just released from a visitor. we [talked] with Doct. D[arling] and his Wife passed our time very agreably till past 11. I finished the Evenings entertainment with smoking one of Browns Cigars, and listening to his description of the Theatrical performance. No Exp

Saturday 20th

Cold, but beautiful Weather. After Supper I called on my brother. in returning home I met Moulinier. he wanted me go to with him to Witness the exertions of The Sable Harmonists.[21] I left before it was out. To Bed 11. Exp 10¢

Sunday Novr 21st

The morning was'nt particularly beautiful, so I did'nt dress before breakfast, but took a reasonable time for that purpose afterwards. Somewhere about 10 oclock I left the house, first went to Kattenhorns, but the good people being all to Church, I soon left there.

Called on Mr Monfrod at his room. the young man was very nearly dressed. We had a long but not very Comfortable Walk of it, being Cold and Windy.

About 11 oclock we returned to my room where we amused ourselves Comforably until One. Had dinner at 2.

I made an Engagement at my sisters[22] for 3 oclock but we did'nt get through with our french in time to keep that. I was there a little before 4. My Share of Coffee and eatables had been preserved for me.

Went home to supper. immediatly afterwards left for Julia's[23] Mansion. my heart is very little engaged there. It is really amusing for me to see her laudable efforts in making ME Jealous. Miss C.[24] was there on a visit. Now Miss C is a brilliant and beautiful Girl, and of course it was my duty to make myself agreable. whenever I try to be so I am most generally successful. I was so much so in this instance, that it required no very penetrating Eye to see that Julia was more out of humor than I have ever been. I promised Miss C to call and see her which I shall certainly do, whenever I have nothing els to do. I left for home at 9 oclock precisely. Went to Bed at 10. Spent 20 cts.

Monday Novr 22nd 1847.

Was really a beautiful day. Business was also very good. The Evening I passed at home. Should have went to the Singing Company, but I amused myself Satisfactory, and that is all I personally care about. Our good and religious *Animaux*[25] went to such a vulgar place as the Theatre. To Bed 10 oclock No Exp.

Tuesday 23rd

Rainy and disagreable Weather. Business very good. I intended to pass the Evening at home, but Mr Brown wishing to go the Theatre again, very particularly requested my Company, which of Course I Could'nt refuse. We Went to the National.[26] Three Comedies of the most amusing kind, made time pass. the pauses we passed in the "Cock loft," amusing ourselves with Angels of "Lightness" Angels of "Darkness" being too "Dark" a term for these "Light" and accommodating beings.[27] Miss Clark appears very pretty on the Stage. Miss [?][28] is also very pretty. we remained until the whole was over. I met Mr. Ireland[29] there. he was in a jolly humor, had been above also. We got home 11 oclock. Exp 15c

Wednesday 24th.

Business dull. I finished my french lesson before Evening. I had a french lesson after supper. Made Miss Mary Price a present of a book being through with my lesson. I went in the Parlour, assisted Miss Jenkins to play Chess until 12, then went to bed No Exp

Thursday 25th November 1847.

To day we had snow for the first time. it is very Cold and disagreable. I was very busy this Morning. Business is very good. The Evening I passed entirely at home. Our little parties in the Parlour are very attractive sometimes. this Evening I made love to[30] Mary Price a young lady of 15 or therabouts. she intends "coming out"[31] next spring. She being blessed with a good looking and healthy person allready begins to experience sexual influence, allthough her behavior towards a young Man is what more aged young Ladies would denominate "verdant," still it is natural, and I like it. I did not go to bed until ½ past 11. No Expence.

Friday 26th

Disagreable and Windy Weather. Business Continues excellent. I have hardly time at present to write my french exercises in the Store.

The Evening I passed at home, excepting a trip I took to see Mayle[32] at the Store, but not finding him I returned direct home. I was bored there by a party of Fanny's friends who talked of nothing but their Eastern doings and Amusements. to bed 10. Exp 5c.

Saturday 27th

We were very busy all day receiving and Shipping Whiskey. being very tired I went to the Atheneum[33] with Mr. Brown, having engaged my Seats during the day. Mr Hackett as Fallstaff[34] was very good. Exp 1.15¢.

Sunday November 28th 1847.

The morning was beautiful, but it became Cloudy, Windy and Cold towards 10 oclock. I was dressed before breakfast, and went out immediatly afterwards to give the Servant an opportunity of Cleaning my room, as I intended to be home again by 10 oclock to write my french lesson before dinner. I went to Henry's,[35] waited until he was dressed, then we both went to my room. he amused himself with my Guitar and I with writing french. I finished just as the dinner-Bell wrung ½ past 1. After dinner from ½ past 2 to 4 I was Employed in reciting my lesson. Then walked and took a view of the river with Moulinier. the river is very high and still rising. I returned home by 5. Amused myself with the young Ladies until Supper.

The Evening I added my little self to a large audience attending Mr Boyentons discourse. It was very interesting. I escorted nearly the whole female population of our house 6 in number, including Fanny of course. before going to bed I had a Smoke with Brown. Exp 30c.

Monday 29th

Ye Gods![36] how Cold it was this Morning. business Commenced dull. Still I was very busy with last week's unfinished affairs. After Supper I intended to visit our Singing Company, but was prevented by events at home. Brown and myself inflicted our Society on Mr Bradley in his office.[37] We Smoked, and played Cards till we had done Smoking. then went in Mrs Howe's room played there also until near 10 oclock. Smoked in the dining-room till bed time.

Tuesday November 30th 1847

It is, and has been very Cold during the last two days. towards Evening it Moderated. Business passably fair. The Evening I passed at home except a short walk to Deserins to drink a glass of Ale. Mary Jane gave me a lock of Mary Price's hair.[38] as a romantic young Lady she of Course thought that she did me a great honor. Mr De'lamaître returned this Evening. We Waited until Mr Brown returned from the Theatre. his Report of the *Viennoises Danseuse*[39] was very favorable. I shall see them to morrow Evening. To Bed ½ past 11. Exp 10.

Wednesday December 1st 1847

Rainy and disagreable the whole day. Business nevertheless very good. The Evening I passed in the Theatre with Mr Brown. The *Viennoises* children appered in 4 of their favorite dances. They certainly surpass every thing in the form of dancing. Their flower dance met with most approbation. During the last piece we went up into the "Cock-Loft" one of its inhabitants took a fancy to me.[40] She Commenced showing it, by running against [me] several [times]. perceiving that she wished me to speak to her, I did so, but no sooner done than I felt her lascivious lips on my virgin cheeks. of course I appeared highly flattered. she continued to make very unmodest advances towards me throwing her vile arms around my hitherto undefiled neck. I was Compelled at last very ungalantly to put a stop to her Amorous Movements. Went to Bed ½ past 11. Exp 30 cts.

Thursday decr 2nd 1847

Weather Continues dirty, nasty, sloppy and disagreable. The Evening I passed partly at home. I played flute till 8 oclock, then went to Kochs[41] a few minutes, from there to my watchmakers,[42] whom I did not find at home. returned and remained home balance of Evening, amusing myself with the g'hals[43] until their Mama's sent them to bed, then smoking a Cigar with Brown, and amusing the Old Woman who was sitting up for her Daughter.[44] The Theatrical party returned 11 oclock. A few minutes after we all went to bed. 15c.

Friday Dec 3rd

Changing Cold again. Business very good. After supper I assisted Fanny with my flute in studying some new music. we played till past 7. I then went in the parlour and played with the little girls until Moulinier [arrived?]. we did not get through with our lesson until near 10 oclock. we frequently get into Scientific disputes and when we do it generally gets late before we finish our *leçon.*[45] Ten I went to Bed. No Expence

Saturday 4th

My Cash balanced Satisfactory this afternoon.[46] After supper I called on Misses Corbins. The young Lady's were in good health. we went to see Mr Murray who intends leaving for New Orleans, where [Granger?] has been during the last two months. I received news from Granger. 9 we took the Ladies home. Went to Bank Exchange, had some Pigs feet &c. from there we went to a Bath house.[47] To Bed 11. Exp 50¢.

Sunday Novr [December] 5th 1847.[48]

Cold and nasty weather. Snowing a little every now and then. I called at Sisters[49] immediatly after Breakfast. poor Daddy[50] is unwilling to let Frank[51] go to Havanna.

I received a letter from Frank on friday in which he states his intention of going to Havanna with a Tobacconist now in St. Louis. father is unwilling to let him go and desired me write his disapprobation of this step.[52] I prefer myself to have frank about so I shall advise him strongly not to go. I shall also write to Agnes[53] who is at present in St. Louis, to use all her influence in preventing his going. from ½ past 10 to dinner I was busy preparing my french lesson which I recited after dinner. Shortly after 3 I went to Kattenhorns played Cards the whole afternoon until past 5. went home to Supper. Sweet Fannie went to church with Mr Delamaitre. I not knowing what better to do went to Kochs where I certainly have not been for 3 or 4 months. Koch Senr[54] was sitting quite cozely 'side his intended—as yet Miss F[riedebor]n,[55] but this long and ugly name she intends to discard and a "Cook" or rather in german "Koch." Rule Came about 8 oclock. he intends making Miss K— Mrs Rule, so as to have at least somebody to rule, according and with (I suppose) a "Rule" of his own. It was dull Company for those not interested so I did not trouble them with my presence very long. went from there direct home. but not to bed for I discussed religious Matters with a very Sober Phiz[56] till ½ past 10. then retired. Exp 5 cts.

Monday Novr [December] 6th 1847

Beautiful Weather is morning. Business Commenced very briskly. I was busily Employed the whole [day]. After Supper I went as I intended to the Singing Company.[57] An Election of officers took place. I did not leave with any high degree of satisfaction, but suppose shall have to attend once a week. I went from there direct home 10. Exp 30

Tuesday 7th

Disagreable Weather again. our Commercial transactions are in a very flourishing Condition. The Evening I passed at Misses Corbens very pleasantly playing Whist[58] &c till 10 oclock then went home to bed having nothing better to do. Exp 10c

Wednesday 8th

Business not particularly lively. Weather damn nasty. The Evening I passed at home with my french and teacher. Went to bed 10 oclock Exp 10.

Thursday 9th

Was a disagreable day in every respect. I was disapointed about Something in the Evening. went to Kochs, returned about 8. passed balance of Evening agreably with the girls. Went to bed 10. Exp 5—

Friday 10.

I saw Anderson perform this evening at Atheneum. *King of the Commons*[59] was performed and most beautifully was it done home to bed 11 oclock. Exp 60

Saturday Novr [December] 11th 1847.

Confound Mayle Larkin he brot in my Store a pretty young Lady who made me Contribute 50 cts for a Library in their Sunday Scool. however she was pretty and there is no use in regretting what's gone. my cash balanced very well this afternoon. The Evening I passed with Mayle at Mrs Corbins playing Cards with her daughters. we played a very interesting game Called *Cousini.*[60] It was 11 oclock before we [were] aware of the time. being once aware of the lateness of the hour of course we retired. gently disingaging ourselves from the girls, we bade them "good night" went direct home. Exp 60.

Sunday 12th

Commenced very fairly. got up too late to dress before breakfast. however I was down to Mayle on Lower Market by 10 oclock, 1 hour later than my appointment. we [went] down to the river to be AStonished at its extraordinary Size. It is higher than I have ever seen it, lacking only 15 feet to make it as high as it was in 1832.[61] it is rising rapidly, and may destroy a great Amount of property before it Subsides. went to Church in order to hear Rev Mr Moffit preach,[62] but he not appearing I left the place indignant with being imposed upon. After dinner I had my french lesson as usual. it being somewhat lenghty, it was 4 oclock when we were through with it. went to Sisters and passed balance of my time there. I had my Supper at home, went out a little to Smoke a Cigar, and give our Sanctimoneus Ladies a chance to go to Church. passed balance in making love to mary. Exp. 25.

Monday Novr [December] 13th 1847

It Commenced Snowing this Morning pretty freely and Continued to do the whole day. by Evening we had 6 to 7 inches Snow on the ground. The river Continues rising 5 oclock P.M. it is on the upper Corner of Water and Main, having risin about 3 feet during the last twenty four hours. The water has allready driven over 300 famillies within City limits out of house and home. It is decidedly a grand sight to see this immense Stream of yellow muddy water gradually approching the business part of front[63] setting its natural boundery at defiance.

The Evening I passed at home, amusing myself with playing on my Guitar, reading and amusing the girls.[64] I went to bed at ½ past 11 oclock. The days Expences 10c.

Tuesday 14th

The river continues to advance. I went down this morning immediately after breakfast. The water had risen about 2 feet during the night it was just touching the Curb Stones corner Syc[amore] & front. Mr Dexter was down early. We Commenced early in the morning to move things out of our Old Warehouse, on Syc[amore] in the new building[65] we were busily employed at this the whole day. all the most valuable articles were removed from warehouse and cellar under Store. It is an exciting time there is no business done of any account.

laborors receive 50 cts an hour.[66] This Evening the water is within 4 feet as high as in "32" and rising at the rate of 1 inch every hour. I being froze quite through and otherwise very tired did not go out after Supper, but worked at my french lesson till 10 oclock. 11 went to Bed. No Expence.

Wednesday Novr [December] 15th 1847

The River has risen about 18 inches last night. this Morning the water covered our Still house[67] to the depht of 6 to 8 inches, and according to Mr Dexters Measurement 13½ inches of "32." the cellars all along lower Market were filled. 12 oclock, the water is under the arch next to our Store 18 inches will bring it on the floor. the water Continues to rise, allthough Slowly. I was in the Store the whole day but had nothing, but Satisfy the Curiosity of idle passers bye. The Ev'ning I passed at home entirely. had a french lesson at first. I then Amused little Mary for a half an hour or so. then went with Brown to Billy Tells drank a glass of ale, went home direct and finished the evening Amusement with Smoking a cigar. To Bed 11 oclock Exp 0000.

Thursday 16th

It Snowed again to day. The river Continues rising. this Evening it was at its hight very nearly and was within 8 inches of the "32" mark. After Supper I went to the Theatre with Brown and Delamettre. Anderson was playing *The Elder Brother*[68] to a passably filled house. he played well. I was very much pleased so were my Companions. Went home and to bed ½ past 11. Exp 55c

Friday 17th

This Morning 8 oclock the river was at its height and within 6 inches of the 1832 mark. during the afternoon it receeded 1 inch. I wrote to Chs D[exter] this day. The Evening I passed at home playing Flute Duetts until 9. Amused the girls[69] till 10. Smoked till 11. Exp 15c

Saturday Novr [December] 18th 1847.

The river Continues to recede although slowly. it fell about 10 inches this day. is still in the Distillery. my Cash balanced very accuratly for this Week. the business of the week has been very Small.

I commenced the Evenings Amusement with playing Some Duetts with a gentleman Border in the Same house. Shortly before 7 Moulinier Came and requested me to accompany him to the Atheneaum. as it was Andersons benefit,[70] and he appeared in two fine pieces, *The Lady of Lyons* and *Elder Brother,*[71] I went with him, and was really well repaid for my trouble and Expence. Miss Logan Sustained him in a most effective and satisfactory Manner. It [was] within 5 minutes of 12 when the performance Concluded.[72] Exp 1.15c

Sunday 19th

I arose too late to dress before breakfast. I and Mr. Delamettre were dressed a few minuites before 10. went togather to Selves to partake of a bottle of Dayton Ale. from there to my Store to note the fall of waters. it fell fully two feet last night. we then went to enjoy a pleasure excursion over the river in to Covington. It was certainly [amazing?] to see the usually modest Ohio river of width of two and three miles in Some places and well repaid for the trouble of getting on the Ferry. I came near getting drowned again in making a long jump on the ferry. I was paying the owner of the Skiff[73] when the ferry pushed off. I made a grand jump and a fortunate one. We called on some female acquaintances of Mr D[elamater]. Being through with this We Went to an Eating house took lunch in the Shape of mince pie and Coffee. The whole of Newport was still under water. returned in time for dinner. Had my french from 2 to 4. then went [to] Brother in Laws.[74] from there I went home, not till I had supper. it [was] 8 oclock. played with the girls till 9. Smoked till 10. then to Bed. My expence wer 75 cts.

Monday Novr [December] 20th 1847.

Most Excellent Weather again. Snowing beautifully. the river fell last night over 2 feet and stands now below front St. the present Cold weather will make it recede rapidly. I suppose business will be dull this week, so I'll devote my time to french, and getting my bills ready for the End of the year.

Business made a gentle Commencement again, merely to intimate that it had not deserted us. I was occupied the whole day in filing this years bills. The Evening I passed at home, the Weather being very raw and windy. played flute Duetts until 9. then joined Mr Bradley's Card Table, and assisted him till 11. We then in Company of Brown [and] Del—r went to Billy Tell's and partook of glass of Egg Nogg[75] or a Sort of milk Punch. Went direct home. Smoked and Chatted till 12 or nearly so. 12 to Bed. No Expence.

Tuesday 21st.

Very Cold yet. river falling rapidly. it is allready 5 to 6 feet below front St. Business is very good Compared to what other Merchants are doing. After supper I went "at the risk of breaking my neck" to Currman's[76] for the purpose of getting my flute Duets and also of playing some with the above named Gentle Man and if Miss C. was handy to have a chat with her. I was eminently Successful in a these things.

C. having an Engagement with his intended, we had to quit at ½ past 8. Stopped at Hunkums[77] to take a glass of Egg Nogg. Then went direct home. Smoked with Brown and Del—r till 11 oclock. Exp 20.

Wednesday Decr 22nd 1847

Cold, Clear and frosty weather. Business has resumed its full and most active course. if it continues so, this will be a brilliant week for us. After supper I had a french lesson which detained me till 10 oclock. Went with Del—r to Billy Tell's. he treated to Egg Nogg. Smoked home until 11 oclock, then went to bed. Exp 10.

Thursday Decr 23rd

Business very good, our Commercial transactions cannot but prove Satisfactory to Mr Dexter. After Supper I had nothing particular to do. So I paid Mr Koch a visit. returned home about ½ past 9 oclock. Smoked with Mr Brown and Mr Del—r till 10. then to bed.

Friday 24th

Commerce Continues flourishing. I am at present so much occupied with it, that I have no time at all for my french. The Evening was passed in Bradleys office playing "Euchre."[78] It being Christmas Eve, the Ladies of our Establishment took the liberty of beseiging our Retreat with firecrackers and torpedoes[79] wounding none and killing less. We afterward Smoked until 11 oclock. then to Bed. Exp 10.

Saturday Christmas, 25th

This was decidedly the worst and most uninteresting Christmas I have ever spent. I was Confined in the Store the whole day. Received no present Except a handkerchf from my Sister. The Evening I passed at home with the girls who gave a party. To Bed 10 oclock Exp 5.25.
[Margin note] I gave presents to the following persons: Mary Price, Mary Jane Jenkins, my Cousins[80] and Mr. Dexters children.[81]

Sunday Decr 26th 1847

A very Cold, but bright day. I got up too late to dress before breakfast. about 10, I was dressed. Went to Kattenhorns where I passed my time in reading and Amusing my Brother in law. Went home to dine. after dinner I went to the post office[82] to deposite a package for Mrs Howe which Cost me 40 cts and which I have allready charged to profit and Loss. Moulinier Came to see me about ½ past 1. we read until ½ past 3, then went to the Cathedral[83] to get hold of Burkhard.[84] we were Successfull, took him along and got him to play the flute part in flute and Guitar Duetts. we had a most Excellent Supper, and about an hour afterwards Punch which was also good. I received an invitation from Mrs Moulinier to dine with them next New Year, which of Course I accepted. I left for home about 9 oclock. found the familly all up yet and enjoying themselves excellently. after they had retired we Gentn Smoked until 10 when we retired also. No Expence—

Monday 27th

Commerce & Trade made a faire Commencement this Morning. I am nearly all the time occupied with the business of the day. Weather moderated considerably during the day. The Evening I passed with Brown and at his Expence at the Atheneum. Booth[85] performed the Character of Shylock to the Satisfaction of a large and fashionable Audience, but omitted the last act,[86] which did not Satisfy myself and Brown. To Bed ½ past 10. Exp 50c.

Tuesday December 28th 1847.

Weather moderate again. Business however does not moderate because the Weather is doing so. The Evening I passed entirely at home with my french Teacher. we had a long lesson. from 10 to 11 I Smoked with B[rown] & D[elamater]. Exp 25c for french Book

Wednesday 29th

Weather is quite mild and moderate. thawing fast. whiskey is declining again. Business very good—plenty to do. I gave a Small party to the Gentleman part of our Establishment at Bradley's office.[87] we played Euchre and drank of course we had some fine Cakes with it. we kept going until ½ past 10, when we retired being driven out of our retreat by the Ladies of our Establishment with fire crackers and torpedoes and other destructive missiles. Exp 70.

Edmund Dexter (1801–62), c. 1860. Dexter took young Mersman on as an apprentice at age 14, for a ten-year apprenticeship. Under Dexter, he learned whiskey distilling and rectifying, as well as good business practices. (Cincinnati Museum Center–Cincinnati Historical Society Library.)

Thursday 30.

Business good. Weather dirty and Sloppy, raining at intervals. After supper I and Mr Dow amused ourselves with playing some duetts. afterward I joined the girls who were playing in the Parlour we amused ourselves Capitally until the Old folks came home. To Bed 12. Exp 15.

Friday 31st

To night the *Liedertafel* gave a ball. I did not feel like going, not having had time to attend the Singing Meetings. I went with Brown to the Atheneum. *The Naied Queen* was performed by Miss Logan.[88] I amused myself very well. Brown did'nt. To Bed 11. Exp 30.

NOTES

1. In addition, Cincinnati had some three hundred small hotels and taverns, many of which provided lodging (CCD 1848–49, 23–27, 117–22).

2. Mrs. Jenkins was not unusual. Of the 163 boardinghouses listed in the city directory, sixty-two (37 percent) had female proprietors (CCD 1848–49, 23–27).

3. USC 1850, M432, roll 687, page 155, lines 1–12; page 317, lines 27–32.

4. A clerk in Edmund Dexter's wholesale business, JJM rectified domestic whiskey and also sold imported spirits (CCD 1842, 29).

5. See the Annotated List of Persons, Places, and Businesses and map 3.

6. By November 1847, Louis Drach had relocated his food and drink business from 289 Main Street to the Bellevue House, north of the city. See map 2. No tavern called "Mike's Headquarters" is listed in the CCD; that may be a name derived from a bartender at the establishment (CCD 1846, 149; CCD 1848–49, 118).

7. JJM drew a tiny hand in the original text here and in the following entry.

8. JJM hired Charles Moulinier to tutor him in French so that he could communicate better with businessmen in New Orleans and St. Louis.

9. JJM's older sister Elizabeth, wife of grocer Arnd Kattenhorn and the mother of four children (Louisa, Sophia, Henrietta, and Arnd Jr.), assumed a maternal role for her younger siblings (Henry, Joseph, Agnes, and Frank) after their mother's death in 1833. See the Annotated List of Persons, Places, and Businesses.

10. Henry Mersman's business, styled as Nulsen & Mersman, sold cigars and other tobacco products at a shop at 210 Main Street. See map 4 (CCD 1848–49, 57).

11. Principé cigars, thinner and shorter than others, provided a brief smoke.

12. Likely Mary Jane Jenkins and Mary Price, teenagers at Mrs. Jenkins's Boarding House.

13. The William Tell Restaurant. See the Annotated List of Persons, Places, and Businesses and map 5 (CCD 1848–49, 63).

14. Possibly the younger Menzel, Jacob, a tobacconist with many talents.

15. Julia Corbin and her sister Mary Corbin were JJM's friends. See map 4.

16. Fanny Jenkins.

17. John Milton (1608–74), English poet and prose writer, is famous for his masterpiece, *Paradise Lost* (1667) (Siepmann, 652).

18. They attended the wedding ball mentioned 14 November 1847.

19. Edmund Dexter routinely shipped large quantities of whiskey to ports along the Ohio and Mississippi rivers. See map 1.

20. It was common to refer to family members formally as "Mr." or "Mrs." An etiquette book of the era noted: "It is low-bred also to say 'my husband,' 'my wife' or, except amongst relatives, to use the Christian name only, in speaking of husband or wife. Speak of your own husband or wife as, 'Mr.' or 'Mrs. B_,' and of your friends also by the surname prefix as 'Remember me to Mr. or Mrs. D.' (Frost, 46).

21. The Sable Harmonists, a minstrel group of six to eight Caucasian men in blackface who toured major American cities, played folk music on banjos, violins, guitar, accordion, tambourine, and bone castanets. Original conundrums, quaint sayings, and comic lectures added to the evening's entertainment (ANY, 5:392, 394, 410; ENQ, 20 November 1847).

22. Elizabeth Kattenhorn and her husband, Arnd, welcomed JJM's extended family (his father, siblings, their spouses, and children) for dinner each Sunday at their home on Seventh Street between Main and Walnut Streets (CCD 1849–50, 159).

23. Julia Corbin.

24. The identity of this woman (perhaps Miss Dorothea Carrman or Karrman) has not been positively established.

25. [Fr.] creatures.

26. The National Theatre featured a comedy, *Follies of a Night,* a drama, *The Imp of the Elements,* and a burlesque, *The Humpback.* See map 5 (COM, 23 November 1847).

27. Commercial sex workers frequented the third tier of theaters, where there were opportunities to solicit clients. During performances, audience members often wandered about, talking with friends and making arrangements for later assignations (Hill [1], 134–35, 199–206; Gilfoyle, 109–12; Cohen, 77–78).

28. Possibly Miss Bruce, who also performed at the National Theatre that evening. Nothing more has been discovered about that actor, whose career seems to have been local and limited.

29. Mr. Ireland has not been further identified.

30. "Make love" was understood in the nineteenth century to mean to pay amorous attention, flirt, or practice coquetry. No sexual activity was implied (OED, s.v. "love").

31. "Coming out" marked the formal entry into society upon reaching womanhood, i.e., becoming eligible for courtship (OED, s.v. "come").

32. Mayle Larkin.

33. The Athenaeum, another of Cincinnati's three theaters, scheduled touring actors as well as local talent. See map 5. That evening's bill included *Rip Van Winkle, Henry IV, Monsieur Mallet or The Post Office Mistake,* and concluded with the farce *Nick, The Cabman* (COM, 27 November 1847).

34. One of William Shakespeare's (1564–1616) best-loved characters, Sir John Falstaff is a drunkard who befriends young Prince Hal in *Henry IV, Part I.*

35. Henry Mersman. See map 4.

36. JJM's choice of words may reflect the general interest in classical civilizations that was fashionable, or it may indicate his knowledge of Shakespeare's *Julius Caesar:* "Therein, ye gods, you make the weak most strong; / Therein, ye gods, you tyrants do defeat" (1.3.91–92)

Although he lacked formal education, JJM attended plays including *Richard III, The Taming of the Shrew, King Lear, The Merchant of Venice, Othello,* and *Much Ado about Nothing.* JJM's exposure to theatrical language appears to influence his choice of words. For example, in chapter 9, he quotes from *Hamlet* while describing an epidemic.

37. JJM uses the term "Bradley's office" in a jocular fashion to refer to Mr. Bradley's room in the boardinghouse.

38. A lock of hair could be a keepsake for an admirer. Mary Jane Jenkins, some eight years younger than JJM, was playing the role of Cupid for Mary Price.

39. *Les Danseuses Viennoises,* a troupe of four dozen ballet dancers from Europe, toured the United States to great acclaim in 1848 (ANY, 5:256, 258, 260, 324).

40. See note 27.

41. The Koch brothers, Henry (John Heinrich) and John D., lived together. See map 4.

42. Fritz Tappe.

43. JJM refers to Mary Jane Jenkins and Mary Price. In the United States, from approximately 1846 to 1866, a "b'hoy" was understood to be a town rowdy, and a "g'hal" was the female companion of such a character. The spelling attempts to replicate the lower-class dialect, as popularized by the play *A Glance at New York in 1848.* JJM saw these spellings in newspapers of the time (Peters, 306–7; ENQ, 7 August 1848).

44. Mrs. Jenkins was waiting for Fanny Jenkins.

45. [Fr.] lesson.

46. On Saturdays, JJM tallied the records for Mr. Dexter's business, summarizing weekly income and expenses.

47. Few mid-nineteenth-century households had the plumbing required for bathing. Cincinnati had at least three large public bath houses: the Arcade Bath House, the Eagle Bath House, and Watson's Bath House. They provided warm and cold baths, shaving, hair-cutting, and shampooing services. See map 3 (CCD 1848–49, 19; COM, 23 March 1848; ENQ, 29 July 1848).

48. On 5, 6, 11, 13, 15, 18, and 20 December 1847, JJM incorrectly wrote "Novr" as the month.

49. The home of Elizabeth Kattenhorn.

50. Frederick Mersman, JJM's father, widowed in 1833, remained single for the rest of his life.

51. Eighteen-year-old Frank Mersman, JJM's youngest brother, worked wherever he could find employment as a laborer. At this time, he was in St. Louis.

52. Within the family and among close friends, the Mersmans likely spoke German. Although the father may have been able to write in German, Frank, who was only four years old when he left Oldenburg, probably could not read it. Therefore, JJM likely wrote letters in English to help his father communicate with Frank.

53. Agnes Lake, JJM's younger sister and wife of circus clown Bill Lake, was traveling with Rockwell's Circus, performing as an equestrian (MOR, 15 November 1847).

54. "Koch Senior," refers to the older Koch brother, John Heinrich. See note 41.

55. Elisabet Friedeborn married John Heinrich Koch on 4 May 1848 in Cincinnati (Hamilton County Marriage Records, A-19:403).

56. "Phiz," an abbreviation for "physiognomy," meaning face, countenance, expression, or some aspect of the face (OED, s.v. "phiz").

57. The *Liedertafel.*

58. Whist, a card game for four players divided into two partnerships, was a predecessor of bridge (Hoyle, 93–95; Beaver [2], 104–5).

59. *King of the Commons,* written by James White (1803–62), was first performed in 1846.

60. No information about a card game named "Cousini" has been found. Perhaps JJM was referring to casino, a card game for two, three, or four players (Hoyle 409–15).

61. The flood of 1847 crested on 17 December, at a point within six inches of the record set in February 1832. The 1832 flood resulted in two Cincinnati deaths, while the 1847 flood, despite widespread property damage, claimed no lives (HOC 82, 96).

62. Raised as a Roman Catholic, JJM attended a Methodist Church on this Sunday to hear Mr. Moffitt's sermon.

63. Front Street, the second street north of the river, was just one city block south of Edmund Dexter's store. See map 4.

64. Mary Jane Jenkins and Mary Price.

65. In 1846, Dexter's business was on the corner of Lower Market Street and Produce Row. By 1848, he had relocated to the west side of Sycamore Street between Columbia and Lower Market streets. See map 4 (CCD 1846, 143; CCD 1848–49, 180).

66. During the emergency, a laborer could earn five dollars for a ten-hour day of work. In comparison, JJM's wages were approximately two dollars per day (an annual salary of seven hundred dollars).

67. Edmund Dexter used stills to rectify whiskey. The flood temporarily interrupted production.

68. *The Elder Brother,* written by John Fletcher (1579–1625) and Philip Massinger (1583–1639), was first performed in 1625 (http://search.eb.com/shakespeare/micro/380/24/html, and http://search.eb.com/shakespeare/micro/211/91.html).

69. Mary Jane Jenkins and Mary Price.

70. A benefit performance was one in which a major portion of the receipts was given to a designated actor or performer (OED, s.v. "benefit"). The benefit night was generally the night before the termination of the engagement (Weisert, iv).

71. *The Lady of Lyons* (1838) was written by Edward Bulwer-Lytton (1803–73); for information about *The Elder Brother,* see note 70 above.

72. Because theatrical performances typically included multiple plays as well as singing and dancing acts, shows commonly lasted until midnight (Foster, 112).

73. Because of the flood, the Covington-Cincinnati ferryboat was unable to get close to its usual mooring. Therefore, JJM had to take a rowboat out from the water's edge to board the larger ferryboat and make the crossing.

74. The residence of Arnd Kattenhorn. See map 4.

75. Eggnog (or egg-nogg), a beverage made with eggs stirred into hot beer, cider, wine, or spirits, was popular during cold-weather months (OED, s.v. "egg nog").

76. Probably Carrman's or Karrman's home. See map 4.

77. Frederick Honkomp operated the Second Ward House. See map 5.

78. Euchre, a card game for two to seven players, was extremely popular in the United States during the nineteenth century (Hoyle, 237–41; Beaver [2], 106–9).

79. Torpedoes, toys made of explosive powder and fine gravel wrapped in paper, made loud noises when thrown against a hard surface (OED, s.v. "torpedo").

80. JJM's paternal uncle, John Henry Mersman (1794–1867), known in Oldenburg as Johann Heinrich Messmann, came to America in 1836 with his wife, Maria Elizabeth, née Schroeder, and settled in Cincinnati. The couple had at least three children, JJM's cousins: seventeen-year-old Marianne, fifteen-year-old John Henry, and six-year-old Samuel Alexander (VOL, 23 September 1867; USC 1850, M432, roll 691, page 14, lines 9–13).

81. On this Christmas, Mr. Dexter's small children included three-year-old Adolphus and five-year-old Julius (USC 1850, M432, roll 687, page 100, line 15).

82. The United States Postal Service charged ten cents per half ounce for letters sent over three hundred miles. For half-ounce letters to California or Oregon, the charge was forty cents (ENQ, 21 February 1849).

83. St. Peter in Chains Cathedral. See map 3.

84. One of the two Burckhardt brothers, probably the younger, Leopold.

85. That night, Junius Brutus Booth appeared in two plays: *The Merchant of Venice* by William Shakespeare, and a farce, *The Review* (COM, 27 December 1847).

86. As a result of time constraints, performing only part of a Shakespearian play was a common practice in the 1840s.

87. See note 37.

88. Eliza Logan appeared in the *The Naiad Queen* (1839) by J. S. Dalrymple (COM, 31 December 1847).

CHAPTER TWO

Theater and Circus

1 January 1848–11 March 1848

Cincinnati's urban environment offered JJM a variety of entertainments. The National, Athenaeum, and German Theaters regularly scheduled touring actors and usually changed their bills nightly. Famous performers, including Junius Brutus Booth, Edwin Forrest, Anna Cora Mowatt, and Julia Dean, appeared with local talent in productions of classics as well as popular fluff. Although JJM lived far from the glamorous stages of New York, he sought to develop a sophisticated appreciation of the arts by attending shows two or three times per week.

The circus held a special interest for JJM. His younger sister Agnes had married a celebrated clown, William Lake Thatcher, in May 1846, and the two began a life on the road, using the stage names Bill and Agnes Lake. A major port on the Ohio River, Cincinnati was the home of several circus troupes. The tent show season customarily extended from the first of May until the end of October. During those warm months, Agnes and Bill Lake saw the Mersman family infrequently because bookings took them to distant cities on the Mississippi and Ohio rivers (see map 1). When ice and snow limited river travel and made tent shows impossible, the equestrians, acrobats, and other performers practiced new routines at their winter quarters.

A horsewoman even before her marriage, Agnes Lake aimed for success as a rope walker, an act she debuted during the 1848 season. JJM adored Agnes; he admired her talent and visited her often when she was in Cincinnati. Of all the people in his life, Agnes was his favorite.

Saturday January 1st 1848

The first day of this blessed year was exceedingly disagreable both in and out doors. It rained more or less the whole day, was very muddy in the streets, and as it was Saturday very few Stores Closed, so that those who are in general

William Lake Thatcher, aka Bill Lake (1817–69), c. 1865. Bill Lake married Agnes Mersman, worked in various circuses, operated his own circus, and was shot in an altercation over ticket money in Missouri. He was a renowned clown, and very popular with patrons. Agnes operated the Lakes' circus on her own after his death. (The York County Heritage Trust, PA.)

mostly disposed toward mirth, jolity and fun were confined to their desks. I dined with Moulinier. he had invited a few mutual friends. There was also a young Lady a Miss Cheever who contributed in some degree towards passing time pleasantly. We played Cards part of the time. I returned to the Store just

in time to Close up. Waited until Moulinier came back, took two bottles of Port Wine[1] along with us. The supper like the dinner was excellent. We Commenced the evenings Amusement with Music, but that having a tendency to make us rather silent and melancholy we changed to something quite the reverse viz[2] Card Playing. Mr Baker appeared to be very fond of it. I as before was Miss Cheevers partner. we played with varied success. at first we lost 3 games in succession, the next 4 we won and so on. we adjourned at ½ past 12 oclock. It is'nt to be supposed, however, that we did'nt do any thing els except playing. we nearly finished the two bottles of wine, had of course plenty of Cakes and other eatables with it. Mr Baker was not precisely typsy, but fully half seas over.[3] It being very late, I at the earnest Solicitation of Baker went and slept with him all night.[4] before going to bed however we took a bottle of Champaigne togather, which about finished my friend Baker. It was two oclock when we got into Bed. I slept Soundly till ½ past 7 next Morning.
[Margin note] My expences for the first day in this year were about 1.50, a good beginning. I have Spent this year about 430.00, 130$ more tha I intended.

Sunday January 2nd 1848

I and Baker were dressed and had our breakfast by ½ 8 this Morning.[5] after lighting a Cigar we went to my Store togather, where I treated my young friend to a glass of good Port. we then proceeded up Walnut togather. I went home, left him going up [?] St. to meet an engagement. I was home writing the whole forenoon, not having my French lesson finished. After dinner, or rather towards Evening, for it was 3 oclock when Moulinier came, I had my lesson. Shortly after four I went to my Sisters, passed my time there till Supper time. After Supper I went to Kochs in order to learn something of our *Liedertafel* Ball. The young blaguards[6] were all sleepy yet. The good fellows Came very near having a fight. Mr Kock Senr got a blow from our good friend and Swill Companion Groenlandt. they were however prevailed upon to cool themselves, before it got to be Serious. I left there ½ past 8 amused myself with the young Ladies at home until the old ones returned from Church, then indulged in an half hours religious Conversation. Smoked a Cigar after the Ladies had retired. Went to Bed 10 oclock Exp 5 cts.

Jany 3rd (Monday)

Business Commenced very good. Weather pleasantly Cool. The Evening I passed entirely at home, but in place of Working at my french lesson as I ought to have done I passed or rather Idled my time away with the Ladies in the Parlour. not that I did'nt amuse myself, for I did. we had lots of fun Myself, Dow, Del—r and the Women. I and Dow treated them to Some music. Smoked till 11 Wrote till 12.

Tuesday Jan 4th 1848

Business very good. Weather pleasant. every thing as it Should be. The Evening I was writing at home until 8 oclock. then went with Dow to the election of officers at the young Men's Mercantile Library Association.[7] Smoked at home till 10. wrote french again until 11. then tired and Weary with a long days business I went to bed. Exp 25c.

Wednesday 5th

Business very good indeed. our whisky Sales are infirior to none. Weather pleasant. After supper I had my french lesson, which of course kept me at home the whole Evening. From 10 to 11 I Employed with Delamettre in Smoking. We also went to the Billy Tell and drank a glass of Ale. for this however we suffered during the night D. had the nightmare, and I voided about pint of live giving material that I otherwise Should have retained. No Expence at all.

Thursday January 6th

Weather beautifully pleasant. Business is also very pleasant going about as brisk as we can desire it. After supper I called on Henry's Wife in order to arrange about the making of Shirts. from there I went to see my old acquaintance Julia P—[8] and her Sister. The young [ladies] were in excellent health, but a little reserved because I had'nt been there for more than 2 months. their brother was Ill. poor fellow he had danced too much. I passed a pleasant Evening. To Bed 11. Exp 5c.

Friday January 7th 1848.

I was busily occupied the whole day. had but little time devote to my french. Weather pleasant. The Evening I passed with Brown at the Atheneum. We Witnessed 3 pieces and they were all three very good.[9] The performance detained us until nearly 11 oclock. We went direct home Smoked our Cigars and Went to bed 12. Exp 1.10.

Saturday 8th

To day is the Anniversary of the glorious Battle of New Orleans.[10] The Evening I passed at home, excepting a short Walk which I took in Company of Mrs Bradley and Mrs Howe to see the fire. it was Shires Old Theatre,[11] which burned very brightly, and had in its exit more Witnesses or larger Audience than it ever had before. It made a beautiful Illumination. the houses and trees were just

Cov'red with Snow, which at the time was falling fast and looked like glittering rubies. I had a french lesson from 8 to 10. Then to Bed. Exp 10

Sunday 9th.

The Earth was Covred this Morning with 4 inches Snow. I waited for my brother till 10, then went to his house. he was undressed yet. did'nt [as] I intended to have went to Covington as the Weather was too disagreable for him. About 11 I went to Kattenhorns, where I had dinner and passed my time till 3 oclock. then I went to our Singing room. from there Some 5 or 6 of us went to Rebstock. I was modest, did'nt drink any thing except a glass of Punch. I had supper at home, passed the Evening there also. It being in my estimation too disagreable out doors. To Bed 10. Exp 15c.

Monday January 10th 1848.

Was without doubt the Coldest Morning we have had this Winter. My hair was gray when I got down to the Store, being Cov'red with frost. Business was dull. The Evening I passed at home, writing my french exercise. I wrote till 10 oclock when, being very tired with leaning over the table and writing, I went down to join Brown who was Smoking. Shortly before 11 all of us went to the Fountain Saloon[12] and partook of elegant refreshment. This was a Temperance Depot so we had no chance to tipple.[13] we returned direct home. Smoked till 12 oclock, then to bed. Exp 15c

Tuesday 11th

Business a little better to day. Weather slightly milder. After supper I had a lesson which of Course kept me at home. from 10 to ½ past I smoked with Brown, read till 11, then to Bed. Exp 10c

Wednesday 12th

Very disagreable day, raining at intervals throughout the day. Business passably good. The Evening I passed at Mouliniers house. The young Man had small party assembled. I went in Company with Mr Baker. The early part of the Evening passed very stiffly, the Company not having been suffisciently long acquainted. immediatly after Supper we played a game with a Plate,[14] the plate of Course was broke which also broke the game. Mr Baker introduced the Card Table. I, Baker, Miss Lodge and Mrs Pullan amused ourselves Capitally playing Whist. I came very near falling in love with Mrs. P—n. She was beautiful. I took Miss Cheever home. To bed 1. Exp 5.

Thursday Jany 13th 1848.

Was the nastiest and most disagreable day that I have ever seen. Business was in Consequence thereof very dull.

After Supper I had my Coat mended at Kochs for which I paid them 50 cts. About 9 oclock I went with Del'r to the Merchants reading room. from there we went to Bank Exchange where I Spent 20 cts for dayton Ale. returned home 10. Miss Fanny Came home immediately afterwards. I was Called upon to treat to Some Pea-Nuts which I had lost some time ago in a bet with the Old Lady.[15] of [course] I had to fork over. After the Ladies had retired I and Brown and Del'r got into a discussion about the propriety of Compliments the difference between Compts and flattery. this kept us busy till ½ past 12 oclock. Exp 40 cts.

Friday 14th.

Weather passably good. Business not bad. The Evening I passed at home, studying french and amusing myself with the girls.[16] Smoked till 10. then to bed. Exp 10c

Saturday 15th

Was beautiful Weather. Commerce prospered Satisfactorily. My Cash was obstinate at first and would'nt balance but by a Careful Comparison of all the Accts I Succeeded in a Close balance.[17] My young friend Baker passed the afternoon with me in the Store. I invited him to Supper. Shortly afterwards Moulinier Came. We all discussed languages and poetry so much that my lesson suffered by it. I went to bed at 11. Expence 5c

Sunday Jan. 16th 1848

Early in the Morning it was a little Cold, but about 9 it Cleared off beautifully. I and Henry went over the river to Mr Puthoffs,[18] I having some business to transact with him. I saw my old flame Mary. not having seen her for nearly 6 months I expected to find her somewhat altered, but she was just the same only a little paler it seemed to me. I had very little Conversation with her, and what I had—was of very slight importance. I transacted my business with her Father to our mutual satisfaction. I have his note for two hundred Dollars payable at the End of this year, also his obligation to pay me Eight Dollars as part of Interest, which I shall notice in this record as soon as he pays it to me.[19] I returned to town about dusk, had to wait for the Ferry boat nearly ½ an hour. I was quite weary when I reached home. Consequently was not to be tempted to go to church with any of the Ladies. I tried to Civilize our virtuous Cook but the girls were in the road[20] so I could'nt Come it.[21] I read till 9, then joined the

Company in the parlour. Smoked after the Women had retired, with Brown till 10. Exp 30c

Monday Jan 17th

Most beautifull Weather. Our Commercial speculation were numerous and successful.

The Evening I passed at Mrs Corbins. the young Ladies were in excellent spirits and evidently glad to see me. I passed an agreable Evening with them. I got a ring from Mary which I certainly did not expect. to Bed 11. Exp 5c

Tuesday 18th January 1848

The Weather underwent a severe transition to day. this Morning beatiful, almost spring—this Evening bitter Cold. I passed the Evening in Mr Bradley's office playing Euchre. We Concluded the amusement by playing for the liquor all-round. I lost and had to pay it. We smoked till nearly 11 oclock. Exp 45c. I lent Edgar W. Scott[22] Two hundred dollars this day. to be repaid at the End of this year with Interest at the rate of Ten per ct Semi-Annually[23] ~ I suppose him very good.

Wednesday 19th

Was a beautiful and pleasant Winters day. Business was rather wintry, not much doing. I had a french lesson after supper. After being through with it, I wrote a third of my next lesson. about 10, being tired with writing and leaning over a table, I went down in the parlour. Shortly after 11 I and D[elamater] retired. Exp 135c. I paid Bradley my Share of a bet about Tosso's Concert[24] 1.25.

Thursday 20th

The Weather continues beautiful & pleasant. Business slightly dull. After supper I called on my young friend Baker. He had to escort some Ladies to a place.[25] So I left, went to my brothers house, passed the Evening there very agreably till 9 oclock. When I returned there was quite a party in my room. I had to assist Fanny in some of her songs with my flute. The generosity of Mr Delamaître was very Conspicuous. he volunteered and did treat us all to Egg Nogg. To Bed. 11. No Exp.

Friday Jan 21st 1848.

It is really too annoying to be stuck up before an old and rusty desk on a beautiful day like this. O that I was rich! I fear whenever I become so, the power of Enjoyment will have deserted me. although a poor Consolation it is nevertheless fact, that over half of this Worlds Creatures are less blessed than even I am. I was busy the whole day. what little time I could spare from business, I applied to my french lesson. I missed a french lesson in the week between Christmas and New Year. this week I intend to regain it so I had, and will have to study hard.

After the lesson I called with Moulinier on Mr Baker. the young [man] was home, but seemed partially out of humour as it was later than I expected and promised it would be. We smoked and enjoyed ourselves Capittally till 11 oclock. I went direct home and also direct to Bed. Exp 5c.

Saturday Jan. 22nd.

Another beautiful day has passed. during the whole of this Week the Weather has been most delightful. Business has also been very good. It was with a peculiar satisfaction I Commenced balancing a tolerably sized Cash Account and with no ordinary pleasure did I produce a balance that did away with the necessity of a second essay [assay]. The Evening I did intend to employ in study, but Mr Brown insisted upon my accompany him to the Theatre. he (Mr Brown) is too Clever a fellow to refuse any thing of this kind. Miss Logan was the principal attraction.[26] To bed 11 oclock. Exp 25c.

Sunday Jan 23. 1848

Was a most suitable day for filling all the various churches, the Weather being all that the most fastidious could desire. I regret that my studies kept me from attending church Service.

I walked a little immediatly after breakfast to smoke a Cigar in the open Air, and give the servant a fair opportunity of Cleaning my room. Returning ½ past 9 and immediatly Commenced writing my french lesson. it was just one o'clock when I finished having written 7 pages of Stubborn Colloquial french. My lesson I had from 2 to 3. then went per appointment to my Sisters. took my flute and some music along. I and my neice's Piano Teacher played some duetts togather.[27] I invited myself to Supper. Played Cards afterwards till 8 oclock when I bade *adieu* to my brother in laws familly. went direct home. Sweet little Mary[28] was at the gate, seemingly watching for my return. I passed a pleasant evening with the young Ladies. the Old people were all in Church. I took the liberty of kissing Mary a few times. read till 10. then to bed. No Exp.

Monday Jan 24th

Weather Continues to be all that the most fastidious female can desire. Business is a shade duller then it has been lately. The Evening I passed with Mr Brown at the National Theatre. I treated to two tickets, it being Mrs Kents benefit.[29] I have not seen a Theatre so crowded for a long time. The performance was Well

Calculated to amuse a large audience, being light & humorous. It was 12 oclock when it concluded. Exp 1.15c

Tuesday January 25th 1848.

From a bright Morning the Weather consigned us to a dark and rainy afternoon and evening. I was very indifferent about the change as I was compelled to remain at home in the [evening] and give my attention to a french lesson. did not go out afterwards, but read till 10 oclock and then went to Bed. No expense.

Wednesday 26th

Was not noted for any thing very remarkable except the Weather, which was remarkably disagreable. I received two Theatre tickets from Mr Dexter to Sarcedas's Benefit.[30] I thought of Mr Monfred, and knowing that the young man has been very much confined the whole winter by his Medical Studies[31] I thought It would be a relief to him to pass an Evening in listening to well arranged nonsense. I went and invited him to go along, which he did. We amused ourselves passably. the performance for the kind was very good. We got home about 12 oclock my expences were about 40c

Thursday 27th

Dull and sometimes rainy Weather. Business was dull also. In my leisure time I attended to my french lesson. The Evening I threw away. Played a game what they call Old Maid[32] which of late has become popular with our good people.[33] from 8 to 9 I studied some french verbs. 10 went with Brown & Dow to Wm Tell. Smoked till 11. then to Bed. Exp 25c.

Friday January 28th 1848

Weather Cold but pleasant again. Business was very good this day. I did not have much leizure time to devote to my french.

Rockwell & Co's Circus[34] returned again to day and with them came my sister and Brother in law Mr Lake. I did not see them until after supper, when we met per appointment at Kattenhorns. Agness looked very nearly as handsome as ever in fact to her husband I believe she looks more so, for the good and to him very satisfactory reason that she is in the "familly Way"[35] a very bad way by the bye, but one in which it seems most Women will fall into. Well! I hope it may be a boy. if it should be I will make him my Hair in case I should die an Old bachelor. Frank did not Come with them. he refused to come, pleading a variety of excuses, half of which were false. Lake was in very good health, has been the whole summer.

We conversed about their troubles, Cares, and Amusements which they met with during the summer until 10 oclock when as they were both very tired and sleepy we all went to our respective homes. when I came home Fanny was playing on the Piano and Singing. of course it was my duty to assist her with my flute, which I did so effectually that she soon got tired of it. Smoked with Brown till 11. Exp 5c.

Saturday Jan 29th

Business very good indeed to day. I did not settle my Cash to day, it being near the End of the month. After supper I studied my french till 8 oclock, Moulinier being very late this Evening. Our lesson occupied us till 10 oclock. I did not go out afterwards but after studying till 10, I retired. Exp 5c.

Sunday January 30th 1848.

T'was rainy this Morning, and I had to go in Compliance with my promise to play a flute part in one of Mozarts best Masses[36] in 5th St Church.[37] this mass or rather Musical Mass was in honor of Mr Henni's presense. The Bishop is on a visit to this City in which his early efforts were first brot into notice, and his character as a man a[nd] student made Conspicuous.[38] I, Moulinier and Baker were treated to a couple bottles of Wine after the service was over by Mr Tappe. I came just in time get some of the remains of a Cold dinner. After dinner having recleaned myself, I went to my Sisters Mrs K[attenhorn]. found my younger Sister Mrs Lake there also.[39] We played Cards the whole afternoon & Evening till near 10 oclock. I then went home read my french lesson till 11. then went to Bed. My Expence 10c.

Monday January 31st 1848.

Was a very good, fine and agreable sort of a day, only a little too cold towards evening. Our commercial transactions Commenced very favorably. I settled my Cash this afternoon, it balanced very Closely. Our sales during January Amount to very near 10,000$ Cash.[40] Entire sales including shipments about 12000$. After supper I accepted an invitation from Mr Brown to go to the National with him. It was Yankey Hills Benefit.[41] He appeared in four pieces. during the Early part of the Evening I amused myself very well, but too much of Nonsense soon satiates, no matter how good it may be. 12, to bed. Exp 20c.

Tuesday February 1st 1848

Beautifull Weather. the ladies are making use of it. the streets especially the more fashionable one's are very attractive. Business is somewhat dull again. I commenced Writing a letter to Clemens[42] this Evening. had no time tho' to finish it, as I had promised my sister to visit her. which of course I had no inclination to break. Went home and to bed 11 oclock. Exp 10c.

Wednesday 2nd

Business decidedly dull, no matter! we have been doing well all this winter. Mr Dexter gave me 9 Theatre tickets[43] this morning, which Came very near making me feel of some importance to my friends. I gave 3 to sweet Fanny Jenkins. She took Mrs Howe and Mr Delamettre with them. I also treated Mr Brown, Dow and Mr Wardner to one each. this left me 3 for which I took my sister Agnes, her husband and myself. Agnes was Splendidly dressed and looked really beautiful. we made a favorable impression upon those around us. the Performance was very poor. It was ½ past 12 when I got in bed.
[Margin note] Exp 20 cts.

Thursday 3rd

Business more favorable again. Weather pleasant again. After supper I made my long defered call on the Misses Corbins. The young Ladies looked bright and happy. Some one of the boarders had a small galvanic Machine[44] there, with which we Amused ourselves Capittally for an hour or so. we then played Cards till 10 oclk when I travel'd home. not finding any body up I went to bed.

Friday February 4th 1848.

It changed from Warm pleasant Weather to Cold raw and Windy and by no means Warm Weather. Business was very good to day. After Supper I had my first french lesson this Week, and after that I finished my letter to Clemens Nulsen,[45] which I [mailed] the next or this Morning. Miss Jenkins now that she has my Piano in the Parlour holds a kind of Musical levee every evening after Supper. I have not participated as yet, nor shall I unless I have nothing else to do. to bed 11.
[Margin note] No expense.

Saturday 5th

I have not been more sensibly affected by the Cold Weather the whole Winter, than this Morning. unfortunately I was very busy this morning, and suffered much. My Cash balanced badly at first, but I detected an error which made the balance fair. The Evening I passed at home, playing Cards in the Early part and writing my french exercises till 10 oclock. Smoked with Brown till 10[46] then to bed. Exp 10c.

Sunday 6th

Most Confounded Cold the whole day. The whole forenoon I passed at home writing my French exercise but did'nt finish then. I also had a regular Scrubbing from head to toe.[47] Immediately after dinner I had my french lesson, and went immediatly after it to my sisters. Henry and Lake with their wives were there. we had a first rate time of it. I eat too much, suffered afterwards Consequently. we played Cards till ½ past 8. before going to bed I wrote a page of french and smoked a Cigar. Expence 20 cts.

Monday February 7th 1848

Weather very Cold again. Commerce made a lively Commencement for the Week. The Evening I passed entirely at home. Entertained Mrs Howe and Fanny till 8 oclock. then wrote 3 pages of french exercises. Studied and Wrote till ½ past 9. finished the Evening with Smoking. No Expense.

Tuesday 8th

Weather moderated Considerably. it was however very windy and Consequently dusty. business good. The Evening I passed with Mr Brown in the National. Mr. C. D. Pitt,[48] an Englishman, performed *Werner* a Tragedy by Byron. he is a fair actor but of so different a Scool that the Audience seemed at a loss whether to admire or Condemn. his acting pleased me passably the piece very much. It was 12 oclock when I got in bed. Exp 25.

Wednesday 9th

Was a most lovely day. business being dull in the afternoon I had plenty time to finish my french. Moulinier came at an early hour. We Were ready at 9 oclock I did not go out but read till 11 oclock. then went to bed. Exp 5.

Thursday 10th

Beautiful and lovely, of which many a lovely woman took advantage. Business was rather dull. After Supper I amused myself with my flute till ½ past 7 then Called on my sister.[49] found her in good health practicing the Guitar. returned home ½ past 9. Smoked and [talked?] till ½ past 10, then retired to my Couch. Exp 10c

Friday 11th February 1848

The Weather is "beautiful Winter Weather" business is very good. We sell our Double Rectd about as rapidly as we can rectify it. After supper I called on my brothers Wife. borrowed Henry's German Copy of Shakespiere[50] and lent it to Mr Baker on whom I called ½ past 7. Passed my time there very agreably till 10. Then went with Baker to Wm Tell and treated him to a glass of Ale. from there we went direct to our respective homes. to bed 11 oclock Exp 15c.

Saturday feb 12th

Passed away without any thing remarkable occurring. Weather was all that could be desired. my Cash balanced to perfection. The Evening I passed at home, Having my french lesson during the early part, and Entertaining Mr Baker and Mr Moulinier as my Guests till past 10 oclock. then went and Smoked with Brown Exp 25.

Sunday Feb 13th

Was certainly the most beautiful Sunday we have had for some time past. Although not dressed I indulged in a Walk immediatly after breakfast. went up to Kattenhorns. returned home 10 oclock. finished my last french lesson. After dinner I called per appointment on Baker, but the young Man disappointed me. I can of course not consider him a Man of Word and strick veracity. The Evening I passed at Julia P's and I must confess very pleasantly, although I have really neglected them lately. I did not leave there until past 10 oclock. No Expense.

Monday february 14th 1848 St Valentines day

I was roused from sleep this [morning] by the rain splattering against my Window, a cause of real satisfaction to me, as I have had a head ache for the last two days from the Clouds of dust that have been annoying Everybody that sported a large nose. I do not think I shall send a Valentine, or receive one. After supper I went to Theatre with Brown and Delamettre. It was Mr Pitts benefit, the Pieces *Merchant of Venice* and *The Lady of Lyons.*[51] both were performed admirably by Mr P. in some of the characters he was but indifferently sustained. Billy Wharam was drunk and Played his last character very badly. between the first and 2nd pieces we went to the St Charles[52] and Commenced tippling slightly. After the Plays were over we went to the United States[53] and enjoyed another stiff Horn, then went home, and Amused ourselves with criticising the play and smoking till 1 oclock. Exp 65.

Tuesday 15th

Raining more or less the whole day. Business was very dull the whole day. I had some [time] to spare for my french. After supper I did nothing particularly Except assisting towards making time pass pleasantly in the Parlour Playing on my flute till the Chambermaid interrupted me. tried to make her give me her Maidenhead,[54] but she had'nt time to give it up. Then went to Kochs, where I met my old friend Menzel. Subscribed to a Maskerade Ball to be given 2nd March.[55] Shortly after 9 I went with Brown to the fair of the Catholic free Scool.[56] I went without any Money, but was Compelled to borrow. from there we went to Billy Tells. Smoked at home till 11. Exp 45c.

Wednesday feb 16th 1848

I received a letter from Clemens and my brother Frank to day. Clemens is in ecstacy with his Bride elect,[57] and Frank is grumbling because I hinted to Clemens in my last letter that if he Contracted any gambling debts I would'nt pay them, and I do not intend to anull this Clause.

I was very busy the whole day. had'nt time to finish my french lesson. During the afternoon in my leisure moments I menaged to finish a letter of 3 pages to Frank.

After Supper I had my french lesson which occupied me till ½ past 9. I went with Moulinier to the Billy Tell. he treated to a glass of ale. from there direct home. Smoked with Brown till 11 oclock. then to bed. Exp 5.

Thursday 17th

Busy the whole day and very much so. After Supper I amused myself at home, with the girls, my flute and french lesson. did not go out at all. To bed 11. No Exp.

Friday 18th

Business was not particulary bright, the Weather not over pleasant. I went to Theatre with Moulr. Mr Pitt performed *King Lear*[58] and did it well. it is however a horid piece and portrays human nature in its worst form. Mrs Dexter was there also. as Mr D[exter] was not there, I, and M[oulinier] endeavour'd to amuse the Ladies (Mrs. D[exter] and Julia)[59] to the best of our abilities. Julia Dellinger does not possess much Theatrical discrimination. Booth[60] in the Concluding Farce was very good. The farce was much relished by the audience after the horifying Sensations produced by *King Lear.* We took the Ladies home. To Bed, 12. Exp 65c.

Saturday February 19th 1848

I was very busy the whole day, althoug not with the aff[61] Business of the Store, but with shipping, bills' Lading[62] and running to and from the River. I had my french lesson immediatly after Supper. it occupied us nearly till 9 oclock. Moulinier had to go to the Singing room. I and Baker went to the fair.[63] we did not spend a great deal of money, for the excellent reason that we had very little with us. About 10 oclock we went out to Wm Tell and enjoyed a glass of Egg Nogg. Baker acknowledged that it was the first glass he had ever drank, and also that he liked it passably well. about 11 oclock we left the fair, and went to my boarding house where we smoked until ½ past. Exp 60c.

Sunday 20th.

It was somewhat Cloudy this Morning but otherwise very pleasant. I and John Bradly had along Walk togather after breakfast. from 10 to 12 I wrote my french for ensuing Week, then dressed myself Carefully for dinner. After which I went to Mr Tappe with Delamaître. looked at some of his Guitars, and other Musical instruments. from there I went to Menzels rooms, but left delr on the way. then Sallied out to see Julia & her sister[64] in order to [invite] them to the Maskerade Ball to Come off in a few weeks. I was ASStonished that my invitation was not accepted with avidity which I anticipated. they Wished to consult their Parents first. Went home to Supper. Passed the Evening at Mouliniers. To Bed ½ pas 11. Exp 15c.

Monday february 21st 1848

Business Commenced Smashingly this Morning. I had no time to look at my french the whole day. The Eve'g I passed with Brown, and at Browns expence in the Theatre. Mr Pitt performed *Gissippus*[65] in the Play of this Name. It was a most affecting and thrilling piece of acting. I have never seen an audience more enthusiastic in their applause. We remained to see the last piece also. for doing so we had to go home in the rain. 12 oclock to Bed. Exp 65c.

Tuesday 22nd

It is Washingtons Birth Day. Dancing Masters seem to be the only persons disposed to Celebrate it by giving a Ball in honor of it. The profits of which—but never mind the profits . . . [66]

Business was very good to day. Weather very disagreable. After Supper I wrote french till nearly 8 oclock then Went to See my Sister[67] with whom I passed my time agreably till ½ past 10. went direct home, to bed at 11. Exp 5c

Wednesday 23rd

Weather beautiful. Business was rather dull, but still I had plenty to day. My french lesson Came immediatly after Supper, but we did'nt finish until after 10 oclock. of course part of the time was passed with Conversation that was'nt much to the purpose. After Moulinier left I went below to Smoke my Customary Cigar. To Bed 11. Exp 10c.

Thursday Feb 24th 1848

Weather the whole day was very windy and unpleasant out doors. Business not particularly brisk either.

The Evening I passed with Mrs Moulinier and Miss Cheever witnessing the Concert of the Amateur Society.[68] the instrumental part was very good indeed Especially the two overtures that were performed. The Quartett's were all poor—very. Solo's only bearable. The Chorus was good, very good. The Hall was over Crowded. I had a headache half an hour after I entered. And was unfortunately ditained until ½ past 10. It was my pleasant duty to take Miss C[heever] home. the young Lady looked really beautiful. My love and ardour had however time to Cool off by the time we arrived at her house. She invited my [me] Warmly to Come and See her, which I promised. To bed 12. Exp 10.

Friday 25th

Yesterday news was received of the Death of J. Q. Adams. He died at Washington. ~~in his~~ The Evening I passed entirely at home writing french.

Saturday 26th

Weather was beautiful. Business slightly dull. I had no Cash to settle this afternoon, waiting very patiently for the End of the month.[69] The Evening I passed entirely at home again, being detained there by my french lesson until ½ past 9 oclock. balance of time till 12 oclock I passed with Mr Brown Smoking our Cigars. [Margin note] Paid Mrs Jenkins for Boarding to date 12.00 also for washing 1.00.

Sunday February 27th 1848

Was undoubtedly the finest Weather we have had for a long time. I and my brother-in-law, Lake made use of the forenoon by taking a buggy ride to Joe Harrisons old Place.[70] on the road I drank a glass of Ale, and when we arrived there I had a glass of Egg Nogg. It seems that the two Could'nt agree togather in my Stomach. the Consequence was that I was sick for the balance of the day.

We returned and were in town ½ past 12. Had dinner at home. After it, from ½ past 1 to nearly 3 I walked about the Eastern part of the City with Mr Delamettre—did not notice many improvements along there. About 3 I left Delr and went to Kattenhorns, had Coffee with the familly in the good old german fashion. About 4 oclock Lake and Agness also came. they had been to the Same place we were in the Morning. I had Supper there, and played Cards with the Balance until ½ past 8. then went home wrote two pages french, after which I went into the dining room where I Smoked till 11. Exp 65c

Monday, feb 28th

Very Cold and disagreable this Morning. Business Commenced tolerbly fair for a retail Business, which after all is the most profitable.

After Supper I promised myself some pleasure in going to Miss Cheever, but the young Lady was not at home. I was not preperred for this, not having my Card Case with me.[71] from there I went home, studied french verbs till ½ past 9, then smoked my Customary evening Cigar. To Bed 11. Exp 5c

Tuesday february 29th 1848.

The last leap year day in this month. was not a very pleasant one being very Cold and windy. The Evening I passed with my sister, Mrs Lake. I waited for her husband very patiently till 11 oclock when he Came. He brot me some dresses[72] for the Maskerade which is to come off in a few days. It was 12 oclock when I left. Went of Course direct home. Exp 15.

Wednesday March 1st 1848

Not an over agreable day by any Means, being too cold alltogather after the weather we have had. Business was very good to day. After supper I had a french lesson. I also purchased a french course of instruction by Dufief[73] from Mr Dwelle[74] for which I paid 3$ I did not go out after my lesson, but having Smoked a Cigar went to bed early.

Thursday 2nd

It was Snowing when I awoke this Morning, and Continued to do so nearly throughout the entire day. I arrived late at the ball this Evening, having to arrange a very troublesome dress i e a polka dress.[75] It was fully 9 oclock when I got in the Ball room.[76] they all unmasked shortly after I came. Every person there Seemed to amuse himself Satisfactorily. the objection that could be made was that the piece was too long entirely. this of course delayed supper time. I had little Miss Koch to the supper table.[77] I did not however feel very galantly disposed. I had plenty of opportunities to dance, and fortunately always had good dancer. It was five when I got home this Morning. Total Ball Exp 3.90.

Friday March 3rd 1848.

I slept quite cozily till ½ past 10 oclock this Morning. I was not tired or any ways much out of Sorts. Mr Dexter had been very busy and was Complaining when I came down. I did not regret my absense. I was employed however all the balance of the day. The evening I passed in lounging about the parlour. the girls would'nt [let] me read. I went however to bed a little before 10 and slept well. No Exp.

Saturday March 4th

I am over the effects of the ball. was bright and busy the whole day. my Cash balanced to satisfaction. did'nt get home till late though. had a french lesson after Supper for which however I was but poorly prepared. Baker passed the entire afternoon and Evening with [me]. after my lesson I and Baker went to the Library rooms,[78] from there to "Bill Tell." Baker would'nt drink. suppose he saw somebody that knew his ralation with the Bishop.[79] from there we both went direct home. Exp 15c.

Sunday March 5th

Beautiful weather, indeed. I called on Baker 8 oclock. took him to my room, where we passed the entire forenoon, reading and studying. After dinner I called on Miss Koch—time lost—then went to K[attenhorn]'s. had Coffee there. Called on Wagner,[80] did not find him at home, on Henry, not at home either. Went home and wrote a few pages of french before supper. About 7 Mr Baker Called on me. we went togather to Mr Moulinier's. Passed a pleasant evening there. to Bed 11 oclock. No Exp.

Monday March 6th 1848

The morning dawned with a transplendant brilliancy upon "Porkopolis."[81] every thing look gay and animated throughout the City. Business kept pace with the lively scene and Compelled me to move about the whole day in a very lively measure in order to do justice to it. The Evening allthoug beautiful I passed with the rest of the Gentleman in Mrs. Howe's room, enjoying with her

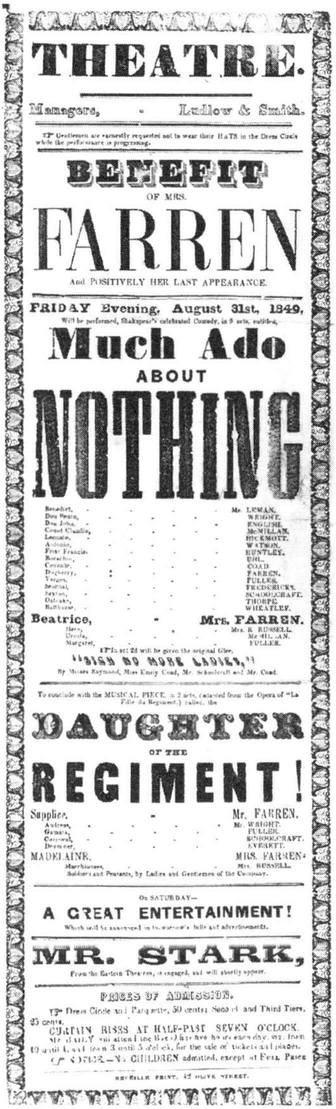

Mrs. Farren Benefit advertisement, 31 August 1849. Benefit performances, with proceeds going to a particular member of the cast or troupe, were one of the ways audiences showed their appreciation for certain performers. (Theater Programs Collection, Missouri Historical Society, St. Louis.)

for the last time a Social game of Old Maid. Mrs H. starts to Morrow for Burlington, O. taking her children along. I did not go out at all. Went to Bed at 11. No Expence.

Tuesday 7th

Business continues to be very good I was Employed the whole day. After supper I had the Gentleman of our Establishment in my room playing Euchre. Brown donated the eatables and drinkables, the latter being in the shape of a dozen bottles of Cider Champagne[82] and a grand pound Cake.[83] We enjoyed it very much till 10 oclk, when being tired we went to bed. No Expences.

Wednesday 8th

Charles Dexter's letter advising his admission to Cambridge University.[84] The young man had a very severe struggle for it. Business continues excellent. Weather disagreable, streets very muddy. The Evening I passed in my room entirely, studying french. I was to have had a french lesson, but Moulinier did not come. he went, I believe, to the Theatre. To Bed at 11 oclok. Exp 15c.

Thursday March 9th 1848

Although very busy the whole day I menaged to steal suffiscient time to write Charles Dexter a letter of 3 pages, being one of congratulation upon his entry in Cambridge, also explaining my unusual long silence, and giving such general information as I thought likely would interest him. I mail'd the letter in the Evening, wishing it safe to hand,[85] for I have little spare time to write letters in. After Supper I called on Moulinier. poor fellow! he has been Confined to his room for the last two days with a Cold. from there went direct home, and about 11 oclock to Bed. Exp 5c.

Friday March 10th

Was a passably lovely day. business however was not very bright. After Supper just as I and Brown were Cloaking ourselves to go to the Theatre Fanny returned from Dayton. that did not prevent us from witnessing Harry Placide in *London Assurance.*[86] I saw Hunt in the same piece some five years ago. H.P. was Capittal. Some of the other Characters were poorly supported. The last piece was a miserable burlesque. we did not stay to see it out. Went home about 11. Smoked till ½ past, then to bed. Exp 30.

Saturday 11th

Was a very pleasant day. the Ladies were out *en masse.*[87] My cash balanced very nearly, overruning some 5$ though. After supper I had a french lesson at Mouliniers. The young [man] has not yet suffisciently recovered to go out in the Evening. to bed 11. Exp 10.
[Margin note] Mrs Puthoff Paid me the 8$ due by Mr H.[88] I paid them over to Henry in full for 6 shirts made by his Seamstress.

NOTES

1. Port is a dark-red wine of Portugal (OED, s.v. "port").
2. *Videlicet,* abbreviated "viz.," is Latin for "that is to say; namely" (OED, s.v. "videlicet").
3. "Half seas over" means somewhat intoxicated (OED, s.v. "half-seas-over").
4. Sleeping accommodations of the era commonly placed two same-sex individuals in one bed without any implication of sexual involvement (Kasson, 14–15).
5. This numerical rendition of the German "*halb acht*" (7:30 a.m.) reflects JJM's fluency in both languages.
6. Phonetic spelling of "blackguard" or scoundrel (OED, s.v. "blackguard").
7. The New York Mercantile Library Association, founded in 1821, set an example that men in other cities followed. By 1835, Cincinnati had a similar organization (Augst, 161). See Annotated List of Persons, Places, and Businesses.
8. Julia Puthoff and her sister Mary. Their brother was named Frank. See note 18.
9. The bill that night included a farce, *Thimble Ring,* and two other plays: *Charles II* and *The Miller and His Men* (COM, 7 January 1848).
10. The Battle of New Orleans, fought 8 January 1815, was a triumph for Andrew Jackson, although it occurred fifteen days after the War of 1812 officially ended (DAB, 9:526–34).
11. Arson was blamed for the fire at Shires Old Theatre, a wooden building that had been unused for two years, and cleared the ground construction of the Burnet House (HOC, 374; ENQ, 10 January 1848; COM, 10 January 1848).
12. Located on the southeast corner of Fifth and Walnut, the Fountain Saloon served only sodas, fruits, and confections in a plush crimson interior. Shortly afterward, the saloon went out of business and advertised furniture and fixtures for sale (ENQ, 19 February 1848).
13. In the early nineteenth century, Americans consumed more alcohol than at any other time in history. However, a revolution in social attitudes occurred midcentury, and outspoken individuals promoted temperance as the solution to the social ills blamed on alcohol. In 1848, Cincinnati had twenty-five clubs opposed to alcohol use: six chapters of the Daughters of Temperance, fifteen chapters of the Sons of Temperance, and four chapters of the Cadets of Temperance (CCD 1848–49, 188, 199–200; Stowell, 1).
14. "Spin the trencher," a popular parlor game, was more commonly played with a wooden bread board or circular tray instead of a ceramic plate. The starting player spun the trencher on its side and called out the name of another player. The named player had to catch the object before it stopped spinning. Success permitted that person to be the next spinner (Beaver, 43–44).
15. Mrs. Jenkins.
16. Mary Jane Jenkins and Mary Price.
17. Every Saturday JJM balanced the books for Dexter's business.
18. At least two dozen individuals with the surname "Puthoff" or "Putthoff" emigrated from Oldenburg to America in the decade beginning 1836. Belonging to two major family branches, many

Puthoffs settled in Cincinnati. Some found homes across the Ohio River in Kentucky. JJM knew Puthoffs in both places, for some were his cousins, and all had been family friends for decades. Francis H. Puthoff, who resided in Covington, Kentucky, had a daughter, Mary (1829–60), who caught JJM's eye. In 1845, Mary Puthoff joined JJM in witnessing Henry Mersman's second marriage (his first wife, Mary Imsicke, had died soon after their 1842 wedding), so she clearly was a close friend. However, JJM must have extricated himself carefully in order to preserve the cordial relations (Mersman-Tebbelman marriage, 19 August 1845, Holy Trinity Marriage Register, unpaginated, arranged by date, HAC).

19. Thus, JJM charged his friend 4 percent interest.

20. JJM means "in the way" or "causing an obstruction" (OED, s.v. "road").

21. "Couldn't come it" means "could not accomplish that" (Brewer, 258; COM, 10 January 1848).

22. Edgar B. Scott was a farmer in Hamilton County, outside the city limits of Cincinnati. Possibly, JJM wrote the middle initial incorrectly.

23. Ohio law limited the interest rate to 6 percent, so JJM's agreement was not legally enforceable if the debtor failed to repay the debt (SLD 1848, xiii).

24. Joseph S. Tosso, a violinist, frequently performed in Cincinnati with Mrs. Scheidler, Mr. Runge, and the *Liedertafel* singing society. Injured by the explosion of the steamer *Blue Ridge,* Tosso was honored by a benefit concert on 21 January 1848. The nature of JJM's bet is not known (ENQ, 13 January 1848; 19 November 1847; 16 April 1848).

25. When venturing after dark, respectable women usually walked with a male companion. "In a city, or any lonely place, a lady must avoid being alone after nightfall, if possible. It exposes her, not only to insult, but often to positive danger" (Frost, 94).

26. The evening's program included the comedy, *The Soldier's Daughter,* with Miss Logan in the principal role, and the drama, *The Ice Witch* (COM, 22 January 1848).

27. Elizabeth Kattenhorn's two daughters, thirteen-year-old Louisa and eleven-year-old Sophia, were JJM's nieces.

28. Mary Jane Jenkins.

29. The performance that night featured a comedy, *Somebody Else;* a two-act drama, *Fortunio and His Seven Gifted Servants;* a "military spectacle," *The French Spy;* a solo dance act; and a comic song. Ticket prices were 50 cents for box seats and 25 cents for the pit. JJM's expenses for the day suggest that he and Brown sat in box seats (COM, 24 January 1848).

30. The bill that evening at the National Theatre included two comedies, *Honest Roguery* and *The Hypocrite,* and the drama, *Fortunio and His Seven Servants.* A dance number and a comic song rounded out the performance (COM, 26 January 1848).

31. A physician's education consisted of attending lectures at a medical college and apprenticing with an established practitioner. There were many proprietary institutions in Cincinnati: the Cincinnati Medical and Surgical College, the Eclectic Medical Institute of Cincinnati, the Medical College of Ohio, the Miami Medical College, and the Physio-Medical College. Licensing of medical practitioners had not yet begun in the United States (CCD 1853, 174).

32. Old maid was a card game for two or more players, using a full deck of cards minus one of the queens. Dealt cards were discarded in pairs. The player with the odd queen was the "old maid" (Beaver [2], 98–99).

33. The residents of Jenkins's Boarding House.

34. Owned by Henry Rockwell (c. 1814–49), Rockwell & Company's New York Circus played in St. Louis from 15 November 1847 until 22 January 1848. During the long run, William Lake served as "Director of the Circle" (i.e., the ringmaster), performed as an equestrian, and led his trained dogs in their tricks. Agnes Lake appeared as a principal equestrian. The show wintered in Cincinnati and subsequently traveled to nine states in 1848 (MOR, 15 November 1847–22 January 1848; Thayer, 458–60).

35. "In the family way" means pregnant (OED, s.v. "family way").

36. Between 1766 and 1791, Wolfgang Amadeus Mozart (1756–91), composed twenty Masses for use in Catholic Church services. Two works that feature the flute are the *Mass in C Minor* (k. 427) and the *Mass in D Minor* (k. 341) (Zaslaw, 3–17).

37. Holy Trinity Church was the Mersman family's parish. See map 3.

38. The 1848 visit of Dr. John Martin Henni to Cincinnati was also described in his biography (Marty, 185). See also the Annotated List of Persons, Places, and Businesses.

39. Agnes Lake had the evening off from the circus because there were no Sunday performances.

40. This is approximately $240,000 in 2005 dollars. Edmund Dexter's whiskey business made him one of the wealthiest men in Cincinnati.

41. The program that evening at the National Theatre included the second act of the drama, *Knight of the Golden Fleece, Honest Roguery,* and the farces *Happy Man, or The Magic Shirt* and *Wife for a Day.* The performance concluded with scenes from Shakespeare's tragedy *Richard III.* A comic song completed the bill (COM, 31 January 1848).

42. John Clemens Nulsen, henceforth referred to as JCN.

43. At fifty cents per ticket, Mr. Dexter's $4.50 largess was a substantial gift to JJM. JJM had seen the plays only two days earlier, but that night he saw again *Knight of the Golden Fleece, Honest Roguery,* and the farces *Happy Man, or The Magic Shirt* and *Wife for a Day.* The performance concluded with a scene from *Richard III.* Most of JJM's guests were boarders at Jenkins's Boarding House, plus his sister and brother-in-law, the Lakes (COM, 2 February 1848).

44. A galvanic machine created an electrical charge, making the hair of anyone touching it stand on end and providing parlor amusement (OED, s.v. "galvanic").

45. JCN's business partner, Frederick William Ficke, had died suddenly in November 1847, so JCN was seeking a new partner who could bring capital to the firm (DDT, 17 November 1847).

46. JJM probably meant 11 o'clock.

47. See chapter 1, note 47.

48. The evening's bill at the National Theatre included *Werner;* a farce, *Alpine Maid;* and a comic song. It was the second night of Charles Didbin Pitt's run in Cincinnati (COM, 8 February 1848).

49. Agnes Lake.

50. William Shakespeare (1564–1616), English playwright.

51. The newspaper announced the show at the National Theatre was for Charles Dibdin Pitt's benefit, but failed to name the plays (COM, 14 February 1848).

52. The St. Charles Exchange Hotel. See map 5.

53. The United States Hotel and the United States Tavern were two separate businesses. JJM often visited the United States Hotel because Dexter & Co. maintained a shipping office there, but this reference is ambiguous (CCD 1848–49, 172).

54. "Maidenhead," or virginity, appears with playful exaggeration (OED, s.v. "maidenhead").

55. Balls provided opportunities for eligible men and women to socialize, and masquerades were both fashionable and popular in the cities (Beadle 11). No information about this social event has been found, but many balls were advertised in the local newspapers.

56. From 14 February 1848 until 21 February 1848, the "ladies friendly to gratuitous education" sponsored a fund-raising fair at the Melodeon Hall. Admission was ten cents. Their goal was to construct a beautiful building to serve as a free school (COM, 16 February 1848).

57. JCN had proposed to Albertine Creuzbauer, whom he had met at Mons. Xaupi's ballroom dancing school in St. Louis. They married 17 May 1848 (WPO, 18 May 1898; St. Louis Marriage Record, 4:190).

58. The evening's program at the National Theatre included *King Lear;* a farce, *Dead Shot;* a drama, *Cavalier;* a dance act; and *Catharine and Petruchio* (COM, 18 February 1848).

59. Julia Dillinger, Mrs. Dexter's unmarried sister.

60. Thomas G. Booth (1821–55), no relation to Junius Brutus Booth.

61. JJM may have meant "aft," a nautical term meaning "behind" or "in the rear" (OED, s.v. "aft"). Therefore, JJM was not busy with stock or the operation of the distillery, likely located behind the store, but with shipping that he handled in the front of the store.

62. A bill of lading was a detailed receipt of transported goods by which the captain of a merchant vessel made himself responsible for the safe delivery to the consignee. A bill of lading was required for freight on steamboats (OED, s.v. "bill").

63. JJM had attended this fundraiser on 15 February 1848. See note 56.

64. Julia and Kate Cobb. Tickets to the balls commonly admitted one gentleman and two ladies.

65. The plays at the National Theatre that evening included *Gisippus* and a farce, *The Young Widow.* A solo dance act filled the bill between the two plays (COM, 21 February 1848).

66. Three balls were given that evening, providing ample opportunities for dancing to the general public of Cincinnati: "Uncle Dick" Richards organized one at the Melodeon Hall; Professor White

offered one at the Assembly Rooms; and the Union Fire Company sponsored one at the Masonic Hall (ENQ, 23, 25 February 1848). There were *eight* balls given in the Over-the-Rhine neighborhood. JJM correctly saw that dancing masters profited from such social events (COM, 24 February 1848).

67. Agnes Lake.

68. The Amateur Society, a group of local musicians, scheduled instrumental and choral concerts at the Melodeon Hall. A subscription of $3 per annum admitted "one gentlemen and accompanying ladies" to a series of three performances (ENQ, 24 December 1848).

69. Mersman usually prepared weekly summaries of business transactions for Mr. Dexter on Saturdays. At the end of each month, he wrote a monthly summary.

70. "Joe Harrison's old place" has not been identified, but it likely was a tavern on the western edge of the city.

71. Etiquette required that those making calls leave engraved cards if the receiver was not "in" for callers (Hemphill, 152; Cards, 1–10).

72. JJM uses the term "dresses" when he actually means "costumes." The German word *Kleid* means a woman's dress, and the plural, *Kleider,* also means "clothes," "costume," or "clothing." This sentence supports the hypothesis that JJM still thought in German and used it in his dealings with family and friends, so his use of English sometimes reflected German grammar and syntax.

73. Nicolas Gouin Dufief (c. 1776–1834), a scholar of foreign-language education, had published extensively and influenced Jean Manesca (1774–1837). Dufief's books include *Nature Displayed in Her Mode of Teaching Language to Man; Method of Acquiring Languages with Unparalleled Rapidity, Deduced by the Analysis of the Human Mind, and Consequently Suited to Every Capacity* (London, 1836), and *A New Universal and Pronouncing Dictionary of the French and English Languages* (Philadelphia, 1810).

74. Mr. Dwelle has not been identified.

75. A lively dance of Bohemian origin, the polka reached the United States in the 1840s. However, no special clothing was required. Perhaps, for this event, JJM selected (from clothing he obtained on 29 February 1848) formal attire: a black cutaway coat, black trousers, white vest, white shirt, black tie, white kid gloves, and patent leather boots. Since he had limited resources, to other balls JJM likely wore the attire of an urban businessman as shown in his portrait (Beadle 9; OED, s.v. "polka"; Manual, 188–95).

76. Etiquette books advised it was fashionable to appear an hour late (Ruth, 109).

77. JJM escorted Miss Koch to the refreshments as each gentleman routinely accompanied a lady (Beadle, 14).

78. Probably the reading rooms of the Young Men's Mercantile Library Association.

79. Exactly how Baker was related to Bishop John Baptist Purcell has not been determined.

80. August Wagner, Anthony Nulsen's brother-in-law, had become a good friend of JJM's.

81. "Porkopolis," a nickname for Cincinnati, came from the hog-butchering activities which were well developed by the 1840s. In 1848, 475,000 hogs were packed in Cincinnati (HOC, 98; NDP, 22 November 1864; Wortley, 169).

82. Champagne is a sparkling wine named for the province in France where it was first produced (OED, s.v. "champagne"). Cider champagne, a uniquely American beverage, was a fermented product made from apple juice (Rorabaugh, 110–14).

83. Traditional pound cake was made with one pound each of butter, sugar, flour, and eggs (about eight to ten) (Rombauer, 626; Simmons, 48).

84. Charles Dexter, admitted to Harvard University in Cambridge, Massachusetts, received a bachelor's degree in 1851 (Harvard University Archives, 250).

85. "Safe to hand" means to arrive at its destination free of damage (OED, s.v. "safe").

86. The program for the evening at the National Theatre included a comedy, *London Assurance,* and a burlesque, *Bombastes Furioso.* An orchestral overture was performed between the two plays (COM, 10 March 1848).

87. [Fr.] as a group.

88. Mary Puthoff paid the interest charge noted in the 16 January 1848 entry; JJM refers to her husband, Francis H. Puthoff, by his middle initial.

CHAPTER THREE

Music and Dancing

12 March 1848–29 April 1848

In JJM's day, Cincinnati was the largest city west of the Appalachian Mountains, and the sixth-largest in the nation.[1] *With a burgeoning population of 115,436 in 1850, it supported entertainments far beyond simple stage productions.*[2] *"The Queen City" was an important stop for artists from foreign lands touring the United States: JJM went to concerts performed by a German orchestra, the Steyermarkische Gesellschaft, and two French dance companies, Les Danseuses Viennoises, and the Monplaisir Troupe. Not only did he attend performances, JJM himself played the flute and guitar, and sang with a chorus, the Liedertafel, a popular German community activity.*

JJM also took lessons from a French dancing master, Charles Ernest, and attended public balls organized by bandleader[3] *"Uncle Dick" Richards. Such parties kept JJM out until dawn, dancing the polka and formation dances such as reels and quadrilles.*[4] *Masquerades sent him scurrying for special attire so that he could "cut a swell."*

Music and dancing provided ample opportunities for antebellum bachelors to meet eligible women, and the list of JJM's flirtations was long. He often called on an assortment of neighborhood girls and ogled females at the theater, both on and off the stage. He turned his charm on housemaids, prostitutes, and guests from out of town. JJM's account of his interactions with women demonstrates how nineteenth-century youths escaped rigid supervision in social situations.

Sunday March 12th 1848

The morning was mild, but appearances indicated rain. nevertheless I, Wardner and John Brandly started on a two mile walk, in the Western part of the City.

Jenny Lind, Swedish singer and actress, c. 1850. Miss Lind is mentioned in several entries in Mersman's diary. She was very popular with theatergoers. (Somers Historical Society.)

We did not however enjoy it. The young hurricanes that were blowing in every direction Created such a dust that devrived [deprived] us entirely of all we went to see. before we could return it commenced to rain gently. We took the hint and returned instantly—It rained till 12 oclock. From ½ past 9 to 12 I was engaged in my study of french. About ½ past 1, I and Delamettre Called on

Baker—were fortunate enough to find the young man *chez lui.*[5] took him along. Went to Moulinier's. he was not ready to go yet. Walked about for a half an hour. It was very Windy, but otherwise the weather was delightfully pleasant. When we called the second time, "M" was ready.

We called on Tappe, but too late, he had allready gone to church. As I intended to visit my sister I did not to church. M[oulinier] & B[aker] went. I and D[elamater] turned our faces homeward. Delar being dry, could'nt well go and "Take" something without inviting me. so we drank a glass of Ale togather at the Pantheon, Cor 5th and Walnut. I went direct up to Kattenhorn's, where my brother and wife were also.[6] We passed a very agreable afternoon, us "males" being engaged at the the Card table. I had supper there, after which Continued our games till 8 oclock, when Henry and I left. at home I studied till 10 oclock, then went with Brown and "took" a glass of "Castillon"[7] To Bed 11. Exp 40¢.

Monday, March 13th 1848

How Cold it is! Exclaimed Sweet Fanny, poking her Snout out of doors just as I entered the Parlour this Morning, and truly the weather was suffisciently severe to cause the exclamation, it being indeed very Cold. Business was tolerably during the day. I was occupied nearly all the time. After supper I amused myself with Sweet Fanny for a half an hour. Fanny has promised her little darling of a hand to a small gentleman with a small name but large immagination having gone through College. his name is "Doll"[8] a very *droll* name. were it not for his Wiskers, it would be very appropriate. I and Delr went to Billy Tell's and enjoyed an Egg Nogg at my private Expense. It was ½ past 11 when we retired. Exp 25c

Tuesday March 14th

Business dull. Weather very Cold. The Evening I passed entirely at home, having a french lesson which occupied my time till ½ past 9. balance I passed with the familly in the parlor. Exp 5.

Wednesday 15th

Confound this Cold Weather. Our business requires open doors, and attendance in the front of the Store, which on a morning like this is any thing but Comfortable. After Supper I studied my past french lessons till a little after 8 then Called on my Sister Agnes.[9] I have not been there for a week or more. did not stay until [Bill Lake] returned, but went home about 10, just in time to have a Smoke with brown and delr. It was nearly 11 oclock when we retired. Exp 10c.

Thursday 16th 1848

The temperature of the Weather moderated Considerably during the day. Business was pretty good. I was a good deal troubled with some bill's of lading in being unable to find the Clerk.[10] The Evening (my only valuable time) I was foolish enough to throw away entirely, with no other inducement then the worthless gratification of wining at "Euchre." We played in my room, and being very Comfortably situated, we kept it up till 10 oclock. Then we Went over to the U.S.[11] and treated ourselves at Brown's expense to whatever we desired. We Smoked till 11, then retired to Bed. My Exp. 10 cts.

Friday 17th

Weather very pleasant again. Business was also bright and brilliant. Our commercial transactions taken upon average for the last 5 months have nearly doubled those of any previous season during the same time. After supper I had my french lesson, which detained me till ½ past 9. I did not go out however, but read and smoked in the dining-room till nearly 11. Exp 5c.

Saturday 18th

I succeeded this Morning in selling 374$ worth of foreign [brandy][12] to a Mr Reinhardt of Madison, the getting up and shipping of which kept me busy the whole day. My Cash balanced very accurately for this Week.

The Evening I passed at home playing flute for ½ an hour or so then finishing my last french exercise. It was precisely ½ past 10 when I retired. Exp 10c

Sunday March 19th 1848

I had to go to the Store this Morning in order to Ship Some brandy &c for Mr Reinhardt. Last Evenings mail boat left him and part of his goods. Passing the Pearl St House on my return I remembered owing the Barkeeper there for 4 Cigars had on the night of the Maskerade Ball 2nd of March. of course I called in and paid it.

from 10 to ½ past 12 I was very busy writing my french exercise for this Afternoons *leçon.*[13] Dressed, had dinner—five minutes afterwards Moulinier Came. We were through 3 oclock. Called on Baker togather, but he had left already. As it was very pleasant we walked to Texas[14] to witness the laying the Corner Stone of a new German Catholic Church.[15] There was a most extensive Crowd brot there principally by Curiosity.

It was too crowded in the immediate vicinity to obtain any chance of witnessing the Ceremonies. So we quit it as soon as we could. from there we rambled all over the city. about half past 5 we went to Mouliniers house to rest a few minutes for we intended to call on Tappe, which we did. The Old Gentleman had one Guitar quite [done], and two others nearly finished. I have promised to take One. if my sister does not want it, I shall keep it myself. About ½ past we returned to Mouliniers I accepted his invitation to sup with him. the supper was very good, combining all of the substantials, and ornamental or sweet-meats.[16] as we had nothing to do in the Evening we took "our time" eating. Mr Baker came about the usual time, shortly after 7. we were detained there by the First Thunder Storm this year, till 11. then direct home. Exp 25c

Monday March 20th 1848

Last night the first Thunder Storm of this year broke loose. it was a very Serious one, and fatal to two human being. A man and his wife were struck and killed instantly while walking togather near Mill Creek.[17] The rain Continued to pour down till 10 or 11 oclock this Morning. Commerce is decidedly dull this Morning—only about 15 bbls[18] Whiskey sold and now it is already 12.

The afternoon was beautifully pleasant and the ornament of Creation "Woman," contributed largely towards the beauty and joyousness of the whole.[19] The Evening I passed with Mr Baker. We Walked about enjoying the pure and balmy air until 9, then visited the Library rooms[20] to look over some new french books lately received. there is at present a fair Collection of French and German Standard Works in the Mercantile rooms.

10 oclock I left Baker and went home. Mary Jane permitted me to read a letter she had just received from Mary Howe, in which there was good deal of general information, but nothing in particular. Delametre invited me to go with him to a person noted for keeping good Ale. I could not possibly refuse it—the Ale really was excellent. it was served out in the old Scotch fashion "Pewter Tanckards." We Smok'd at home till ½ past 11. then retired Weary and tired. Exp 15c.

Tuesday 21st

The Weather Continues delightful, our business was all that we could wish it. I had however a good deal of time to attend to my french. The Evening I passed *chez moi*[21] till 8, reviewing Manesca.[22] then went to see my Sister.[23] She was in good spirits consequently it was easy for me to Amuse her. Went home 10. to bed ½ past 10. Expense 10c.

Wednesday March 22nd 1848

The rainy and exceedingly disagreable Weather disappointed many as one in the City. This day was set apart to pay a Publics respect, in performing the

Funeral Ceremonies of John Q. Adams.[24] Judge Walker delivered the Oration. The Evening I passed at home entirely. I had a french lesson, although not a very good one, as Mr Baker read out the questions, and private conversation and talking was more attended to then my French.

After my visitors departure I sat down in the dining room and Smoked my usual Cigar. Brown and Delr joined. To Bed ½ past 11. Exp 10¢.

Thursday March 23rd

Weather tolerably pleasant. Business quite satisfactory for Mr D[exter]. The Evening I passed with Mr Brown in the National Theatre. it was Mrs Warrens Benefit.[25] as I had not been to Theatre for nearly two [weeks] I concluded to Sacrifice a dollar for the would be coquettish Mr[s] W. She performed the Queen in *La Tour de Nesle.* The house was but thinly populated. Miss Logan in *Simpson & Co* was precisely the same as she has been. We went home after the 2nd piece. Smoked our Cigar at home as usual. To bed 12. Exp 1.05.

Friday 24th

Mr Dexter is sick to day. I was very Busy the whole Morning. I wrote a french letter to One of our Customers, the first attempt.[26] The Evening I passed at home entirely reviewing Manesca. To Bed 10. Exp 30.

Saturday March 25th 1848

The Weather although not decidedly bad, Was extremely Coquettish. One third of the time slightly raining, another third sun shine, and remainder both togather. towards Evening it brightened up a little, which brightened the feelings of every one in our familly. for why? 'Cause Wm Lake my brother in law had a benefit this Evening at the Circus.[27] It proved to be a real Benefit. when I came in, about ½ past 7 the House was nearly filled and kept filling till it was the best House that has been there this winter excepting the Clown's benefit. The performance was best and most pleasing I have ever seen in any Circus. Agness on the Slack wire did very well. She fell off 3 times, but on the whole she made a very favorable impression on the Audience.[28] She had presents thrown in the ring to the value of 40$. The affair Cost me about Eight Dollars[29] altogather. It was nearly 12 when I got home, and I went home direct. Exp 7.85.

Sunday March 26th

Was a decidedly disagreable day, unsafe for a person to venture out *Sans parapluie*[30] as it was raining every few minutes. Immediatly after Breakfast I went to

Mouliniers house to take a french lesson. returned about ½ past 10. Went to Lake's room. his nett profits for his Benefit will be about 60$.[31] Had dinner at home. After it enjoyed a Walk to the river with Del—e which cost him 20 cts for Cigars and Ale. About 3 oclock went to Kattenhorns. Came just in time to take Coffee with them, a time honored Amusement with the Germans. The Afternoon we passed with playing Cards. I had my supper there also. We played till nearly 9. then I went home—

March 27th Monday.

Very disagreable weather. Business was dull. I should'nt at all be displeased if we had a dull week of it. After Supper I reviewed french till 8 oclock, then went to see my Sister,[32] but she was'nt home, so I had my trouble for nothing. returned direct home. Amused the Ladies till nearly 10. after they had departed I and Del—r Smoked our Customary Evening Cigar. To bed 11. Exp 10.

Tuesday 28th

Weather is getting pleasant again. I was very busy during the entire day, did'nt have time to look at my french. After Supper I gave a little party in my room to the Gentleman of the Establishment. it was not however entirely of my own giving. I furnished a bottle of fine old Bdy,[33] Brown two bottles of Champagne and Del—r the Confectionaries. we had a fine time of it. Played Euchre till nearly 12 oclock and were fully "half Seas over"[34] when we quit. before we went to bed we Smoked our Cigars in the dining room as usual, totally disregarding the lateness of the hour. Exp 60c.

Wednesday 29th

Our Business is going it like Hell to use a strong and vexatous expression. I feel myself Wearing out rapidly for 700$[35] a year. After supper I had my French lesson. After which I and Moulinier called on Mr Tappe to get our Guitars. neither were finished. So we returned as we went—Empty. To Bed 11. Exp=5¢

Thursday 30th March 1848.

Business continues provokingly lively. I have no chance to peep into my french at all. I am expecting a cessation from one week to the other, but we can hardly do all that we might do had we the material.[36]

After Supper in place of Studying I went to the National Theatre with Brown.[37] there met John Quincy Harrington. I had not seen him for years. he has been engaged in New York for some time acting Low Comedy. the meeting cost me 20 cts for two fine Brandies. The performance was tolerbly good. We did'nt get home till ½ past 11.

Friday 31st.

A very rainy and in every respect disagreable day. business was nevertheless tolerbly fair. at least I was busy the whole day. After supper studied till 8 oclock then Called on my Sister. I had to go for her, in the rear part of the circus. Amused myself and her till near 11, then went home. it was raining very severe. when I got home my Clothes were more than damp. To Bed 11. Exp 10. I paid Moulinier for 3 months French instruction from January 1, 1848 to April 1, 1848 Ten Dollars—[38]

Saturday April 1st 1848

All fools day. I—fortunately escaped becoming a subject to it. Business kept me Employed the whole day. After Supper I had my french lesson then went with Moulinier to Tappe. I gave up my Old Guitar and kept my 5 dollars. from there direct home. Exp 15c.
[Margin note] Paid Boarding and Washing to April 2nd. 15.80¢.

Sunday April 2nd 1848

I was up betimes this morning. when the breakfast Bell rung, I was dressed. immedeatly after it, I went to my Brother in Laws "Lake." they were nearly ready, had every thing packed, and William was just sending off the trunks.[39] Mr Wilson a young Mechanic with whom Lake is intimate was there also. After all the Luggage had been sent down, we all four went to Kattenhorns. left Agness there, then went to Henry's House. he was not dressed yet—that operation having been materially retarded by the Sickness of his Child. from Henrys we returned to the Circus. Saw the 3 dogs[40] of Williams put in charge of an attendant. then returned to K[attenhorn]'s. My Sister had gone to Church, Kattenhorn had also Sneaked off Somewhere, so Lake and his Wife had nobody to take leave off. Father went down to the boat with them. I went home first to get Some Cigars for William. when I came down they were all safely stowed away in the Cabin. Henry Came down immediatly afterwards also. Daddy Came very near crying, but Agness Coolness prevented it. I remained till the boat went. She turned up the River a little piece, when she returned, she glided past the city with a Swiftness seldom equalled, the Circus Band playing some of the Favorite Airs of the day. . . . . I returned home ½ past 11. the excitement and Farewell "Horn"[41] of Brandy made me feverish. The Afternoon I passed with Moulinier, Baker and Burkhardt, Walking around and viewing the improvements of the City. I had two Severe "Nose bleedings" to day.

The Evening I passed at Kochs. being tired, I rested there on the Sofa at my ease, Suffering myself to be amused. To Bed 11. Exp 75c

Monday April 3rd 1848

Pleasant weather. Business also very pleasant, being able to do it all with ease, and have a little time left for my french Study. I took my book home with me intending to Study, but found it impossible to refuse Mr Browns invitation to accompany him to the Atheneaum, to see Mrs Wilkinson.[42] She appear'd in *The Wife.* I did not like her acting so well as I anticipated, having seen Mrs. Mowett in that beautiful piece.[43] by the bye Mrs W. is a very pretty little Woman. this pretty fact made her find more favor with me, then her acting would have done. we did not Stay to see the End of the Evenings Entertainment, but went home at 11. Smoked till ½ past, then to bed. Exp 15c

Tuesday 4th

Disagreable Weather again. business however is very good. I intended to study after supper, but Mr Moulinier came just as I was commencing to write, to point out the necessity of going to Mr Runge's concert. of course I went, Mr Runge being an acquaintance of mine also. Mrs Sheidler sung well, Runge also—on the whole it was a passable affair.[44] from there direct home. Exp 65c. [Margin note] Paid Koch my Tailor 5$ on account.

Wednesday 5th

The Weather has Cleared off again and every thing looks spring like and beautiful. I was very busy the whole day and not idle during the Evening, having a difficulte but interesting french lesson to recite. from 10 to ½ past I employed in reading and Smoking in the dining-room. No Expence.

Thursday April 6th 1848

Was a Somewhat dull day for business althoug lovely weather. The Evening I passed at home entirely reviewing Menesca[45] till nearly 10, when, being very tired I went to Melodeon,[46] drank a glass of Ale, and returned immediatly. read and Smoked till ½ past 10. then went to bed. Expence 15c.

Friday 7th

Was one of the most busy days we have had lately. I was occupied and busy all the time, did'nt think of my french. After Supper I went to the Atheneaum, it being Fenno's[47] Benefit. poor fellow! It did'nt prove a benefit to him. the house was'nt half full. The performance however was not good enough even for the indifferent house they had. Mrs Wilkinson will not I suppose descend long to act in a place where she is so poorly supported. this Evening I had to fork over the Dollar for tickets.[48] Brown however menages to pay twice to my once. he being a Clever fellow I permit him to have this pleasure. To Bed ½ past 11. Exp 1.10.

Saturday 8th

The beautifull Morning made the Market quite animated and gay. the Ladies were out in abundance. Our Cash could not be made to balance by twenty nearly 24$. After Supper I had a french lesson which of course kept me at home the whole Evening, and very busy also as I had a somewhat difficult lesson. To Bed 11. Exp 10c

Sunday April 9th 1848.

Was throughout a very agreable day, although the Sun did not show himself until ½ past 10. immediatly after breakfast I, Del—r and Doctr Darling started on a long walk. they being witty and humorous fellows, I also being in very [good] spirits, we had a agreable time of [it]. every thing in our way seem'd to Contribute towards our amusement. by 10 we were back. I had my last french lesson to write up, which occupied all my time before dinner.

I and Del—r attempted to take a walk after dinner but he was too lazy. So I left him and Went to Kattenhorns, where as usually on Sunday I had my Coffee. I was detained there longer than I intended. Captain Kessler's[49] Funeral procession halted there nearly an hour or so. From there returned home where I passed the remainder of the afternoon, playing with Mary Jane Jenkins for passtime.—I had nothing else to do—

After supper I called on Moulinier. I found there quite a collection of musical genius's. Tosso, the two Burkhardts and some few others. they (the musical men had a stiff time of it among themselves), I and Baker left shortly after 10. Made a halt at Corner 5th and Walnut[50] to refresh ourselves with a glass of Ale. To Bed 11. Exp 25c

Monday April 10th

Most beautiful and lovely Weather, but business commenced dull. the Error in my last weeks cash was Mr. Dexter. he paid out some money without giving the Desk Credit for it. The Evening I and Brown passed in the Atheneum.[51] both Mrs. Lewis and Mrs. Wilkinson performed! poor House! Exp 20¢.
[Margin note] Bot an Edition of Shakespiere for 4$.

Tuesday April 11th 1848

Business is suffisciently lively for this season of the year. towards Evening I was very busy receiving whiskey.

The valuable time from 7 to 10 I was foolish enough to throw away entirely. Played a two handed game of dull Euchre in which by the bye there is no Amusement. then went with Brown (having lost the grog) to have a glass of Ale. returned direct home—Smoked till 10. Then to bed. Exp 15c.

Wednesday 12th

Excellent Weather. business was very good to day. The Evening I passed at home entirely, excepting only a walk to an ale-house immediatly after my french lesson with Moulinier. returned directly home. Smoked till 10 oclock. then retired Weary and Sleepy. Expenses 20c.

Thursday 13th

Disagreably Cold Weather. Business very lively all day. After supper I was foolish enough to go to the Atheneaum. Mrs Wilkinson appeared in 3 pieces but we (I and Brown) only saw two of 'em after which we went home.[52] I immediatly to bed. Exp 1.05

Friday 14th

Very good Clear weather, but also very windy and dusty, consequently not particularly agreable. During the afternoon I had some time to devote to my french but was on average actively employed the whole day.

Immediatly after Supper Commenced reviewing Manesca, and had finished nearly two lessons, when I was particularly invited by Mr Bradly to join a Euchre party in his room. We played till half past 10. B— treated at the U.S. Hotel. To bed 11. Exp 5.

Saturday April 15th 1848

Most beautiful and lovely Weather this Morning. Business was dull, but on Saturday I always find plenty of Employment in arranging the past Weeks business, which to day, as usual, kept me busy the Entire day. My Cash in the afternoon balanced accurately. I balanced the Weeks business to the Satisfaction of my Employer. After supper I was to have had a french lesson, but receiving a particular invitation from Mr Brown to accompany him to the Theatre to see Forest in *Virginius*, I had no reason to regret going. It was indeed a good piece of acting. We did not stay to see the farce.[53] from ½ past 10 to 11 we Smoked at home, then retired. my Exp 20c.

Sunday 16th

Was one of the lovliest day lately enjoyed in this good City. as I missed my lesson last Evening I was Compelled to go to Mouliniers house early in the Morning. by this arrangement I lost the entire forenoon, for after we had finished, I waited till M. dressed himself. then we went out walking togather. I did not get home again till near 12 when it was high time for me to dress myself before dinner. . . . . Immediatly after dinner I called on Baker but it seems that in general he is every where except at home. being unsuccessful there, I went to Henry's. he was out also. then went to Kattenhorns. had coffee and a sort of fancy lunch, a very pleasant thing to take on Sunday afternoons. I and Katn went to Drachs on Syc[amore] Hill. we had been there but a short time when we were joined by Mr Wagner. We tippled till nearly Sun Set. however we did not drink any thing except Ale. The Evening I passed at home reading over some of my french lessons. Exp 25c.

Monday April 17th 1848.

Business Commenced quite Animated this Morning. having gone to bed early last evening, I was in good spirits and fully competent to do justice to our numerous patrons. at the same time when a leizure moment presented itself to do the days study of my french. There is at present quite a variety of Amusements in the city. Genl. Tom Thumb[54] holds 3 levees each day to Crowded houses, Uncle Dicks Ball[55] to night, to morrow night the Concert of the *Liedertafel*[56] of which by the bye I am no longer a member. having been one over three years, I resigned the honor early this year. Mrs Wilkinson is still at the Atheneaum and last, though most important of all, *Forest* is at the National, Performing to Crowded houses, and Audiences that are Capable of appreciating his supr Genius. I received a letter from Frank this afternoon, wrote an answer immediatly, also wrote to Clemens Nulsen. I had to Call on Mr Daum[57] immediatly after supper, was detained there till 9 oclock. it being too late to do anything else I went home, read till 11. then to bed—No Expense.

Tuesday 18th

Business very dull. Weather excessively disagreable. towards evening we had a small Snow Storm. this however did not prevent every body as it were from going to the National Theatre, for there was certainly the largest audience I have ever seen there. Mr Forest performed *Metamora,* his celebrated Indian character.[58] he was however very poorly supported, the piece being a strange one to all the other actors. To Bed 11. Exp 1.55.

Wednesday, April 19th 1848

Weather Windy and Cold. Business was slightly troublesome but not Extensive. After supper I had my french lesson. did not go out afterwards, but read till 10 oclock. Exp 5.

Thursday 20.

Weather cleared off beautifully this Morning. it was however very Cold. business was not over brisk. I had suffiscient leizure to Study my usual share of french.

did not go out after supper. reviewed my past lessons till after 9. read *Dombey & Son*[59] till ½ past 10. then to bed. Exp 10.

Friday 21st

beautiful and lovely weather. our business was slightly dull. I had so much the more time for my french. After supper I went to the Theatre with Moulinier and Delamattre. Forest played *The Gladiator,* and most grandly did he play it. I do not beleive that the National Theatre has ever been so crowded as it was this evening. the Second Tier of boxes was almost entirely occupied by Ladies.

I considered myself fortunate in getting a place where I could see standing. A young Lady, Miss Wil—n was in a seat right beside me. I knew her when she was quite a child, but never having had a formal introduction I did not Venture to address.[60] Moulinier is acquainted with her. If in a year or so my position in Society should be elevated to that of a Merchant I shall Certainly seek an introduction. On her account I remained to see the last piece, which I otherwise should not have done. the piece in itself however was worth seeing as Logan[61] took a prominent and favorite character in the piece. ¼ before 12 I retired, fully satisfied with the Evenings entertainment. Exp 85c.

Saturday April 22nd 1848

Weather very fair indeed. business was dull. I was however occupied the whole day with writing business letters, filling out bills of lading and in the afternoon balancing my Weeks Cash. After Supper I had my french lesson. did not go out afterwards. I paid in going to Supper Eggers & Wolkop for a Copy Shakespiere

4$ or all I am indebted to them.[62] Kochs my Tailors 6.50¢ being the entire balance of my Account with them. After Moulinier left me I read till 10, then went to bed. Exp 10c[63]

Sunday 23rd

The morning was bright and beautiful. Lake and my Sister returned early this Morning.[64] L. was in my room before I was dressed. immediatly after breakfast I went to Kattenhorns where I met Agnes. She had a fine boy, or rather gave birth to a male child while in Louisville, but the poor little thing was dead.[65] The Accouchement confined her only some 5 or 6 days. She has allready commenced taking her part in the performance, as though nothing had happen'd.

The Company was in town only an hour [or] so, being compelled to Start for Maysville[66] immediatly. I did not go down to the boat with them, they being in a Carriege.

About 10, I called on Monfort, now an M.D. was so lucky as to find him at home. we walked until we were tired, then went to my room, where we passed our time agreably till dinner. I did not go out during the afternoon till towards evening, it being too dusty. I amused myself at home with Mary Jane and Fannie. Called on Moulinier after supper. did not make any Stay. went to bed at 10 oclock. Exp 15c.

Monday April 24th 1848

Beautiful Weather. we need rain very much however. Our farmers I have no doubt would prefer to see thunder Storms and rain in torrents, in preferance to this.

Business Commenced somewhat lively this Morning. I have no objection to have it continue so. The Evening I passed entirely at home reading and reviewing Menesca for two mortal hours. balance of time till 11 I passed below Smoking. Exp 5c. Paid A. Bender for a Hat, had [bought it] 11th Jany 3.50c.

Tuesday 25th

It is somewhat Cold again. Our Commercial transactions are not of the most extensive kind at present although we are buying and shipping as fast as we can rectefy. After supper I went with Moulinier, whom by the bye I treated to a ticket to the Concert of the *Steyermarkische Gesellschaft.*[67] The performance was really grand and beautiful, far superior to any orchestral Music ever heard in this City. it was duly appreciated by an Audience who was capable of deciding on Musical Merit. The Finale was a Rail Road Galop[68] the most characteristic I have ever heard. all the various noises attending the starting of a train were most perfectly imitated. The piece instead of concluding with a general burst up, was brot to decent halt, like a well regulated train of Cars should be. To Bed 11. Expense 1.15.

Wednesday 26th

I was busy the whole day with making out whiskey accounts, writing letters and taking bills lading. The Evening I passed at home having a french lesson which kept us busy till ½ past 9. did not go out. Exp—10 cts.

Thursday April 27th 1848

Il a fait bien beau tems toute la journée. Les affaires sont aujourdhui tout à notre gré. Je veux beaucoup que je puisse finir ceci en français, mais cela m'est impossible. J'ai été au concert du Steyermarkische gesellschaft *ce soir. je m'étais bien Amusé. mais je n'ai pas eu une aussi bonne place comme j'avais la première fois.* [The weather was nice all day today. Business has been very favorable recently. I would like to finish this in French, but that is impossible. Tonight, I went to the concert of the Steyermarkische Gesellschaft. I enjoyed it very much. But I didn't have as good a seat as I did the first time.] Our whole Establishment (all the boarders both male and female) was at this concert. The Music in general was fully as good as on Tuesday evening. The Hall was Crowded. there were not seats suffisient to accommodate all. I came there Some what late but just in time to get almost the last one vacant. Smoked with Del—r and Brown till 11—

Friday April 28th 1848

Business during the entire day was very [brisk]. I had no time to devote to my french at all. The Evening I passed entirely at home reviewing Menesca till a little after 9 and then usual I went in the dining room, the place where some of us boarders are permitted to smoke our Cigar in the Evening. to do this with our Customary Conversation took us till 10 or perhaps a little past, as we generally have a great deal to say. Exp 10.

Saturday April 29th

Was with the exception of some Shipping Business very dull. My Cash balanced quite satisfactorily. After supper I had my french lesson. I did not go out afterwards as I had some preparations to make for to Morrow. To Bed 10 oclock. Exp 10c.

Julia Dean, American actress, c. 1846. Miss Dean, an actress in "dramatic" performances, graced the stage in both Cincinnati and St. Louis. This lithograph is from her performance in *The Hunchback.* (Julia Dean in *The Hunchback* [1846], the Harvard Theatre Collection, the Houghton Library.)

NOTES

1. New York, Philadelphia, Baltimore, Boston, and New Orleans had larger populations (DeBow [1], liii).
2. Cist (3), 44.

3. In these early days of American dancing, the dance master or leader of the orchestra called out the steps that couples performed in time to the music (Durang, 28).

4. Formation dances called for the participants to stand in lines, circles, or squares at the start of the music. A full description of such dances may be found in Beadle, 15–32; Durang, 24–186; and on the Web at the American Memory Homepage of the Library of Congress (http://memory.loc.gov/ammem).

5. [Fr.] at home.

6. Henry Mersman and his wife, Adelaide Tebbelman Mersman, frequently ate Sunday dinner at the home of his sister, Elizabeth Kattenhorn, and spent the afternoon visiting there.

7. Castillon brandy is a strong alcoholic spirit distilled from wine, named for a village in the Bordeaux region of France (Johnson, 242–43).

8. Mr. Doll has not been identified. No record of a Jenkins-Doll marriage has been found.

9. Agnes and Bill Lake were practicing their acts for the new season with Rockwell & Company. The circus gave preview performances throughout March. To stimulate attendance, the show awarded prizes to performers and audience members (ENQ, 22 March 1848).

10. JJM searched for the clerk of the steamboat which carried Mr. Dexter's goods as freight. See chapter 2, note 62.

11. The United States Hotel and the United States Tavern were less than a block apart. Both served beverages. See map 5 (Cist [3], 167).

12. See JJM diary, 19 March 1848.

13. [Fr.] lesson.

14. "Texas" was the name of a neighborhood in northwest Cincinnati. See map 2. (HOC 409).

15. St. Joseph Church, at Linn and Laurel streets, was built in 1846, but the congregation grew so rapidly that a new building was needed just two years later. Bishop Purcell, assisted by "nearly all the Catholic clergy of the city and attended by a vast assemblage," conducted the cornerstone laying on 19 March 1848. See map 3 (ENQ, 25 March 1848; Lamott, 141).

16. Sweetmeats are fruit (such as peaches, pears, and melons) and nuts preserved with sugar (OED, s.v. "sweetmeat"; Webster, 817).

17. Mill Creek, a small river on the western edge of Cincinnati, was also the name given to a township north of the city. See map 2. On this date, no newspaper reported human casualties, but one recorded the death of a horse due to lightning (COM, 20 March 1848).

18. Abbreviation for "barrels."

19. Apparently, many women were about and JJM appreciated having them near his shop.

20. Young Men's Mercantile Library Association.

21. [Fr.] at my home.

22. "Manesca" refers to Jean Manesca (1778–1838), author of *An Oral System of Teaching Living Languages: Illustrated by A Practical Course of Lessons in French through the Medium of English* (New York: Lockwood & Son, 1845). This text had numerous editions. Manesca also wrote *An Examination of Mr. Dufief's Philosophical Notions, with a Criticism upon His System and Mode of Teaching Languages in Four Letters* (New York: Clayton & Van Norden, 1825).

23. Agnes Lake.

24. The people of Cincinnati had a particular fondness for John Quincy Adams, as he had visited the city in 1843 and helped dedicate the Cincinnati Observatory. They named Mount Adams in his honor. When news of his death reached the city on 24 February 1848, the courts adjourned for the afternoon. The memorial procession on 22 March 1848 included military troops, benevolent societies, college educators, elected officials, lawyers, judges, and fire companies. Ten white horses with black plumes from Rockwell & Company's Circus drew a ceremonial wagon. At Wesley Chapel, a Methodist Episcopal church on Fifth Street between Sycamore Street and Broadway, four clergymen read prayers and scripture and a chorus sang hymns and a funeral anthem. Judge Walker's oration gave "credit both to the speaker and the subject" (COM, 25 February 1848; 10, 23 March 1848; ENQ, 22, 23 March 1848).

25. Mrs. Warren, likely local talent, has not been further identified. The drama of *La Tour de Nesle* was followed by two farces: *Simpson and Company* and *The Widow's Victim.* JJM purchased box seat tickets at fifty cents each (COM, 23 March 1848).

26. Trade with French-speaking customers in New Orleans and St. Louis provided the stimulus for JJM to study French.

27. William Lake, a major draw for the show, received a benefit performance, which increased his compensation (COM, 25 March 1848).

28. This was Agnes Lake's first performance as a rope walker (COM, 25 March 1848).

29. Admission cost fifty cents. In addition, JJM probably treated friends to refreshments and threw cash into the ring. Thus, he spent half a week's wages on one evening's entertainment.

30. [Fr.] without umbrella.

31. About $1,440 in 2005 dollars.

32. Agnes Lake.

33. Brandy.

34. "Half seas over" means tipsy or somewhat intoxicated (OED, s.v. "half-seas-over").

35. JJM's salary as a clerk was about $16,800 in 2005 dollars.

36. JJM indicates that the public's demand for whiskey exceeds Mr. Dexter's ability to provide it.

37. Yankee Hill appeared for his last evening in a drama, *The People's Lawyer,* and a character sketch, *The Yankee Peddler* (COM, 30 March 1848).

38. Thus, JJM paid the 2005 equivalent of $240 for twenty-four lessons in French, on Wednesdays and Saturdays.

39. William Lake was departing with Rockwell & Company for a run in Louisville, Kentucky. See also note 64.

40. The clown's three dogs, possibly Rolla, Bibo, and Napoleon, were featured performers (COM, 25 April 1848).

41. "Horn" harkens back to the time when drinking vessels were made from trophy animals (OED, s.v. "horn").

42. This was the first night of Mrs. Wilkinson's engagement at the Athenaeum. *The Wife,* by James Sheridan Knowles (1784–1862), was first performed in 1833.

43. Anna Cora Mowatt had played at the Athenaeum 22 April through 3 June 1847 (ENQ, 27 April 1847).

44. The program at the Melodeon Hall, which began at 7:30 p.m., offered both vocal and instrumental music. It featured William Runge, and Messers Tosso, Sofge, and Scheidler, in addition to Mrs. Scheidler. Singing of "La Marseillaise" was the high point of the evening. Tickets cost fifty cents (ENQ, 4 April 1848).

45. See note 22.

46. The Melodeon Building housed a first-floor bar as well as third-floor performance space.

47. Augustus William Fenno, the acting manager of Rockwell's Athenaeum Theatre, also played roles in the performance that evening: Rolla in the tragedy *Pizarro* and the title role in *Ben, the Boatswain* (COM, 7 April 1848).

48. Seats in the dress circle cost fifty cents each (COM, 7 April 1848).

49. Captain Hermann Kessler, a trained artillery officer originally from Saxony, died while serving in the Mexican War with the Ohio Fourth Regiment. His funeral procession included German Lafayette Guards, military companies of Covington, the German Benevolent Society, and a large number of Cincinnati residents. The regiment had left Ohio on 1 July 1847 with 860 men and returned a year later with 162 fewer (COM, 10 April 1848; ENQ, 10 April 1848; 25 July 1848; Klauprecht, 179).

50. At least two "watering holes" were at that intersection: the William Tell Restaurant and the Pantheon. See map 5.

51. The performance that evening, the first night for Mrs. Lewis and the seventh night for Mrs. Wilkinson, commenced with a drama, *The Forger,* followed by a farce, *Dead Shot,* and a second drama, *The French Spy* (COM, 10 April 1848).

52. The show at the Athenaeum included a drama, *The Green Banner of Ireland,* and a farce, *The Young Widow.* JJM skipped *The Dumb Girl of Genoa* (COM, 13 April 1848).

53. The farce that accompanied *Virginius* at the National Theatre was *A Loan of a Lover* (COM, 15 April 1848).

54. Tom Thumb's performances at the Masonic Hall included storytelling, singing, dancing, and an impersonation of Napoleon in full military costume (COM, 17 April 1848).

55. "Uncle Dick" Richards, dancing master, hosted a ball at the Melodeon Hall (COM, 17 April 1848).

56. The *Liedertafel,* led by Mr. Scheidler, performed a vocal and instrumental concert at the Melodeon Hall featuring Madame Scheidler, and Messrs. Tosso, Runge, and Sofge, for the benefit of the German Revolutionary Fund (ENQ, 17 April 1848).

57. Valentine Daum, proprietor of the Napoleon Tavern, was likely a customer of Edmund Dexter's (CCD 1846, 138; CCD 1848–49, 118).

58. The third night of Edwin Forrest's six-night engagement at the National Theatre, *Metamora, or The Last of the Wampanogs,* was followed by a farce, *The Swiss Cottage* (COM, 18 April 1848).

59. *Dealings with the Firm of Dombey and Son,* a popular novel by Charles Dickens, was published in installments in 1847 and 1848 (http://www.bibliomania.com/0/0/19/36/).

60. A gentleman would converse with a lady only after the two had been introduced (Beadle, 18).

61. Cornelius Logan played the lead in the farce, *Animal Magnetism* (COM, 21 April 1848).

62. See JJM diary, 10 April 1848. Dinner for three people likely cost far less than four dollars, so the German booksellers Eggers & Wulkop gave JJM a bargain price for the book.

63. JJM records the day's expenses, not the payment of his old debts, which totaled $10.50.

64. Rockwell & Company's Circus played for ten days in Louisville, Kentucky, and then went to New Albany and Madison, Indiana, for one-night stands. They performed in Covington and Newport, Kentucky, before stopping briefly in Cincinnati on Sunday, 23 April 1848, when there was no performance (Thayer, 459).

65. A search of Louisville newspapers did not reveal any mention of this incident.

66. Maysville, Kentucky, was the stand for Rockwell's Circus on 24 April 1848 (MAY, 24 April 1848). See map 1.

67. The *Steyermarkische Gesellschaft* (Styrian Music Band), a German, nineteen-piece orchestra, performed six "grand instrumental concerts" at the Melodeon Hall from 26 April to 4 May 1848. Each concert featured different works of popular and classical music. Waltzes, polkas, and folk dance music interspersed selections by Beethoven, Weber, and other notable composers. Tickets were fifty cents; children, half price (COM, 25 April 1848; VOL, 28, 29 April 1848, 2, 4 May 1848).

68. *The Railroad Gallop* by Hungarian composer Joseph Gungl (1810–89), was the last number on the program, which included works by Liszt, Donizetti, and Strauss (COM, 25 April 1848; Randel 341).

CHAPTER FOUR

The Miami and Erie Canal

30 April 1848–4 May 1848

Cincinnati's growth depended on transportation by water. Steamboats, first introduced in 1811, plied the Ohio and Mississippi rivers, connecting the Queen City with other domestic and international ports. By 1842, there were 450 steamers on the western rivers.[1] In 1847, the number of steamboat arrivals in Cincinnati was 3,729, an average of more than ten per day.[2]

Canals swelled trade on the Ohio River by connecting the state's interior with profitable markets hundreds of miles away. The Miami and Erie Canal, begun in 1825, reached Toledo in 1845, providing continuous passage of 249 miles from Lake Erie to the Ohio River. Canal ditches typically were forty feet wide at the top and four feet deep, thus accommodating heavy loads of flour, tobacco, and whiskey.[3] In April 1848, 2,020 passengers and 5,943 tons of goods arrived in Cincinnati on canal boats.[4]

In this section, JJM described a trip he took on the Miami and Erie Canal from Cincinnati to Piqua, a distance of 100 miles. JJM and his brother Henry sought tobacco for cigar production and traveled on a packet boat, probably towed by three or four horses. The crew likely consisted of a captain, two drivers, two steersmen (one each for day and night), and a cook. Spare animals rode on the boat.[5] The one-way fare of $2.50 included meals.[6]

By the 1830s, tobacco was the major cash crop of southern Ohio,[7] and Henry Mersman sought to eliminate any middlemen who would cut into his profits. Packed in wooden hogsheads,[8] the leaves would reach Cincinnati ready for Henry's workmen to make cigars.

INSTRUCTION IN THE FRENCH LANGUAGE.

C. MOULINIER,

East side Race between Fourth and Fifth Streets,

CINCINNATI,

TEACHER IN THE FRENCH LANGUAGE.

Pupils will be taught at his rooms or at their own residence as may suit their convenience.

C. Moulinier advertisement, 1842. Mersman employed Moulinier's services in learning to read, write, and speak French, while in Cincinnati. (From the Collection of the Public Library of Cincinnati and Hamilton County.)

Sunday April 30th 1848

The morning was bright and beautiful. I had hardly dressed myself when my youngest Brother[9] came in my room. He had just arrived from St. Louis. the little fellow has grown and develloped himself some, though not a great deal. I was almost sorry that I was Compelled to leave just then, but having once made all the necessary arrangements, I could'nt recede. Frank takes my place in the house during my absence. After Breakfast we went to Kattenhorns togather. Father was of Course overjoyed to see Frank and to have him back once more. when the necessary Welcomes and greetings had been gone through with, I made Frank sat down to [play] and show his Skill on the Piano. He has practiced to some extent, but has not troubled himself extensively with the intricacies of music as a study.

It was necessary for us to be on board of the Canal boat by ½ past 10, so as soon as I had partially satisfied myself of Franks Capability I went to Henry's. he had not finished his Toilette yet. about ½ past 9 he bade his Wife farewell and we left. went to Kattenhorns again. Henry was better pleased with Franks playing then I was. Daddy was quite satisfied with it.

Frank brought about 5$ worth of music with him from St. Louis. Some very good pieces by the bye. We drank our parting Glass about 10 oclock or a quarter past. Kattenhorn was not there. Went on board ½ past 10. ¼ before 11 she started.

How dull it is on a Canal, or any other boat. on starting all are strangers to one-another. Very few only venture to open their mouths, every one being uncertain what kind of reception his remarks will have. the dullness of our Company was however Considerably lessened by a very loquacious and also a very brazen faced old Jew (who ever saw a Jew devoid of impudence) he had the kindness to make a fool of himself for our general amusement. I was really thankful to the old blaguard[10] (for that he certainly was) for breaking the Ice of reserve. for as soon as every one had once spoken, we all got along very pleasantly.

The first little Shanty of a village we came to was Cummingsville. what a nest! more Horses and Cattle there [than] human Inhabitants. I noticed Platt Evans[11] little Country Seat a little this side of it. It is really a beautiful situation, adapted for raising every kind of produce and vegetables except Wine. I am told, however, that he raises this also. otherwise the farms between Cinc'ti and Cummingsville do not wear the aspect of Scientific Cultivation. Lockland wears the aspect of a pretty little business place. I noticed some two or three mills, a button factory, Saw, and rolling mills. Saw Mr Dubbs[12] there, had the pleasure of drinking his health, of course at my Expense. from Lockland to Hamilton there is nothing I believe that bears any name. In Hamilton we arrived about 6. the sun was just sinking behind the Hills. The little place is very pleasantly situated. It has a most beautiful Canal basin. (I was told the best and most perfect in the State) I suppose it is from 175 to 200 feet in wendth, and from ½ to ¾ of a mile in lenght. The packet always stop there about ¼ hour. As soon as we had left Hamilton, I went in the Cabin as the Evening Air in the Country is generally very damp and chilly. In looking at my face which I had'nt seen the whole day, I was astonished to see that my favorite member in my Phiz[13] had suffered very severely during the day. The cold draught & hot Sun had inflamed my nose that it was as red as a Topers.[14] Our consolation: Henry and August[15] were in the same dilemma.

I dreaded the whole day the Coming of the Evening, not knowing what to amuse myself with, to pass time. but in my anticipations of Ennui I was agreably disappointed, for no sooner were the Lamps lit then some one proposed a game of Euchre. as I had a pack of Cards, We soon found plenty of Candidates, and thus amused ourselves Capitally until 9 oclock, when they Commenced preparing the Cots in which the Passengers are stowed away on each side of the boat like Corpses in a charnel-house, 3 over one another. The Captain Called out the Names of the passengers as they followed in rotation in his Book, and as they Came in succession each one took the best Cot left by his predecessor. I slept like a Top—excepting the time passed in a lock, when the jarring and pitching of the boat kept me awake. I was however suffisciently tired to sleep again immediatly. About 6 in the morning we were all roused from our slumbers & summoned to rise. at 7 we had breakfast just as we were entering Dayton. As the packet stops about ½ hour in Dayton we took a promenade around the city. The place however was unusually dull. Farmers are all busy at their work, and they are the only beings that bring Animation and Trade into a Country Town. Instead of going on the packet again in the City we went out of the Eastern part of it, along the Canal about two miles, to where it Crosses the River. Dayton abounds in extensive public Works, quite a variety of locks, almost any number of bridges both over Canal and river. the Canal passes over the river immediatly on the other side of it. on the opposite side is the Reservoir or feeder, this I did not see. They are at present building a new Court-house, which, when finished to match the Commencement, will be a grand and imposing structure. the Material is entirely of Dayton Stone. Walls from 24 to 30 inches thick. It has 6 large Stone columns in front. If there is any thing to mar the harmony of the whole, it is its narrowness, it being too narrow for its otherwise massive and solid proportions.[16]

The Dayton Ladies I think are slightly inclined to corpulency, judging from specimens I have seen. I suppose this proceeds from good living and continual damp atmosphere. We had a party on board, going Maying.[17] they appeared as happy and lively as Larks, only went a few miles to a pleasant Grove near the Canal. as Soon as they had left we Commenced playing Euchre. A favorite amusement of the boat hands seems to be that of shooting at Snakes and large sized Bullfrogs, which are met with very plentifully between Dayton & Troy.

We arrived at our place of destination[18] about 10 minutes to 12. My Brother Henry had to transact some business here. Mr Rappe the first Farmer we called on was not inclined to sell his Tobacco, intending to ship it to Phil'a.[19] he was hospitable enough to treat us to a plain but palatable Country dinner. after which we immediatly left for some others that we were told had their Crops still on hand. What a tramp we had of it, over fences, up and down hill, little ditches and large Trees, to Say nothing of the Cursed briars and undergrowth.[20] Fortunately we met the man we Came after in the field plowing. he had the good sense to offer us some fresh Milk to quench our thirst before he offered his tobacco. after an hour and halfs examination and bargaining, Henry bought the tobacco. From this Mr McGrew we went to another farmer Martindale of whom we bot 3000 lbs his entire Stock at 4½ cts a half cent lower than McGrew's. we expected to remain all night with Martindale, but he put us off with the excuse that he had but 2 rooms in house, one of which his Daughters (two pretty girls) occupied the other himself, Wife and Small Crop of Children. although we Were all three very tired, still rather than beg a nights lodging we preferred to go to the next Tavern which was two miles distant in a little place Called Vandalia, Containing about 13 or 14 houses and 50 to 60 human inhabitants. when we arrived we were about as tired as City Mortals well Can be.

Our fare, lodging and attendance with mine host of Vandalia was quite satisfactory to us. We had fortunately a few good Cigars in our boxes yet, for this is a luxury not to be procured in a country tavern. having Enjoyed our Evening Cigars after a substantial supper we went to bed although it was only 8 oclock. I do not Wonder any more that country people go to bed early. I was in favour of it myself on this especial evening. I slept like a top the whole night, had a better bed then I have ever had in Cincinnati.

Vandalia Tuesday Morning May 2nd 1848

We arose and dressed in time for the regular Country Breakfast hour ie 6 oclock. having enjoyed good repose, we were quite refreshed and ready to undertake the journey back to Rappe's place on the Canal. Our breakfast was also very good. Charge for the whole only 50 cents a piece.[21] We set out immediatly after 7 oclk to return to the Canal, having Concluded all our business transactions. hardly had we travelled a mile when we were overtaken by a slow, moderate but steady shower of rain which Continued for about an hour Wetting our Clothes to the Skin. this was not our only misfortune. We also had the ill-luck to loose our way. through this mishap we lenghtened the distance about 2 miles. as however some good luck will generall succeed a series of misfortunes, so in this instance, by loosing the way, we pitched upon an old Farmer who had about 2000 lbs of tobacco left, which we bought at 1 ct per lb, a Clear gain of 30$.

As we struck on the Canal we Came right on a milk and Butter Establishment, where Canal boats supply themselves with these dainties. having had a right smart mornings Walk, we also laid in as much as we had Storage room for.

Arrived about 10 oclock at the place from which we Started. in order to make time pass more rapidly we played Cards till we Saw the packet coming, being about 12 oclock, just in time to have dinner on board. The Company on this boat was not near So Sociable as on last Sunday, a lot of Self Conceited Country Gentlemen as ignorant as Asses and as bigotted as ignorance could make them. Some of them had their better half's with 'em and the Worst part of a familly ie the Children. there was no enjoyment of any kind on deck and they made the Cabin unbearable.

I could not help reflecting on my progress and advancement in life when we passed a place, some 3 miles this side Piqua,[22] which I recognized as the Scene of my boyish labours 12–13 years ago, when I was, what the Labourers termed their Water Boss or a boy that had to bring them Water when they were thirsty.[23] If during the next Ten years my position in life advances proportionally, I shall have reason to thank God and be Content.

We arrived in Piqua about ½ past 4. took a room at the Piqua Hotel, the best one there. had supper at the usual Country hour 6 oclock. Called on some acquaintances, pass'd the Evening at Holzimans & Detmer[24] playing Cards, not for Money but for liquor. I and August lost both rubbers.[25] August and myself tried hard to have some fun with some girls, but we did not succeed. retired 10 oclock.

Piqua Wednesday Morning May 3rd 1848

I slept well the whole night. there is some enjoyment in going to bed early. in the first place it is supposed that one is tired of Course, and then it is really a pleasure to pop down into a fine bed where you can hardly feel the substance you are laying on. Breakfasted at 6 the usual hour. after it, we had a general shave in a fashionable Piqua barber shop. It certainly did not lack much of being equal to any in Cincinnati. We then Called on Mr Clark[26] a young Grocer with whom Henry was acquainted. he assisted us very generously with our business, and also pointed out to us the peculiarities and changes of the place, and with his assistance arranged our business satisfactorily during the day.

Piqua I believe has improved more then the most Sanguine Residents anticipated 10 years ago. The Catholics have a very elegant little church there.[27] altogather there are some 7 or 8 churches in the Place.[28] a large and commodius Town Hall graces the upper part of Main St.[29] like most Country Places, Piqua is a temperate place, not a licenced drinking house in it. Our Walk this Morning was a pretty Extensive one. when we returned about 10 oclock I was very tired. So I went up into my room with August and Commenced this small travelling Sketch of this my first excursion for twelve years. ere I had however finished half, I was agreably interrupted by the dinner-Bell. recommenced immediatly afterwards and finished this far—by looking at my Watch I find it is 10 minutes to 3—August is asleep on a bed by the side of my writing-Table. (August is my brother's clerk.) poor fellow! he is tired and Worn out, having had the largest share of our troubles. The Evening we passed in the same manner as last, ie playing Euchre I had to pay again. to bed 10.

Dayton Thursday May 4 P.M.

I am sitting in Swaynies Hotel.[30] it is ½ past 3 precisely. arrived here 10 minutes past 2 by Stage. Immediatly after breakfast this morning we packed up our things and Were ready just as the Stage halted across the Street at the Post Office. As there were but 3 persons in it I succeeded in persuading Henry to Come in, So we left Piqua very abruptly without time to bid any of our acquaintances *adieu.* every thing went well until we reached Troy. here we were overtaken by a Thunder Storm. a very vivid Flash of lightning frightened the Horses just as we were out of the Stage. the Driver a noble little fellow succeeded in turning the Horses around the corner of the next street which was only 20 paces ahead of him, running them over a large stump of a tree, before which it remained standing, while the Horses run on ~~for~~ a few Squares farther. the runing before the stump broke the tongue,[31] which left the Stage standing before it. we were detained in Troy about 2 hours, while a new tongue was made for the Stage.

This little accident frightened Henry so much that he refused to proceed any farther by way of Stage. as he has a Wife and Child I did not like to urge or plague him especially as the Weather threatened more rain, thunder &c.

While there (waiting for the Stage) we took a walk through the Place. it has not improved at all. Main is a somewhat regular street, has some pretty large buildings in it, but every thing looks old already, no new improvements going on. in comparing it with Piqua, Troy is receding.

Nothing occurred to make us regret having taken the Stage,[32] as we arrived safe and sound in Dayton. I and August orriginally intended to remain a day & night in Dayton, but in walking through the Place from one End to the other which we did during the afternoon, we found every thing so quiet and dull that We resolved to leave it for Cincinnati the Same evening, before Henry had arrived with the Packet, and giving him a voice in the breaking up our first arrangements.

By the time the Packet arrived we had our little Trunk at the packet-office. Henry did not offer any objections, he was also glad to get home. We took [off] the same Evening for Cincinnati. had Supper on board. Our Evening party was not so pleasant as on the first boat. Two orators from some village volunteered to inflict the Company with Songs, in which infliction they Succeeded admirably. Our boat went along rapidly. I slept well, when I arose this morning we were on this Side of Hamilton. After a very good breakfast all the male Passengers went on deck to enjoy the fine Morning, and most of them a good Cigar at the same time. Every thing appeared handsomer and of more importance now, then when going out. perhaps I was in better humour, nearing home every moment. We arrived in Cincinnati shortly before 11. I went direct home to change my dress, put on fresh linen, and shave myself. every one Complimented me on my unusual dark Complexion. I did look very dark. my beard also was of an unusual lenght. I succeeded however in giving myself a decent appearance befor dinner, at least as much so, as my sun burnt Complexion would admit of— I found Mr. D[exter] sitting in an easy devil may care position in his favorite place in the Store, looking as grim as an Old Turkey-Cock. when however the light of my Countenance broke ~~in~~ on him, his face gradually relaxed, and he delivered himself to this Effect. Well! I am glad you are back. I swear I could'nt 'ave stood it much longer. —Stretches himself— What a time I have had of it. On Monday and Tuesday I had to Send for the Doctor. Should'nt have though of going out of the House, had it not been necessary. Poor Old Cock, he was very Sick during the early part of the Week. well! I had my troubles also. I finally arranged all my business to my satisfaction. he finally got well again—Wonderful Similarity.

I did intend to visit the Theatre after supper, but my face was so inflamed and red that I was 'fraid to venture out. 'Till about 9 oclock we were in Mr Bradley's room playing Euchre. I, Brown and Del—r then Walked out for a half hour or so, the Evening being beautiful. from ½ past 9 to ½ past 10 We Smoked in dining Room, then to Bed—

NOTES

1. Loomis, 23.
2. Hall, 223.
3. Loomis, 11.
4. ENQ, 10 May 1848; WPA (2) 59.
5. Loomis, 23.
6. COM, 10 March 1848.
7. Jones, 250.
8. Hogsheads were large casks that held goods for transport (OED, s.v. "hogshead").
9. Frank Mersman had worked for a St. Louis tobacconist, but now returned to Cincinnati, jobless.
10. Phonetic spelling of "blackguard" or scoundrel (OED, s.v. "blackguard").
11. Platt Evans (also Evens) (1791–1873), born in New York, was a merchant tailor who owned a shop on Main Street and a farm in Cumminsville, five miles west of Cincinnati, that became a landmark (CCD 1840, 174; COM, 5 November 1873).
12. John H. Dubbs (1808–?), a native of Pennsylvania, was the proprietor of a small hotel in Lockland, Ohio (USC 1850, M432, roll 686, page 413, line 39).
13. "Phiz" means face or physiognomy (OED, s.v. "phiz").
14. A "toper" is a chronic drunkard (OED, s.v. "toper").
15. Henry Mersman and August Rittmeyer, the laborer.
16. The Greek Revival courthouse, begun in 1845, was completed in 1850. The structure, constructed of massive blocks of limestone, became a symbol of Dayton, and still stands in 2005 (Borchers, 13; Ronald, 38–39; Steele, 185).
17. "Maying" is the celebration of May Day by picking flowers and picnicking (OED, s.v. "maying").
18. Apparently, near Troy, Ohio, the seat of Miami County.
19. Philadelphia, Pennsylvania, had markets which might pay higher prices for Ohio tobacco.
20. Henry, JJM, and August Rittmeyer headed south as they sought farmers with tobacco.
21. The cost of bed and breakfast per person.
22. I.e., south of Piqua.
23. JJM worked as a waterboy during the construction of the Miami and Erie Canal in 1835 while his family resided in Minster, Ohio.
24. Jacob D. Holtzerman and George Dettmer, German immigrants, established a wholesale liquor business in Piqua in 1838 (USC 1850, 432, roll 711, page 380, line 15; Rayner, 60, 70, 183).
25. The card game may have been euchre or whist, card games for four players, which use rubbers for scoring (Beaver [2], 104; Hoyle, 237–42).
26. Harry Clark (1823-?), a native of New Jersey, operated a grocery in Piqua (USC 1850, M432, roll 711, page 370, line 24).

27. St. Mary Church in Piqua was dedicated in 1846 (Lamott, 152–53, 341).

28. There were actually ten churches in Piqua: one Episcopal, one Catholic, three Presbyterian, two Methodist, one Baptist, one German Lutheran, and one Christian (PIQ, 15 April 1848).

29. Completed in 1844, the first town hall was a three-story brick building surmounted by a cupola containing a bell (Oda, 6).

30. Built by Alexander Swaynie (1804–77) in 1839, Swaynie's Hotel in Dayton provided first-class accommodations for about a hundred guests (Steele, 173; Reemelin, 180; USC 1850, M432, roll 713, page 151, lines 13–42; page 152, lines 1–42; page 153, lines 1–20).

31. The "tongue" is the pole extending from a vehicle between the animals drawing it (OED, s.v. "tongue").

32. JJM and August Rittmeyer took the stage from Troy to Dayton, and therefore arrived before Henry Mersman, who traveled by canal boat.

CHAPTER FIVE

Cigars and Saloons

6 May 1848–9 August 1848

Cigars, first introduced in the early 1800s, had, by JJM's day, supplanted pipes in popularity as a means of smoking tobacco.[1] *Tobacco—from Ohio, Missouri, Kentucky, Virginia, Cuba, and Spain—made its way into products manufactured in Cincinnati. In 1850, the federal census enumerated 219 tobacconists and 170 cigar makers among Cincinnati's residents.*[2] *A count in 1851 found 62 tobacco factories in Cincinnati, with a total output of $931,000. Such factories employed as many as 150 workers.*[3]

JJM mentioned cigars virtually every day of his life in Cincinnati. His father and brothers, all tobacconists, made their livings by manufacturing and selling cigars. Many of their German-speaking friends—Baker, Becker, Beneke, Dieck, Fahlbush, Meyer, Pauk, Tebbelman, and three Nulsens (Anthony, Francis, and JCN)—also depended on the tobacco trade. The common expertise shared by the men provided the basis for JJM's social network.

JJM enjoyed smoking, and made a ritual of finishing each day with a cigar. His visits to saloons and other nightspots invariably ended in a cloud of blue smoke.

JJM's happy-go-lucky existence contrasted dramatically with that of the married women he mentioned: Agnes Lake, Elizabeth Kattenhorn, Mrs. Granger, Mrs. Murray, and the former Miss Karrman, each of whom struggled with her lot in life. Financially dependent on men, coping with illness and pregnancy, the young matrons experienced a lifestyle vastly different from the one JJM enjoyed.

Saturday, May 6th. 1848

The sound repose I enjoyed the whole and long night, having gone to bed early, refreshed and made me fully Capable of resuming the business as heretofore. I

WILLIAM TELL RESTAURAT,

BY FREDERIC DISERENS,

South side of Fifth street, between Main and Walnut,

CINCINNATI.

Lately rebuilt and enlarged, is now prepared to receive Boaders by the Day or Week.

Extra Meals at all hours.

Oysters and all kinds of Game in their season.

Cooking done to send to all parts of the city.

N. B. Persons boarding at this House, who cannot attend regular meals, can call at any hour, without additional charge.

The William Tell Restaurat [*sic*] advertisement, 1846. The William Tell was one of Mersman's favorite saloons. He refers to it in his diary, often as the "Billy Tell." (From the Collection of the Public Library of Cincinnati and Hamilton County.)

was up betimes also. Business is however very dull at present, hardly any thing doing. every one seems afraid to part with Money for an uncertain equivalent, and hardly any thing is considered safe. The Cash as kept by Mr Dexter balanced very Closely, the Weeks was good. The Evening I passed entirely at home, reading till 9 oclock, then went out with Del—r to Day's Saloon where we enjoyed a plate of rich Ice Cream. from there we went to an Ale cellar under the Melodeon to [follow] the Ice Cream with a glass of Ale. It was very Warm this Evening, so we took a [cigar] under the porch[4] where we coold off right pleasantly. To Bed ½ past 10. Exp 20c

Sunday May 7th

Beautiful Weather, the Morn'g especially was very agreable. after breakfast I and Del—r took an extensive walk over north-Western part of the City. from 9 to 12 I was busily Engaged reviewing and studying French. I have forgotten to some extant already but as I read it over, it comes back to memory again.

After dinner I and Del—r smoked our Cigars under the porch. this I suppose will be our favorite Smoking [place] during the Summer. 3 oclock I went to K[attenhorn]'s. there was a small party assembled. About 5 returned home, read till supper. Walked with Brown along some of the fashionable streets, while smoking our Havana's.[5] from 8 to ½ past 9 I was at Moulinier's. To Bed 11. Exp 35c.

Monday May 8th 1848

Business is encreasing in dullness every day. Whiskey drags to day at 14 cents.[6] Southern advices are very discouraging. whiskey is down to 14¼ - 14½, in New Orleans, 16. dull.

After supper I called with Brown and John Bradley at the National Theatre. we were there joined by Del—r before the play commenced. Forest performed in *Damon and Pithyas,* a beautiful piece and *Therese the Orphan of Geneva* also very good.[7] I was very well amused. went home about 12. the performance had not Concluded when we left. I was very sleepy. To Bed 20 min. after 12. Exp 1.60.

Tuesday 9th

Beautiful and pleasant Weather again. Commerce with us commenced very flourishingly this Week. The Evening I passed in various ways. from ½ past 7 to 8 I exercised myself on the flute while Delamettre was emigrating to a room above. Del—r has been my room-mate the whole Winter. I should have parted with him with regret, if any body except Frank[8] had taken his place. We are now to have our room to ourselves again, for which we are to pay 5½$ per Week.

Shortly after 8 I and Del—r Walked out. Corner of 4th and Main We met Brown. poor fellow! he was quite alone, and without protection, so I and D[elamater] took him in Charge. after walking about some time for the benefit of B's health we proceeded to Billy Tell's to refresh him, not forgetting ourselves. Brown then to return our kindness took us to Dieks[9] and treated us to a good Cigar. to Smoke these with satisfaction we went direct home. To Bed 10. Exp 20c.

Wednesday May 10th 1848

Of all disagreable days we have had lately, this surpasses them all. a slow Continual rain of the coldest kind, & accompanied with the [worst] Wind I have ever felt in May, pour'd down the whole day. Commerce was agreably brisk. The Evening I passed principally at home playing Duette's with Fanny.[10] about 9 I went to the German Orphans Fair.[11] It was a mixed and Common affair. I did not stay long. was home again before 10. Smoked till past 11. Exp 60 cts.

Thursday May 11th 1848

Were I disposed to swear about it, I should say that it was damn bad Weather, damnably disagreable, rainy the whole day. After supper I had a french lesson again. being through with this I went to Billy Tell's treated my self to a glass of

Ale. then went home Smoked with my usual Smoking Companions till 11, when I retirrd. Exp 10c.

Friday May 12th

Very pleasant Weather again. Slightly Cold yet, but other wise all that Can be desired. business very dull. Nothing doing at all. After supper I and Frank called on Sister Mrs K[attenhorn]. we were however very Coldly received. So we did [not] stay long. Frank went to the German Theatre. I, home. Studied french, translated about 30 lines from the german.

I fear father and Elizabeth will fall out. She is a vulgar Woman, although my Sister, and treats Father as though he was dependant on her, which he is not having I beleive suffiscient Money to board with until he dies.[12] We Smoked our Cigar as usual. retired about 11. Exp 5c.

Saturday May 13th 1848

This would be a pleasant day, were it not so Windy. being so, it is of course impossible to be pleasant. Business was dull. the time for leizure and indolence has evidently come at last. My Cash balanced very accurately this afternoon, a very desirable thing for me. The Evening I passed with my french Teacher.[13] having my lesson first, then went with him to his house. was treated to a glass of Ale, which I relished much, it being old and good. from there I went direct home.

Sunday May 14th

Was decidedly the plaisantest Sunday we have had this Season. About 9 oclock I, Del—r and John Brandley started per Omnibus[14] for Sportsmens Hall, a place I formerly visited pretty frequently, but which has for the last two years been quite neglected. It is now kept by John Ganter, who is making extensive additions to the building. We amused ourselves first rate during the two hours we were there, looking over the grounds, garden &c and pitching Qoits[15] about ¼ past 12 we returned to the city, arrived just in time to hear the dinner-Bell ring. Shortly after dinner I called on Henry. he was not at home. Amused his wife until 4 oclock. then return'd home. Brown was in the parlour, troubled with Ennui. to disperse which we went out to the Grave-yard on 12th St.[16] Had plenty of Company there. the place seems a Sort of resort for lazy Loafers. Having Smoked my usual Cigar after supper I called on the Misses Corbens. I have not been there for Some time. Mayle Larkin is boarding there. he seems to be entirely Cut out of the good graces of Mary. poor fellow! To Bed 11 oclock. Exp 45c.

Monday May 15th 1848

Weather Warm although pleasant. Business, considering the general dulness in the city, made a passable commencement. The Evening I and Brown passed in the National togather.[17] The French Balet Company[18] made their first appearance this evening. They are not equal to the Ravels[19] as Pantomimists, but very active dancers. the pantomime which they performed, devoid of the dancing, would have been very uninteresting. Met Mr. D[exter] & old Logan[20] taking a Horn at Pap Hughes.[21] I and Brown were doing the same thing. The performance concluded ½ past 10. To Bed 11. Exp 5c.

Tuesday 16th

Retail business continues fair. Weather warm. during the forenoon a good shower moderated the heat considerably. Commerce flourished with reasonable activity. The Evening I passed entirely at home, having a lesson which detained me till ½ past 9. So I had just time to smoke a Cigar which I did and then went to bed, it being about ½ past 10. Exp 10c.

Wednesday 17th

It rained nearly the whole night, is raining this morning. I anticipate more—it is So very Warm yet. towards evening it brightened up, giving us a clear fine moonlight night for our deprivations during the Day. After Supper I was emphatically at large, having nothing particular to do, and it was too beautiful out doors to study at home. so I went down to the Merchants Reading rooms and Amused myself there till ½ past 9.[22] when I got home Bradley was standing ready at the Gate to take me and Del—r over to the U.S. Hotel and there treat us to a good [horn]. the Bar Room of U.S. looks well after its refitting and enlargement. I, B[radley] & D[elamater] Smoked in the dining room 'till nearly 11. then went to bed. Exp 5c.

Thursday May 18th 1848

Excessivly warm weather. business very dull. To day We Commenced moving out of our old Warehouses in to the New Store.[23] the removal will take at least a weak. After supper I went and got my flute having had some repairing done to it, enlarging embochure, and having the joints Corked. I was charged 1.10 which was not too much. from 8 to ½ past 9 I, Brown, Bradley and his Son played Euchre in my room. I lost the liquor. from ½ past 9 to nearly 11 we Sat and Smoked in the dining-room. then to Bed—Exp 1.30.

Friday 19th

Excessive warm weather. business very dull. Whiskey is down to 13⅝. Money very hard to get. Confidence in the Mercantile World is considerably Shaken by extensive failures and embarrassment of large Houses.[24] The Evening I passed at home first playing on my flute till I was tired. from ½ past 9 to nearly 11 we played Eucre in my room. Although invited, I did not go out to drink with the Company and only smoked one Cigar during the evening, two being otherwise my general allowance. Exp 25c.

Saturday 20th

Continues very warm. business dull. To days mail brot me a very interesting letter from Charles Dexter. as we are moving at present, I shall defer replying until we are permanently fixed in the new Store. The Evening I passed at home with my french Teacher.[25] from 9½ to ½ after 10 I kept Brown Company smoking. Exp 5c.

Sunday May 21st 1848

Was a most disagreable day. Very warm and raining every other hour or so. I promised Mr Tappe yesterday to play Second flute at the Consecration of the new Catholic Church on Congress St.[26] Service was to Commence 10 oclock. So about ½ 9 I sallied forth, at a time when the heavens were overcast by dark Clouds, every one of which was leaking awfully, rendering my somewhat antiquated Umbrella a very poor protection against the rain.

The Consecration took place about 10, while the church was Empty. About 11 Service, or Mass, Commenced. Our exertions to produce good music were pretty successful. The Church was very Crowded. the Windows opened from below, leaving the atmosphere above where we were very impure.

I had a cold dinner on this account, it being near 2 oclock when I got home. being however very hungry, it tasted well.

from 2 to 3 I was very busy dressing myself, in my holiday attire.[27] Called at Henry's, found nobody at homme except his Wife. did not Stay long. from there I went to my old friend Wagner (Clemens brother in law) I passed a very agreeable afternoon with him. I like him better than any german in Cincinnati, having far more Common Sense. It was oppressively warm, and but for Wagners good Soda I should have melted away. About 5 I went to Kattenhorns for a few minutes—did not see Sister—from there direct home. Endeavoured to amuse Mary Jane[28] till supper time. 'beleive I was pretty Successful. After supper I and Brown took a Walk while Smoking our evening Cigar. Endeavoured to see My young friend Baker who owes me the five dollars I lent him some time ago. To Bed 10 oclock. Exp 10 cts.

Monday May 22nd 1848

Weather once more bright and beautiful altho' very warm. Business was not so very bad, not even as much so as I anticipated for the present Season. I did not have much time to devote to my french during day. In the evening I was too tired to do any thing at it. So accepted Mr. Brown's invitation and Went to the Atheneum with him.[29] Mrs Wilkinson Continues the presiding Star of the House. her acting in the *Italien Wife* was very good. We did not stay for the last piece. before going home however we indulged in a "Julip"[30] at the U.S. Hotel for which I had to fork over. To Bed 11. Exp 25c.

Tuesday May 23rd

Our "moving" is progressing rapidly, to day all the rectefiers will be placed in the new building. the large cisterns are already there. Business and Weather both favourable. After Supper I had a french lesson. did not go out afterwards except to drink a glass of Soda. to bed 10. Exp 15 cts.

Wednesday 24th

Business Continues good. The Evening I passed at home entirely amusing myself with my flute till nearly 9. balance of time till ½ past 10 I threw away entirely. only Smoking with Brown. Exp 10

Thursday 25th

Weather very Coquetish, raining every now and then. towards evening it came steady and continued till—I don't know how long as I went to bed 10 oclock, being very sleepy and tired. Business tolerbly fair during the day—Exp 15 cts.

Friday May 26th 1848

Weather is beautiful, although a little warm. the frequent Showers lately have brot forward all the various Spring fruits to an unusual early perfection. I have not as yet indulged in any of the early fruits, except, Currant Pie. I have no taste or desire for any of them. Strawberries especially have until [now] Commanded a high price. Business a shade duller than the previous part of the Week. We are progressing slowly with our moving operations. all the rectefyers are to be re-bottom'd and retined [retinned], which will take some time to finish.

After supper I had my second french lesson this Week. my lessons occupy the whole evening, passing of course a large portion of the time in mescellanious Conversation. I accompanied Moulinier to the reading room,[31] read and looked over the various Magasin's there. about 10 I returned home, found

BANK EXCHANGE HOTEL,

And Dining Rooms,

GEORGE SELVES, PROPRIETOR,

Third street, opposite the Franklin and Lafayette Banks,

CINCINNATI.

Bank Exchange Hotel advertisement, 1846. This amusing ad, from the Cincinnati City Directory of 1846, points out that the turtle soup served at the Bank Exchange dining room was so popular that turtles lined up to have their heads cut off, just to make customers happy. (From the Collection of The Public Library of Cincinnati and Hamilton County.)

Brown and Del—r out doors under the porch enjoying a good Havana. Could'nt resist the temptation of joining them. To Bed 11. Exp 10c

Saturday 27th

Business to day was very lively. I was more or less occupied all the time. read a letter from Charles Dexter[32] to his Father. The young Gentleman appears to be getting ahead rapidly, & is evidently satisfied with himself. My Cash balanced very accurately to day, a most satisfactory Conclusion to the Weeks business. After supper I studied my french lesson till nearly 9. then went out, bot a pair of Socks on Main St. Went up called on Brother in law a short time. treated myself to a glass of Ail, and about ½ past 9 I went and indulged in good Bath on Court S.[33] from there direct home. To Bed 11. Exp 50c

Sunday May 28th 1848

The day was beautiful although very Warm. Immediatly after breakfast I went down to the Store had the Pony Saddled and rode out of the City on Mount Auburn.[34] I met Tony Nulsen ascending the Hill with his little Son,[35] took the little fellow on the Horse before and treated him to a pleasant ride as far as Drachs. Stop'd there myself a few minutes to refresh myself with a glass of lemonade and light my Cigar. the view from that Place is really beautiful, embracing the Entire bottom on which the city is built, excepting only Fulton and the very northern Part of Texas.[36] The high and regular chain of Hills on the Kentucky side formed a difinite outline Seemingly reaching half way up in the clouds. After enjoying the prospect a short time—my Havanna also—I contin'd my ride. The Sceenery on Walnut Hills is also lovely, the Residents all along there display a great deal of taste in ornamenting their gardens & Houses. This being the first time I have been out on Horseback this year I cut my ride short, fearing the effects of a long one on my "foundation" returned to the city by the Vine St road, a very disagreable one by the bye, being lined on one side with lime kilns that never seem to be idle.[37] From 10 to 12 I studied french. I had no sooner swallowed my dinner than Moulinier Came to give me my lesson. being through with it we Called on Tim O'Connor. All three went out on the Observatory Hill.[38] Passed the whole afternoon under the Shade of thick leaved birch Tree. the agreable Coolness & refreshing breeze well repaid us for the trouble of ascending. I had Supper at home. did not go out afterwards—

Monday May 29th 1848

During the day we had two or three very severe showers, cooling the air to a comfortable temperature. Business was very good the entire day. The Evening I passed without doing any thing particular. went down to Kochs whiled away a half hour there, then went with Koch and Menzel up [?] Street, left them corner of 9th, called on Kattenhorn to inform him of some changes in the Market. from there I went home. To Bed ½ past 10. Exp 10c

Tuesday May 30th

Yesterday and last nights rains Cooled the atmosphere very effectually. Business was very good. I hardly [had] time to prepare my french lesson for this Evening. by severe application however between 7 and 8 until Moulinier came, I menaged to get ready. after my lesson I took a short walk with M— treated him and myself to a glass of Mineral Water. to bed 10 oclock. Exp 15.

Wednesday 31

Was a very busy day for me. during the forenoon I was employed in Collecting the monthly accounts and during the afternoon in setling my monthly Cash acct. The Evening I passed at home with my little brother Frank studing till 10, when we retired. both very sleepy. Exp 5.

Thursday June 1st

Commerce still Continues very flourishing. I could have Sold 200 bbls Whisky to day if we had had them to spare. through severe application I menaged to gain suffiscient time to nearly finish my french lesson. I have to take 3 lessons this Week. my trip to Dayton and Piqua put me back 2 lessons.[39] did not go out at all. To Bed 11. Exp 10c.

Friday June 2nd 1848

It was very warm again to day. I was busy the entire day, excepting about 2 hours towards Evening. of these I made use of in writing partly my french lesson. I lost a Philipine[40] with Sweet Mary Corbin, and was under the disagreable necessity to refuse her kind invitation to a Picnic Party to come off to morrow. of Course I cannot expect Mr Dexter to put himself to any inconvinience on account of mere Amusement especially as his presence is so necessary in the new building at present. After Supper I Called on the Misses Corbins to explain these reasons personally. They were kind enough to evince a reasonable regret at my unability to attend. was introduced there to a Miss Agnew, a rather good looking Lady with Sentimental Curls falling in rich profusion around a passably formed head, hiding or rather diminishing the Size of a goodly Sized noze. She appeared to be well versed in the art of Coquettry[41] neither particularly favouring or offending any one of her numerous admirers, of which there were Some 7 or 8. Met Mrs Murray (of Granger Memory) there also.[42] She was Sick. About 10 oclock I went home. was so excessively foolish as to some [smoke] a cigar before going to bed. Exp 10c.

Saturday June 3rd 1848

Pleasant and agreable Weather. Business very lively. my Cash account Came out "Square" After Supper I had another french lesson making three this Week. after it, I was so foolish as to Smoke a Cigar. Went to bed at 10, read till 11. Expence 10c.

Sunday June 4th 1848

This day was Set apart for the 4th Anniversary of the German *Liedertafel.* Our mode of Conveyance was different this time than it has been heretofore. We Went per Ferry Boat. At 7 we were to Start, but a few minutes before this time it was raining horibly. this of course caused a general delay giving every one chance to enjoy breakfast before going. A few minutes before 9 our boat left—Started from foot of Main St. going up was very pleasant, the wind had by this time chased every cloud from the heavens, making the Weather all that could be desired. if any thing it was Slightly too warm yet. The party on board I suppose Numbered from 80 to 100. of the young Ladies there were a great many what might be termed the old Stock, ie they have been young Ladies "Long time ago." I found it no easy matter to ascend the Hill.[43] what must many of the more Corpulent Germans have suffered. Vogel,[44] a beast who weighs over 300. I did not think it worth my while to pay attention to any of the German Ladies there. Some few that I did Condescend to notice were married. made myself intimate there with a Mr Baker, who appeared to be about the most decent young man in the Crowd. As soon as we were Cooled off a little we Commenced tippling. We did so rather too energetically for an hour afterwards. I was elegantly Cocked, not drunk—but just in that State when Heaven and Earth begins to go Slowly around. not wishing to get drunk, I left off and did not touch Wine again till towards Evening. The dinner consisted of about the Same Compounds as usual, nothing extra and suffisciently good to quiet the cravings of the Stomach. at the Table I endeavoured to do my duty in waiting upon the females in my immediate neighbourhood, noticing most of the Gentleman Singularly remiss in this respect. After dinner the arrival were numerous and in a Short time every available place of Comfort was taken.

Some of the Old Social games played heretofore at every festival were not attempted at all this time. Those who had girls and were tired of drinking and drinking Company would quietly steal away, and enjoy things among themselves. About 3 oclock the Company was organized and attempted to sing, but most of the members had looked in to the bottle too deep to retain any distinct idea of Harmony. every thing however passed off very pleasantly. I did not hear an ill natured word spoken. Some of the girls were pretty good looking, but no decided beauty did I see. Consequently gave myself no great trouble in waiting upon any particular one. About ½ past 6 we left the top of the Hill ½ past 7 the Fery Boat left. every One was on board. by the bye I omitted to mention one thing. Mr Mensel[45] made a poor speech because it was too short. Groenladt[46] spoke longer but very little to the purpose. Mr Stallo's speech was suffisciently

Enthusiastic to meet with approbation of all. towards Evening it rained a little again but none got wet. the boat returned in far less time than it took her to go up. Avery one was more Silent than Coming up this Morning. It appeared to me that many of the girls wore disappointed faces. suppose their anticipations were not realized. It was about 8 or ½ past I suppose when I got home. I did not go out again during the Evening, but went to bed before 10. Exp 1.45c.

Monday June 5th 1848

Very Windy to day. The Hurricane not only making all the dust he can, but now and then in his fury throws up Small stones, forces awnings from their Comfortable Situations, and kicks up a most thundering row. Business Commenced very lively to day, keeping me Engaged all the time. After supper, I visited the Circus.[47] Lake officiated as Clown and in my opinion acquitted himself very well. the performance was very good. I left however at 10 oclock. Went direct home. Exp 60¢.

Tuesday 6th

Beautiful Weather. every one, especially the Ladies, is enjoying it. My Brother in law Wm Lake gave me call this afternoon, which cost me Two dollars for a bottle of fine old Mada[48] and two do [ditto] Old Castillon Bdy,[49] one do of Whiskey. About ½ past 8 I went to the Circus to take Agnes down to the boat. She had her Horse there. the Menager furnished me with another so we rode down. we had not been there long ere Agnes discovered that she had to go up again. Poor girl She half Complained of her Husband. Say's that he Commences to drink again and is Cross to her sometimes. I consoled and advised her as much as was in my power. Lake has been talking of going to South America.[50] I have done all I could to dissuade him from doing so. These people are so unsteady that one is totally at a loss how to advise. When we arrived at the Tent the performance was nearly Concluded. I remained till all was over. Lake has left me one of his Dog's (Rolla).[51] the poor beast has a severe Cough and requires rest and a quiet life for Some time. I bade Agnes & Lake farewell Cor. 6 & Race, perhaps for the last time. Went home very Sad. To bed 11. Exp 15c

[Margin note] I have also agreed to keep Agnes Guitar. If either She or Lake Should return in want, I intend to pay twenty dollars for it, this being the amount it has cost them in money— J.J.M.

Wednesday 7th June 1848.

The Coughing of the dog—whom I was Compelled last night to put in my room—awoke me this Morning at ½ past 4. I believe he must have awoke the inmates of the neighbouring rooms Several times during the night. this Morning early I took him over to Henrys Store and consigned him over to his Charge. The parting with Agnes and Lake always makes me Sad to part. It seems to me so uncertain whether I shall ever See them again, but they both seem to have a roving disposition and this I can not help. may God guard and look mercifully on them.

After Supper I had my french lesson for which I was fully prepared. Went out for a few minutes afterwards with Moulinier merely to treat him and myself to a glass of mineral fluidity. returned direct home and Went to Bed. Exp 15c.

Thursday 8th

Weather pleasant and agreable. Business lively & do [ditto]. Entering our parlor at dinner time to day, whom Should I see but my Old friend Granger. He returned direct from *Mexico,* but a few days ago. the Gentn looked somewhat the worse or better for the roasting he has undergone, appeared to be otherwise in excellent health. his Wife was just on the point of Starting for Indiana when her husband arrived. poor Mrs G. I met her a few days since on 5th street. She then looked as blooming as a young girl of 18 or 19, but now the Consequences of her husbands return and presence are already visible on her pale and Care worn Countenance.

The Evening I passed with Del—re in Atheneum. Mrs Coleman Pope appeared in two characters, and acquited herself passably well.[52] To Bed 12. Exp 65c.

Friday June 9th 1848

Business is not so lively to day as it has been during the Week. I received a letter or rather merely a note from Lake, desiring me to forward Some linen that his Washer Woman omitted to deliver while here. I have sent Frank[53] out there to enquire about it. She left the articles with Mrs Runnels, who promised to Send them along with some of her own that she intended to send to her husband. I shall write to Lake to Morrow Morning by the Louisville Packet and explain every thing to him. Lake's Dog Rolla I have placed in Charge of a German Doctor who, having been a Sporting Character pretends to know all about Dog's and their deseases. he expects to Cure him entirely in two Weeks which if he does, I shall remunerate him handsomely.

The Evening I passed entirely at home, Smoking during the early part of it with two fellow-boarders under the porch, and from ½ past 8 to ½ past 9 I amused myself with playing on my Guitar. As it rained I did not venture out at all. To Bed 10 oclock Exp 5c

Saturday June 10th

Cloudy and disagreable Weather. I wrote to Lake this Morning and put the letter on *Pike No 7*.[54] Business dull, who cares!—The Confounded Cash would'nt balance this afternoon. It detained me till late in the Evening. The Evening I passed at home with my french teacher. with our french exercise and Guitar playing it got to be past 10 when we were through. I went with Moulinier for few minutes to treat him to a glass of Mineral Water. To Bed ½ past 10. Exp 15c

Sunday June 11th 1848

Most lovely Weather this Morning. I was up early, having to get shaved before breakfast. Immediately after it my Brother[55] Called on me. I went to his Store with him, enjoyed a good Cigar there. About ½ past 9 I returned to my room Shut myself up there, and Wrote a long letter to Clemens,[56] in reply to his favour of last Saturday. this occupied me the whole forenoon. After dinner I went with Daddy whom I found loafing about the House to Henry. he was not at home. I got Daddy to Stay there. Called on Wagner, did not find [him] home either. from there I proceeded to Our Mr Pauk. was so fortunate as to find the girls at home. An Old, young Man by the name of Mehner[57] who is paying particular attention to the Oldest, was there already. It was so very warm that we preferred to Stay at home. Miss Carrman that used to be but now is Mrs, I do not know what her name is,[58] Called there also. Poor girl she is a good deal of joints. her face is quite thin, and Care worn. She looks to be half way on the familly road.[59] Says she is troubled with fits of weakness, or rather Fits caused by Weakness. I had no reason to regret the time passed there. Came too late for the regular supper, not being hungry. I was Content with the leavings. The Evening I passed with Del—r. we first Smoked a Cigar immediatly after Supper. then took a walk of 5 or 6 Squares, then went to the U.S.[60] with Doctr Darling, then Smoked again, then had Ice Cream then Concluded with Smoking another Cigar. to bed 10. Exp 30c.

Cincinnati July 12th 1848.

My Journal has had a rest of One month and One day, the last Entry is on Sunday June 11th. on Monday we Commenced Moving vigourously. In the moving of our Effects I attended in the Old Store to the taking them down properly, and Mr Dexter to the placing of them in the New One. The Exertion for Mr Dexter during the first day was too much for him. for on Tuesday he was taken Sick, with a Complaint similar to the Piles,[61] and the same one he suffered so much, about two years ago. Of course every thing immediatly devolved on me. What was the work of two active Men, I had to do and Menage alone, and as ill luck would have it, Business in the new House Commenced very briskly ere we were hardly in it. I have the Satisfaction of knowing that I fullfilled my duty, although it was a very laborious one, both Mentally and Phisically, the latter because all the men were unacquainted with the Manner of doing things in the new building, and in fact I was at a loss sometimes myself.[62]

Business, which Commenced very lively in the new place, retarded our moving or rather the finishing of it over a Week. a few days after our Commencement of rectefying, I had to Commence Shipping to New Orleans. this I had to Continue as often as had a Suffisciently large Lot to Ship. Frequently in the evening I was so tired and Worn out that I [barely] had the strengh to Walk home. then as Soon as had my Supper I had to Call on Mr Dexter. of Course my own Sympathy would have led me to him very frequently also, but all this required time and finished by keeping me Employed 15 hours out of the 24. My french lessons I menaged to get ready by studying on Sunday and late in the Evening.

During all this time I was but Once in the Theatre—NO! twice. Once to see the Model Artists[63] and on fourth of July. by the bye on 4th inst, I had the Store open till dinner.

Dined at home. immediatly after dinner Mr Moulinier Called on me. We went to Burkhardts togather. about 3 oclock we made up a party of 5, went down to the River and through my influence obtained a Yawl.[64] had a very agreable Yawl ride and Swim in the Licking River.

The Evening we passed in the National Theatre.[65] On thursday the 6th Mr D[exter] came down to the Store for the first time. I was indeed glad to see him about again, not only because it will give me a great deal of time again, but also because it released him from a disagreable Confinement which [occurred] during the very hot weather that we have had all along for some 3 Weeks.

Business during this Week has been very dull, but to make up for this we received returns from both New Orleans and Mobile[66] which proved very satisfactory. for the future, every day will have its Entry.

Sunday, July 16th 1848

I fear my Journal will not receive the attention now that we are in the new Establishment,[67] that it has had for over three years.[68] The latter part of last Week I was so busy every day, that I had not suffiscient time to finish my french writing. I certainly delight in doing a fair business, but when it is so Continual and so pressing that it requires all one's time, the pleasure of it Ceases and it becomes Labour. However as the men become ascustomed to our new arrangements, they require less watching and superintendance, and I suppose when they are as Conversant with every thing as formerly in the Old place, I shall nearly have my Old quantity of leisure again.

My little brother Frank has gone to St Louis again. He left on Friday the 6th of July, leaving me to settle for his last weeks Boarding. he did not even bid me farewell.

This Morning was a beautiful One. immediatly after Breakfast I and Mr Shotwell[69] indulged in a walk for the Benefit of our health, not that we at all sick, but as preventative. from 9 to 12 I studied french. tried to Amuse myself with my Guitar, but the E string broke & would not be repaired. After dinner I, O'Conner and Moulinier went out to see a Captain Ekert, Some 4 Miles out of the City. He was not at home when we arrived so we strolled about his Grounds until he Came. we were then well treated. His Grounds, wine, & ale vaults are all in Excellent Condition. The Capns Residence is really a Splendid Edifice and if he was only somewhat of a litterary Man might lead a very happy life there. but of this he did not give the slightest indication, being from all appearances a plain practical and self made Man, one who has had the good fortune to be successful in life as a Steamboat Captain.

We missed the Omnibus that took us out there, so we waited until 7 oclock, all that Came by in the mean time being Crowded. and then we started on foot back, this being the best Conveyance we Could procure. we walked to the Brighton House a distance of two miles, when we were overtaken by a "Buss" not quite so Crowded as the former one's. this we patronised for the balance of the way.[70] Arrived in town about 8. I accepted Mouliniers invitation to take supper with him. About 9 I went home, passed an agreable hour with "Mary Jane" smoking my Cigar at the same time. I had'nt smoked since dinner. to Bed ½ past 10. read till 11. The day's Expenses 50 cts

Monday July 17th

Was a most lovely day. Commerce Commenced very lively this Morning. I was busily Engaged the entire day. And when Evening Came I thought myself suffisciently tired to stay at home. My leisure time in my room I devote at present to the study and practice of my Guitar, and sometimes, when I am Amourously disposed I devote a little time to flirting with Mary Jane. I did not however do so this evening. Was in bed before 10. read till 11. Exp 10c

Tuesday July 18th 1848

Weather almost too Warm to be pleasant, even for this season. Business good. After supper I Called on Tim O'Conner. not finding [him] home I went to the

Atheneaum and there found Tim, seated quite in front, so as to be able to see the rather good looking Countenance of Miss Dean with Convinience.

We enjoyed it very much. Miss Dean played Julia in *The Hunchback*[71] a character in my opinion better adapted to her, than any I have as yet seen her in. Wharam did justice to the difficulte part of Sir Thos. Clifford. To Bed 12. Exp 75c.

Wednesday 19th

was a most disagreable warm day. the most most provoking occurrence in this day's Existence was that Business was most disagreably brisk. The Evening I passed at home with my french Teacher. after the lesson we called at the "Tell"[72] and refreshed ourselves. To Bed 10. Exp 15c

Thursday 20th

Although We have had some very wet Showers, it still continues very Sultry and hot. I made another financial transaction to day. Loaned to a Mr Becker, Lithographer on Walnut St One hundred Dollars for his note, with a good endorsement for 107$ payable Jan 1, 1849.[73]

The Evening I passed at home Amusing myself with my Guitar. To Bed 10. Exp 10c

Friday July 21st 1848

Commerce has left us in gentle repose to day; we have been most agreably idle. I had excellent time to do justice to my french lesson. I did so.

The Evening I passed with Tim O'Conner in the Theatre, admiring sweet "Julia"[74] in *The Wreckers Daughter,* and as the Duchess in *Faint Heart ne'er Won fair Lady,* in both of which she sustained her parts admirably. Billiam Wharam, the blaguard, was d'hrunk, which melancholy fact was particularly noticable in the latter piece. Some of the others were defecient in their Parts. the Audience however fortunately were suffisciently interested in the preciding spirit to overlook the imperfection in the minor characters.

The Wreckers Daughter is but an indifferent Piece, having a very lame and almost silly Conclusion.

I hope fair Julia will have an opportunity to try her power at the National where with a supr stock she would be better supported. Tim had the good Manners to treat between the first and [second] piece, a most fortunate thing as I had no money with me. I got in Bed at 12 oclock. Expence 70c

Saturday 22nd

Weather not particularly beautiful, but pleasantly Cool. Business so-so. My Weekly Cash balanced very satisfactorily. The Evening I passed at home. till nearly 9 I was playing on my Guitar and waiting for my french Teacher. It was nearly ½ past 10, when I had finished. read till 11. Exp 15c

Sunday July 23rd 1848.

I got up just in time to have a warm breakfast. when through, some 4 of us went and procured good Cigars, then started for a Walk. Went on 3rd St Hill,[75] examined the reservoirs, inhaled the nauseous gasses emanating from the Laboratory[76] situated just West of them. after satisfying ourselves that the [laboratory] ought not to be so near neighbours, We Slowly descended the Hill again and Wended our way homeward.

I was occupied during the forenoon with Writing a letter to Clemens,[77] Concerning a debt that my little Brother Frank Contracted when in St Louis last. It seems that Frank has not proceeded direct to St Louis this time. Clemens' letter is dated 15th July. Frank left here on 8th in the Evening and ought to have been there on 11th. I requested Clemens to acquaint me with the Amt &c did not promise to pay it however. after having dined and smoked a Cigar with the rest of the *joli*[78] young Gentlemen in our establishment under the old Porch on the Southern Side of the building, I, Del—r and that young imp of nonenity John Bradley went out on a hill North of the City ascending by the Vine St road.

We did not Succeed in finding a shady place of such beauty and Comfort as we had pictured to ourselves, but had one where we could perceive every thing that was going on. Two fellows had a girl in tow. no sooner had they got Her safely over a high fence and in the Woods, than they were followed by 8 or 10 Boys from 16 to 20 years old. What fun they had, We did not Stay to see. The Evening I passed home, playing with Mary Jane Exp 30c

Monday July 24th 1848

Business Comfortable. Weather quite the Contrary, being hotter than we had it this Summer.

Received a letter from a friend of my little Brother Frank, who lives in St Louis of 14th inst. The letter notices Rockwells Circus being in St Louis.[79] From this, it appears to me evedent that Frank has gone some other place, leaving myself, or Henry to settle with Clemens, knowing or supposing that his Piano will pay this, as well as his old Debts.

The Evening I passed at home, playing on my Guitar till 10, then went to bed and there read till 11.

Tuesday 25th.

Warmer Still. Every healthy person in the street looks as if he had been pulled out of a lard Oil barrel. the Evening I passed at Henry's House, his little daughter was suddenly taken Ill with an inflamation in head and Brain.[80] Ye Gods![81] how I perspired this Evening in runing from One Swill Shop to another to obtain some Ice, was however at last successful. The prompt attendance of a good Doctor with all the necessary Medicnes soon releived the poor thing in some degree of its suffering. It was a sad spectacle however to see the mother weep and Wring her hands as if the Child was dying or allready dead. It Would have died from suffocation, had it not been immediatly releived by a Lady-Neighbour who had evidently had experience in these juvenile attacks. In returning Home I called at the store to advise Daddy of the Childs recovery, but the Old Gentn was asleep. To Bed 11 oclock Exp 15c

Wednesday July 26th 1848

Warm Sultry Weather towards Evening we had rain, which did not have a very cooling effect though. One of the Laboures or rather our Foreman by the name of Christian,[82] an odd genious, was suddenly taken sick this afternoon with the Colera Morbus.[83] poor fellow he thought himself dying; although his attack commenced with the best possible symptom, that of vomitting Blood. Mr Dexter acted very generously towards him, procuring him a Carriege and negro attendant to wait upon him.[84]

After supper I had my french lesson. Went with Moulinier to Annans Book Sale. Neither of us purchased any thing. Most of the Books that sold there could I suppose be imported for half price. To Bed ½ past 10. Exp 10c

Thursday July 27th

Business not near so dull as it might be, although not particularly bright. It is raining every few hours. Shortly before there was a furious shower.

The Evening I passed at homme without doing any thing particularly. We (the Boarders of the House) amused ourselves with a Boy, a precocious Phrenologist.[85] the little fellow Convinced us however that he was more Master of the Science than we anticipated. upon examining the Cranium of a Mr Johnson, he described his principal characteristic's most accurately. To Bed 10. Exp 10c

Friday July 28th 1848

The Warm Weather has given place to suffisciantly Cool in temperature, but the change is nevertheless very disagreable. We have now every other hour a severe shower. Streets are very muddy, almost unpassable.

Business to day was exceedingly dull. no matter! we can afford to have a dull spell. besides our double rectefied is selling Constantly to advantage in New Orleans and Mobile. I have, thank dull-times, sufficient time to prepare my french lessons.

The Evening I passed at home, without doing any thing useful however, fooling away time that is precious to me. Towards 10 oclock I went with Del—r to Billy Tell's. we took a "Stiff Horn" of Jamaica.[86] from there we Strayed on 6th St. and Came very near taking some more Jamaica, but my horror of getting tipsy prevented this, so we simply had a dose of Mineral "Wather" to Cool the Effects of our first libation. Del—r called for the Cigars. we went direct home, smoked till past 11 then retired to our respective chambers. Exp 20 cents

Saturday July 29th

Disagreable rainy Weather. No Business doing of any account. during the afternoon I had nothing at all to do, having already finished my french lesson, and no Cash to balance.

The Evening I passed with my Teacher[87] in my room. Recd from Mr Dexter Twenty five Dollars. Paid Mrs Jenkins for Boarding and Washing in full to August 1st 18.35 and 1$. I subscribed to a New Church. from 10 to nearly 11 I was in a Barber Shop, having my Hair Cut.[88] Exp 25c.

Sunday July 30th 1848

Was one of the nastiest and most disagreable Sundays immaginable. After Breakfast I and Johnson took a short Walk. had to hurry home, for fear of being treated to a shower. the forenoon I passed in my room entirely, reviewing Manesca. I could not play on the Guitar because one of the Strings was broke.

Had dinner at usual time ½ past One. Smoked my customary Cigar after it, in company of the Gentn smokers of the Establishment. Called on Christian[89] about 3. He has nearly recovered from his sickness and altogather so from his fright. from Christians place, I went to Wagners. was so fortunate as to find him home. permitted myself to be treated to a good Glass of wine and Cigar. passed a few hours pleasantly with him. About 5 or ½ past I returned home

After supper, as I was walking down Walnut St, I was called in by Mr Dieck. He, like a genuine Dutchman[90] treated me to a Glass of beer having the Article in the house. he purchases and drinks wholesale. while standing in his door cosily discussing nonsensical matters, Miss K—ch[91] passed. the young Lady smiled so sweetly at us (I flattered myself it was me) that I formed a sudden resolution to go and pass the Evening with her. Of course I did so, for in this respect I do—and go—where I please. I was passably Amused, learned the latest slanders in the German World.[92] Had her society Entirely to myself. Went Home and to Bed at 10 oclock. Exp 25c

Monday July 31st. 1848

Pleasant, but somewhat Cold Morning broke in upon "Porkopolis"[93] belating[94] every body, myself not excepted. my morning dose [doze] was so sweet to me. Commerce commenced lively this Morning. Mr Dexter seems to thing that his disease[95] will breake out again. I hope sincerely he may be mistaken. Mr Dexter intends setting out for the East on the 10th of next month. this will give me another troublesome period. After Supper, I and a couple of young fellow boarders took a long walk. I was tired when I got home. Went to Bed 10. Exp 5

Tuesday August 1st 1848

Business very good. Mr Dexter placed the Cash and all his accounts in my hands this Afternoon, it being the first of the Month. I suppose I shall not be releived from this responsibility until first of October. I only wish for health and a Clear head and I have no doubt what I shall be able to render a satisfactory account of my doings when he returns. The Evening I pass'd Entirely at home, Playing on my Guitar &c. Exp 10c

Wednesday 2nd

Beautiful and pleasant Weather. was occupied with Business the entire day. My french has been quite neglected as yet this week.

The Evening I passed at home. played on my Guitar till 9 oclock then went down in the Parlor and Welcomed Brown home. He seems to bear Matrimony with the Heroism of a Martyr. To Bed 10 oclock. Exp 10c

Thursday August 3rd 1848

Coquettish Weather. it seemed uncertain, whether it would Rain or Sunshine. it gave us a touch of both. the small retail business kept me Employed the Entire day. When Evening came I was but poorly prepared for my french lesson. I had delayed it however one Evening already, and could not pospone it any farther. To Bed 10. Exp 5c

Friday 4th

Business was duller to day. I received a letter from Clemens to the effect that Frank Owe's him 35.50 and that Frank had joined the Circus[96] and kept aloof from him (Clemens) for fear of being dunned for the Money. Henry intends to pay this debt, and secure himself with the Piano, and I have promised to pay half of whatever balance there may be after the Piano is disposed of.

After supper I went with Johnny Bradley in the Manegerie.[97] the collection is not very large but the specimens are very good. A Miss Clark who had the temerity to Enter the Cages, seemed to be Entirely at home among Wild Beasts. Went home to Bed about 11 oclock. the Evenings Expences were 35 cts

Saturday 5th

Bright in the Morning. during the afternoon we had rain. I settled my Cash before 3 oclock. it did not balance very accurately. By 4 I was ready, and we— I, Henry and August[98]— started for Cheviot to see Henry's Wife.[99] got there about 7. had supper immediatly afterwards. it was very muddy from the afternoons rain. attempted to inspect the garden, but could not venture from the broad pathway as every Shrub and plant was Wet.

The Evening we passed in the Parlour with the girls, of which there were two tolerably fair specimens. We had a fine Evening of it, the girls assisted us Manfully in drinking two bottles french wine. as soon as we were thawed a little we treated them to some of our german Songs. I and August could not get a chance however to be alone with the girls. their "Ma" kept a most Motherly guard over them.

About 11 oclock we retired to our Chamber. had to sleep in a room in which there were 3 others already. we two, made five.[100] I did not sleep very well, not knowing the persons who were rooming with us, and having some valuable effects with me.

Arose about 7 next Morning. dressed and had breakfast a few Minutes afterwards. Until ½ past 10 I read and looked over the books of the young Ladies. they appeared to possess a taste for literature, having a good Collection of the best English Poet's. When they descended from their dressing room, we left for the Church. listened to a very good Sermon, for which I paid 10 cts.

After dinner we passed about 3 hours in Company of the Girls, and about 3 oclock We started for home, or rather for Millers,[101] as we stopt there and indulged

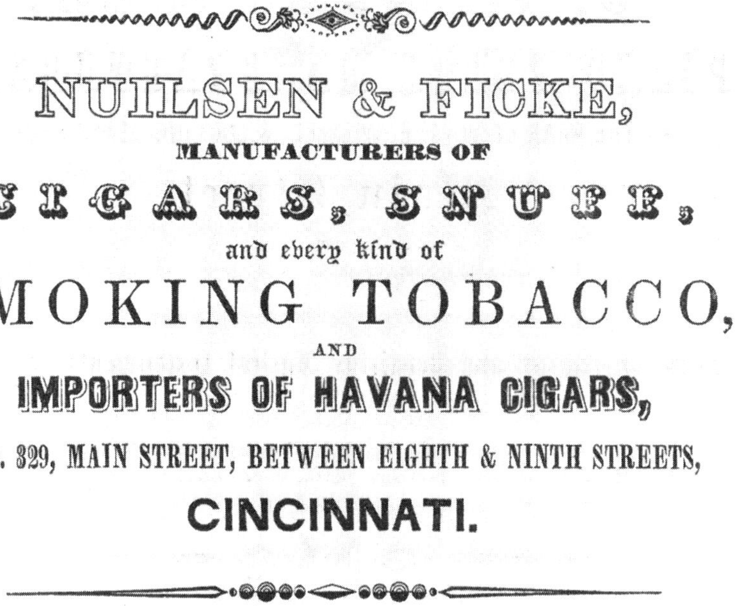
NUILSEN & FICKE,
MANUFACTURERS OF
CIGARS, SNUFF,
and every kind of
SMOKING TOBACCO,
AND
IMPORTERS OF HAVANA CIGARS,
NO. 329, MAIN STREET, BETWEEN EIGHTH & NINTH STREETS,
CINCINNATI.

Nuilsen and Ficke advertisement, 1841. Clemens Nulsen's brother was in the tobacco business in Cincinnati. (From the Collection of the Public Library of Cincinnati and Hamilton County.)

in a bottle of Champaigne. left there at 4. from there to the Brighton House proved a long walk being a little over 4 Miles. An Omnibus was just ready to start when we arrived there. jumped on, and 6 oclock I was once more in my own room. The Evening I passed at home with Mary Jane.
[Margin note] My Entire Expences for this trip were 1.45.

Monday August 7th 1848

Business Commenced dull this Morning. The Weather is exceedingly beautiful. I had some time to devote to my french to day. The Evening I passed at home having a french lesson, the one I omitted last week. Went with Moulinier to his House. was then treated to some Claret wine and Cakes. while Amusing ourselves in this way the fire Bells gave the alarm of a fire. on looking we saw a lurid light apparently only about 2 Squares distance, but in going there we found it in the extreem Western part of the city.[102]

When I reached home again, it was 11. Some of my fellow boarders were standing on the Pavement. on Del—rs invitation I went Bill Tell's with them to be again refreshed. returned immediatly in order to Smoke our Cigars in the dining room. To Bed 12. Exp 10c

Tuesday 8th

If anything, a little too warm. otherwise it is very pleasant. Business is dull.

After supper I accompanied Del—r to the Atheneum.[103] the Entertainment Commenced with a grand Effort at *Othello.* as an Effort it was good. But the Concluding piece, *A Sight at New York in 1848,* Exceeded every thing in the Shape of Mirth and ludicruousness I have ever witnessed. the various characters are most Excellently portraid. its spiciness however consists in the oddity of the characters not in real Witticism of Speach. To Bed at 1 oclock. Exp 40 cts

Wednesday 9th 1848

Very Warm—damn Warm—too hot for business. After Supper I had a french lesson, which kept me at home till ½ past 9. then went with Moulinier out walking. he treated to the Ale. left [him] Cor 7th & Vine going up to Burkhardts. I went home direct. Stopt in the parlour a few minutes to plague Mary Jane, if it is possible for me to do so. to Bed 11. Exp 10c

NOTES

1. At the same time, chewing tobacco was replacing snuff (Burnam, 88).

2. Cist (3), 49, 51.

3. Cist (3), 244.

4. It was considered rude for a gentleman to smoke in a room which ladies frequented (Tuttle, 88).

5. Cigars from Havana, Cuba, were among the most desirable.

6. The commodity price was fourteen cents per gallon; barrels, made to order, held between thirty and fifty gallons. Most likely, forty gallons was the size used by Dexter, and is the volume used for all whiskey calculations in this book. Therefore, on this date, one barrel of raw whiskey in Cincinnati cost $5.60 (personal communication, Jerry Dalton, master distiller, Jim Beam, Inc., Clermont, Kentucky, 6 December 2004).

7. That evening, Edwin Forrest played the lead in both plays at the National Theatre. There was no farce scheduled (COM, 8 May 1848).

8. Frank Mersman, JJM's brother.

9. Dieck & Fahlbush, cigar manufacturers.

10. Fanny Jenkins.

11. Held at the Masonic Hall, the fundraiser lasted two days and featured the raffle of a "magnificent chair" (ENQ, 19 May 1848). It benefited St. Aloysius Orphan Home, which housed about one hundred German Catholic boys on Fourth Street west of Western Row (CCD 1853, 74; Cist [3], 151).

12. Frederick Mersman had sold the family farm before departing Oldenburg, and had enough money to purchase investment property in Ohio in 1839. Probably because of language difficulties, the receipt was made out to JJM, then fifteen years old (cash files for Joseph Messman, 15 August 1839,

Final Patent 11487, Government Land Office, Lima, Ohio, Land Case Files, RG 49 Bureau of Land Management, NA).

13. Charles Moulinier taught JJM on Wednesdays and Saturdays.

14. Horse-drawn wagons, omnibuses, left from the corner of Lower Market and Broadway every ten minutes during the day and traveled to Sportsman's Hall and other destinations (CCD 1850, 47; COM, 26 September 1848).

15. Quoits was a game played with rings of rope or flat metal thrown at an upright peg, much like horseshoes (OED, s.v. "quoits").

16. At present, the site of Washington Park in Cincinnati.

17. That evening the National Theatre presented a comedy, *The Married Rake,* followed by a ballet pantomime, *La Jeune Dalmate,* by the Monplaisir Troupe (COM, 15 May 1848).

18. The Monplaisir Troupe toured major United States cities in 1848 (ANY, 5:412, 428–29).

19. The Ravels (fl. 1832–65), a French dance company that toured the United States repeatedly, featured four brothers, Gabriel (1810–82), Antoine (1812–?), Jerome (1814–90), and François (1823–81), among the lead dancers (HAS, 303–4).

20. Cornelius Logan, manager of the National Theatre, was apparently a friend of Mr. Dexter's.

21. The identity of Mr. Hughes and his connection to a saloon have not been determined. Perhaps he was a bartender; no proprietor by that name has been discovered.

22. The Young Men's Mercantile Library Association provided opportunities for self-education (see also Augst, 158–206).

23. Edmund Dexter was moving his store from Lower Market Street between Main and Sycamore streets to 49 and 51 Sycamore Street, between Second and Market streets. See map 4.

24. The events in Europe during 1848, i.e., political unrest, slowed mercantile transportation between the United States and Europe. This resulted in a scarcity of paper money and coin in the reserves of larger banks, causing panics in the banking world (ENQ, 17 May 1848).

25. Charles Moulinier.

26. St. Philomena Church, on the north side of Congress Street between Pike and Butler streets (see map 3), served a German-speaking congregation. The cornerstone was laid in 1846 (Lamott, 335; CCD 1853, 92).

27. The Mexican War ended 19 May 1848. JJM may have been celebrating this event along with many others throughout the United States. Residents of Cincinnati had supported Texas's struggle for independence and supplied cannon used in the conflict.

28. Mary Jane Jenkins.

29. The summer season had begun at the Athenaeum with reduced ticket prices: the dress circle was twenty-five cents and the upper circle only ten cents. The evening's performance included *The Wife, Sailor's Hornpipe,* and *Lady of the Lions* (ENQ, 22 May 1848).

30. Also called a "mint julep," the beverage is commonly made with bourbon whiskey, sugar, water, and flavored with mint. Usually served chilled, it is a traditional drink of the southern United States (Carson, 214–17).

31. The reading room of the Young Men's Mercantile Library Association.

32. Charles Dexter was a student at Harvard College.

33. The Eagle Bath House was located on Court Street. See map 3.

34. Mount Auburn, located to the northeast of downtown Cincinnati (see map 2), provided a view of the metropolitan area from an elevation of some 500 feet (Cist [3], 107).

35. Anthony Nulsen's son, Anton Clemens Nulsen, was two years and nine months old. Born 7 August 1845, his godfather was John Clemens Nulsen (Anton Clemens Nulsen entry, Nulsen Family Bible in possession of Leif Nulsen, Indianapolis).

36. "Texas" was the name of a neighborhood in northwest Cincinnati. See map 2 (HOC, 409).

37. Limestone quarries on Mount Auburn produced building materials for the city. Lime (calcium oxide) was made by heating limestone, which is mainly calcium carbonate, to drive off carbon dioxide. Lime mixed with water and sand created a mortar used in brick construction.

38. Mount Adams was the site of the Cincinnati Observatory. See map 2.

39. JJM missed French lessons on Wednesday, 3 May and Friday, 5 May 1848.

40. Philippine (filopena) is a custom of German origin in which a gift may be claimed by the first of two people who have shared a nut with two kernels to say "philippina" at their next meeting; a gift claimed in this way (OED, s.v. "philopena").

41. "Coquettery," flirting or tantalizing men, sometimes made suitors anxious (OED, s.v. "coquetry"; Rotundo, 112–13).

42. Murray and Granger were business partners, but no further information has been found. Their wives apparently remained in Cincinnati while the men went to Mexico and other distant places.

43. This was possibly Bald Hill, six miles east of downtown Cincinnati, a popular picnic location.

44. Vogel has not been identified.

45. Probably Gustav Adolphus Menzel, the lithographer.

46. Herman M. Groenlandt, a portrait artist, was very active in German groups.

47. Rockwell & Company's Circus played for a week in Cincinnati beginning 4 June 1848 (COM, 4 June 1848).

48. Madeira is a white or amber-colored wine, like sherry, named for a group of islands off the northwest coast of Africa belonging to Portugal (OED, s.v. "madeira").

49. Castillon brandy is a spirituous beverage distilled from wine, named for a village in the Bordeaux region of France (Johnson, 242–43).

50. Even in the mid-nineteenth century, some American circuses traveled to South America, seeking new audiences and adventure (Thayer, 303, 347, 352).

51. Bill Lake, a clown, had an act that featured several performing dogs (COM, 25 April 1848).

52. The performance included *Soldier's Daughter* with Mrs. Coleman playing the Widow Cheely, and *Rent Day* with Mrs. C. Wilkinson playing Rachel Heywood (ENQ, 8 June 1848).

53. Frank Mersman was otherwise unemployed.

54. The *Pike No. 7*, a 480-ton sidewheel packet that carried mail, regularly traveled between Cincinnati, Ohio, and Louisville, Kentucky. Rockwell & Company played in Louisville on 12 and 13 June 1848; JJM hoped his letter would reach his brother-in-law before the circus left that town (LDC, 12 June 1848; Way #4492, 371).

55. Henry Mersman.

56. JCN.

57. Louis Mehner, a grocer, had a shop on Lower Market Street (CCD 1848–49, 113).

58. Miss Karrmann was now married to Otto Onken, a lithographer (Onken-Karrmann Marriage, 3 February 1848, St. Matthaeus German Evangelical Church, Cincinnati, Ohio, Marriage Records, 75, FHL Microfilm 1548046; CCD 1848–49, 131).

59. "On the family road," or "in the family way," means pregnant (OED, s.v. "family way").

60. Probably the United States Hotel.

61. Hemorrhoids, a painful condition caused by inflamed veins around the anus.

62. JJM oversaw the installation of rectifying equipment and the initiation of distilling procedures.

63. The Model Artists, living statues posed as classical works of art, were an avant-garde entertainment that toured the nation between 1848 and 1850. Because of their abbreviated costumes, their performances were marked with controversy. They appeared in Cincinnati 22 June to 4 July 1848 (ENQ, 25 June 1848).

64. A yawl is a small boat propelled by oars or sail (OED, s.v. "yawl").

65. On 4 July 1848, the last night of the season, the National Theatre presented three plays: *The Star Spangled Banner, Fourth of July in the Morning,* and a "comical, tragical, melodramatical, operatical sketch" called *Councilman's Dream or The Model Artists.* The curtain rose at 7:45 p.m. instead of the usual 7:30 p.m. (COM, 4 July 1848).

66. Edmund Dexter routinely shipped whiskey from Cincinnati to New Orleans, Louisiana, and Mobile, Alabama. Steamboats provided transportation down the Ohio and Mississippi rivers to New Orleans and then east across the Gulf of Mexico to Mobile. The total distance, some 1,600 miles, took two weeks. Customers made payment only after the merchandise had safely arrived.

67. See note 24.

68. JJM notes that he had kept a diary for three years, suggesting that there was an earlier volume, now missing. Only a portion, this single volume, has survived to the present.

69. Theodore Shotwell, a dry goods salesman.

70. A horse-drawn omnibus ran from the Brighton House to Fourth and Main streets frequently during the day (CCD 1850, 47).

71. At the Athenaeum, the performance of James Sheridan Knowles's play *The Hunchback* was followed by two solo dances and a farce, *Willful Murder* (COM, 18 July 1848).

72. William Tell Restaurant.

73. Thus, A. F. Becker agreed to 14 percent interest. (He paid seven dollars interest for the use of one hundred dollars for six months.) At the time, usury laws in Ohio limited interest to 6 percent annually (SLD 1848, xiii).

74. Julia Dean appeared at the Athenaeum (COM, 21 July 1848).

75. JJM's walk took him to the east side of the city, to the base of Mount Adams.

76. The nature of this laboratory has not been determined, but it was possibly part of the city's waterworks (HOC, 388–93).

77. JCN.

78. [Fr.] handsome.

79. Rockwell & Company played in St. Louis on 17 and 18 July 1848 (MOR, 17 July 1848).

80. Henry Mersman had a daughter Josephine, born 1846 (USC 1860, M653, roll 976, page 112, line 27).

81. "Ye Gods" may reflect JJM's exposure to theatrical language or to the general popularity of classicism. See chapter 1, note 36.

82. Christian Vefean survived this episode (CCD 1850–51, 277).

83. "Cholera morbus" was just one of the many terms by which doctors called a disease characterized by abdominal cramps and diarrhea. Other names applied to such an ailment included "dysentery," "summer complaint," and "inflamation of the bowels." In 1881, the disease modern physicians call cholera was proven to be caused by a bacterium, *Vibrio cholerae*, spread by contaminated food and water (Fisher [1], 189–211).

84. Ohio law forbade slavery. Therefore, Mr. Dexter hired a free man to care for the worker.

85. Phrenology, a pseudoscience that claimed the shape of a skull reflected personality characteristics, was a popular pastime (Tuttle, 23–25; COM, 31 October 1848).

86. Jamaican rum, an alcoholic liquor distilled from molasses, commonly exported from the Caribbean island, was a popular beverage in the United States (Rorabaugh, 61–69).

87. Charles Moulinier.

88. Evening hours for barber shops accommodated the work schedules of their patrons.

89. Christian Vefean.

90. *Deutschmann* or "German man."

91. Not identified.

92. Cincinnati's German-speaking community included some 30,000 individuals (Cist [3], 47).

93. See chapter 2, note 81.

94. Here, a verb form of the word "belated" means "delaying."

95. Edmund Dexter suffered from hemorrhoids. See note 62.

96. Frank attached himself to Rockwell & Company when the circus played in St. Louis. The show proceeded to travel by wagons and play in rural Missouri (Thayer, 459).

97. Van Amburgh & Company's Menagerie, an exhibit of exotic animals, played on the corner of Canal and Race streets in Cincinnati on 3–5 August 1848. Admission was 25 cents. One hundred dapple-gray horses drew the carriages and cages and Miss E. Calhoun gave "an interesting illustration of the ascendancy of the intellect over the wild tenants of the forest." There was no mention in the newspaper of a "Miss Clark." (COM, 21, 23 July 1848).

98. Henry Mersman and his laborer, August Rittmeyer.

99. Adelaide Mersman was likely visiting relatives in Cheviot and escaping the summer heat in the city after her two-year-old daughter's illness.

100. Households commonly lacked separate beds for guests (Kasson, 14–15).

101. Apparently a tavern or restaurant west of Cincinnati: no further identification has been made.

102. The flames were a house fire at the west end of Third Street at about 10 o'clock. The blaze was extinguished without much loss (ENQ, 19 August 1848).

103. The performance started at 8:00 p.m. *Othello* was followed by *A Glance at New York in 1848* (COM, 8 August 1848).

CHAPTER SIX

In Charge of the Store
10 August 1848–1 October 1848

Now in the tenth year of his apprenticeship, JJM had learned from Edmund Dexter how to keep business records, manage inventory, negotiate sales, and supervise laborers. Such long-term training was common at that time, while opportunities for classroom education were limited. JJM had mastered the secrets of rectifying whiskey and observed that it was far more profitable than the tobacco business.[1] *Responsible and honest, JJM fulfilled Edmund Dexter's requirements for an assistant. Dexter's confidence in JJM was evidenced by his plan to take a seven-week vacation on the East Coast, from mid-August through September 1848, leaving JJM in charge of a business that sometimes had monthly sales of ten thousand dollars.*[2]

Letters maintained JJM's contact with Edmund Dexter, but the young man was on his own to make decisions about daily operations. JJM relished being in charge and longed for the day when he would have the status of merchant instead of clerk. JJM continued to enjoy his leisure hours with a mixture of amusements and educational endeavors. He repeatedly visited the Over-the-Rhine district, saw plays, attended concerts, and even ventured on excursions outside the city.

JJM used his diary to keep track of his development and measure his progress in life.[3] *Periodic summaries of his net worth served to mark his achievements. His primary goal was to become a wealthy, self-made man.*[4] *His main companions—Brown, Delamater, and Moulinier—shared the same objective.*

Thursday 10th 1848

Mr Dexter left to day for New York. I sincerely hope he may have a pleasant time of it. When the Omnibus[5] Called at the Store it was so Crowed inside that the Old Man had to mount the Drivers Seat, which exposed him during a 15 minutes ride to the hot rays of the Sun.[6]

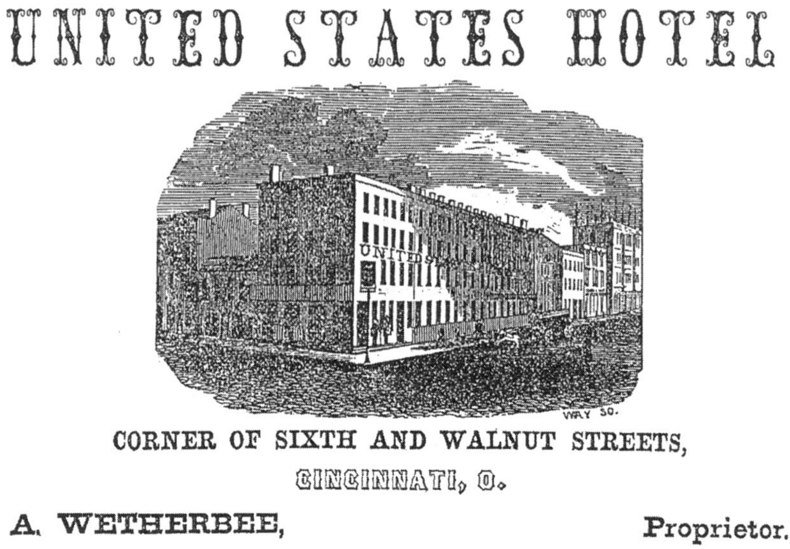

United States Hotel advertisement, 1849–50. This downtown Cincinnati hotel was one of many frequented by Mersman. All major city hotels of the time had dining rooms and saloons. (From the Collection of the Public Library of Cincinnati and Hamilton County.)

The Evening I passed entirely at home. until 9 oclock I was up Stairs performing the last duties to a dying fellow Creature. the poor fellow had been suffering for the last two weeks. His relations reside in Lousianna, and his last thoughts were devoted to a dear sister. his fate was indeed a hard one, to die among strangers, without the kind Sympathies of one relative to Confide his last wishes and desires to. he was however well attended to and received all the attention that could possibly have been bestowed on him. his death was a gradual one, his breath failling him gradually. Some 5 minutes Elapsed ere we could perceive that he had ceased to Exist. I and Johnson laid him out in fitting position for the Coffin.[7] I went to Bed 10 oclock. Exp 25c.

Friday August 11th 1848

Commerce was slightly more favourable than it has been lately. After supper I had a real *jolli*[8] party in my room. among the favoured One's was my Old friend Brown, who is married now. Peace to his Memory! We played till ½ past 10. Then Went to Billy Tells,[9] and Enjoyed a good Milk Punch. Shotwell treated to the Cigars. from there Went home, parting from Brown Corner 5th & Walnut. Had we Contented ourselves with this slight Dissipation all would have been well. but Johnson who intends to leave for Chacago next Monday, thought it fit and appropriate that we should have a Small parting Spree, and expressed himself to this Effect. Del—r who, (whenever he has one glass is allways willing to take another,) immediatly assented. as for myself against Older Majority, what Could I do? I reluctantly yielded. Went strait for the U.S.[10] back to our boarding House. Sat there some 10 minutes, then to Coffee House on 6th St.[11] from there Billy Tell's again, and so on until it was 1 oclock, and We had drank 6 brandies and 1 Milk Punch. Johnson was so fortunate as to vomit when we reached home. I and Del—r could not do so. Exp 65c

Saturday 12th

I got up late this Morning was not in Store till after breakfast. My Cash and the Business of the Week balanced Satisfactorily. The evening I passed at home with my french teacher. after we were through we went to Burkhards a few Minutes. I did not stay long. To Bed 10. Exp 10 cts.

Sunday August 13, 1848

I was up ½ past 5. 6 I being fully dressed I went to see after my breakfast. had to wait a quarter of an hour for that. being through with that I felt the necessity of discharging the superfluities in my stomach. after that I lit my Cigar and waited impatiently for the Company with which I intended to take a trip to the springs.[12] We calculated to start at 6, but it was ½ 7 when they Came.[13] In Covington we were detained fully a half an hour. any how it was 10 oclock when we arrived there. I was in a Carriege with Mr Jamboni,[14] the lately imported Italien who sings so Capittally. as he spoke very little English I had to make use of all the french I was master of.

Immediatly after our arrival I played a game Ten Pins with Gibbiere,[15] beat him all hollow.[16] after that I and Tim O'Conner amused ourselves on the Porch with the ring-game. The dinner was good. I and Tim did justice to it. Mr McCarthy[17] was there also. I drank a glass of wine with him at Table. After dinner I and Tim having lit our Cigars, sought a shady and cool looking place. there we slept till past 3. we then got all our Company togather and had a general kick-up among ourselves. 5 oclock we started for home. I arrived just in time for supper. did not go out afterwards. To bed 10. Exp 1.75.

Monday August 14th 1848

Weather most intensly hot, 93 in the Shade. Business Commenced dull. there were 3 persons killed by the heat during the day. Two Sun Strokes one by drinking too abundantly Cold Water.

The Evening I passed in Henrys Store. I had a capital shower bath there which quite refreshed me. In going home I treated Henry and August to a Glass of Ale. to bed 10. Exp 20c

Tuesday 15th

Two more Cases of death occurred through heat this day. the hot Weather if any thing encreases in intensity. Business a little better. I attempted to play on my Guitar after supper, but it was too warm to stay in it. Excepting a gentle Walk I was at home all evening. Went to Bed about 10 read till 11. Expence 20c [Margin note] I wrote Clemens to day, informing him that I would pay Franks note.[18]

Wednesday 16th

Warm Weather Continues—without any abatement. Men and beast suffer very much at present. Business was dull to day. it is dull all over the City. After supper I amused myself with my flute till 8 oclock. about this time Moulinier came and we went to work at my french lesson. It was 10 oclock when we were through. I Went out with M to take a little exercise before retiring. To Bed at ½ past 10. Exp 10 cts.

Thursday August 17th 1848

Weather has Moderated considerably. Business continues dull. the Evening I passed principally at home, amusing myself with my Guitar. Spent over an hour at the Mercantile rooms.[19] To Bed 10. The days Exp 10¢.

Friday 18th 1848

Business slightly better. I had very little time for my french. The evening I passed at home playing on my Guitar. About 8 I went in Company of Menzel Jr and Peter Rule, two old tippling Companions of mine over the Canal[20] to a new Grogery, where we tippled on a new kind of drink till 11 oclock, playing at the same time Domino[21] who should pay for it. I lost as usual. Got to Bed about ½ past 11. spent during the day 35c

Saturday 19th

Was so busy at store the whole day that I had no time to settle my Cash. After Supper I had a french lesson, and after it I went to Billy Tells, drank a glass of Ale, which gave me the Belly Ache. To Bed 10 oclock Expense 15c

Sunday 20th

Was again a busy day, may the Lord forgive. The forenoon from 8 to ½ past 12 I was busy settling my Cash and preparing Statements for my letter to Mr Dexter. After dinner from 2 to 5 I was busy writing to Mr D—. I gave him a full and accurate Statement of all my business transactions since his departure.

After Supper I called at Mouliniers. Charles was not *chez lui.*[22] I passed a very agreable Evening with Mrs M. To Bed 11. Exp 20c

Monday August 21st 1848

I received a letter from Mr Dexter to day. He has been so fortunate as to have had a pleasant and quick trip. Commencement of business for this Week very good. The Evening I passed with Del—r in the Atheneaum. the principal piece was *Mose' Weding* a sequel to *A Glance at New York.*[23] I did not enjoy it at all being entirely too uncomfortably situated for any enjoyment. it compares however unfavourably with its predecessor. It was 11 oclock when I got to Bed. Exp 40c

Tuesday 22nd

I loaned Mr A. F. Becker another Fifty Dollars, making with what I have advanced him allready and interest 160$ for which Amt I have his notes (two, Eighty dollars each) endorsed by Lyon & Smith.

Business today is dull as regards sales. I made some purchases that kept me busy. The Evening I passed at home, playing on my Guitar and a few games of Euchre with Johnny B—y [Bradley] won the treat from him. went to a place on 4th Street with him to receive it. When I got back, I wrote French till ½ past 10 then to Bed. Exp 15c.

Wednesday, 23rd

Business has lately kept me so well employed that I did not have time to finish my lesson for this Evening. might have finished it before Moulinier Came, but was detained at supper Table by Mary Jane. he came very early however so I had not time to talk to her. Our Lesson was finished at 9. I accompanied M— nearly home treated to a glass of Soda. To Bed ½ past 10. Expense 15c.

Thursday August 24th 1848

Business Continues dull as to Sales. my purchases keep me busy. From Store I went direct to Mouliniers where I had a good supper. Charles gave a small musical party. Mr Giamboni, the two Burkhardts, Softje and a Mr Douglass were the Amateur performers. I, an old Gentleman from Dayton, and Mrs M[oulinier] composed the audience. We had some good music, and enjoyed ourselves Capitally. when we retired it was ½ past 12. I went direct home. Exp 10c

Friday August 25th

Weather is very agreable and pleasant just now. business was a shade better. The Evening I passed at home, doing however nothing particularly that was of value except playing on my Guitar. I had Mr Granger for my Bed-Fellow this night.[24] He arrived in town yesterday from the interiour of Indiana where his wife is now. the Gentleman has quite a dark complexion, which he acquired in Mexico, and which has been heightened here by Continual exposure. Went to Bed ½ past 9. Exp 15c

Saturday Aug 26

I was more Employed with Business than I have been lately. My Cash Account balanced very Satisfactory this afternoon. I prepared my Statements for my letter to Mr Dexter ere closing up. After Supper I was home with my French Teacher. To Bed 10 oclk. Exp 15c

Sunday August 27th 1848

I and Granger were up be-times, at least dressed before breakfast. being through with it we enjoyed a Short Walk of a Cigars duration or while I Smoked my Cigar. 8 oclock I Seated myself in my room and in a letter of 3 pages detailed to him [Edmund Dexter] my Business transactions for the week. I was unwell and not at all in a humur for writing. the Consequence was that the letter was a poor affair.

About 11 I took it to the Post office,[25] but upon enquiry found it too late for that days Mail.

I passed the afternoon principally under the Porch smoking with the other young One's. I, Del—r and Shotwell attempted to take a walk but found it entirely too warm, so we made it Short and returned home.

After Supper I [and] Granger walked for about an hour or so. as soon as we were back he went about some business and I entertained Mary Jane till 9, when she was summoned by the old Lady[26] to go to Bed. after smoking another Cigar I went also it [being] ½ past 9. Exp 40¢.

Monday 28th

Business Commenced favourably this Morning. Weather pleasant and agreable. Mr Granger left this Morning for Louisville, Ky to attend the races.[27] I had a set of Euchre Players in my room, myself, Shotwell, Lockwood[28] and McGrew.[29] I and Lockwood got licked at both Euchre and Whist. ½ past 9 I broke up the party by refusing to pay. To Bed. Expense 20c

Tuesday 29th August 1848.

The [weather] is and has been really beautiful lately, neither too warm nor too Cold. Business to day is somewhat dull. I did not purchase any whiskey to day.

The Evening I passed at playing on my Guitar in the early part of and Euchre afterwards till 10. the[n] went down stairs and smoked a cigar with some of my fellow-boarders. To Bed 11. Exp 15c

Wednesday 30th

Business was a little more lively to day Weather very pleasant. After supper I had my french lesson to attend to, which kept me employed till 10 oclock. then to bed. Exp 5c

Thursday 31st

Business good. Weather pleasant. The Evening I passed without doing any thing particular except playing on Guitar. I fooled some time away with Mary Jane. To Bed 10. Exp 10.

Friday September 1st, 1848

This was quite a busy day with me. The foreign news advanced all kinds of Produce.[30] Whiskey jumped from 16¼ to 16¾c I replied to a letter received from Mr Smith[31] day before yesterday. I did not get time to look at my french. The Evening I passed at home. played on my flute till 8, then wrote nearly my entire french lesson. To Bed 11. Exp 15c—

Monday Morning September 11th 1848

I have been so extreemly busy during the whole of last week that my journal has been entirely neglected. my french also, had to be attended at home in the Evening. The Evenings I passed all at home devoting a little time to music, principally in studying my lessons. I had two letters from Mr Dexter during the week. the old Gentleman seems to amuse himself Capitally. Seems to take great delight in Bathing.[32] his last inform'd me of his being in New York again.

My commercial transactions were quite extensive I received 206 bbls Whiskey on Saturday. My Cash on Saturday balanced very closely. I wrote to Mr D[exter] on Saturday Evening and mailed the letter early on Sunday Morning. On Thursday Evening last week I was at a Small party given by Mrs Moulinier. Met a Miss Callison there, a sweet little piece of Mortality. Pity She is going to N.O.[33] shortly.

Yesterday forenoon I was at home, playing on the Guitar part of the time and studying french or rather finishing my last lesson. Went to Post Office immediatly after dinner. return'd direct home. Charles Moulinier and Burkhart[34] Called for me about 2 oclock. We went down to Mr Scheidlers to arrange about the Concert of Monsr Giamboni our Italien, but as Mr S. was not at home we could make no diffinite arrangement. We however saw him at the *Liedertafel* Rooms. from there we went to Burkhardts house got Leonard,[35] and Sallied over the Canal to a place where good wine was kept. We four finished four bottles. I ate Supper at B[urkhardt]'s. Went home pretty cocked Exp 1.20.

Monday September 11th 1848[36]

Was a most lovely day. the weather for the last two weeks has been uninterruptedly beautiful. If anything mars it, it is the dust which fills the street immediatly upon the slightest provocation. I bot no whiskey to day, wished I had. the Evenings advises from N.Y. show an advance. Perhaps I shall have fully as fair a chance to morrow. Business to day was dull.

After Supper I played on my flute till nearly 8 oclock. I was seated in front of an open window with a door immediatly behind me open, and being just from the Supper table, warm and heated from having drank two Cups of Coffee, I caught suddenly a very severe Cold. in fact when going down Stairs I attempted to speak to one of the girls I could'nt find my voice. and to make it worse still I went to Theatre with Mr. Lacy, where we sat half the night, looking at an uninteresting performance.[37] When I got home I felt it firmly seated in my breast. Went to Bed 12 oclock. Exp 35c

Tuesday September 12th

It was quite Cold and disagreable to day. I felt my Cold getting [worse.] towards Evening I could hardly speak. Commerce was dull. Very! The Evening I passed at home Comparing a french flute that Mr Lemaire has to mine. The instrument has a softer and sweeter tone than Mine. I shall endeavour to trade with him. I did not go out at all. Went to Bed about 9. read till 10. No Expence—

Wednesday September 13. 1848

Trade was a shade better to day. had'nt much to do however. towards evening I was busy. about 4 oclock I bot 110 bbls whiskey from C[orr] & P[oland] at 18 ½ which detained me at Store till 7 oclk.[38]

Immediatly after Supper I went with my flute to Lemaires. after much hagling we Came to terms. I had to Give 6$ to boot.

Went home, found Charles[39] waiting for me. had my french lesson. To Bed 10. Exp 6.10.

Thursday 14th

Weather was quite warm again to day, although cloudy, and now and then a slight sprinkling of rain. Commerce was quiet to day. After supper I went immediatly to Mouliniers. they were waiting for me. Confound the thing I did not have my anticipated Amusement at all. when our little party left Mr McGurks they were all in a flury, and the young Lady I wished particularly for my partner was given to Moulinier. I had Mrs M[oulinier] and Miss McGurk. The Apollo Room is smaller than any other Concert Room, but is very tastily fixed up. the ventilation of it is bad. the windows being all in the rear of the building, and in order to produce a current of air, it is necessary to have the doors open, which however makes it very disagreable for who may chance to be seated near it. Miss Dean refused to deliver the address because her name was not on the Concert Bills to this effect.[40] I was afflicted the whole evening with a severe headache. It was ¼ past 11 when I retired. Expense 1.65c

Friday September 15th 1848

The Sun was out bright and beautiful again this Morning. Last evenings foreign news[41] had rather a dampening Effect on the whiskey Market this Morning. I was foolish enough to buy 140 bbls at 18½.[42] this afternoon I heard of a sale [at 18] ¼. The Evening I passed at home. my cold is vanishing again. To Bed at 10. Exp 10c

Saturday, 16th

Whiskey sold to day as low as 17¾. was busy the Entire day setting up the weeks business. In the afternoon I counted my rectd whiskey. find 1600 bbls.[43] Cash

Balanced accurately. After supper I had a french lesson, and from 10 to 12 I was busy writing my weekly letter to Mr Dexter.

Sunday 17th

Was up early. went to Store before breakfast to enclose a note of Mr Scheidlers in my letter, and to add a N.B. to the Effect that it was raining at that moment.[44]

The forenoon I passed at home finishing my last french lesson. Could'nt play on the Guitar as one of the strings was broke. went to the Post office after, but did not receive any thing from Mr Dexter. returned home shortly after 2. Mr B—d[45] chanced to pass by. I went along with him. found Giamboni at his house, Moulinier also. about 3 we made a party out for the purpose of going on Vine St Hill, but our Leader, Mr B's brother in law,[46] got drunk before we got up. was at home in the Evening. To Bed 10. Exp 15c

Monday, Sepr 18th 1848

Quite cold and autumn like this Morning. Business very dull. this dullness is general as the River is so low that nothing can be done.[47] After Supper I amused my self with my flute till past 8 oclock, then went down D[ieck] & F[ahlbush], got a good cigar. returned. sat down in the dining room with the Old Lady and Mary Jane[48] to smoke it. when it was consumed, I, Del—r and Shotwell went down to the Billy Tell[49] procured ourselves a glass of something good. on returning Del—r bot some apples. I ate one. the Ale and apple togather disturbed me. I had to visit *mon pot de chambre* two or three times, *mais après tout ceci, je pisais dans le lit, que le diable emporte ce malheur. je ne puis pas réelément m'empêcher de le faire quand j'ai bu un peu trop.* [I had to visit my chamber pot two or three times, but even after all that, I pissed in my bed. May the devil take away this illness! I really cannot avoid it when I drink so much.] To Bed 10. Exp 15c

Tuesday 19th

Beautiful Weather. no prospect of rain. if old neptune was aware how necessary it is for us to have some water in order to get our Double Rectd off, I guess he would see about it immediatly. I had a letter from Mr Dexter to day. he thinks still that whiskey will rate high. it is now worth only 17¼, but nothing can be done with it. The River is so extreemly low. Boats are not attempting to take any freight for ports not 20 miles off. I beleive it is lower than it ever has been. After Supper I played on my flute till 8. then, hearing Browns voice below I went down and [invited] him Delr and Shotwell in my room to a game of Euchre. I &

B[rown] were victorious. B. treated to 2 bottles Scotch Ale at Peter Thompsons I to the Cigars. Went to bed 11. Exp 30c

Wednesday Sepr 20th 1848

Recd a letter from Edmund[50] this Morning. replied immediatly. The Weather has undergone another Change. it is Cloudy, in fact this Morning it rained. Should it have any effect on the River things will advance. I determined to risk it, so I bot 146 Bbls whiskey 17¼¢. there cannot be a loss at this figure, at least not of any account.[51]

After supper I played flute till Moulinier Came which was about 8 oclock. We were through with our lesson at ½ past 9. did not go out, but after having Smoked a Cigar in the dining room, Went to Bed. Exp 10c

Thursday 21st

This was the Coldest Morning we have had this Season, which lately has been thoroughly Fall. but apart from the uncomfortable Coldness it was beautifully bright and pleasant. Whiskey was dull this Morning at 17c.[52] damn the thing! it is impossible to know what to do with it.

The Evening I passed at home playing on my flute during the Early part, then studying a little french, and concluding with Entertaining the Ladies who were in the dining room, and were just getting blessedly dull among themselves. To Bed 10. Exp 10c.

Friday 22nd

Weather is bright and beautiful again. No prospest of rain. news from Pittsburgh in this respect in the afternoon was also particularly discouraging. The Evening I passed at home, finding suffiscient amusement with my flute. To Bed 10. Exp 5c

Saturday Sepr 23rd 1848

Weather continues bad for commerce, but for Gentleman loafers about Town it is the *beau ideal.*[53] My Cash balanced satisfactorily for the Week. Our business has been very poor indeed. After supper I had my french lesson. Charles [Moulinier] came early. So I was through a great [deal] earlier than usual. After parting with him, I Seated myself in the dining room to Smoke and read. the former I *did* the latter I could'nt. Cause! Why? The women[54] would'nt let me. Kept talking to me all the time. To Bed 11. Exp 15c

Sunday 24th.

Was a beautiful and lovely day, (they are too abundant) warmer than it has been lately. It was entirely a day of rest for me, as I had no business in the Store, and no letter to write to Mr Dexter. The forenoon I passed at home, with my Guitar, and reading french.

After dinner I went to the Post office, found nothing of importance there. from there to Mouliniers. Burkhardt was there. I was just in time to assist at the preserves.[55] From there we went to B[urkhardt]'s amused ourselves there with music till 4. then went over the Canal had a bottle of wine at a place where we were two Sundays ago. Lit our Cigars and Strolled up Vine St. Walked over the Hill's to Drach's where we met Some acquaintances of B's and Moul—rs, also some *Liedertaflers.* they as usual kept themselves separated from the rest. I & Moul—r called at Mrs McGurke's after Tea. Sweet Cary C[allison] was as lovely as ever. To Bed 11. Exp 40c

Monday September 25th 1848

There is no business doing at all of any extent in the city. I had nothing to do the entire day. No prospect of rain. advices from Pittsburgh are similar to what the statement from here, there would be.

I studied my flute till 8 oclock. then went with Shotwell & Lacy to a Fair at Masonic Hall.[56] The attendance was very poor. we however amused ourselves capitally. it was ½ past 10 when we got home. Before going to bed I smoked a cigar with Del—r. Exp 65c.

Tuesday 26th

The warm humid atmosphere to day causes the beleif that rain is not distant after the many fallacious reckonings lately, I am somewhat Skeptical as to the verification of present appearances: The foreign news has no depressing Effect on our Market here.[57]

William, (our drayman)[58] whom I sent out to Lebanon to bring the Familly home,[59] returned this evening alone. They will follow in a few days. After supper I and Moulinier went to the National Theatre. J. R. Scott was playing *Richilieu,* and ably Supported by Miss Logan. however the female Characters in this piece are minor one's. Mr Scott did full justice to the old Cardinals Character and frequently received the enthusiastic cheers of a respectably sized and decerning audience. His representation of <u>Wm</u> in *Black Eyed Susan* was also well Conceived by the young Man. I was agreably Amused the whole Evening.

Moulinier left shortly before 11. I did not go till the performance had Concluded. when I got home it was 12 oclock. Exp 1.20c—

Wednesday Sepr 27th 1848

It is most disagreably dusty, in fact has been for some time. There is every appearance of rain, but as yet not a drop has fallen. River Continues about stationary. there is no margin for any decline.

The Evening I passed at home having a french lesson to attend to. To Bed at 10. Exp 10.

Thursday 28th

Weather looks as if it were going to rain every minute, but beyond its appearance no change has as yet taken place. I bot 75 bbls Whiskey 16⅝. Should it rain soon this will prove a fine purchase. After supper I went to the Atheneum with Lacy and Shotwell. Mrs Lewis played Claude Mellnotte and Mrs Wilkinson the "Lady" It proved *Melange*[60] of good acting and Miserable ranting on the part of Mrs L. Mrs W. sustained her part admirably. The last piece was "fudge."[61] I was again so unfortunate as to take a severe Cold. The Construction of this place is peculiarly adapted for giving its patronizers a Cold. to bed at 12.

Friday 29th

The Encreasing probability of rain caused Whisky to advance to 17¢ I had an invitation to visit Miss Cary Collison, but could not go. went with Chas. Erbest to my future Boarding House to look at a room. from there we went to the "Fair" with Charles.[62] We amused ourselves passably, at least we stayed till ½ past 11. When I got home it was nearly 12. Exp 90c.

September 30th Saturday.

This Morning it rained, actually rained, and with an appearance of Continuance. 17½ was offered for whiskey this Morning, but Sellers were Contending for 18. The Foreign news this Morning is unfavorable. it seems to have had no effect on the Market.[63] My cash in the afternoon balanced as it should do when I have the controll over it.

After supper I had a french lesson. we were through ½ past 8. balance of the evening till 10 oclock I was in the dining room smoking, and amusing Mary Jane. then, Went to Bed. Exp 10¢.

Pearl Street House advertisement, 1841. This Cincinnati hotel was located at Pearl and Main streets. (From the Collection of the Public Library of Cincinnati and Hamilton County.)

Paid Mrs Jenkins to date for Boarding & Washing 16.25¢. The old Hag charged me 25 cts for Heming two linen Henkchs [handkerchiefs] done by Mary Jane.

Sunday October 1st 1848

The forenoon I passed in the German Catholic Church on 5th St[64] assisting with my Flute in a Musical Mass, in honor of the Anniversary of its dedication. Moulinier was there also. The music was passable. I did my share towards making it so. It was very warm up there, Church being crowded. I had a head ache the whole day. Immediately after dinner I went to Henry's New House on Vine St.[65] He is very comfortably situated. We played Euchre there the entire afternoon. about 4 oclk We had Coffee and its accompaniments. before supper I went down to Williams. Mr Dexter has not arrived yet. The Evening I passed at home packing up some of my Sundries. Exp ===

NOTES

1. Cincinnati had at least two dozen firms that made rectifying their primary endeavor (CCD 1844, 78).
2. The equivalent of about $240,000 in 2005.

3. Many men of this era made diary entries to chart their emotional and financial development (Augst, 62–66). Statements of JJM's net worth appear in the following diary entries: 15 February 1849; 29 January 1851; 20 March 1855; 28 September 1862.

4. By 1850, the Self-Made Man was the dominant conception of American manhood (Kimmel, 42).

5. Omnibuses that provided transportation to any portion of the city could be found at all hours of the day at the corner of Broadway and Second Street (OED, s.v. "omnibus"; CCD 1850, 47–48).

6. Edmund Dexter traveled by omnibus from his store to a boat. He could have boarded a steamboat at the public landing to travel up the Ohio River to Pittsburgh, and continued east by coach; or have taken a canal boat north to Lake Erie and New York State. Both routes were commonly used.

7. No report of this death made it into any Cincinnati newspaper, so the identity of the boarder remains unknown.

8. [Fr.] pretty.

9. The William Tell Restaurant.

10. Likely, the United States Hotel, which JJM preferred to the United States Tavern.

11. Possibly the Galt House. See map 5.

12. Latonia Springs, a mineral spa located about four miles south of Cincinnati in Kenton County, Kentucky, thrived as a resort from 1829 to the Civil War (Gastright, 26–28).

13. A literal translation of *halb sieben* or 6:30 a.m.

14. Signor Natale Giamboni, from Havana (according to newspaper reports), gave a concert at the Apollo Hall on 14 September 1848 (COM, 14 September 1848).

15. Possibly a nickname for Mr. Jamboni or Giamboni.

16. "Beat him all hollow" means to surpass completely (OED, s.v. "beat").

17. Not identified.

18. Because of the proposed business partnership, JJM wished to maintain good relations with JCN.

19. The reading rooms at the Young Men's Mercantile Library Association.

20. The Miami and Erie Canal, which cut through the middle of Cincinnati, was called the "Rhine" by local residents. The entire neighborhood came to be called the Over-the-Rhine district (Wimberg, 4).

21. Dominos, a game played with rectangular tiles of wood, bone, or ivory, originated in fourteenth-century China. The tiles, marked with all possible combinations of numbers that can be rolled with the dice, numbered twenty-eight pieces. JJM gambled with only the bar bill being at stake (Beaver, 87–91; Hoyle, 303–4; ESG, 52–57).

22. [Fr.] at home.

23. *A Glance at New York in 1848*, a popular play by Benjamin Baker (1818–90), featured the character Mose, the "Bowery b'hoy" (COM, 8 August 1848).

24. "Bed fellow this night" does not imply sexual activity. Boardinghouses commonly lodged two people in one bed, even unacquainted travelers.

25. The United States Post Office, located in the Masonic Building, corner of Third and Walnut streets, had Sunday hours from 8 a.m. to 10 a.m. To send a half-ounce letter less than 300 miles cost five cents; over 300 miles cost ten cents (HOC, 96; CCD 1848–49, 199; LCD 1848–49, 25).

26. Mary Jane Jenkins and Mrs. Jenkins.

27. Louisville, Kentucky, was a popular location for horse racing (ENQ, 6 June 1848).

28. Lockwood, possibly Ezekial or William, was likely a member of the family of the Lockwood Brothers who operated a clothing store at 73 Pearl Street.

29. McGrew has not been identified. A half-dozen young men with that surname lived in Cincinnati. This was evidently a resident of the boardinghouse. Also, "McGrew" may be an error in recording the name of William McHugh.

30. Revolutions in Europe dominated the international news in autumn 1848, and the markets responded with increased prices for many commodities. On this date the *Cincinnati Daily Commercial* reported potato rot in Ireland, a state of siege in Paris, an Austrian invasion of Italy, and unrest in Germany (COM, 1 September 1848).

31. Mr. Smith has not been identified.

32. This is probably a reference to swimming in the ocean.

33. New Orleans, Louisiana.

34. Most likely Frederick Burckhardt, the older brother.

35. Burkhardt's first name in the city directory was listed as "Leopold," but friends called him "Leonard" (CCD 1849–50, 49).

36. A second diary entry on this date. Apparently JJM wrote this entry before going to bed, and the previous entry that same morning.

37. The plays presented that night at the National Theatre were *Hamlet* and *The Trumpeter's Daughter.* Mrs. Kent, Miss Logan, and Mr. Murdoch performed (COM, 9 September 1848).

38. Mersman's purchase of 110 barrels, each with 40 gallons, cost $814.

39. Charles Moulinier.

40. Newspaper advertisements announced that a concert at the Apollo Hall by the Amateur Musical Society would feature Sig. Natali Giamboni of Havana, and that Julia Dean would recite an address. "The hall is 75 feet long, 35 feet wide, and 25 feet high. The apex of the dome is 43 feet from the floor" (ENQ, 14 September 1848; COM, 14 September 1848).

41. The foreign news reported that the prices of breadstuffs in England had declined and that crops in Ireland were threatened (COM, 15 September 1848).

42. In the morning, JJM purchased 140 barrels each with forty gallons at 18½ cents each, and thus spent $7.40 per barrel or $1,036 in all.

43. A barrel of whiskey probably contained forty gallons. Thus, Dexter's inventory on this date, 64,000 gallons, was valued at approximately $11,360, or about a quarter of a million dollars in 2005. See also chapter 5, note 6.

44. N.B., abbreviation for *nota bene* or "note well." JJM's postscript informed Dexter of an expected market change: because of the rain, the Ohio River would rise. Because of the ease of transport, the price of whiskey would likely increase.

45. Probably "Burckhard."

46. Leopold Burckhardt had married Margaretha Zollies on 17 April 1846. Presumably she had a brother, who was Burckhardt's brother-in-law (Burckhardt-Zollies Marriage, 17 April 1846, Herbert, 40).

47. Low water hindered transportation, particularly at the Falls of the Ohio River, at Louisville, Kentucky. Therefore, JJM could not sell his merchandise to anyone who would wish to ship outside of Cincinnati.

48. Mrs. Jenkins and May Jane Jenkins.

49. William Tell Restaurant.

50. Note that JJM refers to his employer by his first name. Left in charge of the business, JJM regards himself as the social equal of the merchant.

51. JJM purchased 146 barrels, each with forty gallons, at 17¼ cents per gallon, and thus spent $6.90 per barrel or $1,007.40 in all.

52. JJM's transaction lost ¼ cents per gallon. Since each barrel held forty gallons, he lost approximately $14.60, the equivalent of his wages for two weeks.

53. [Fr.] beautiful ideal.

54. Female residents of the boardinghouse, possibly some combination of Mrs. Jenkins, Mrs. Granger, Mrs. Darling, and Mrs. Howe.

55. Preserved fruit was a common dessert; JJM indicates that he reached his friends' home too late for dinner, but in time for sweets.

56. The Daughters of Temperance opened their fair on Sunday evening 24 September 1848, seeking to raise money for the relief of ladies who suffered neglect on account of their husbands' intemperance (ENQ, 25 September 1848).

57. The *Cincinnati Daily Commercial* reported declining prices of grain in England, while the *Enquirer* headlines advised of advances in lard and breadstuffs in European markets (COM, 26 September 1848; ENQ, 26 September 1848).

58. William McHugh hauled barrels of whiskey to and from the steamboat landing.

59. Perhaps Dexter's wife and children were vacationing outside of Cincinnati and not traveling with the family patriarch. The Dexters' connection to Lebanon, Ohio, is not known.

60. [Fr.] a mixture.

61. "Fudge": nonsense (OED, s.v. "fudge").

62. Charles Moulinier joined the other young men, Charles Herbst and JJM, and the three attended the Daughters of Temperance Fair again. See note 56.

63. Newspapers on this date reported a rebellion in Ireland, declining prices of commodities in Liverpool, and an uprising in Spain (COM, 30 September 1848; ENQ, 30 September 1848).

64. Holy Trinity Church, the first filial church of St. Peter in Chains Cathedral, was dedicated on 5 October 1834 (Lamott, 135).

65. Henry Mersman's residential address was the north side of Center Street, between Race and Elm streets. He had moved there from Main Street between Sixth and Seventh streets (CCD 1843, 239; CCD 1849–50, 197).

CHAPTER SEVEN

Mosher's Boarding House

2 October 1848–28 November 1848

For two months, JJM resided in a second boardinghouse, run by the widow Elizabeth Mosher. What precipitated JJM's move from Jenkins's Boarding House is unknown, but the new residence was a few blocks farther east and closer to his work (see map 4).

Mosher's Boarding House was smaller than JJM's previous residence; it may have had only a half-dozen bedrooms. The inhabitants included the proprietor's daughters (Mary Mosher, Libby Mosher, and Harriett Mosher Jacobus), her son-in-law (Theodore Dwight Jacobus), and a few others: Hal Brayley and William Lacy (roommates); Charles Herbst and JJM (roommates); and Mr. and Mrs. Wilkins. Mrs. Mosher leased the building rather than owned it, so when she developed cash-flow problems after JJM's arrival, she terminated her business, forcing everyone to scramble and find new lodging.

In this section, JJM manifests a preoccupation with rain and the water level in the Ohio River. Rivers were the primary trade routes, and freight rates on steamboats profoundly affected commerce. Low water in the Ohio and Mississippi rivers increased the risks of travel and therefore resulted in higher shipping costs. Rain (up to a point) caused transportation fees to fall. The prices of goods then reflected a complicated calculus based on supply and demand.

In addition to his usual entertainments, JJM discovered national politics in the form of the presidential campaign of 1848. Representatives of the candidates spoke to the crowds that gathered on street corners in Cincinnati. JJM, although not yet a citizen, had resided in Ohio for more than a year and thus was eligible to vote.

YOUNG MEN'S MERCANTILE LIBRARY.

Young Men's Mercantile Library advertisement, 1875. This private library, organized in 1835, is still active today. In 1848, it had 1,100 members. (From Daniel J. Kenny, *Illustrated Cincinnati* [1875].)

Monday October 2nd 1848

It rained pretty much all last night. about 11 there were some very vivid flaches of lightning without its usual companion "thunder" This Morning it continues to be cloudy and threatening. however towards noon it brightened up, and during the afternoon it was pleasant.

About ½ past 3 I commenced Moving. it seemed that the ugly old place had entwined itself around my heart, for I was really sorry to leave it. I gave the old Lady and Mary Jane[1] a hearty kiss when bidding them farewell. I gave Her (Mrs Jenkins) One Dollar for the last two days.

I and Charles Herbst (a very dutch[2] name by the bye) went to the Atheneum after supper. It was Mrs Lewis' Benefit. She performed *Jack Sheppard* to the satisfaction of a crowded House. I did not like it myself. The Farce of *Somebody Else* followed. I was well pleased with the manner in which it was got up. Mrs Kent performed a prominent character in it. She recd a very enthusiastic reception.

We did not stay to finish the performance. left after the second piece. went to the Billy Tell's.[3] Charles Treated to Coffee and pie. from there direct home to Bed. Exp = 1.15.
[Margin note] I received a letter from Mr D[exter]. fullfilled his instructions.

October 3rd.

No Rain fell last night. it Continues Cloudy. Advices from Pittsburgh do not notice a rise.[4] Whiskey is dull this Morning I did not however buy any The Evening I and Charles[5] passed togather. we went to a meeting (Whig)[6] on 5th St. patiently listened to a political [speech] for over a half hour. then, to indemnify ourselves went to a Restaurat on Syc[amore] and feasted on hot coffee and boiled Eggs. Exp 50c

Wednesday October 4th 1848.

Weather Cleared up again and to day it is again a bright Indian Summer day. Business was a little better to day. Mr Dexter is certainly expected to arrive to day. After supper I had a lesson. being through when it was only 8 oclock, I and Charles went with Moulinier to Burkharts. expected to hear some good Music, but the Messrs B's were engaged and went from [there] "to hum." Moulinier amused himself with evident satisfaction with "Sarah."[7] Went home ½ past 10 oclock. Exp 10

Thursday 5th

E[dmund] D[exter] has not yet arrived. Commerce quiet. Weather pleasent. had the good sense to go to bed 9 oclock and save Exp—

Friday 6th

E[dmund] D[exter] returned last evening with Lady and Miss Fessenden. The Old Gentlemans appearance indicates a decided improvement of health. he is much pleased with the trip, and not at all displeased to be complimented upon his improved looks.

After Supper I went to Mrs Mouliniers. Her Company had not arrived yet although I came late. They Came about 8. We had a pleasant time of it. It was past 12 when I got home Exp 10c

Saturday 7th

Butifull Weather. Business dull. My cash in the afternoon balanced suffisciently well to dispense with the trouble of going over it again. The Evening I passed entirely at home. Exp 10c

Sunday October 8th 1848.

Beautiful Weather. had breakfast at 8 oclock in my new boarding house. many of the married people were even then not forthcoming. Immediatly after breakfast I went to the Store. had not been there long ere Mr Dexter Came also. We had a busy forenoon of it. I had the satisfaction to see all my accounts Come out well, balance as accurately as Could be expected. we were busy till 1 oclock. I had no time to dress before dinner which came punctual at 1.

I had hardly finished when Charles Moulinier came to give me the last French lesson in Menesca.[8] After 16 months hard study I am at last done with Menesca, and am really loth to part with him as he has given me some valuable information. however I intend to review him alone. My next lesson is reading and Memorising.

Being through with my lesson I Charles, and Moulinier went to Burkharts. Sarah— Mouliniers latest flame—was also [there]. the young Lady was so anxious to be Married, that out of a feeling of generousity I consented to officiate as bridebroom [bridegroom] on the occasion and M— as the priest. my young wife proved a faithless one, for she permitted M— to kiss her 3 minutes after the Ceremony.

About ½ past 4 we went over the Canal to our old Swill place.[9] had one bottle only. from there went home. After Supper I went with a Couple of Germans boarding with me, to Rebstocks, where we cracked a bottle of good Rhine wine. To Bed at 10. Charles do.[10] Exp 1.10.

Monday Octr 9th 1848

Business inclined to be dull. Weather beautiful, and River falling again. of Course produce will sink with it. Mr Dexter was down early. things will go on again as usual. I shall now—until business commences—have more time again for my private affairs. The Evening I passed in the National, It being for the Benefit of Mrs & Mr Connor. I had no opportunity of Judging of their Merit. Mrs C has a very poor voice, not at all adapted for tender display. One of the Germans[11] was also there in fact he treated to a ticket. between the first and 2nd Piece the Democratic Torch light procession[12] passed along 4th, so the sight of that was included in the evenings entertainment. The performance Concluded late. by going direct home I got in bed 12. Exp 15c

Tuesday Octr 10th.

Business decidedly better. was more or less occupied the entire day. The Evening I passed at home, without however effecting any thing, being to sleepy from last nights vigil. Whenever I stay up too late, I am sure to feel it the next day. To Bed 10. Exp 10

Wednesday Octr 11th

Weather has been and continues pleasant although the nights are cold. After Supper I had my french lesson, an unusual sort of one. poor Menesca is discarded. being through with the exercise we went to, or proceeded up to Burkhardts but ere we got there I and my room-mate concluded upon going to the National. It was Conners Benefit. He performed *Richilieu* and *Robt de Moore.*[13] To Bed 12 oclock. Exp 35c

Thursday Octr 12, 1848.

Business so so. I was occupied however to some extent with our purchases. leisure time I devoted to my french. After supper I went to Henry's Store. He was not there. from there I went to the Barbers & had my hair cut. then direct home. I Paid Mrs Mosher Twelve Dollars for 4 weeks boarding or in full to the 30th having come on the 2nd inst. Studied french till 9 then went to bed. Exp & Bording 12.10.

Friday Octr 13.

Was a lovely and also a blessedly dull day. I dwelt among the French having ample time to study my entire *leçon.*[14]

After supper I went out for a few moments to get an English Paper. Not being able to get it, I returned immediately to my room. Studied till 10 oclock. Exp 10c

Saturday 14

Weather had that damp humid character that indicates and preceeds rain. Commerce was languid. My Cash in the afternoon balanced as closely as we generally desire.

Had my french lesson in two devisions, before and after supper. We were through at 8 oclock. I, and my room mate than went out, first to some Tailors as I need Clothes, but could not make any Choise. listened for an hour or so to a Barnburner Speech.[15] Home 10 oclock. Expense 15c

Sunday Octr 15th 1848

I arose ½ past 7. had breakfast at 8. Sat in the dining-room a half an hour or so. than Went to Kochs to select some Clothes. after an hours tumbling over of good's I succeeded in suiting myself for 2 coats, 1 vest, 1 pair 'pants togather amounting to 41$, which I am promised by next week Thursday. I shall need them that evening to cut a "Swell"[16] among the Dutch arristocracy, which will assembled or at least profusely represented at the Assembly Rooms on the occasion of the first *Liedertafel* Ball this Season.

From there I proceeded home. had just taken my Coat off—and was on the point of naturalizing my self still further when Mrs Jacobus Entered my Room, to request me to accompany her husband who wished to indulge in a walk and who was still weak from a recent sickness. Mrs J, being a pretty little woman, of course I went. Jacobus did not prove *Si malade*[17] as I expected. we cracked two bottles of Scotch Ale at BK-Exchange,[18] where after a good walk we remained till dinner time.

Had dinner at home. immediately after it I went up to Burkhardts. Moulinier was not there. I did not stay there long. Went to my brothers new residence.[19] He was not *chez lui.*[20] I remained to have Coffee, after which, having my Stomach full, I went Home again. After supper I did not go out at all. went to Bed at 9 read till 10. No Exp—

Monday Octr 16, 1848

By Jupiter, Neptune, or any other heathenish Diety having Command of the Watery department. Last night He gave us a touch of Thunder Storm and treated us besides to a respectable quantity of rain. Whiskey in Consequence advanced this Morning to 17 cts at which price Mr Dexter bot some.

Business was very fair. I was able to obtain an advance, ie 18 cts per gallon.[21] The Evening I passed partly in my room and part[l]y in the reading room of the young Mens M[ercantile] L[ibrary] Association. was introduced to a young man named Marsh. ere going home we stopped at the City Hotel and indulged *chacun à son gout.*[22] To Bed at 10 oclock. Exp. 25

Tuesday 17th

Was a bright and lovely day again. Whiskey sold to day for 16½. River is still very low. freight to N.O. for Whiskey 2.25 per barrel.

Business tolerday fair. we are not purchasing at all at present.

Marsh came to our room immediately after supper. Amused ourselves home till nearly 9, then went out to take a walk. Chance led us past Masonic Hall where one of the Fire Company's holds a fair. having nothing better to do we went in. There were 3 specimens of St Louis Firemen, quite Poetically dressed.[23] The Confounded Scrape Cost me only 80 cts, 79 too much. To Bed 11 oclock. Exp 90c

Wednesday Octr 18, 1848.

Cloudy and Cold Weather. if it was a trifle warmer I beleive it would rain. Sold Mr James McGregor[24] 75 Bbls Whiskey to day at 18c for which he paid 2.25 cts freight to New Orleans.[25]

Supper over, I finished my french lesson with Moulinier. we were through at 8. Went to Kochs to see about some clothes. My good friend M—r took it into his wise Head to treat me to a glass of Ale at Billy Tell's. Prince John Van Buren[26] was addressing a large crowd of Whigs,[27] Barn burners,[28] Loco's,[29] and Dead-Heads[30] on 5th St. my curiosity to hear him was'nt strong enough to induce me to stand in a dirty street, with a Cold wind blowing & being already afflicted with a slight Cold. I went home after listening about 5 minutes. To Bed 10 oclock. Exp 10c

Thursday 19th

Raining again to day. Our Staple[31] is again in demand. I took my time in dressing for the Ball after supper. In fact it was nearly ½ past 9 when I reached the rooms.[32]

The attendance was larger than I expected, and composed of many new faces, which to the young men was certainly agreable. I amused myself capitally although I had no Lady with me.

Miss Grothouse received a large share of my attentions. Mrs Wagner was also there. Mrs Thiesing also. I got home about 4 oclock. Exp 5$

Friday October 20th 1848

I and Charles arose about ¼ past 9 this Morning Our good Landlady was kind enough to furnish us with a breakfast at that late hour.

Arrived at the Store about ½ past 10. Mr Dexter had not been doing any thing the entire morning. Business throughout the day was dull. was'nt Sorry for it. although I experienced no inconvinience or disagreable Effects, still I was drowsy, and prefered repose. in fact was too fatigued to study.

Saturday Octr 21, 1848

Beautiful Weather, very. Business dull to day. In the afternoon we were busy with receiving raw whiskey. My Cash after some trouble was balanced satisfactory. The Evening I passed at home, having a french lesson. To Bed 10 oclock. Exp 10c

Sunday 22nd

Lovely Weather. We arose too late to dress before Breakfast. had a bath after it. went out about 11 oclock, over to Newport to view the Government improvements at the Barracks.[33] Crossed the licking [River] and went to Puthoffs.[34] I notified F. Putthoff that I wanted my Money when due. It being near 1 we were invited and partook of a "hasty dinner" There.

Shortly after 2 we were at Mouliniers. Charley was not at home. about 4 went to Burkharts did not find any body at home. After Supper went to Burkhardts. from there to Werners. Home 11. Exp 65¢.

Monday October 23rd 1848

Raining this Morning. Whiskey is again held at 17c Mr Dexter refused to buy an engaged Lot[35] last Saturday at 16½. This morning he had to pay 16¾ for the Same Whiskey.

The Evening I passed without accomplishing any thing of value, but amused myself capitally. Until about 8 I was in Mr Wilkins rooms. Mrs W— tried to sing and I to accompany her on the Guitar. I then attempted a few Guitar Solo's. after this I examined Mrs W's polite correspondence, and finished with playing a rubbar at <u>Euchre</u> which Mr and Mrs W won. before we had finished our game Mrs Jacobus entered and requested me to call in her room, that I was particularly wanted there. being through & having lost, I bade goodnight to Mr & Mrs W. and went in Mrs J's room. She had a visitor (an Eastern acquaintance) there. It seems I was wanted to fill a "Set" at "Whist" I did so with pleasure. I and Mr Jacobus Came out A. No 1. when we broke up it was ½ past 10. I had just time Smoke a Cigar before retiring. Exp 10c

Tuesday 24th

Weather has changed again. to day it is Sunshiny and pleasant. Business is dull. Whiskey is firm at 16¾ and 17c.

Immediately after Supper I went to my Tailor, but my Coat was not ready. returned direct home. Studied till 11 oclock, then went to Bed. Exp 10c.

Monday Octr 30th 1848

Mr Dexter is and has been for the past 3 days confined to the House. is at present afflicted with a kind [of] internal pile.[36] The business of the Store and my own affairs have prevented me from devoting customary attention to my Journal. The balanced of the Ev'nings last week excepting one I passed at home. That one I went with Lacy, who is at present boarding in the Same House with me, to the National Theatre to witness and admire the Heron familly. The Children are Certainly very precocious and acted admirably, but the best of Juvenile perfections do not please me suffisciently to pay 50 cts to see them. I regretted my "change."[37]

Yesterday forenoon I passed at home with my french. did effect a great deal tho' had dinner at home. Having enjoyed a good dinner I went to Mrs Mouliniers. the good Lady was just preparing to go to Church. I and Charles went to Burkhardts. had not been there long when Tim O'Conner came upon [us] very unexpectedly. he has not been visible for some time. Sweet Sarah was there also. I had a very pleasant time with her. when we left (about 5) I took the Liberty to kiss her. She returned the Compliment. Went to Rebstocks had a bottle of Rhein wine or rather two bottles for 5 of us.[38] Burkhardt treated the crowd to a supper. Went home about ½ past 8. played with the girls at home till 10. then to bed. Exp 65¢

Monday Octr 30, 1848

Weather somewhat upleasant. toward Evening we had a regular Storm. I called on Mr Dexter after Supper. Charles Moulinier was there giving Edmund[39] a lesson. About 8 we left and went to the Theatre. Mr Booth performed *Richard III* and did it admirably.[40] The Audience was large and select. all appeared to be amused. Mr B's voice, from the effects of drinking is at present unfit for any character except such an unatural one as Dick the IIIrd. To Bed at 12. Exp 65c

Tuesday 31st.

Cold clear and pleasant weather. prospect of a stage of water is again diminishing. Was very busy during the day with collecting and delivering McGregors 700 bbls Whiskey.[41] After Supper I played Cards till 8. then per appointment went to Sofge's for a lesson on the Flute. ½ past 9 was home again. About 10 I and Jacobus went to the Bank Exchange.[42] friend I treated twice while there. when we got home it was 11 oclock. Exp 5c

Wednesday November 1st 1848.

On this, the first Morning in the Month we were treated to small Snow Storms . . . River rising again at Pittsburgh. The Evening I passed at home till ½ past 9 studying, then went out with Jacobus to the St Charles. he treated to Oysters,[43] I to Liquor. Exp 25c

Thursday Novr 2nd, 1848

Beautiful weather again. River is falling at "Headquarters," ie Pittsburgh. Produce here is of course falling again. The Evening I passed altogather in my room, having a french lesson, after which I studied until about ½ past 10, when I went to bed. Exp 5c

Friday 3rd

Business to day was good. I received a paper from Charles Dexter to day. the young Man has indeed been neglected, of late, but very unwillingly. between my own studies and encreasing duties at the Store I have hardly a moments spare time.

Saturday 4th

Was a decided nasty disagreable day. Business was tolerbly fair. towards [evening] I bot from C[orr] & P[oland] 80 bbls whiskey at 16½ the receiving of which detained me a little later than usual.[44]

During the Evening we young'un's had a little Spree. about 7 we Commenced playing Cards. played till near 10 oclock. then went out *en masse*[45] to the St Charles. had a glass' "refreshment" there. from there went to the Bank Exchange where we took another dose. returned to the St Charles indulged in a third.

Went to 5th St[46] to take another, but my Sage suggestion prevailed. we went home without further indulgences. Played on our return till ½ past 12. Exp 65c

Sunday Novr 5th 1848

When I arose, which I did about 8 oclock, the Sun was Shining in full glory. it was a beautiful Morning. 4 of us, (I mean 4 of us young men) took a walk immediately after breakfast, to enjoy the beauties of a fine, Cool and pleasant Morning, and to give the Chambermaid an opportunity to Clean our rooms. I enjoyed it very much, as I felt feverish from last nights dissipation. returned about ½ past 9. the balance of the forenoon I Employed in studying my french lesson. ½ past 12 I Commenced dressing and had just finished when the dinner bell rung. Shortly after dinner my good *precepteur de la belle langue française*[47] came to give me a lesson in it. when we were through with it, it was 3 oclock. We then went to Mesers Burkhardts. the whole familly was at home, including Sarah, or Miss Cook, who, although she resides next door with her Sister, is nevertheless one of the assembled Company on Sunday afternoon. Tim O'Conner was there also. We had a decided pleasant time of it. Fred[48] played a few pieces choice Flute music.

I loaded a Pistol for Tim.[49] He intended going to a whore house and anticipated some difficulty.

We all had supper at Burk's. Sarah during the afternoon invited me to call and see her after Supper, but having played with her all afternoon I had no desire to do so. Went home about 8. Amused the girls "to hum" till 10. then went to Bed. No Exp.

Monday November 6th 1848

Beautiful but somewhat Cold Weather. Retail Business tolerbly fair. we expect to load A Flat Boat this week.[50] If we do I shall be actively employed. must endeavour though to produce better french lessons than last week, and if I have any spare time I shall write to Charles.[51]

Immediately after Supper the entire male population of our Establishment went out to view the processions: Whig, democratic, and Barnburners. the Whigs were on Horseback and presented a very good appearance. Democrats were few and far between. Barnburners held an illuminated meeting on 5th St but their Sentiments were not heard as the numerous [people] that had Assembled made too much noise for any speaker to be heard. I was home again before 8 oclock and staid there studying my french lesson. Exp 20¢

[Margin note]: Paid Mrs Moser boarding and washing to date.

Tuesday November 7th 1848

Was a most important day for every true hearted American. on this day the whole American Nation cast their vote[52] for a Candidate who favours those principals that every free citizen chooses to consider the most beneficial for his Country. I gave my vote[53] to General Taylor a thorough honest old Whig. The interests of the Mercantile Community, of the Mechanic, and the entire labouring Class are certainly intimately connected with the whig principals. The Evening I passed with my Flute Teacher.[54] went home about 9 oclock, studied till ½ past 10. Exp 15c

Wednesday November 8th 1848

Clear, fine, but very Cold weather. Business is not so bad as it might be, considering the high rate of freight. I had a french lesson this evening, but it was a poor one. it is too cold in the Store for study. If I set down to write I am so far removed from the Stove, that my fingers are benumbed in five minutes. After supper I went to Henry's Store to get a box of Cigars, for which bye the by I did not pay for. Saw Albert Töppelman and Grothouse his partner. they have been doing business in Chicago Ill's, but, poor fellows! They had just got their Establishment going, when their Entire Stock was destroyed by fire. Covered by insurance 300$. loss about 550$.

from there went direct home. had just Commenced studying when my troublesome friend Jacobus Entered to invite me to play Euchre in his room. I was foolish Enough to do so. lost thereby the better part of the Evening for Study. Exp 10

Thursday 9th

I omitted to mention that I wrote to Clemens[55] yesterday. Sent the letter by a Mr Rosenfeld who is in the Employ of Clemens. Business very good to day. Weather Clear and Cold. River falling at Pittsburgh. The Evening I passed entirely at home, Employing my time in the study of music and French. Studied hard till ½ past 10, then went to bed. Expense 5c

Friday November 10th, 1848

Business is becoming good. I have no time french at the Store. About 8 P.M. I went to Sofge's & had my flute Lesson. went direct home. Exp 5c

Saturday 11th.

Most confounded busy with shipping. I copied Six letters filled out 12 bills lading & the small Local business was also very good.

After supper all of us young men, 5 in Number,[56] went to the National Theatre. C. D. Pitt was performing Claude Mellnotte[57] & Petruchio[58] in the latter piece, both of which he did very fairly. the Audience seemed pleased with his Efforts. his wife in the last piece was passably [good] She is rather good loocking. got home at 11 oclock. Exp 70c

Sunday 12th.

It rained during the greater part of the forenoon. I suffered severely from tooth ache during the night. did not rise till 8 oclock. the forenoon I passed at home, studying my french lesson. Moulinier Came about 2. ½ past 3 we had finished our lesson. went up to Burkhardts where we passed the balance of the afternoon agreably. Went home to Supper. Jacobus was as drunk as a beast well could be. to please his wife I played Cards with him till 9 then went in the girls room till 10 when I went to Bed. Exp Nothing.

Monday November 13th 1848.

Rainy and disagreable weather. Business not particularly bright. Still we had something to do. The Evening I passed at home, amusing myself with my flute and French. To Bed at 11. Exp 15c

Paid for boarding to date 3$ and Sofge my Music Teacher 8$ on which I have had 5 lessons.

Tuesday 14th.

Raw disagreable weather. River rising again at Pittsburgh. The larger class boats are getting ready here for New Orleans. Business to day was tolerbly fair. it is too cold to sit at my small desk and write. So, between Cold weather and business my french lessons at somewhat neglected at the Store. The Evening till 8 I passed in my room. at 8 I went to Sofge's and had my flute lesson. To Bed 11. Exp 5c

Wednesday 15th

Was one of the busy days. we shipped 633 bbls Whiskey to day, 612 to New Orleans at 50 cts per bbl freight, 20 cts a bbl lower than any that has been shipped yet.[59] After Supper I had a french lesson which employed me till nearly 8 oclock. hardly had Moulinier left, when Shotwell came in with my old friend Mr Delamattre. the young man loocked precisely as he did last year about this time. We played Euchre till ½ past 9, then went to the St Charles and I treated the Company to a Horn,[60] thus committing the Sin of making them Horny. To bed ½ past 10. Exp 35c

Thursday November 16th. 1848

A cold raw day. River is again falling at Pittsburgh. freights are steady at 70 cts to New Orleans.

The Evening I passed at home, without however affecting any thing beneficial, as we played Whist nearly the entire Evening. To Bed 11. Exp 5c

Friday 17th

I did intend to go to Mr Werners Concert[61] this Evening, but my flute lesson prevented me from doing so. returned home about 9. Exp 5c

Saturday 18th.

Was a somewhat busy day. Weather is quite cold again. The Evening I passed at home playing Whist from 9 to 12 before that time I studied. Exp 10.

Sunday 19th.

Did not get up till 8 oclock, which was after the second bell had wrung. The Morning I passed at home studying french, back lessons, of course. Immediatly after dinner or about 2 oclock I walked up to Henry's House, found the whole familly assembled. His wife is again blessed with another little baby, a girl, making his familly 4 large.[62] The little thing was about 2 weeks old. I returned home before supper. Afterwards I studied till 8, then went in Jacobus's room. he had quite a party of Ladies there. about 9 went with Marsh to BK Exchange,[63] had Oysters Scotch Ale &c. to bed 11. Exp 25.

Monday November 20th 1848

Most outrageously Cold this Morning. in fact the Coldest Weather we have yet been treated to.

Business Commenced very lively. I had to lay hands on myself.[64] did not regret this, as it was too cold to write. After Supper I went up to Henry's Store, and paid him 3.50 for One box Cigars. owe him at present for another.

Went up to get my flute but it was'ent ready. returned direct home from there. played on the Guitar till 9. from that time till ½ past 10 I was in Brayleys room playing Whist. Exp 10c. Paid Boarding & Washing to date $3.35c.

Tuesday Novr 21st.

Beautiful weather, but cold. Business to day was good, at least I was occupied the entire day. directly after supper I went up to get my flute. from there went to Sofge's. had my lesson by 9. Mr S. treated me to a ticket for Madam Ablamowics Concert.[65] went direct home. Smoked in B. L. & Co's room[66] till ½ past 10. Expence 1.60.

Paid One dollar fifty cents for repairing my flute.

Wednesday 22nd

Confounded Cold this Morning. Business tolerbly fair during the day. My Old friend J. C. Nulsen arrived late last Evening from St. Louis. I did not see him until in the Evening when I went to Wagners. The young man looked fully his former self. We passed the evening in the German Theatre.[67] To Bed 12. Exp 60c

Thursday Novr 23rd, 1848.

Business was very good. I have not touched my french lessons this week. Clemens visited me at the Store about 11. from what I could gather from his Conversation he is willing to accept me for his Partner. I have been seriously thinking of it myself, and have Come to the Conclusion that it will be to my interest to Start in business with him. went to Henry's Store after supper, but Clemens did not keep his promise of coming there. returned home about 8. Played Whist until 11, then went to bed entirely tired out. Exp 10c

Friday 24th.

Business good, weather disagreable. After Supper I called at Wagners per appointment with Clemens, but the young Man in a very unbusiness like Manner, had cleared out already with his wife to Fahlbush. I returned to Henry, talked with him over our prospects in case I connect myself with Clemens. Went home shortly after 8. played Whist till past 10. Went tired to bed. Exp 5c

Saturday 25th

Après avoir en souper, J'allais trouver Mr Dexter chez lui pour parler de nos affaires. Il me disait qu'il a toujours compté de m'établir aussitôt que Son fils Charles Serait

revenue. qu'il leverait Mon Salair 100 gourdes chaque an. je revenais chez moi à dix heures, et me couchait à onze. [After dinner I went to see Mr Dexter to talk about our business. He assured me that he is still thinking about settling with me as soon as his son Charles comes back. He also added he would raise my salary $100 per year. I came back to my place around 10 PM, and I went to bed around 11.] Exp 10c.

Sunday Novr 26th 1848.

Immediatly after breakfast I went to Henry's House. although it was 9 oclock he was still without his *déjeuner.*[68] Toney Nulsen arrived shortly afterwards also. we went to Wagners. Clemens was already up, in fact nearly dressed. We went up to Drachs place on Syc[amore] Hill. Cracked about ½ doz pint bottles Catawba wine[69] for which Henry paid. while setting over the bottles and smoking our good Cigars, Henry introduced the difficulty existing between him and Clemens. from what was made out it would seem that I was the Cause, although unintentionally and not now remembered by me. Seeing that the difficulty Could not be settled any other way except I took all the blame upon myself, to reconcile all parties I did so. We returned about ½ past 12. I went home to dinner. About 3 oclock I returned to Wagners. it was confounded Cold. Shortly after my arrival Mrs W— handed the coffee around. as I had been smoking and felt cold it was a real luxury to me. The afternoon we passed very pleasantly playing Whist. I and Clemens were playing against Tony and Fahlbush. we won every game except one.

After supper we continued our game and were equally successful. It is true by playing we had to neglect the Ladies, but as they were all Married except one who was ugly we were pretty easy on this Score. Went home 10 No Expence.

Monday Novr 27th 1848

Business was dull to day. Weather raw and unpleasant: I was projecting all day whether it would not be best to go along with Clemens to St Louis[70] and have a look at things there before I leap. The Evening I passed with Clemens and in fact nearly the entire relationship of Nulsen & Mersman were assembled at Toney's at least all those that count any thing in the business world.[71] The good folks Amused themselves with playing Puhl [pool]. it was no Amusement for me, as I can not play at billiards.[72] Home at 11. Exp 45c.

Tuesday Novr 28th.

Clemens was to have left to day, but the good boat *Geo Washington*[73] gave him another to pass with his friends.

Bartlett's Commercial College advertisement, 1850. A business school in Cincinnati, it offered courses in bookkeeping and business management. It was one of at least five such schools in Cincinnati in 1849. (From the Collection of the Public Library of Cincinnati and Hamilton County.)

Father called on me this Morning and advised me to ask Mr Dexter's permission to accompany Clemens. I did so after dinner and obtained it. The boat will leave to Morrow at 10 oclock certain. This Evening I was busily Employed in packing up my Effects and getting ready. Called at Henry's also, deposited all my due bills with him.[74]

As Mrs Mosher will probably remove ere I return I left all my things in charge of Mr Charles Herbst my room-mate. To Bed 11 oclock—

NOTES

1. Mrs. Jenkins and Mary Jane Jenkins.
2. *Deutsch* or German.
3. William Tell Restaurant.
4. Merchants in Pittsburgh, the origin of the Ohio River, reported changes in water levels, which

would eventually reach Cincinnati. JJM remained alert to these reports because they affected transportation costs. See map 1.

5. Charles Herbst, JJM's roommate.

6. The Whigs were a nineteenth-century American political party, organized in opposition to Democratic President Andrew Jackson's social policies. After 1850, a split over the slavery issue caused many northern Whigs to join the newly formed Republican Party (EAPH, 441–42).

7. Sarah Cook.

8. See chapter 3, note 22.

9. Swill is a large draft of an alcoholic beverage (OED, s.v. "swill"). The "old Swill place" may be the Bavarian Brewery. See map 5.

10. "Do" is the abbreviation for ditto. Charles Herbst also went to bed at 10 p.m.

11. Residents of his new boardinghouse. See JJM diary, 8 October 1848.

12. Street rallies by political parties were an important part of the 1848 presidential election campaign (COM, 5 October 1848).

13. The performance at the National Theatre included *Richelieu,* with E. S. Conner playing the title role. Schiller's tragedy *The Robbers* was conflated into three acts and Conner played the role of Charles de Moor (COM, 11 October 1848).

14. [Fr.] lesson.

15. The Barnburners were a radical northern Democratic Party faction (1842 to 1848) that went on to support the Free-Soil Party between 1848 and 1854. They opposed the expansion of slavery into western territories and nominated former President Martin Van Buren in 1848, winning roughly 14 percent of the popular vote. The term "Barnburners" came from its members' alleged willingness to burn down the barn (the party) to get rid of its enemies (EAPH, 147–48).

16. To "cut a swell" means to make a good impression (OED, s.v. "swell").

17. [Fr.] as sick.

18. The Bank Exchange Hotel and Restaurant. See map 5.

19. Henry Mersman's new residence was located on Center Street, between Race and Elm streets. See map 4 (CCD 1849–50, 197).

20. [Fr.] at his house.

21. Dexter bought at seventeen cents per gallon and JJM sold at eighteen cents per gallon, thus earning forty cents per barrel.

22. [Fr.] each to his taste.

23. The Invincible Fire Company No. 5 of Cincinnati had a fund-raising fair for a week beginning 16 October 1848. Among the guests were members of the Union Fire Company of St. Louis (COM, 18 October 1848).

24. James McGregor has not been identified.

25. McGregor purchased seventy-five barrels each with forty gallons at eighteen cents each, and thus spent $540 in all. The shipping charges were seventy-five barrels at $2.25, or $168.75 for transportation.

26. John Van Buren, the son of former President Martin Van Buren, was campaigning for his father, the Free-Soil Party's candidate in the 1848 presidential campaign (COM, 4, 16, 18 October 1848).

27. See note 6.

28. See note 15.

29. Radical New York Democrats who, in 1835, organized to oppose financial policies such as state banks, paper money, tariffs, and monopolies, called themselves the Locofoco Party. The party was never a national contender and did not survive the depression of the late 1830s, but opponents frequently applied the name to all Democrats (ENPH, 5:142).

30. A "deadhead" is one who, on account of his influential position, receives favors for which others have to pay, e.g., journalists. Unlike the other terms, this does not refer to a political party.

31. Whiskey was the principal item in Edmund Dexter's inventory.

32. The Assembly Rooms, a public hall used for social events, was likely the site of the ball.

33. The United States Army had established Newport Barracks in 1803 at the mouth of the Licking River (WPA [2] 538). A recruiting station and depot, the post underwent a building program beginning in 1845. Adding more quarters for officers and soldiers, grading the river bank, and enclosing the

perimeter created a controversy, particularly concerning the site of the proposed buildings, that continued until 1848 (collection of Joseph Donnelly, compiler. Mss fD685, Transcripts of letters, records, etc. relating to Newport Barracks. Cincinnati Museum Center, Cincinnati Historical Society Library). See map 2.

34. The Puthoff family in Covington, Kentucky, are described in chapter 2, note 18.

35. Dexter had a contract to purchase raw whiskey at 16½ cents per gallon but did not complete the transaction because of high transportation costs. He subsequently regretted that decision.

36. An internal pile, or a hemorrhoid, is an inflamed blood vessel near the anus.

37. JJM considered his coins wasted.

38. JJM, Tim O'Conner, Charles Moulinier, and the two Burkhardt brothers made up the group; Sarah Cook was not included.

39. Edmund Dexter or, less likely, Edmund Dexter Jr. (1836–79), his second son, received tutoring from Charles Moulinier because French was useful in business.

40. Junius Brutus Booth was engaged at the National Theatre for this night and the one following (COM, 30 October 1848).

41. See JJM diary, 18 October 1848.

42. Bank Exchange Hotel and Restaurant. See map 5.

43. The oyster season in Cincinnati, from 1 September through April, depended primarily on shipments from Baltimore. Shell oysters, six hundred per barrel, traveled packed in seaweed; canned oysters, the largest packed seven dozen to a can, retailed at $1.50 per can (Cist [3] 366–67).

44. JJM purchased 80 barrels, each with 40 gallons, at 16½ cents per gallon, or $528 for the lot.

45. [Fr.] as a group.

46. The William Tell Restaurant appears on map 5.

47. [Fr.] teacher of the lovely French language, i.e., Charles Moulinier.

48. Frederick Burkhardt.

49. Tim O'Connor.

50. A flat boat, used for downstream transport, drew less water than a steamboat.

51. Charles Dexter.

52. Election day 1848 was the first time in American history that the entire nation voted for president on the same day (COM, 6 November 1848; U.S. Code Title 3, Chapter 1; http://moritzlaw.osu.edu/electionlaw/comment0315.html).

53. JJM was twenty-four years old, so 1848 was his first presidential election. Although he was naturalized years later, in 1865, citizenship was not yet a requirement to vote. Under Ohio's constitution of 1802, voting was open to white males over the age of twenty-one, residents at least one year, and taxpayers. Ohio's 1851 constitution limited suffrage to white male citizens, thus disenfranchising many immigrants (Ohio Const [1802], Art IV, § 1; Ohio Const [1853], Art V, § 1; http://www.ohiohistory.org/onlinedoc/ohgovernment/constitution/cnst1851.html).

54. Henry E. Sofge.

55. JCN.

56. Probably all of the single men at the boardinghouse, including JJM, Harry Brayley, Charles Herbst, William Lacy, and Tim O'Connor.

57. Claude Melnotte was a leading character in *The Lady of Lyons*, by Edward Bulwer-Lytton (1803–73).

58. Petruchio was the male lead in *Catharine and Petruchio*, based on Shakespeare's comedy *The Taming of the Shrew* (COM, 11 November 1848).

59. By using a flatboat instead of a steamboat, Dexter saved $122.40 in shipping costs.

60. "Horn" refers to a drinking horn, a vessel made of an animal's antler (OED, 4:1055).

61. Mr. Werner, the pianist, performed with his wife and Mr. Tosso in a concert at the Melodeon Hall beginning at 8:00 p.m. Tickets were fifty cents (ENQ, 17 November 1848).

62. This daughter died before the 1850 census was taken.

63. The Bank Exchange Hotel and Restaurant. See map 5.

64. Usually JJM supervised laborers who moved barrels of merchandise. On this date, there was so much work that JJM himself did manual labor.

65. Madam Ablamowicz's next major concert, which JJM attended, was scheduled for Tuesday, 9 January 1849.

66. Most likely the room of Harry Brayley and William Lacy. JJM playfully created a name for an imaginary firm, "Brayley, Lacy & Company."

67. Two plays were performed: the drama by Charlotte Birch Pfeiffer, *Hinko, King and Free Man* and *The Younger Son.* The curtain rose at 8:00 p.m. A single ticket for a seat in the parquet cost fifty cents; in the gallery, twenty-five cents. Subscribers for four shows received preferred seating, bargain prices, and an invitation to a ball.

68. [Fr.] breakfast.

69. Catawba wine, likely a locally produced product, was made from the grapes immortalized by Longfellow's poem (see Preface). In 1850, Hamilton County, Ohio, produced 35,000 gallons of wine (Rorabaugh, 105).

70. St. Louis was becoming known as a good place to make money. High wages and a large German population added to the attraction for JJM (Adler, 95, 108).

71. Very likely those in attendance included the hosts, Anthony and Maria Nulsen (JCN's brother and his wife); Augustus and Philippina Wagner (JCN's sister and her husband); Albertine Nulsen (JCN's wife); Francis and Dorothea Nuilsen (JCN's oldest brother and his wife); Henry and Adelaide Mersman (JJM's brother and his wife); Arnd and Elizabeth Kattenhorn (JJM's sister and her husband); JJM and JCN. Therefore, as many as thirteen adults gathered to celebrate the new partnership that would start business in St. Louis. There is no mention of children; presumably they remained at their homes with the servants.

72. Billiards is any of several games played with hard balls that are driven with a cue on a cloth-covered table (Bartlett, 130–34; Earl, 271–313).

73. The *George Washington,* a 303-ton sidewheel packet with a wood hull, was constructed in Cincinnati, Ohio, in 1845. It exploded near Gulf Port, Mississippi, in 1852 with the loss of seventeen lives (Way #2315, 186). The one-way fare on first-class boats from Cincinnati to St. Louis was about six dollars but could be negotiated (LDC, 9 June 1848).

74. Because of the dangers associated with travel, JJM deposited with his brother Henry Mersman all the promissory notes that he held from other businessmen. Thus, if he failed to return from his journey, his wealth would not be lost to his family.

CHAPTER EIGHT

Farewell to Cincinnati
17 December 1848–17 February 1849

JJM began his ten-year apprenticeship with Edmund Dexter on 18 January 1839, so as 1848 drew to a close, he faced an important decision: What to do next?

The answer was not far away. For six years, JJM's brother Henry had partnered with another immigrant, Anthony Nulsen, in a tobacco business. By 1848, Anthony's younger brother, John Clemens Nulsen (JCN), was looking for a business partner. JCN had opened a tobacco store in St. Louis in 1845, but his associate, Frederick W. Ficke, died suddenly two years later. Needing capital to shore up his venture, JCN invited JJM to join him. JJM made a trip to St. Louis to explore his prospects. Accordingly, JJM agreed to become JCN's partner and expand the business to include whiskey rectifying.[1] *However, relocation meant that JJM would leave his father and siblings, the first time in his life that he had been separated from them. Before that could occur, JJM had to settle his affairs in Cincinnati.*

During JJM's final days in the Queen City, he lived at Ross's Boarding House, also on Third Street (see map 4), even closer to Dexter's store than his previous residences. His friends, Charles Herbst and Hal Brayley, also boarded there. The three bachelors enjoyed the usual entertainments—balls, plays, cards, books, and women—as JJM consolidated his finances. He collected on debts that were due him and secured the capital that he needed for his new endeavor. He added twice-weekly flute lessons to his schedule of twice-weekly French lessons, always seeking to improve his skills. After a round of parties and good-byes, JJM set off for life as an entrepreneur in Missouri.

Sunday December 17th 1848.

Yesterday about ½ past 8 oclock I set my foot on Ohio's shore again, after an absence of 18 days, Certainly the longest I have indulged in for Eleven years.

Louisville, Kentucky, riverfront, c. 1850. A series of rapids and small waterfalls on the Ohio River at Louisville made it necessary for most riverboats to navigate a series of locks around the rapids. Only the most foolhardy of riverboat captains would "shoot the falls." (The Filson Historical Society, Louisville, KY.)

I must now attempt a description of my trip from a few notes I took, but Mainly from Memory.

On Wednesday the 29th I left the Store and bade Mr Dexter farewell about ½ past 8 in the Morning. Expecting the boat would leave at 10 or ½ past, went direct home, to do some little packing. then gave my trunk in charge of one of Henry's Boy's[2] who took it to the Boat. Charles Herbst went down to the Boat with me. we were told there that she would not leave until 4 oclock.

I dined to [that] day with Henry. immediatly after dinner I bade everyone at his house "good bye," then went to Wagners. passed the afternoon there until 4 when we all toddled down to the boat accompanied by Mrs Wagner, Mrs Nulsen[3] and their respective Husbands. as the boat was not ready yet we "Males" went to the City Hotel and took a farewell Horn. before leaving I called on Charles Moulinier to bid him farewell. about 5 the boat finally made unmistakable preparations for leaving. The last parting kisses were exchanged and final farewell's interchanged. the Ladies as a matter of course indulged in tears. this pleasure was denied us "worser Halves" my kind friend Charles[4] jumped on to another boat. ours shoved off, went above the City a short distance. when she returned it was with full speed. my good friend Charles stood on the Huricane deck of a neighbouring boat. When we passed he waved his hat, stood there until the encreasing darkness rendered us invisible to one another. Shortly afterwards we had supper. Clemens' wife showed plainly that she had been indulging in tears.

My old acquaintance Mr Dugan was on board also. after supper we got up a game of back set Euchre. I and Dugan lost at it, Clemens won about a dollar. We then played Loo.[5] at this game and the previous one I lost 5 dollars, that is 4.15 of my own money. once I won 85 cts counting this as loss, I was 5$ minus when I quit, which was about ½ past 9. Dugan continued playing at Poker[6] and loosing. When he quit he was minus 25 dollars. He was in the clutches of Skillful Men who did not scruple to bleed him as copiously as his Means would permit.[7] Next Morning we were in Louisville. immediatly after breakfast I and Clemens called on my Brother Frank. the young rascal had not got down to the Store yet, although it was 8 oclock. our boat had to pass through the Canal[8] so we had plenty of time to take a good look at the city before there was any necessity to think of ~~the boat~~ her.

Louisville is a mean ugly looking place from the river. the Landing is but poorly paved. an old venerable Creek[9] is permitted to devide it. It is true they have built an elegant bridge across it, but had they Changed its Chanal and Carried it into the river above the City it would have been far better. The City has began a splendid Court House, but the State in which it has existed for the last Ten years is a disgrace to its builders.[10]

We also attended an auction Sale of Tobacco. Some very fair samples sold at reasonable prices. about 10, we left the City, walked along the Canal—overtook our boat ere she was about ¼ mile in it—about half way there is a dutch Tavern where we treated ourselves to glass of ale. Frank, here, as well every where we went, seemed to be acquainted. we then visited the celebrated Kentucky Giant, John Porter;[11] what a beast he is to be sure! The House he occupies was built by him for his own accommodation. every thing is on the gigantic order. doors about 2 feet higher than usual. his Gun is about 6 feet long, walking Cane the size of two Stout Cincinnati dray pins.[12] but in spite of his gigantic proportions he seems week and feeble, moving about with difficulty. I and Clemens had some trouble to get on our boat in time for dinner. About 4 we were finally Clear of the Canal and then with light hearts proceeded on our way. I had made up my mind to play no more Cards for Money. The Evening I passed in reading *Mathilda*—[13] Nothing remarkably occurred during the balance of the trip. indeed, it would have been an exceedingly dull one, had it not been for some Louisvilleans we had on board. they made the Evenings at least pass off agreably with dansing. the last (Saturday) Evening they kept up the danse till 11, then took it into their wise Skull's to have a song. Singing was kept up till nearly 2 oclock on Sunday Morning. Louisville G'hals are some punkins[14] to keep a Crew awake!

During the first night I had some trouble to get asleep, the continual shaking and noise of the Steam rendered every attempt abortive, but during the succeeding one's it seemed to Contribute if any thing to sound snoozing.

Arrived safely in St Louis on Sunday Evening. You God's[15] what a muddy city! I never saw a richer and more plentiful collection of mud in my life. I permitted myself to be directed to the Misouri Hotel by my friend Clemens. had my room shown me and retired to bed. I caught a Cold the first night. my room was large with a high Ceiling, but very damp. immediatly after breakfast I went to Clemens' Store. He was already there. his Retreat seemed to be a snug little Business place, but it will not suit to put Liquors in it, being too narrow and small altogather.[16] During the forenoon we visited the Post office, Lempe the Celebrated Beer Man, and a variety of Clemens customers. I accompanied Clemens to his house at dinner, was introduced to the familly. His mother in law[17] is certainly a very agreable old Lady. His Sister in law,[18] judging her by her actions, is decidedly a very Modest little girl, although in years she is his wife's senior. one of his brother in law's is a good hearted and good loocking young Man, but is just begining to enjoy the liberties of a Man, and it is hard to foretell what he will be, as he seems to be rather impulsive.[19] My good friend Clemens is certainly blest with a good wife,[20] and he seems to appreciate her too. if the young man takes Care of himself he Can not but be happy for Life.

During the Afternoon I removed my Effects from the Hotel to Clemens house where I was at home during my Stay. Clemens took a very severe Cold the second day on the boat, which did not leave until 5 or [6?] days after his arrival.

The first and second day I did nothing. it was raining incessantly. I did not attempt to black my Boots. Ennuie however was driven away by the old ladys conversational powers. had plenty of good cigars to smoke, and while smoking I amused myself with reading a german copy of *Ivanhoe.*[21] On Wednesday I presented my friend Shotwells introductory letter to Mr Thompson, Clerk at Russell & Bennetts. he was so obliging as to give all the information in his power. The following day I called on Mr Braun.[22] he was not at home, but I gathered as much information from his head Clerk as I should have done from him. I made some enquiries from other Sources. from [what] I could gather I came to the Conclusion that the rectefying business must be good there in a short time, in fact is now. I intended to leave on Sunday but could not obtain a boat. the boats that were advertized to leave on Monday did not do so until Tuesday.

Before going I concluded a diffinite arrangement with Clemens. our firm is to be Nulsen & Mersman.[23] we made partial arrangement for a Store on Main St. where we shall have to pay 1000 dollars a year rent. If the business proves half what it ought to, we shall get along excellently. Rittmeyer[24] is still with Clemens and appears to be a piece of furniture belonging to the Store. On Tuesday Morning I bade the familly farewell. The *Wirlwind*[25] was to start at 10 but did not leave until ½ past 12.

Clemens went down to the boat with me. We talked over some of our plans while setting in the Cabin. about ½ past 11 the 3rd Bell rung. We took our parting Embrace, and he went on shore. the planks were taken in, but a few passengers and some freight arriving our departure was delayed. A disagreable Scene occurred just at this time. There was only one plank out which was not Securely fastened. four got on at once. the plank pitched over and 3 were precipitated in the water. Clemens stood on the shore about ½ an hour. When about 12 he waved his hat and Sloped. I certainly felt very Sad. as soon as he had left I went into the Cabin and did not emerge again, until the boat had gone up and turned. we passed the City in full speed and announced our departure with a Canon Shot. had dinner about ½ past 1. The day was very Cold. the river filled with Ice. large pieces now and then were already frozen. I was the whole afternoon in the back part of the Cabin, reading a Novel that I had purchased in St Louis, *The Adventures of Faublas.*[26] a somewhat interesting thing, though slightly smutty. The next Morning at 5 we were at Cairo, shortly afterwards in the Ohio river. There was at least an immediate differance of 10 pr Ct in the temerature the day was a lovely one, and nearly half of the Crew was passed on deck. I with the exception of a few hours kept in the Cabin, amusing myself with *Faublas.* did not wish to take Cold, having seen the disagreability of it in my friend Nulsen. Our trip was a fortunate one and about Medeum in quickness. On Friday about 10 we were in Louisville. Saw my brother Frank there. the little fellows personal Toilet did not Show any thing new since I last saw him. being but thinly clad the poor boy had Caught a Severe Cold. I gave him good advise but no Cash. He seems well satisfied with his present Employer. about 11 our Crowded boat left again. by the bye I nearly omitted to mention that we Came over the Fall's at Louisville.[27] another boat attempted it but did not succeed. This day I passed in studying French as I had finish *Faublas.* During the Evening I Engaged in a game of Whist merely playing for the Cards and liquor, as I intend to keep my resolution of never gambling for Money again. about 9 oclock the boats "Doctor" (part of the Machinery)[28] broke which detained us two hours. I slept Soundly. The Next Morning when I arose about 6 we were within 14 miles of "Home." ½ past 8 I was in the Store. Mr Dexter was busy and on this account if on no other was glad to See Me. I immediatly resumed my former duties. sent William[29] for my Trunk, and during the forenoon sold 200$ worth of Mdse.

About 11 I called at my former boarding house, but it was locked. Mrs Mosher had failed.[30] went up to N[ulsen] & M[ersman]'s Store. shook hands with Toney, Henry not being at home. Had dinner at the St Charles for which Mr Dexter paid. during the Afternoon I called on "Harry"[31] and found that we were boarding on 3rd St near broadway.[32] was in the Store the entire afternoon.

Father and Henry Called on me about 3 to Congratulate me on my safe return. The Cash would not balance. I did not care a fig, as I did not have any thing to do with it. had supper at ½ past 5. immediatly after it went up to Henry's with Charley.[33] then to Mr Andrew to get my watch. about 10 I went to bed.

Sunday December 17th 1848

I arose this Morning about 7 dressed before breakfast. had it about 8. Shortly afterwards went with Charley & Hal[34] walking. returned about 9. half past went to Henrys[35] house. his wife was well, baby sick. Called on Toney.[36] the foolish Man had gone to Church with his wife. She must have had a new dress to show of in. well well! so wags the world. Husbands must obey their wifes now and then.

from there went to Wagners for whom I had a letter. all my and Clemens relations appear to be highly pleased at the idea of our intended Partnership. after having entertained Mrs Wagner for half an hour [or] so, we went up to Rebstocks where we indulged in two bottles of Rhein wine.

I dined with Henry. directly after dinner I left, went down to my old friends Moulinier. My old friend Monfort, was there also. the young Man since I last saw him has been to all the Eastern cities. I partook of Mrs Moulinier's Elegant desert. half an hour afterwards we were at Burkharts. Sweet Sarah[37] was there as usual, evidently glad to see me. about 3 we sallied forth, walked until we were all tired. Stoped at Karrmans drug Store. Mr Douglass and Fredc K and two others were there, amusing themselves with Music. I was slightly sick. went home about dusk. took Tea—and about 8 I retired to my bed—

Monday Decr 18th 1848.

There is at present nearly as much Mud here as there was in St Louis two weeks ago. present appearances indicate more rain. Business oppened very fairly this Morning. After Supper I called on Kochs to have my coat repaired, then at Henry's House to get my flute. from there direct home to bed. Exp 10c.

Tuesday decr 19.

Business continues very good in the retail way. I have as yet done nothing to my french exercises. Mr Dexter is making use of his liberty again by absenting himself nearly all day from the store. Mr Sofge called on me during the Afternoon. in the Evening I had a flute lesson, from there direct home to bed. Exp 5c

Wednesday 20th.

Weather rainy and disagreable, fully as much so as it was in St Louis. during a rainy season all western Cities can boast of being a little dirty. Business for this weather very good. After supper Moulinier called to give me a french lesson, although I had no Material ready for a lesson. it was short and easy. about 8 I went out with Hal' over the Canal. Called at Kochs. bot John's Cloak for 16$. Home, and to bed at 10 oclock. Exp 10c

Thursday December 21st 1848.

Weather continues most Confoundedly disagreeable, raining at intervals of every hour or so. Commerce in spite of all opposition flourishes finely.

After supper I practiced on my flute for a half hour. then called with Harry and Charles[38] on Mr Frintz.[39] from there we went to Mrs Mosher on Elizabeth St[40] at least a mile from our boarding house—to get there we had to traverse the muddiest Section of the City, beating St. Louis all hollow. The familly were just through with supper although it was 8 oclock. they all appeared in good Spirits, and were quite lively in spite adversity. to amuse ourselves the better we played a short rubber of Whist, which I and Jacobus won. Half past 9 we returned home. Stopped at the Billy Tell; took a piece of Pie and Cup of Coffee each. To Bed at ½ past 10. Exp 15c

Friday Decr 22nd

Business very good. towards Evening it turned quite [cold?]. After supper I had a lesson of Sofge. returned home about 9. read and studied french till 11 oclock, then retired to bed. Exp 10c.

Saturday 23rd.

Weather disagreable. Business good. after supper I intended to give a grand Spree to my room-mates, Charles & Hal, but could not obtain oysters, the article being Scarce.[41] had my french lesson. To Bed at 10 oclock. Exp 10c.

Sunday December 24th 1848

The entire forenoon I passed in my room. did not have breakfast until 9. Immediatly after dinner I went to Henry's. there I passed the whole afternoon playing Duetts on the Guitar with Henry. from there I went to Kattenhorns where I had my supper. About 9 I returned home. wrote half of my french Exercise and at ½ past 10 I went to Bed. Exp 10c.

Monday 25th Christmas. 1848.

I was in the Store fully as early as usual. remained there till 12 oclock, then went to Kattenhorns to dine. Stopt on my way to make the necessary purchases for my little nieces.[42] I gave them each an Anual,[43] the three costing 2.60. In return I received from my sister Mrs Kattenhorn a superfine white silk hankerchief, a good dinner & Supper.

Two oclock I returned to the Store. Kept it open till 4 oclock, then returned to Kattenhorns where I remained till 9. Home and in bed at 10. Exp 3$.

Tuesday 26th

Last evening intelligence was received that the Cholera existed Strongly in New Orleans, Vicksburgh and Memphis.[44] Weather to day fine and Cold. Commerce dull. I notefied Mr Becker of the expiration of his Note. received all my Notes from Nulsen & Mersman. Called at Kochs to procure a Ball Ticket for this evening.[45] this being in all probability the last Ball I shall honor with my presence in Cincti, I could not resist the temptation of going.

I did not make any attempt to be particularly dressed, so I was ready before 8 oclock. The Concert had not yet Commenced, did so about ¼ past 8. Charles Moulinier was there also. Mr Runge's Leadership is certainly far more effecient than Mr Scheidlers. the singing was far more Scientific, displayed more taste, and certainly was more pleasing. At 10 the dansing Commenced. Not being able to get any thing better I had to put up with "Louisa" for my partner.[46] however after the first danse she did not have that honer again. There were some handsome german girls. twice, through favours that were shown me, I came near making a Scientific Love declaration, but some preventive fortunately occurred just at the time I was at the point of making a fool of myself. I amused myself Capitally. all my old friends were assembled. Wagner kept perfectly sober. Toney[47] was slightly Corned. Rehfuss, Beneke, Kolb, Pöppelman were all in high glee. the dansing went off very lively. the gentleman actually did their duty in point galantry. My attentions at one time were somewhat pointed towards a Miss Remlinger.[48] She made such decided advances that I had to kiss her in the Ball room. the poor fellow who brought Her there thought he had a right to be jealous. I did not once danse with a Married Lady, altho' most of my intimate female friends were there. I certainly regret it now, but too late. When I went home 4 oclock it was snowing. I caught a severe Cold. Total Exp <u>3.20.</u>

Wednesday decr 27th. 1848.

I arose this Morning at 10 oclock, having given Mr Dexter the keys of the Store last evening. at 11 oclock I was comfortably seated in the eating room of the St Charles, making most successful attempts at breakfast.

You Gods! What a cold you have afflicted me with, just because I did'nt take particular care of myself last evening. my nose was runing the whole day, and the Continual blowing of it made my head ache, just punishment for imprudent enjoyment. fortunately our business was very trifling to day. So I hardly any thing to do, but to Set half asleep beside the Stove. about 8 oclock I went to bed. No Expense except for my breakfast which was 25 cts.

Thursday 28th.

Business dull to day. Weather quite nasty. My cold under existing state of things is sure to stick to me. Immediatly after supper a fire broke out in a building on Walnut St. once occupied by My friend Clemens and Johnson,[49] but lately by Calhoun & Co as a varnish and alcohol depot. These Combustible Materials made a bright blaze. The fire was Communicated to the building North, and after a few hours when all was supposed to be out, the Southern one suddenly blazed forth also. about 2, Messrs Mitchell & Co's bed factory caught fire.[50] this produced the brightest blaze I have ever seen. The fire bells were ringing nearly the entire night. from 8 to ½ past 10 I was in the Catholic fair[51] with my friend Marsh. The Scrape cost me only 85 cts. to Bed 11—

Friday Decr 29th 1848.

After leaving the fair last evening, I went to the new restaurat on 3rd St called "La Belle." Every body there said it surpasses every thing of this kind in the U.S. It certainly looks Magnificent. I doubt now whether the profits there will pay the establishment in two years.[52] My Cold this Morning is just as bad as yesterday. Mr Dexter is confined to his bed. I am busy shipping and receiving whiskey.

After supper I called on Doctor Potter to arrange the payment of Mr Johnsons Note. after much talking I accepted the Doctors check on Ellis & Morton dated 14th January in payment for the Note.[53] from there I went direct home. read till 10, then to bed. Exp 5c

Saturday 30th.

Weather very mild, but Cloudy and disagreable. Business is getting dull. boats are refusing to depart for New Orleans.[54] Produce of all description is declining rapidly. Whiskey is down to 15 cts. Pork 3$, was 3.90 and 4$ in the early part of the week. the report from below is to day 75 to 100 Deaths per day. After supper I went with Charles Herbst to the National. we had not been there more than 5 minutes, when who should enter but Charles Moulinier with Sarah Cook dressed in her best. during the last piece I was quite attentive to Sweet Sarah. Mr Dexter came there also about 9. Murdoch played in *Money* and *Pizarro*.[55] did justice to both characters. got home ½ past 12. Exp 75¢.

Sunday, December 31st 1849 [1848][56]

Got up about 8, had my breakfast ½ past. 9 I was at Henry's. He would not go along to Scotts, so I went to Toney.[57] He went with pleasure. We did not get Started till near 11. had our dinner at Sportsmen's Hall, now kept by Ganter. He was so good as to invite us to dine with, which of course we could not refuse, it being precisely 12 oclock.

We arrived at Scotts 2 oclock. were so lucky as to find him at home. about 3 we had a Country dinner with him. immediatly after dinner He invited us in his private parlour, and after much persuasion signed the Notes I had prepared.

At 4 we started to return. arrived at Ganters about dusk, took a warming Horn. at 6 were in Shaffers Stable.[58] I had to fork over two dollars.[59] went to Kattenhorns to get some supper. about 9 I went Home, having a fresh Stock of Cold in my body. Exp 2.60.

January the 1st 1849. (Monday)

I was in the Store the whole day. when I opened the doors in the Morning I found a letter from Johnson enclosing 40$. This I shall pay over to Doctor Potter.

After supper I called on him. his wife extended the Compliments of the Season to me. About 7 I went with Charles & Harry[60] to Mrs Arons. this Lady's Table was well supplied with the luxuries. left there at 9. went to the American[61] for an hour. To bed 11. Exp 45c.

January 2nd 1848. [1849] (Tuesday)

This Morning thank fortune it is quite Cold. a clear Northern wind prevails, making every one bless the inventor of Cloaks and overcoats. I omitted to Mention in my yesterdays notice that Mr P. Andrew refused to endorse Scotts Notes.[62]

This Mornings report from New Orleans by passengers is that on Christmas day there were over 170 deaths there. Boats here can not procure Fireman at 50$

per month.[63] Whiskey this Morning 14¼. Pork is lower also, how much I do not know. After supper I had a Flute lesson from Softge. returned home about ½ past 8. wrote a letter of 4 pages to my future partner J. C. Nulsen, mostly about business Matters. this I shall mail to Morrow morning. To Bed 11. No Expense

January 3rd. 1849

This Morning Snow to the depth of 2 inches cov'red the ground. Continued Snowing all forenoon a cold North wind blowing all the time. If this is'nt death to Cholera I don't know what is! Whiskey 14c. Pork is a little better this Morning, as the weather is about the most propitious we have had this winter. After supper I had a french lesson, and after that I studied *la belle langue jusqu'à onze heures, alors étant bien fatigué je me couchais* [the beautiful language until 11 o'clock, then, being very exhausted, I went to bed]. Exp 10.

Thursday 4th.

Business has improved again. produce is again looking up. Whiskey to day 14¼¢. Weather turning very cold. After Supper I did not do any thing particular having nothing to do, I was all evening doing it. To Bed 10 oclock. Exp—

Friday January 5th 1849

Weather Clear, but intensely Cold. Business fair. We shipped to day a 100 bbls again to New Orleans. After supper I called on Mrs Jenkins, and Mrs Granger who has been bording at Mrs Jenkins for a week past waiting an opportunity of getting a boat. I was so successful as to procure one for her.[64] to Morrow afternoon she leaves on the *New Orleans*[65] to rejoin her husband in New Orleans.

Returned home about 9. passed an hour or so in the parlour with the Ladies, then to bed. Exp 5c.

Saturday 6th

Received a note to day from Scott saying He would be in Town next week and pay me. Weather Clear and Cold. business fair.

The Evening I passed with my friend Charles Herbst in the Theatre, in the American (late Atheneum). Witnessed the musical abortion of *Blue Beard.* the extra incidents in this piece such as one of the Horses falling from the Staging, and the wrong and Confused Maneuvering of <u>Hot House</u> Soldiers were worth more than the piece.[66] Went hom ½ past 10 oclock. Expense 1.10c

Sunday 7th.

I was at home till past 11, than went up to Henry's where I dined and passed the afternoon. my Fathers Brothers Child, Marianne, was there also.[67] I bid her an eternal *adieu,* as I am not likely to see her again. Had supper at Kattenhorn's. went home about 8 oclock, read for Charles and Harry[68] until 11. Then tired and Weary went to Bed. Exp 0000

Monday January 8th 1849

During last night it snowed a little, but this Morning it was quite mild altho' cloudy. Commerce makes but a poor Commencement this Morning. for myself I have no reason to Complain as my good friend Franck Puthoff had the goodness to send me my money this Morning by his Son in law. Two hundred Dollars are by no means to be sneezed at in these Cholera times. immediately after dinner I took I took the money up to Henry. I deposited Mr Potters check dated the 14th of January with him last Friday. this with Beckers two Notes makes 435 dollars that Nulsen and Mersman[69] at present hold of my Money. they have promised to pay me at the rate of 3 per ct *per Annum* until I want to use it.

The Evening I passed with in the National Theatre with Hal— we got in with a Jolly crew there, all English men. Mr Murdochs efforts were eminently successfull. He played Walter Raymond in the Play of this Name, and Dick Dashall in *My Aunt.* After Performance Concluded about ½ past 10, instead of going home we went to Thompson's,[70] spree'd it there till ½ past 11. I was heavenly, having imbibed 4 Gin Cock-Tails.[71] Exp 90c.

Tuesday 9th.

I did not feel the effects of last nights dissipation at all this Morning. Business was slightly dull. Weather intensely Cold, dealing death and destruction to Cholera. After supper I went Madam Ablamowicz grand Concert of Sacred music.[72] I went to my flute Teacher[73] to play some flute Duetts with him. To Bed 10. Exp 10c.

Wednesday January 10th. 1849.

Weather Continues very Cold. Ice floating quite thick in the river, so that navigation is considerably impeded by it. Whiskey is slightly dull again. The Evening I passed at home, having a lesson from Moulinier. did not go out afterwards, but retired to bed 10. Exp—5c

Thursday 11th.

I sent a Note out to E. W. Scott to day. he being at P. Andrew's, returned an answer the He would Certainly Call on Saturday this week and settle it. Weather very cold. Whiskey down to 14¾ again. River nearly blocked up with Ice. The Evening I passed in the National witnessing Mr Murdoch in two of his favorite pieces, *Walter Raymond* and *The Dramatist.* The first piece did not amuse me as much as on last Monday. it was not given so spiritedly as then. Went direct home. To bed at 11. Expense— 80 cts.

Friday 12th

Weather is moderating again. bot this Morning 103 bbls Whiskey at 14½. advanced afterwards to 14¾ at which it closed firm.[74] Business More brisk. After supper I went with Charles Herbst to Madam Ablamowicz grand Concert of Sacred Music at the Presbn Church on 9th Street.[75] She had a Crowded "House" or rather church. Her recitative Solo's I did admire. She embelishes where embelishment is not intended. went home with a severe head-ache about ½ past 10. No Expense—

Saturday January 13th 1849.

Hal Brayley returned last night about 2 o'clock. poor Fellow! he was half froze to death. This Morning it is raining freely, Ice and other tokens of frost rapidly disapearing from the streets. business more animated as there is no longer any apprehension of suspension of navigation.[76] Commerce with us is "no whar"— The Evening I passed in my room. I gave an oyster supper to four of friends, Charles Herbst, Harry Brayley, Charles Moulinier and James Waddle. We had a capital time of it. the oysters were put up in fine style by our accommodating cook Peggy. about 12 we broke up perfectly satisfied. The scrape cost me 1.75.

Sunday 14th.

Very disagreable Weather Sleeting nearly the entire day. The forenoon I passed at home copying Liquor Receipts [recipes] I bot from Harry Brayley and two wine receipts I received from a German yesterday for which I gave him 2$. Harry did not charge me any thing, altho' his recipe's are of value.[77] Dinner I had at home. immediatly afterwards I went up to Henry's. He was not at home. Frank was tuning his Piano. Daddy looking at him and smoking like a young Steam Boat. about 3, August's Sweetheart and Louisa, our old Louisa![78] arrived to pay their respects. after having partaken of Coffee we all sat down to the Table and played "Old Maid" Luck was against Daddy and the Girls. went home in time for Supper.

The Evening I passed in the Parlour with the Ladies weather being too bad to go out. To Bed 11. No Expense.

Monday January 15, 1849

Commerce made but a poor Commencement. as the time for my departure approaches, I begin to lose my usual interest in the Business and almost wish I was out of it.

The Evening I and Charles H. passed in the National witnessing the almost unsurpassable *Monplaisir Troupe* in the Pantomime *Le Diable à quatre.* Some of the Dances were really unsurpassable and were received with deaffening applause. my dry friend Burkhardt was there also. we were home at ½ past 10. Exp 50 cts.

Tuesday 16th

Business quite dull. The River in spite of the very Cold Weather continues rising and is already very high. After Supper I called on Toney Nulsen at the Store. From there I went to my old Barber Juda[79] and had my Hair cropped. 9 I was at home, 10 in bed. Exp 20c

Wednesday 17th

Commerce really does not deserve attending to. Very Cold, no prospect of moderation. Had a french lesson, which I finished rather abruptly as I had to be ready at 7 to go the National with Hal—

The *Monplaisir's* did their best to please a large and fashionable Audience. Danced the various *Pas* introduced in *L'Almée,* with a grace and perfection unsurpassable. The *petite operette of Poor Soldier* was also well performed. I went home about 11 highly satisfied with every thing. Exp 75 cents.

Thursday January 18th 1849

This day is my 10th anniversary at Mr Dexters. I entered my present situation on the 18th January 1839. Never shall I pass another with him. may the Same kind God who has so far favoured me so Much continue to bestow his favours on me.

Business was a little better to day. Weather very Cold. River still rising. The Evening I and Charles Herbst passed with our mutual friend Joseph Marsh.

about 9 we all rolled around to the American *La belle restaurat* togather. tippled very Sociably togather there till nearly ½ past 10. Exp 40c.

Friday 19th

River still rising. Whiskey to day was brisk at 15⅛. Business improving. Weather is moderating. towards Evening it had the appearance of Snowing.

I and Hal Brayley went to the Atheneum, *pour voir*[80] *Dombey & Son* lately dramatised, and *The Forty Thieves.* after the first piece which proved to be a poor attempt, we took a good Horn. We took a Seat in a different part of the House. I noticed a woman Setting in a Seat before us, looking at me very attentively. as the piece was drawing to a close she leaned back and requesting me to walk home with her, observing at the same time that her Companion had evidently abandoned her. She had the appearance of being a decent Country woman, and like an innocent young man gave her my Arm as soon as the Play was over. She boarded at the Planters House. on the way she kept squeesing my arm. I knew I had a chance, went up Stairs with and to bed also, gave her two rounds. then jumped up, gave her a dollar, took a Horn below, was home as the Clock struck 12. Exp 2.10.

Saturday January 20th, 1849.

Confound this weather. The Cold drissling rain during the night had made the Pavements so Slippery that it was difficulte to walk On it. Saw a Corpulent Chap fall corner Sycamore and 3rd. He rolled halfway down to lower Market ere he could regain his feet. My Cash balanced quite accurately to day. Business was dull.

The Evening I passed in the Parlour, studying my french lesson. 10 oclock I was in bed. No Expense.

[Margin note] Paid Ross for Boarding to date inclusive—

Sunday January 21st 1849.

Mild, moderate, foggy weather. was up in time for the regular breakfast, a fact well worth noticing. The Morning I passed entirely at home. towards 11 oclock Charles Moulinier came to give me a french lesson. I was just going to Commence dressing myself. Finished by half past 12. Immediatly after dinner I went up to Henry's was there the entire afternoon without any Company or amusement whatever except the Doctor as Henry's little [girl] is sick, and Miss Lange[81] who was reported to be handsome, but any Girl who looks with her right Eye on the left side Can not lay great claims to beauty. Frank came home to supper. He had been at Benders all afternoon. Left there about half past 6. Called on my "Sham Wife" Sarah Cook.[82] She certainly looked handsomer this Evening than I have ever seen her. We passed a very pleasant Evening togather In spite of her Married Sister who had not the good sense to leave us alone. I punished her by Staying till past 10 oclock. Went direct home to Bed. No Expense.

Monday January 22nd, 1849

Business commenced very actively this Morning. by the bye when I awoke it was ¼ before 8.[83] fortunately my second self "Billy"[84] came just about the same time.

The Evening I passed in my room having a set of jolly acquaintances to play Euchre with. we amused ourselves Capitally till 11, when at request of their Host my good friends had the goodness to retire. I beleive I got to sleep by ½ past 11. Exp 5c

Tuesday 23rd

This Confounded Man Scott has not paid me yet. I must push him now, or loose the 220$. Clemens[85] is somewhat tardy also, ought to have had a letter ere now.

Was busy the whole day, no spare time in the Store for me, when there is any business doing.

The Evening I passed at home writing my french exercises and also this, and yesterdays Entry. Shall be in bed by 10 as I do not intend to go out. No Expense.

Wednesday 24th

The Lord knows what trouble this day will bring forth. Should it be his Supreeme will, He can make it a day of Joy. Glory be to his Name![86] It was wet and Sloppy. business dull. The Evening I passed entirely at home, being occupied in the early part with my French Teacher. We endeavoured to get up a game of Whist, but could'nt come it. Passed balance of evening in the parlour. about ½ past 10 I retired to bed quite tired. Expense 30c

Thursday January 25th, 1849.

Weather very damp and disagreable, raining at intervals throughout the day. River at Pittsburgh rising again, altho' still of sufficient hight for navigable purposes. Commerce was dull. our days business was tolerbly fair.

The Evening I, Charles and Hal[87] passed in the National Theatre. the principal attraction that induced us to go was *A Glance at N. Y.* Chapman as Mose,

Mrs C. as Lize: It being a rainy Evening that attendance was rather limited. The Scenery was far superior to its former production at Atheneum, altho' the acting hardly as good. Went direct home. Exp 50

Friday January 26th.

The afternoon I passed in a magistrates office, being Witness in case. *Ed Dexter v.s. Steamer Phoenix.*[88] heard some interesting and valuable legal opinion as to liability of Steam Boat Owners for the doings of their Clerks and Captains. was persuaded by Henry to go to a German Ball given for the benefit of the German emegration Society. Got there about ½ past 8. The *Liedertafel* was just treating the Audience to some of their most finished Efforts, after which the familly Strasser[89] contributed all in their power. Henry took his Wife Home. returned just as the dancing Commenced. Frank was also there, Tony, Wagner, Tiesing[90] and in fact quite a Host of acquaintances both Male and female.

Miss G~~rotho~~ [Grothouse] contributed extensively towards my enjoyment. my old Sweetheart Miss Meyer[91] was there. my old Love sweet Kate D[92] was certainly the handsomest Woman there. I danced with nearly all my female friends, wishing to make them all friends before going away. To Bed 4. Exp 3$

Saturday January 27th 1849.

I was up this Morning in time for the usual breakfast and in Store about the usual time. I hardly experienced the effects of last nights fatigue. Business pleasantly dull. Went out to Andrew for the purpose seeing Scott. waited until I did see him. He promises faithfully to pay me next week. Moulinier called immediatly after supper but not having studied any thing, of course could not take a Lesson. about 8 I, Charles and Moulinier went and indulged in a refreshing Bath at the Arcade.[93] from there I went direct home with my Bedfellow Charles.[94] Exp 35c

Sunday January 28th.

Was a Cloudy unpleasant day. The forenoon I passed at home until about 11 oclock, picking out all the Piano music belonging to Frank and some that I intended to present him with. about 11 I went up to Henry's Store, taking the music with me. Frank was there alone. we went up to Henry's House. He, himself was not at home, probably at Toney's playing Cards. I did not Stay for dinner. his wife appeared somewhat out of humour. Had my dinner at Kattenhorns. they had just gone to bed to indulge in their Customary afternoon's Nap. I went home from there with Charles, to Charles Moulinier. We were most deliciously treated by Mrs. M. Charleys Mother. Cakes, preserves, brandy peaches were profusely distributed. about 4 we all went to see our old friend Tappe. He has a Lot of Guitars nearly finished out of which I am promised a "Pick." Supper was given me at Kattenhorns. played Cards there till 7. went and Called on Miss Cook, was so unfortunate as to find her out. returned to K's where I Played Cards till 9. Then direct home. No Exp.

Monday January 29th 1849.

Business Commenced very dull this Week. how it will End I can not say, as I shall quit it forever on Thursday.

After supper I and Charles[95] had a visit from Marsh who detained me at home till it was too late to do any thing. we amused ourselves however Capittally Criticising or rather slandering old Mrs Mosher. About 8 I went up to Kochs to have some old Clothes repaired. they had already Closed. I left 'em in care of their Sister. from there went to the Mercantile Reading Room,[96] got interested in the French Journals. from there direct home. to bed 10. Exp 5c.

Tuesday 30th.

Rainy disagreable Weather all day. we did nothing except ship a 100 bbls Whiskey.

After supper I went with [Hal Brayley] to the American. The great attraction there was *The Buckey Gold Diggers* or *Dutchy in California*.[97] the entertainment commenced with *Love in all Corners*, an amusing and laughable farce. Mrs Adams appeared to decided advantage in it. I noticed Mr Dexter there also. presume he came merely to take charge of Mrs A— between 1st & 2nd piece I and Hal found some mutual acquaintances, some who had already explored the regions above, the abode of Angels of Paradise.[98] of course we could not resist the temptation of paying these accommodating beings a visit. There was a collection of 30 to 40 Members of this independent order of odd Women,[99] some beautiful and Choice specimens. None of us felt inclined however to patronise them. The Bar up Stairs is very handsomely furnished, and I suppose supplied with good liquor. I drank Ale. went direct home in bed at 11. Exp 45c

Wednesday January 31st, 1849

This is my last day Servitude. I have now been with Mr Dexter 10 years and 13 days, having entered his service January 18th 1839. Ten years! what a long time to look forward to, but alas how brief, when looked back upon. I can not realise that I have been there 10 years, and but for this valuable Journal would not know how time had passed, what had occupied my mind during leisure hours. I certainly am in possession of a great deal of knowledge and some few accomplishments of which I was then ignorant. in fact as my early education had been totally neglected, I had nothing to boast of except plenty of space in my cranium to put knowledge into, and I can not but attribute it to Mr Dexters judicious advice and recommendations, that I have so incessantly applied myself and have become what I at present am, i.e. fully competent to Cope with the world, and fight my way with the permission and blessings of the Allmighty towards an easy Competence.

We were Somewhat busy during the afternoon. in the Evening we balanced our monthly Cash account. every thing Came out Correct. I delivered my keys to Mr Dexter. He locked the doors himself. to Morrow My old friend Moulinier will take my place. may He fill it, and keep it, with as much honor and satisfaction to all parties, as I have done. I had just finished my Supper when Marsh Called. we took a short walk to my Tailors returned home by way of St Charles, where we indulged in a "Horn," had a long Talk with him about Miss Grener.[100] poor Marsh is in love. To Bed at 11. Exp 15¢.

Cincinnati February 1st 1849

I was just dressed in time for breakfast, and hard Scratching at that. Until I am established in St Louis I shall have no commercial proceedings to note. During the day I called on some of my friends. in the Afternoon wrote a letter to Clemens, concerning business only. After supper I and Hal called on Mrs Mosher. The entire familly was sick, the old women flattered herself that she was troubled with Cholera. Mary and Libby[101] were also quite unwell—Mrs Jacobus any thing but healthy. Miss Grener was the only one who bore up with a firm will against a Severe Cold. We did not Stay long. ½ past 8 we were seated in Mr Waddle's room playing Whist. Home at 11. Exp for Music 2.25.
[Margin note] Music purchased 2.25.

Friday 2nd Feby.

Up in time for breakfast. raw disagreable weather throughout the day. The Morning I passed at the Rail Road Depot, or rather in Andrews office, waiting for E. W. Scott. He did not Come in. I waited until 12 oclock, Then returned home. If he does not pay me shortly now I must sue him—and will. Immediately after dinner I arranged all my letters. my future one's will be mostly business Letters. No letter yet from Clemens. The Evening I and Charles Herbst passed in the National. it was Harry Chapmans Benefit. Mrs Drake, Harry's Mother in law, appeared in *The Mother's Revenge* a thrilling piece, with which the adience seemed to be highly delighted. in Conclusion *Poor Pillicoddy* by Harry. all were pleased with it. To Bed 11. Exp 60 c.

Cinc'ti February 3rd, 1849

Most beautiful and lovely Morning. I and Charles did not get up in time for breakfast. Half past 9 I was at the Rail Road waiting for Scott. he came there about 11, promised to procure the money during the day. I hurried up to Kattenhorns to get some dinner, and by 1 I was back at the R.R. S[cott] did not Come until 4 o'clock, and then he was *Sans l'argent.*[102] He ordered Mr Andrew to pay over to me the receipts of next weeks Whiskey.[103] The Evening I passed in my room entertaining a party of young Men with Whist and Euchre. also wrote a letter to Charles Underwood. To bed ½ past 11. Exp 10.

Sunday February 4th.

Got up at 8 oclock this Morning. Half past 9 Mr Marsh called. about 10 I was ready—upon referring to my Journal I find with regret that it is nearly a year since I went to a Catholic Church for the purpose a Christian should go. Rev Mr Wood delivered the Sermon, which was tedious and at no point very bright.

Charles Moulinier was Waiting for me when I came out. he accompanied me as far as my Sisters. I had my Dinner there, rather later than the rest.

The Company that was expected did not arrive until 3. that part of it Constituting the Male Sex Amused itself with playing Cards. I, Kattn, Wagner, Tiesing, Duhme,[104] and Daddy. little frank was up-Stairs playing with the Girls.[105] 4 oclock we had Coffee, ½ past 6 Tea. for an hour and a half or so the back Parlour was abandoned to the Children, one playing on the Piano, the others dancing. 10 I was home and in bed—I was! No Expense.

Monday, February 5th 1849.

This Morning I woke about 7, was astonished to find it so light and brilliant out doors. upon looking out I found about 3 inches Snow on the ground. appearances indicate more of it. had the ground been frozen we should have had some fine sleigh riding— about 9 I and Charles went to Peters Music Store. bot Music to the Amount of 95 cts, all for Guitar. Called on Profr Bartlett at his Commercial Rooms. He showed us a very superior interest Table.[106] Called on Henry during the forenoon. was home again by 11. arranged [and] sowed a Lot of German

Papers I have before dinner. Called at Mr Dexters after it, found no Letter from Clemens. The Afternoon I passed in my room arranging and binding my Music.

After supper I called Sarah Cook. I never saw the young Lady so reserved, modest and well behaved. rather suspect that my friend Charles Moulinier has given her hopes of which of which I certainly Never thought. I left about 9 oclock, went to the reading room, found my Christian friend Mr Marsh there also. We Amused ourselves Capittally in looking over a Fac Semile of General Washingtons Accounts with the U.S. during the Revolutionary War.[107] And that Splendid Collection of Indian Portraits painted by Lieutenant Wilkes Exploring Expedition.[108] We Started for home about ½ past 10. Stopped at the St. Charles.[109] Marsh treated. Miss Deans portrait hangs very prominent there. it is raffled out, valed [valued] at 100$. 20 Chances, 5$ per Chance. I am not in. In Bed at 11. did not go to Sleep till 12. Exp 100.

Tuesday Feb 6, 1849

It is very Cold this Morning. Houses and out of the Way Streets are still Cov'red with Snow. The River is at present higher than it has been this Winter. Still rising here, but falling at Pittsburgh. I was up and dressed this Morning in time for the regular breakfast.

The Morning I passed at home binding Music. about ½ past 2 P.M. although very Cold I went out to P. Andrew in order to dun my neglegent friend Scott for my 220$. He has at last succeeded in selling his Hogs to Mr Bogan and Made arrangements with him to pay my Claim. to Morrow I shall Call on Mr Bogan and see what my prospects are now. No Letter yet from Clemens—After supper I and Hal went to Mr Waddle's Room, where we Amused ourselves excellently playing Whist with a mighty dirty Pack of Cards. From there direct home. To Bed 10. Exp—

Wednesday Feb 7th

Last night was Certainly the Coldest this Winter. a few such will fill the river with Ice. During the forenoon I dodged around the Market House to find Butcher George Bogan. did not succeed. Immediately after dinner I and Charles H[erbst] Walked out to their Factory,[110] situated slightly beyond the Brighton House. gained nothing for my trouble but his promise to pay me as soon as Scott brings his hogs.

After supper I, Hal and Charles called on Waddle, but were surprised he had broken appointment. McDade[111] treated the Crowd When we left about 10 oclock.

Thursday February 8th 1849.

Weather not so very Cold as yesterday. I passed the entire forenoon at N[ulsen] & M[ersman]'s Store. I permitted myself to be informed this [morning] by our Letter-carrier that the St Louis Mail has failed for the last 6 days. Immediately after dinner I and Charley H[erbst] went to my brother's House, took Therefrom my Guitar, and transported it ourselves to our friend Tappe who has agreed to exchange it. He will have four or five ready next week. After supper Hal, Charley[112] and my extensive Self went to the National Theatre. The first, a very good Farce *Day after the Wedding,* was very creditably played by Jackson and Miss Mathews.[113] *The Fair One with Golden Locks* followed, principal character by Placide. This Burlesque Tragedy seemed to please every one. To Conclude *The Man and the Tiger* an English Comedy of some merit. I certainly did not anticipate to be so well amused. To bed 11. Exp. 40c.

Friday 9th.

This Morning was clear sunshiny, but damn Cold. As soon as I receive a letter from Clemens I shall know what to do. I did not go out, except a few minutes to the Commercial Reading room.[114] Studied French all forenoon. After Dinner I went in the 1st place to Henry's Store, then to Kattenhorn. The Old fellow was slightly inclined to tipsyness. He made me offers of Service such buying raw Whiskey for me. Anyhow I have his good will.

During the Evening I visited my old friend Diek. His Wife Seems to Stand Matrimony well. She looks far more *Embonpoint.*[115] Nay—She is really thicker. 9 I was home, was in the parlour till nearly 11, then to Bed. Exp 5c. Paid Ross for Boarding to date 4$.

Saturday January [February] 10th 1849.

Most beautiful and lovely Morning, although rather Cold for a Slow Walker. The greater part of the day I passed in N[ulsen] & M[ersman]'s Store. Nulsen's brother[116] was there all forenoon, explaining the existing disadvantages of his present partnership. He offered to consign Lard oil to myself and Clemens.

Comerford[117] called there about ½ past 2. We made no arrangement as I have not yet received any thing from Clemens. During the greater part of the afternoon I was employed in contracting with C' about Cisterns and rects and writing a letter to Clemens again. This makes 3 that I have written to him without receiving any reply.

Marsh called on us after supper. We Went to Derby Bradley & Co's Book Store. I bot a Collection of Old English Plays in 12 vol's and Willis' Works[118] in one, all for 8 dollars. from [there] to the Reading Room.[119] Saw Wm Lacy and Mulholland. from there to St Charles.[120] ½ past 10 in bed. Exp 15c.

Sunday 11th.

Beautiful Weather. I called on Lacy, but Mrs Moshers house has only a broken Bell Pull so I could not get in. from there went to the River. nothing unusual going on there. About 11 I went to Kattenhorns, where I had dinner. half an hour afterwards I went to Henry's. He was just ready to go out. We went to Toney's.[121] Nulsen was there already. Henry, Nulsen, Ficke and two Frenchmen Commenced playing Torock, a new German Game at Cards.[122] I and Frank play'd Draft.[123] I could'nt stand it long. So I and Frank Went to Kattenhorns, where we played Cards for fun. Had a good Supper there, after which we played again. 9 oclock I was home and ½ past in bed. Exp 10c.

Monday Feb 12th 1849

The Morning opened beautifully. I was up early. after breakfast I called at My old place. Mr Dexter was Sick, having a very Severe Cold. Went with Charles Moulinier to the Post office. No Mail from St. Louis. from there to N[ulsen] & M[ersman] where I passed the principal part of the forenoon. Had dinner at home. After it, I went to Koch's my Tailors. returned them a Shirt I bot last Saturday, which did not fit me, and bot 4 others that are warrented to fit. from there to N & M. about 4 oclock I and Henry went to Charley Kopf, to See about Some Wines. We are to Call again to Morrow at 4 P.M. Went to Herman Wellman who has rented the large Hall in Fortman's[124] new building. he intends to have 4 Tables[125] up in a short time, and expects them to Clear about 10$ a day, with an invested Capital of 12 to 14 hundred Dollars. I and Henry played Two games. he lost one and I do [ditto], but he gave me 50 in the 100—Had Supper at Henry's, Met Shotwell and Lacy on Walnut. took them to the Ale house under the Melodeon which cost me 15 cts. Home 10 oclock to bed ½ past. Exp 50c.

Tuesday 13th.

Beautiful Mild Weather, although towards Evening very Cold. I received two letters from Clemens this Morning. the damn Scoundrell who owns the house we intended [to rent] asks 1200 dollars Rent for it. during the forenoon I was occupied writing a letter to Clemens. Called on Mr Dexter after dinner. he advised going to St Louis personally, which advise I shall follow. Pack up as Soon as possible and per first boat go. The Evening I and Marsh and Hal passed at Mrs Mosher's. I might enjoy some sexual fun there, had I time to cultivate it. To Bed 11 oclock Expense for the day 60 cts

Wednesday 14th February 1849

I made a most Confounded mistake there in the previous entry every thing I said there belongs in to days. to day I had Clemen's letters. This Evening I was at Mosher's. last Evening I and Hal were in the Atheneum. yesterday I passed at Henry's Store principally, and in the Evening I and Hal, Bill Lacy and Shotwell amused ourselves Excellently in admiring *Ernest Maltravers* and *Last Days of Pompie.* Exp 50.

Thursday Feb 15th.

To Day I was most Confounded busy, endeavouring to get ready for this evenings boat but Could not do so. I had Dinner at Kattenhorns. immidiately after it took an Omnibus and rode out to G[eorge] & P[eter] Bogans. was so fortunate as to find Scott there and above all so extreemely fortunate as to get my Money, my Dear 220 Dollars. as soon as I could, I returned to Messrs Nulsen & Mersman, gave the Money to Nulsen, and as part was in checks, He took it direct to the Bank. Then went down to Mr Dexter, settled with him. He allowed me 75$ for the last Month, and paid me 133 dollars.[126] from here I went to H[enry] & J[ohn] Koch. my Account with them was just 68 dollars. I paid them 18 dollars in money and my Note payable August 8th for 50 dollars,[127] and received their Receipt in full. returned to N & M's paid Nulsen 15 Dollars borrowed Money, 3.50 cents due for One box Cigars, and 45 dollars to my deposit fund. They have now in their possession 700 dollars of my own Money, and 500 dollars belonging to Father, which makes 1200 dollars, to be paid to me whenever I demand it. The evening I and Charles H[erbst] passed at his Aunts Mrs Arons, making Music. To bed 10 oclock. Exp 5c.

Friday February 16th, 1849

Very Cold Weather, and quite disagreable, being both Windy and dusty. in spite these drawbacks, General Taylor,[128] who arrived about 9 oclock A.M. had the most enthusiastic reception, ever given here to mortal Man. The number of People in the streets exceeded by far the entire number drawn togather by Harrison, Van Buren, and Jas. K. Polk.[129] I and Moulinier went to Mr Dexters House, where, after waiting an hour or so, we had a full view of him as the procession moved on. in fact, I suppose in honor, and out of gallantry to the many Ladies he saw standing in Mrs Dexters Parlours, He Stop'd before the House a

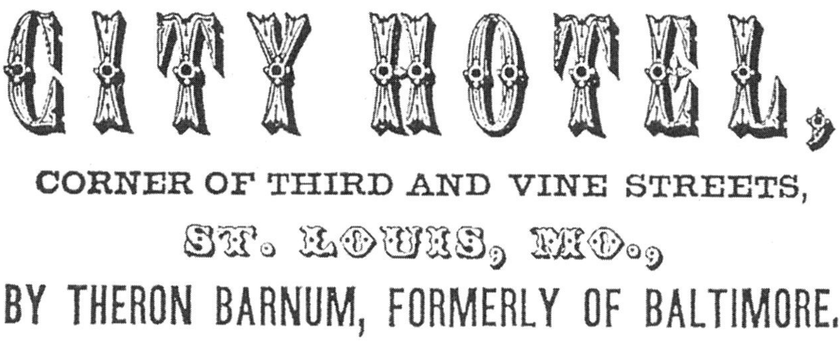

City Hotel advertisement, 1851. This St. Louis hotel offered both lodging and food. It was located at the corner of Third and Vine streets. (Missouri Historical Society, St. Louis.)

few minutes, but being So beseiged by the Crowd who desired to Shake hands with him, the old Gentleman motioned the driver to proceed. He was kissed by every Lady in the Pearl St House on entering the Parlour.

I shall not be able to go until next week, and about 9 oclock this Morning I telegraphed[130] Clemens to this effect.

The Evening I and Hal Spent at Mrs Mosher's, playing Whist with Miss Greener and Mrs Ernst, Wife to my old dancing Master. from there direct home. To bed 11 oclock. Exp 5c.

[Margin note] Deposited with A[nthony] Nulsen 40$ for Safe-Keeping until I go. J.J.M.

Saturday February 17, 1849.

Early in the Morning I went to the River and ascertained that the *Thos Jefferson*[131] leaves on Monday. If she does, I shall go with her. during the principal part of the day I was busy packing up my books, of which I have a larger pile than I immagined. towards Evening I called on Henry's Wife at her new dwelling on Centre St.[132] went home to Supper.

The Evening I and Hal passed in the National Theatre[133] admiring Mr. Logans new piece, *1949*. It is very good. To bed 11. Exp including for Washing to date 1.45c.

NOTES

1. Nulsen and Mersman saw no ethical dilemma in basing their fortunes on the sale of alcoholic beverages. Ironically, four of Nulsen's siblings (Francis, Philippina, Amalia, and Henry) had converted to German Methodism shortly after arriving in Cincinnati and were strict teetotalers. Two of them

(Amalia and Henry) went to St. Louis as missionaries in the 1840s, but the community was large enough to absorb both types of Nulsens, the drinkers and the nondrinkers.

Amalia and her husband, Dr. Ludwig S. Jacoby (1813–74), returned to Europe in 1849 and introduced Methodism to German-speaking lands during the next twenty-two years. Henry converted to Methodism in 1843, assisted Jacoby in St. Louis, and in 1851 began thirty-eight years of mission work in Europe (Barclay, 3:982–98; Simpson, 490–91; Douglass, 50–56, 117, 127; Ludwig Jacoby file, MHS vertical file; "Rev. Henry Nuelsens Letztes Dictat," April 1911, Nippert Collection of German Methodism, 1779–1974, box 3–68, folder 3, CHS; WPO, 21 August 1911; GLO, 21 August 1911).

2. A laborer who worked for Henry Mersman.

3. Anthony Nulsen's wife.

4. Charles Herbst.

5. Loo, a card game for up to seventeen players, uses a hand of three or five cards. If less than five play, a deck of thirty-two cards is used; otherwise a deck of fifty-two cards is dealt (Beaver [2], 109–11; Hoyle, 264–67).

6. Poker, a card game for two to fourteen players, uses a deck of fifty-two. Each player endeavors to hold a better poker hand of five cards than any other player (Hoyle, 5–27).

7. The *Cincinnati Enquirer* on 9 March 1848 warned readers about instances of "open barefaced robbery by the gentlemanly game of poker" played on steamboats. "[These cardsharps] . . . are a nuisance—an unnecessary evil—and should be banished from all the boats."

8. The Louisville and Portland Canal, built in 1830, enabled steamboats to bypass the Falls of the Ohio (Yater, 38–39). Steamboats paid a toll of fifty cents per ton (Hall, 82). In 1848, 1,523 steam boats and 248 flatboats and keelboats passed through, paying tolls that totaled $158,068 (LCD 1851–52, 21).

9. Louisville was founded at the mouth of the Beargrass Creek in 1773 (Clark, 240).

10. The Jefferson County Courthouse, begun in 1837, was finally completed in Louisville, Kentucky, in 1859 (Yater, 78).

11. James D. "Jim" Porter (1810–59), who stood seven feet nine inches, weighed 300 pounds. Known as the Kentucky Giant, he took up innkeeping in 1848 at Porter's Tavern on Front Street in Shippingport, below the Falls of the Ohio ("Jim Porter," vertical file, Filson Club Historical Society).

12. A dray is a heavy, sometimes two-wheeled, cart used for hauling. The pin is a rod extending from the cart to which a team of horses is tied (OED, s.v. "dray," "pin").

13. *Mathilda,* a popular novel by Mary Shelley, was first published in 1817.

14. "Punkins" (pumpkins) was a common term of endearment (see COM, 15 September 1848).

15. See chapter 1, note 36.

16. The shop was too small to accommodate rectifying equipment, including a still.

17. The former Caroline, Baroness Hornig von Hornburg, Mrs. Karl Friedrich Creuzbauer was from a distinguished military family of the Grand Duchy of Baden (today a part of the state of Baden-Württemberg in southern Germany).

18. Claudine Creuzbauer, JJM's future wife. JJM does not identify her by name until the entry dated 12 June 1850.

19. Most likely Edmund Creuzbauer.

20. Albertine Creuzbauer Nulsen.

21. *Ivanhoe,* a popular novel by Sir Walter Scott (1771–1832), was first published in 1819.

22. Possibly Ferdinand Braun, a wholesale grocer and liquor dealer (Braun, Krug & Co), at 32 and 34 Main Street (SLD 1851, 63).

23. The new partners chose the same name as the Cincinnati partnership of their older brothers, Anthony Nulsen and Henry Mersman.

24. August Rittmeyer, JCN's clerk, was born in Nörten, in the Kingdom of Hanover, JCN's hometown, and had earlier worked for N & M (Cincinnati).

25. The *Whirlwind,* a 226-ton sidewheel packet with a wooden hull, was built in Elizabeth, Pennsylvania, in 1846. It ceased operation by 1853 (Way #5762, 484–85).

26. *Les amours du chevalier de Faublas,* a popular novel by Jean-Baptiste Louvet de Couvray (1760–97), was first published in 1825.

27. The Ohio River was high enough for the steamboat to bypass the Louisville and Portland Canal and take the more dangerous route directly over the rapids.

28. The doctor, or main feed water pump of a steamboat, was a high-pressure source of water for the boilers (http://www.steamboats.com).

29. William McHugh, the drayman.

30. JJM's former landlady, Mrs. Mosher, who had leased the boardinghouse, had cash-flow problems and was forced to terminate her business.

31. Harry Brayley.

32. At Ross's Boarding House.

33. Charles Herbst.

34. Probably Charles Herbst and Hal Brayley.

35. Henry Mersman.

36. Anthony Nulsen.

37. Sarah Cook.

38. Harry Brayley and Charles Herbst.

39. Possibly Michael Frintz, a German-born tailor ten years older than JJM (USC 1850, M432, roll 689, page 124, line 32).

40. See map 4.

41. In the months of December, January, and February, when the demand for oysters was greatest, Cincinnati received twenty-five barrels of shell oysters and 2,560 cans of shucked oysters per day. Although the shell oysters were consumed locally, many canned oysters were shipped to other towns in the interior. As a result, the supply—about a quarter million per day—did not keep up with the demand (Cist [3], 366–67).

42. JJM bought Christmas presents for his sister Elizabeth Kattenhorn and her two daughters, Sophia and Louisa Kattenhorn, who were approximately twelve and fourteen years old.

43. An annual is a journal (OED, s.v. "annual").

44. Cholera, spread by contaminated food and water, was carried by infected passengers and crews on steamboats. The residents of Cincinnati read newspaper articles that reported the disease was approaching ever closer, but were unable to stop the outbreak from reaching their community (COM, 9 September 1848, 27 and 29 December 1848).

45. The *Liedertafel* Singing Society gave an annual ball at Christmas.

46. Louisa Kattenhorn, JJM's niece, was not the object of his romantic interest, but she was available for the first dance.

47. Anthony Nulsen.

48. Mary Remlinger was a twenty-year-old German immigrant who lived in a boardinghouse next door to Henry Mersman (USC 1850, M432, roll 687, page 134, line 3).

49. Around 1845 Johnson & Nulsen had operated a tobacco shop on Walnut Street between Franklin and Second streets (CCD 1846, 220).

50. According to the newspapers, the fire started in James Calhoun's store (the Queen City Varnish Company) on Walnut Street and then spread to Banning's cheese warehouse and Sabin's commission house. Firemen saved the property from total destruction (CCD 1848–49, 182; COM, 29 December 1848).

51. The fair, for the benefit of the Cathedral School House, had taken eight months of planning by women of the congregation (ENQ, 7 May 1848).

52. Named for the Ohio River ("La Belle Rivière" or "the beautiful river" immortalized in Longfellow's poem), the restaurant was out of business by 1853 (Longfellow, 107–9).

53. Even the physician had cash-flow problems, so he wrote a postdated check.

54. The threat of cholera discouraged many from going to New Orleans (COM, 6 January 1849).

55. A benefit performance at the National Theatre for Mr. Murdoch, *Pizarro* was conflated into three acts (COM, 30 December 1848).

56. Source text reads "1849," but it was actually the last day of the year 1848.

57. Anthony Nulsen.

58. August Schaffer worked as the stableman at the Black Bear Tavern (CCD 1846, 330).

59. JJM paid for the rental of two horses for the ride to the country.

60. Charles Herbst and Harry Brayley.

61. The Athenaeum Theatre had been refurbished in the Moorish style and reopened in December 1848. Renamed "Rockwell's New American Theatre," it had improved seating, a "gallery for colored persons," and a separate entrance to the third tier from Sixth Street (ENQ, 10 October 1848, 6 January 1849).

62. Since Andrew refused to guarantee Scott's promissory notes, payment might never be made.

63. Even offering high wages for steamboat firemen did not attract workers during the epidemic.

64. Because of the cholera outbreak, few steamboats were making New Orleans their destination. The first cases appeared in Cincinnati in late December and early January, but newspapers attempted to hide the "shameful reports" (COM, 27 December 1848 and 6, 8, 9, 10, 18, and 22 January 1849).

65. The *New Orleans,* a 299-ton sidewheel packet, routinely traveled between Cincinnati and New Orleans. Built in 1848, it sank at Cairo, Illinois, in January 1855 (Way #4178, 345).

66. "The stock companies making up the American theatre were for the most part composed of casual collections of actors and actresses whose histrionic deficiencies appear to have been monumental" (Dulles, 108).

67. JJM's uncle John Heinrich Messman (1794–1867), who had immigrated to Cincinnati in 1836, had a daughter, nineteen-year-old Marianne, born 22 December 1829 in Damme, Oldenburg (Kirchenbuch 1650–1875, Damme, Taufen 1820–39, 329, FHL 909912; Ostendorf, 256; VOL, 23 September 1867).

68. Charles Herbst and Harry Brayley.

69. Nulsen & Mersman (Cincinnati) served as JJM's bank.

70. Most likely the coffeehouse run by Peter Thompson.

71. The term "cocktails" came into use in the early 1800s (OED, s.v. "cocktail").

72. Madam Ablamowicz's concert featured selections from oratorios such as *The Messiah* and *The Creation.* A chorus of sixty amateur performers joined her (COM, 10 January 1849).

73. Professor Henry E. Sofge.

74. On this date, JJM purchased 103 barrels, each with 40 gallons, and made a profit of ¼ cents per gallon or $10.30 in a single day. That was the equivalent of a week's wages for JJM.

75. Madam Ablamowicz performed again with a chorus of sixty. Selections from Handel's *Messiah* and Rossini's *Moses in Egypt* were featured (COM, 12 January 1849).

76. If ice closed the river to traffic, merchants would be stuck with their goods.

77. Examples of such recipes are in the appendix.

78. JJM's niece, Louisa Kattenhorn, in the company of August Rittmeyer's sweetheart, was paying a social call and demonstrating that she was grown up.

79. Judah Judah's barber shop (258 Main Street) was one block north of Nulsen & Mersman's store (216 Main Street). See map 3.

80. [Fr.] to see.

81. Miss Lange has not been identified, but may be a relative of the shoemaker Christian Lange.

82. JJM and Sarah Cook had participated in a mock wedding. See JJM diary, 8 October 1848.

83. JJM overslept and was late for work. Dexter's store routinely opened by 7:30 a.m.

84. "Billy" or William McHugh was Mr. Dexter's laborer.

85. John Clemens Nulsen, JJM's new business partner, henceforth referred to as JCN.

86. The cause of this outpouring of religious fervor is unknown.

87. Charles Herbst and Hal Brayley joined JJM to see a show that began at 7:00 p.m. with a comedy, *Midnight Hour.* It was the second performance of *A Glance at New York in 1848.* Seats in the dress circle cost fifty cents, and the parquet, twenty-five (COM, 25 January 1849).

88. The sidewheel steamboat *Phoenix,* built in 1846 in Cincinnati, weighed 189 tons and made Cincinnati her home port (Lytle, 172). No documentation about the litigation has been found.

89. The Strasser family, a local group of German singers, performed in musical comedies at the German Theatre (VOL, 12 May 1848).

90. Frank Mersman (JJM's younger brother), Tony Nulsen, August Wagner, and Ernst Thiesing.

91. Miss Meyer has not yet been further identified.

92. Kate D. has not yet been further identified.

93. The Arcade Bath House offered warm baths, hair dressing, and wig making (ENQ, 29 January 1848).

94. Charles Herbst shared lodging with JJM.

95. Charles Herbst.

96. Young Men's Mercantile Library Association.

97. That evening Rockwell's Theatre offered *The Buckeye Gold Hunters, or Dutchey in California* (ENQ, 30 January 1849).

98. "The Angels of Paradise" were commercial sex workers who frequented the third tier of the theater. See chapter 1, note 27.

99. JJM jokes about the commercial sex workers by comparing them to a well-established fraternal organization, the Independent Order of Odd Fellows.

100. Miss Grener (or Greener), a boarder at Mosher's Boarding House, has not been identified.

101. Mary and Libby (Elizabeth) Mosher, both daughters of Elizabeth Mosher.

102. [Fr.] without money.

103. Scott, a farmer, anticipated converting his corn into whiskey which Andrew would purchase. Here, Scott directed that his expected income be paid directly to JJM. Bartering was the way cash-poor farmers handled many debts. See also the entry on 6 February 1848.

104. Arnd Kattenhorn, Ernst Theising, Augustus Wagner, Hermann Duhme, and Frederick Mersman spent the afternoon together.

105. JJM's brother, Frank Mersman, was playing with his nieces, Sophia and Louisa Kattenhorn.

106. An interest table helped businessmen calculate transactions.

107. *General Washington's Expense Accounts,* the personal records of Washington's expenditures during the American Revolution, was originally published by the United States Treasury in 1833. Republished in 1841 with additions, it found an enthusiastic audience among government officials and the public (Washington).

108. Charles Wilkes (1798–1877), rear admiral, United States Navy, commander of the United States Exploration Expedition, explored the Pacific Ocean and circumnavigated the globe from 1838 to 1842. Wilkes's account of the voyage, published in 1845 as *Narrative of the United States Exploring Expedition During the Years 1838, 1839, 1840, 1841, 1842,* included drawings, maps and other accounts of the trip. He completed nineteen additional volumes in the next three decades (SIL, http://www.sil.si.edu/digitalcollections/usexex).

109. The St. Charles Exchange Hotel was on JJM's way home from the Young Men's Mercantile Library Association.

110. Bogen's lard oil factory was about two miles north of JJM's Boarding House.

111. Possibly James McDade, a salesman (CCD 1853, 247).

112. Hal Brayley and Charles Herbst, residents of Ross's Boarding House, joined JJM.

113. Neither Mr. Jackson nor Miss Matthews has been further identified. Apparently they were local talent and their careers took them no further.

114. Bartlett's Commercial College, at the Melodeon Building, had a reading room (COM, 20 October 1848).

115. [Fr.] stout.

116. Tobacconist Francis Nuilsen, Anthony Nulsen's brother, partnered with Herman Ficke in a business styled as Nuilsen & Ficke (CCD 1848–49, 180).

117. Comerford made equipment used in rectifying: stills, cisterns, and vats of all sizes.

118. Nathaniel Parker Willis (1806–67) was an American poet, essayist, and dramatist.

119. Young Men's Mercantile Library Association.

120. The St. Charles Exchange Hotel.

121. Anthony Nulsen.

122. Tarock, also called tapp or frog, is played with a fifty-four-card deck. It spread from southern Germany to the United States in the nineteenth century (Parlett 266–68).

123. Drafts or draughts (checkers) is a board game for two players (OED, s.v. "draughts"; Scarne, 504).

124. Franz Fortman owned the Bavarian Brewery. See map 5.

125. For an investment of $1,400 in billiard tables, Wellman expected to clear $60 weekly or $3,120 annually. Thus, he would have a 100 percent return on his investment in just 52 weeks.

126. Mr. Dexter paid JJM seven hundred dollars annually, or fifty-eight dollars per month. JJM's wages for the two last months totaled $58 plus $75 (which included a bonus) or $133.

127. Thus, JJM benefited from an interest-free loan of fifty dollars for six months from his tailors.

128. On 6 February 1849, Zachary Taylor began his journey from Vicksburg, Mississippi, to Washington, DC, to assume the presidency. Traveling by steamboat, his journey included stops in Louisville, Madison, and Cincinnati, accompanied by parades, speeches, and receptions. On 16 February, Taylor arrived in the Queen City, and participated in a parade with the mayor, the governor, military personnel, marching bands, and civic organizations. A reception at the Masonic Hall was followed by a formal dinner at the Pearl Street House. The next morning, Taylor left for Carrollton, Kentucky, and points east. He arrived in Washington on 23 February and was inaugurated on 5 March 1849 (ENQ, 6–22 February 1849; Farrell 16).

129. William Henry Harrison, John Van Buren, and James Knox Polk each visited Cincinnati on separate occasions, and JJM compared the crowds they attracted to the numbers that Taylor drew. Harrison was honored with a large public funeral in Cincinnati in April 1841; John Van Buren drew large crowds when he campaigned for his father in 1848; and James K. Polk campaigned in Cincinnati in 1844 (Goss, 196; COM, 20 October 1848).

130. The telegraph, developed by Samuel Morse in 1844, transformed communication in the United States. By 1851, in excess of fifty telegraph companies operated around the country (Coe, 32; Scharf, 2:1422–30).

131. The *Thomas Jefferson*, a 279-ton sidewheel packet with a wooden hull, was built in Cincinnati in 1846. The boat carried passengers and freight between Cincinnati and New Orleans, but sank at Waterloo, Louisiana, in 1849 (Way #5369, 451).

132. Henry Mersman's new residence, on the north side of Center Street between Race and Elm streets, was more fashionable than his previous home above the store on Main Street.

133. A benefit for Mr. Logan, the performance featured two plays: *The Italian Wife* and *1949, or Cincinnati a Hundred Years Hence* (COM, 17 February 1849).

CHAPTER NINE

Starting in St. Louis

18 February 1849–2 August 1849

Concerned about the dangers associated with travel, JJM recorded a will in his journal. His fears were realistic, for the average steamboat survived only about four years.[1] Flimsy construction, gross overloading, and careless handling made the vessels dangerous public conveyances. Running aground, collisions, and boiler explosions were alarmingly frequent. In 1849 alone, eighty-eight steamboats were totally destroyed.[2]

JJM's destination, "The Gateway to the West," had doubled in size every decade for the previous fifty years. Now with nearly sixty-five thousand inhabitants, St. Louis was teeming with newcomers: German and Irish immigrants, as well as fortune hunters heading to California.[3] One-third of the population spoke German.[4] However, the city lacked essential services. Sewers were nonexistent, storm water collected in basements, and garbage accumulated in alleys. Few residents had public water, so most depended on wells, which often were near privies.[5]

JJM arrived in St. Louis just as another traveler appeared:[6] cholera, a disease that causes diarrhea and death due to dehydration. Spread by contaminated food and water, cholera killed 10 percent of the population, about 7,000 people, in May, June, and July.[7] In addition, a devastating fire on 17 May 1849 destroyed fifteen city blocks and twenty-three steamboats. Anti-immigrant street violence filled the summer weeks with terror.[8] JJM sometimes wrote his diary in French, trying to pass time when business came to a complete halt.

Miraculously, JJM survived the crises. When cooler weather arrived, everything improved: N & M opened their new store with great hopes. They figured that whiskey was a sure-fire money-maker—and they were right.

St. Louis levee, c. 1848. This view, looking north up the Mississippi River, shows the profusion of riverboats at the St. Louis landing. (Thomas M. Easterly, Missouri Historical Society, St. Louis.)

Sunday Friday [February] 18th 1849

Last night the Coquettish Weather treated us to 3 inches deep Snow. it continues however to be very cold. I was home until past 10 oclock, then went up to Kattenhorns, and as my new Boots pained me very much, did not go out again. it is too troublesome to walk with new Boots on a very Slippery pavement.

Although I promised Mr Wagner to call on his Wife this afternoon, I staid at K's about 3, just as we had finished our Coffee in pease, Miss Orderman the youngest and latest importation Came in.[9] She is any thing but handsome, but appears to be fully as accomplished as her Sisters, who have all been so fortunate as to get husbands. She left before Supper, I and Father immediately after it. I had to take Father home, he being uncertain whether he would be able to find the house again.[10]

Henry and Frank did not Come home to Supper. I remained there till 9 oclock, bade farewell to Adeline and her sister,[11] went direct home. wrote this notice, and as the boat will probably go to morrow, and I with her, it [may be] my last entry I shall ever write so I wished to bring it up to date of my leaving.

I have 740 Dollars with Nulsen and Mersman. 40$ of these I shall take along, leaving a balance of 700 dollars. 300 dollars I bequeth and will to my Father, 200 to my brother Frank, 200 to my Sister Agnes—Wife of Wm Lake. To my brother Henrys Wife my Gold Watch, and to my brother Henry my Guitar. To my sister Mrs. Kattenhorn all my Piano, and Piano and Flute music. My Flute and Flute Music I give to Frank on Condition that when he receives them he promises faithfully never to Sell or part with them. My books may be divided between Frank, Henry and Louisa and Sophia Kattenhorn.

Joseph J Mersman.

Saint Louis, Monday February 26th 1849

Cincinnati! thou dear native place. I we are at last Separated, perhaps never to meet again. Well! fare the well. Mayest thou Continue to advance and improve as I have witnessed thee for the past 12 years. I and you had a Sorrowful and unexpected parting on last Monday the 19th of February—I was most busily employed the entire day. as Soon as breakfast was over I and Charles H[erbst] went down to the *Thos Jefferson.*[12] The Clerk Mr Jos Avery affirmed possitively their departure this evening. Went from the boat direct to Wagners to bid farewell and to take any letter Mrs W—might have to send.[13] She had none. from there to Kattenhorns, partook of their fare, perhaps for the last time. bade them farewell immediately afterwards. Went home. had Dinner there also. I and Chas went to the boat again, as I did not intend to pack up until the last day. Captain Symmes[14] informed us, and affirmed it with an unnecessary oath that he would go this evening. Started home, packed up as quick as I could, got one of William's draymen[15] to take all my Effects on board. having seen every thing safely stowed away, I run up to N[ulsen] & M[ersman]'s Store, found Nobody there but Henry. left my respects for all enquiring friends, Shook hands with Henry. Stop'd at Dexter's. the old Man was not at home. left my regards with Charles Moulinier, bade him and all my former Domestic's farewell. Shortly after arriving at the boat Charles H[erbst] joined me. He came down to see me off. The Boat shoved off about 6. My faithful friend Charles watched my departure from off the *Memphis*[16] we Stood gazing at one-another, until darkness made us invisible.

The Ice was runing very thick, Sometimes cov'ring the entire river, and of a thickness and Solidity that made the boat Shake like a leaf to go through it. from 9 oclock till 6 next Morning, our Captain Amused himself with trying to pull the *Pike No. 7* from Shore.[17] She was aground ¾ of a mile above Lawrenceburgh, Inda. I went to bed about 10— Slept all night like a top.

Next Morning our Captain informed us that his boat was aground also, but was Confident would get her off. did So by 9 oclock, when having once more tried to pull the *Pike* off, and finding her too firmly aground, She was left to her fate. we proceeded on our way. the Ice got to be less troublesome the farther we Came down. I amused myself Capitally with reading *Cinq-Mars.*[18] went to bed at 11. it being Stormy, the boat pitched about a good deal, preventing me from Sleeping to Some extent.

Wednesday morning when I got out I found myself in Louisville. immediatly after breakfast I went to a Bookstore on Main St, and having purchased the required quantity of paper wrote a letter to Henry my brother and Charles Herbst, put them in the Post office myself, then hurried back to the boat, which was to leave at 10. had myself Shaved there by a Dutch[19] Barbier before getting on board. I need not have been in any hurry. laid there the entire day. The following Morning at 11 She left her Moorings and proceeded slowly through the Canal.[20] it wanted but 10 minutes to 4 when we were Clear of the last lock.

The balance of the way we got along tolerbly Swiftly. passed our times pretty much as time is usually passed. having finished *Cinq-Mars* I read *Fortesque,* a well written novel by Sheridan Knowles.[21] Saturday I finished the 2nd Volumn. I did not play Cards on this boat except 2 Sets of Euchre for Amusement only. refused every demand to play for Money. our boat arrived here about 2 oclock this Morning. I arose about 5, dressed, went to Clemens Store. Rittmeyer was just opening it. went direct to the House. Clemens had just got up, was making fire for his Wife. had breakfast ½ past 7. Went with C— to the Post office. nothing there! to the boat, my box of books in the hold yet. to McKenzie.[22] He refused to Rent his House for less than 1200$ a year, and Seemed to be averse to letting us have it, because he also keeps a few liquors such as Cordials and Wines. passed the balance of the forenoon ~~with~~ in the Store, brooding with Partner over our future and mutual distiny. it is very hard to get a Suitable Store. Our Motto however is a good one, ie—"Never give up the Ship."[23] I intend to wait a few days yet ere I write to Cincinnati. May have something better to report. Until I am acquainted here and pass every evening differently I shall only make one weekly entry in this Journal as my business Set of Books, will Show all my business transactions in detail. this entry I shall endeavour to make at the end of every Week. I am at present setting in Clemens' House where I shall remain. It is ½ past 9. I am going to bed. may the Lord have mercy on me.

St. Louis Sunday Morning March 25. 1849

A most lovely day. at first, the Continual rainy and disagreable weather muddy streets and &c made me very Melancholy and dispirited, but I very soon got used and accustomed even to this. Now that Nature begins to Smile again, I feel as Life had reanimated all my senses and Capabilities of enjoyment. there still however exists a Serious drawback to my happiness. with the most unwearied exertions we have not been able to obtain a Store suitable for our intended business. the one we depended on all along was rented, or said to be so, when I arrived here, but I am Confident that the owner who, by the bye, also keeps liquors, did not wish us for Neighbours. at this Season it is utterly impossible to obtain a Store. I and my old friend Clemens Nulsen Commenced our Partnership on the 1st day of March 1849. We have togather about 4200$[24] actual Capital. I am to pay Clemens 6 pr cent for his excess of Capital, which however I hope to make up very Soon. We have lately seriously thought of building a house on 3rd St. near the Market and to this effect have written to Nulsen and Ficke, and I to my Brother in Law A. Kattenhorn to loan us each a 1000[25] dollars. we wrote last Sunday the 19th inst. Sent our letters on Monday by Mail, expect an answer to Morrow by Telegraph. If we get the money, we shall Commence immediatlay, so as to have the house ready by the middle of June. If aid is refused us from our Relations, we shall have to make the best use of our Credit, and try to make Some other arrangement. we shall most probably be able to do with the aid of Clemens Father in Law Mr Creutzbauer who very fortunately owns 20 acres of land in Corondelet, 7 miles from St Louis. Time and Fate so far have dealt rather hard with us.

We have been disappointed in the expectations nearest to our hearts. Business has yealded about my wages as Clerk at Ed Dexter's. Clemens' wife has now been sick for 3 weeks in Child-bed.[26] Instead of a Boy, he has to Content himself with a Girl. The little stranger made her entry in this world on the 5th of March, the day on which General Taylor was inaugorated President of the United States.

I have written to my friends in Cincinnati as follows, Charles Moulinier, William Lacy, my Brother two letters, my brother in law A. Kattenhorn, and my old Companion W H Brayley, who is at present in Madison Inda, has a situation in a Liquor establishment. I wrote to him in Cinc, a few days afterwards, received a letter from him dated Madison, advising his removal. From my old friend Charles Herbst I have nothing yet. I am and have been, Thank God! in good health. My time has passed rapidly. during the day I am in the Store attending to the business, and in the evening at home, reading or studying French. I have not been out one Single evening. find plenty of Amusement at home. this faithful Journal has met with most undeserved neglect, but I have been so unsettled and Spiritless. I Shall henceforth be more regular. Total Expenses boarding excepted, Since I have been in St Louis, about 1.60 cts. I pay 2.50 a week boarding—

Sunday April 1st 1849.

A most beautiful Sunday. I have never seen a brighter Sky in Cincinnati. Business last week was very dull. we made our expenses, perhaps a few dollars more. that is all. Our good friends in Cincinnati have not [favored] our petitions with any reply yet. The Lot I fear will slip through our fingers if we do not receive a reply shortly. I am very low spirited, and sometimes Cannot help contrasting my present life, full of trouble and anxiety, with the easy and independant one I lead with my old Patron Mr Dexter. but if we do not get any assistance from Cincinnati from Kattenhorn and Nulsen and Ficke we are of course incapable of building through our own Means, and will have to Content ourselves with renting a house and simply making our living. however next Sunday's entry in this Journal will detail our future prospects, and as I have no other prospects except those Connected with my dear friend Clemens, why! the Conclusion is very simple and plain. I must try and get along with them the best way I Can. There is one Consideration, if we build we shall be very Crampt in money matters for a Couple of years to Come. If we do not, we have plenty of Cash to Commence decently.

During the day I was in the Store. last Monday I and my Partner took a Buggy ride out to his Father in laws Farm,[27] took out with us 1000 grape Plants received from Cincti.[28]

I have passed every evening at home, except one, when I went out with an indifferent Character named Bernsdorf. my useless Expenditures during the week have amounted to 1.20¢.

Saint Louis Sunday April 7th 1849.

I have just finished a letter to my brother in law Kattenhorn. Last Sunday we received a letter from Nulsen & Ficke which brot us the pleasing intelligence that Kattenhorn had agreed to lend us 1000 dollars and that they N & F were willing to let their Account stand for one or two years. All of last week we were busy having our Lease made out. we came very near loosing the property or the Leasing of it, as a man by the name of Schultz was also hard after it. We now hold a Lease from Peter Lindell direct. he (P.L.) is the Propriater of the Lot we have leased. the Lease runs for 30 years. it is at present in the Recorders office to be recorded. Last evening we concluded our Contract for the house with D. Aufdenfelde. for building the house, finding all Materials, he get 2635 dollars. the House is to be finished by the first of July. In order to make all our payments this year that we have agreed to we shall have to do a tolerble fair business. I have made up my mind to work hard this year, and Clemens I am sure will also do his duty.[29] every thing that honesty and industry can do, will be done. Business this week has been tolerably fair. I presume we have made 50$ or 25$ Clear Money, but we Credited one bill of 66$ that may be lost, although there is no probability of it just now. it has been a Week for me full of trouble and anxiety, with the Lease, the Contracting for building &c. I have written my own Plans and specifications, and four different sets of them to four differant builders. in this way we saved 10 Dollars.

I have paid Nulsen for four weeks boarding Commencing on 2nd inst. Small expenses during the Week about 50c

St. Louis Sunday Morning April 15th 1849

I have already written 3 letters this Morning. one to Hal Brayley who is at present in Madison Inda where [he] has a place in a Liquor Store, One to Charles Heberhart asking information about the Manufactoring [of] Mould Candles,[30] to please Mr Creutzbauer and one to Aaron H Bean New York, concerning our business. every letter had 3 pages written full. Should have written to Mr Dexter also but am too tired.

Business during last week has been tolerbly fair. that is we have done more than made our expences. my share of this weeks profits are fully equal to my former salery. Yesterday I went to the Recorders office and got our Lease again. it has all the necessary endorsements on it, and should it prove afterwards wrong, it is the fault or vilany of the County officers. our good friend J. C. Edgar, took it into his head to make a Plan and specifications for our house, for which we had to fork over Ten Dollars, although we never ordered it.

I have passed every evening at home. do not Care to go out or make any acquaintances just now. after our new business is established a little and we are a little more favourably known, acquaintances are more advantageously made. I shall then Cease to be a Hermit.

Last Sunday afternoon I and Clemens passed in the Store settling our Cash. this Afternoon we intend to visit his Father in law who is Sick with Some kind of fever.

Mrs Nulsen is still very Sick. the Doctor fears she is getting the Consumption.[31] Expenses for the Week 50 cts

Saint Louis April 22nd 1849 (Sunday)

The Weather during last Week was well adapted for building, now and then very windy. St Louis through its low situation is subject to frequent little hurricane's. Next Week the builder will Commence laying the Cellar wall's of our house. Yesterday we received a 1000 Dollars from my Brother in law Kattenhorn, for which we have sent him our Notes, the first for 555 dollars payable on 1st of May 1850 the Second payable on the 1st of May 1851 for 600$ This is Calculating interest at the rate of 10 per cent and in the first allowing him 5$ for discount which he paid in Cincinnati. I have also written to Henry this Morning. My

Brother in law Lake and my Sister Agnes are again in Cincinnati. I have advised Henry to keep my Guitar and allow Lake 25$ as the good People are at present poor, having lost their all, by the last Company which failed.[32] Our Business was pretty fair last week. we Cleared about 50 dollars of [after] all expenses.

I passed every evening except one at home, and that one was passed very agreably in Company of an old Cincinnati acquaintance William Sleeth who has a situation in a Dry Goods Store on 3rd St immediately opposite our new house. we intended to go to Strakosh Concert but went in the Theatre to see the *Monplaisir troupe.* The Ladies here are far more dressy than in Cincti and dress much more lasciviously, their bubbies are quite exposed. I have no objections. Conquests must be easier here to make. My Small Expenses including washing were about 2.60.

St Louis April 29th 1849.

I do not know yet how business has been during the whole of last week. In the Store it was dull, but Clemens who left for Quincy on Monday evening may have done pretty fair. yet I fear that He has not been alltogather Successful, or he would have returned last evening or rather this Morning at 1 or 2 oclock. Our first loss in business took place this week by Wieman & Lampe. it seem that on last Monday night Lampe was murdered on the Levee.[33] his body found tuesday Morning. Wieman fled the same night taking with him all portable and valuable effects. I have done Some tall walking in endeavouring to get a sight at the remaining articles, but so far have been unsuccessful. to morrow I shall probably have an opportunity to claim what is our own of remaining goods. and as they had every thing on Commission we shall have no difficulty in getting every thing belonging to us. I have had more runing to do this Week than I have ever done before. Sometimes I am so downhearted that I almost wish I was still with my old principal, living at my ease, but the die is cast. I can never do any thing except be a merchant and make my living by trade. time will show how we Succeed. we certainly have a great deal of Money to pay during the Coming year. I have also had some five or six runs after Lindell to give us permission in our Lease to make a Composition roof. I want this permit to be written on our Lease. The Lot was Measured by the Deputy Surveyor yesterday. I have passed every evening at home this week, except when I had to go for Medecine. Expenses during the entire week including washing 1.50.

Sunday May 6th 1849. (Evening)

I and Clemens have just returned from the "Farm" where Clemens has taken his wife last week Thursday. her Physicians have all recommended Country

Air— The Old Lady her Mother has taken it into her Noddle [noodle] that she is able to Cure her herself. hope and wish she may be successful. Our bussiness last week was but poor. from Wieman we can not recover any thing Cause "nothing left" and plenty of Creditors, all sucked in, Brothers in Misfortune. Our profits were about 25$ Clear. business in general however is very dull, every one complains. I received a letter from Charles Moulinier last week. troubles in business and other anxious [thoughts] have put me out of humor of corresponding with my friends. Our building last Week progressed but slowly. the neighbouring Lot to ours has also been leased. the Lessees intend to build also this summer. we have permission to build our wall over 6½ inches which is a clear gain, then they pay us for what they use of the wall.[34] for this consideration we can bear some detention, otherwise it would be annoying. we also [have] a prospect of leasing our present Store and getting 250$ for the key but this bargain is not yet Concluded. The Cholera is at present encreasing[35] last week there were about 160 Deaths, half of them Cholera Cases. I am thanked be the Lord still in good health. I am at present boarding in the City Hotel[36] and sleeping with Clemens in his house. My Expenses during last week were about 1.50.

Sunday May 13th 1849

Business during this Week was very dull. The great Plague of the Year Cholera is driving every Country [person] and Merchants from Surrounding Cities away. The City looks like a desert Compared to its usual animated appearance. Last week ending the 6th there were 78 deaths from it, altogather 173. this week ending yesterday 278 deaths 189 from Cholera. People parting for a day or so, bid farewell to each other. My Partners familly are fortunately in the Country.[37] I and Clemens sleep in the Same bed, in Case of a Sudden attack to be within groaning distance. during the day my thoughts are too much occupied to dwell upon Cholera. especially this last week I have been Somewhat troubled with our building, builder, building Materials, &C. On last Thursday evening was in Theatre, witnessing Mrs Julia[38] in *Hunchback*. the Theatre was almoast empty. 3 Ladies in the whole House. on settling our Cash yesterday we found we had still Cleared about 10$ each. Some of our valuable Citizens have already become victimes to the dreadful Scourge. To day early I and Clemens went in the buggy to his Father in law's.[39] his wife was bitter [better], free from pain and Coughing. the old Lady Mrs C[reuzbauer], somewhat Sick from freight. We returned home via Montezano house. our Seller[40] Bernsdorf is Bar Keeper there. Sold them a box of Cigars. Went home, had Supper at City Hotel. Went out immediately afterwards on a skin chase. did'nt Succeed. Went to Flora Garden. nothing there. I and

Clemens returned home with Stiff P's. Exp 40c. during the Week 2$.
[Margin note] Received no private letters this week.

Sunday May 20th 1849.

This has been a Week of great events Combining the Sadest and most Melancholy that Can happen to a Nation internally. In New York there has been a large and extensive Mob business transacted.[41] the good People thought that Macready had no right to lay Claim to equal pretensions with Bull headed Forest, and as they had their doubts of Mr F's own Courage and ability to right himself, they volunteered on Condition that Mr F. should appropriate a Certain Sum towards Making them drunk to Mob Mac' So after Mac's return from Cincinnati where by the bye he was duly appreciated they (the People) undertook to mob the Theatre, and as the Theatre was entirely innocent at least as much as Mr Macready, the Mayor of the goodly City of New York called out the Police and Military force to revenge the Theatre, which they did excellently well by shooting some 20 or 30 of the Chief rioters, proving to them unanswerably that the Theatre was the Strongest party, although its windows Suffered very much, being all Smashed. Mac' escaped in Soldiers disguise. he left for parts then unknown, but now ascertained, ie Boston. From whence he will return to England, never to come back.[42] poor fellow he is n't Scoundrell enough for America, especially New York, that great American City. it is Strictly American. the great depot of Scoundrelism, bigotry and narrow mindedness. the Collection of Narrow[-minded] Cocoa Nuts must be great there.

The Cholera at present is raging at present more or less throughout all the western Cities. here it Continues with unabated force. this week 160 deaths from it alone, entire [all causes] about 270. in Cincinnati it is not near so Severe.[43] there have been very destructive fires in 3 or 4 of the up-river towns. but the great fire of the age has been in St. Louis.[44]

It Commenced on Thursday night about 10 oclk, before the inhabitants new precisely its whereabouts. 4 Steamers of the first Magnitude were destroyed. one of these boats when in full blaze, broke loose. had it not done so our Establishment would have been destroyed. When floating down Stream this burning Steamer Set some 10 boats on fire. from these the flames Continued spreading until 24 Steamers were no More. all the Mdse on the Levee was burnt. The burning Stuff on the Levee set fire to the buildings. Suffice to note that by dawn of day 15 entire blocks were destroyed.[45] I and Clemens went to bed about 1 oclock when no longer any apparent danger for our Store existed. a few days afterwards we sold the Lease on our Store for 250 dollars, 50$ advance on previous offers.[46] The day after the Catastrophy I Spree'd with Mullan out of Joy for our preservation.

To day we went out to the Farm with an Omnibus.[47] Wise went with us, also Dushushal as far as *Vide Poche.* on returning we had to Walk to the Arsenal about 6 miles. There we waited for an Omnibus. We were too late to get Supper, so we went to bed without it. Expense for the Week 1.50.

Sunday May 27th 1849.

Our building is progressing but slowly. they are still at the Cellar wall's but they are nearly finished. next week they go on the brick work, when things are expected to go quicker. Received a letter from my brothers Frank and Henry and Harry Brayley, poor fellow. he lost his all by fire also. he has established himself now in a little grocery business in Madison.[48] I have written to him. Business this week has been very dull had it not been for a good Sale today we should not have made near our expenses.

Clemens left Friday Morning 24th for a place 45 miles back in the state to buy some tobacco for N[ulsen] & M[ersman], Cincti. I sincerely hope he may be Successful. if he is entirely we shall make [money] by it. if not, we shall charge his expenses on the next hhd.[49] I have not been in Theatre or any where this week. Wrote Kattenhorn and Frank,[50] also sent them papers of the Fire. To day I wrote the longest letter I have ever written 8 pages to my old friend & Teacher Charles Moulinier. I was at it nearly all the forenoon. I had dinner with Herzer. we intended to go out in a Buggy to the farm,[51] but were disappointed in getting one. went in an Omnibus to the Arsenal. there hired an Ice wagon who took us out all the way—It was absolutely necessary to go out with Some Medicine or They would not have had the light of my Countenance. returned in time for Supper, which I had home, ie City Hotel. Expenses during this Week 60 cts.

Sunday Evening June 3rd. 1849. 9 oclock

I and Clemens have just returned from his Daddy in Law's farm. went out this Morning about ½ past 7. Otto Creutzbauer was with us. arrived there about 9 oclock. Among us we had a very pleasant time of it. the only drawback is the walk from the Omnibus station to the farm. My Partners Wife[52] is Still very Weak. She recovers but slowly. the old Lady[53] was Complaining. Continues to dread and fear the Cholera.

Our building has advanced very rapidly last Week. the wall's for 3rd Story are already one third finished. We have to occupy it by first of July.

Clemens' expedition in quest of Tobacco has been entirely unproductive. All the good Stock had been bot up. what was left was held too high by the owners. We were lucky enough however, to buy a Hhd[54] on friday at so low a price that we Could easily advance 130/100 per 100 easily, thus making about 18 dollars.

Business during past two Weeks considering the exceeding dull times has still been remunerating averaging 15 dollars a Week over expenses, but we had to seek a great deal of it. I was twice in Theatre during this Week, and endeavouring to admire The St. Louis favourite, "Mrs Farren" in *Lady of Lyons.* I did not admire her, but in *Love's Sacrifice* I thought better of her. Still she has some bad "habits" she will never be able to abandon.

My Expenses this Week through buggy riding Were rather heavy. also had a pair' Boots footed. altogather I received or took 9$ which is nearly gone.

Sunday June 10th 1849.

The Weather during past Week has not been so Constantly in favour of our building as previously. operations have been somewhat retarded by rains. on Thursday night I witnessed the severest Thunder and lightening that has ever presented itself before. The flashes were so rapid and vivid that the Sky was most brilliantly illuminated all the time. Clemens was out on the farm with the women and fortunately for old Mr Creutzbauer happen'd to be in town. Business during this week was better than it has been lately. We received a lot of Cuba Wrappers[55] from Troisgross & Lampree New Orleans, which will produce us 25 per cent. I lent 7 dollars to a Charles Sontagg[56] from Cincinnati. he promised to repay it yesterday but strange to say has not done so. Should he swindle me it will be the last time I shall lend Money. I certainly have more need of borrowing than lending. I have not written to any of my friends this week nor have I received any letters. I was twice in Theatre, the first time being Mrs Farren's benefit, and the second I took Rosenfeld there at my expense. the piece performed was *The Bravo or The Venetian.* I was well pleased with it, altho' it seems that the wise public here does not wish Mrs Farren to appear [in] any except her old Characters which are all soft Love Nonsense no tragedy I believe among the number. The 2nd night there were 2 Ladies in the house but very fortunately handsome representatives. This day we have passed on the farm. Expenses during week 2$—

Sunday June 17th 1849

Another week has been added to the number allotted to me. Many of my fellow beings have gone to that bourn[57] from whence no traveller returns. the Cholera has this week added at least 400 victimes to the large amount that have already suffered. Clemens has this Week also been troubled with an indigesting Stomach Caused by Cold. So far however every thing has gone well among those interested and dear to us, and through a merciful providence we all *hope* to escape. I came very near to making a fool of myself this Week, in fact I did. I went with Herzer to an accommodation House.[58] fortunately every strumpet was engaged, and I had no opportunity of committing any folly. Business has been dull. had it not been for the Leaf Tobacco we have on hand we should not have made expenses. as it is we did more than that, altho' our expenses are high just now, having to pay Store rent, ground lease and rent of dwelling house.

I received a letter from Charles Herbst yesterday. he is still in Philda. have not [heard] from Moulinier and Hal [Brayley] since my last. Our building is progressing finely at present. the roof is already on and next week will be so far finished that we can move in the early part of the following week. We were out on the farm as usual to day. went out in a Buggy that was fortunately to be had yet from Linkenmeyer.[59] it Cost us two 50/100 Dollars. I was once in Theatre this week, Mrs Farrens Benefit. she played in *Lucretia Borgia* and some other tragedy. did very well. Expense 1.50

Saint Louis June 19th 1849. 6 in the Morning

I feel it my duty to make an entry here in order to Explain a Circumstance that took place last Evening at Bach's beer house. I, Clemens, Otto Creutzbauer, and a young Man by the name of Herzer, went about ½ past 8 to drink a glass of beer for which we agreed to play Domino. I and O. Creutzbauer were the worst players. Nevertheless I won sooner or later in every game. This made Herzer and Nulsen Somewhat out of humor with me, they being the best players. They Thought They could easily poke it on to me. After Three games had been played, two of which Otto lost and Nulsen one, or rather Otto lost them all and Nulsen lost the last game with me. while playing the last game, it occurred that Nulsen thought I had set out[60] the previous game and that it was his set. I was quite Certain of the Contrary and soon Convinced him, but while Contending for the set out, Herzer rudely thrust himself in our Conversation and declared that he was Certain I had set out. I paid no attention to him at first but kept arguing with Nulsen. Herzer was also talking all the time. at last when I had convinced N— he affirmed and Said possitively that I had set out Three times in Succession. I was already provoked at his uncourtous behaviour and in the heat of the Moment, as soon as he said, I had play'd out three times I said "That's a lie." I was sorry the next Moment, but as I was in the right I thought it my duty to stick to my assertion. he jumped up in a moment and left the house, calling on Otto to go with him wich he did. I and Nulsen finished the game which I won. I do not know what Herzer intends doing. he is but a low Character who lives the Lord knows how. he was in the U.S. Service in Mexico[61] and is of a good familly. Should he challenge me, I think it my solemn duty to refuse fighting a Duel.[62] he may attempt and succeed in destroying me in a way even more dishonorable. Should he kill me, it is my earnest my dying wish that every thing Should be done to bring him to the Gallows. My Brother Henry is especially Commanded hereby to do all that Can be done in bringing him to justice. I think a 1000 dollars well laid out among two of the best Lawyers here in St Louis would hang an innocent Man. This plain and true statement for I hereby Swear it is every word true, shows that I without absolutely degrading myself Could not have acted otherwise. Every thing must be done to have my Murderer killed, and I hereby revoke and annull all my former will's and devote all my Means to the prosecution of the person who shall Murder Me, and hope my dear Brother Henry Mersman will faithfully execute this my last Will and Wish.

Joseph J. Mersman
To Henry Mersmann Esqr[63]
Cincinnati, O

Saint Louis Monday June 25. 1849

I was prevented yesterday from making my usual Entry thro' sickness. On Saturday night I was Careless enough to eat too much. Early yesterday Morning I had to rise and visit the Privy. I felt immediately that I had the dysentery.[64] during the Course of the forenoon I was Compelled to repeat my visit 6 times during afternoon 3 times. towards Evening I had a very violent Head-ache.[65] I was of course home the entire day. fortunately Nulsen brot his familly home again last Tuesday, otherwise it would have proved a Weary and tedious Sunday. Mrs Creutzbauer respects the Cholera too much to venture in its presence, so she has retired to her old home [near] Big River, where she intends patiently await the departure of her Enimy. The deaths from this great Plague during [the past week] have averaged 100 a day not including those that [result] from other Causes. Business is suspended Except what appertains to sickness and Death.[66]

My Ex-friend Herzer did not see fit to molest so far. do not however trust him. Should not like to meet him in a lone place at night. he does not Condescend to recognise me. Well! he is the only ennimy I have in St Louis Mo.[67] This Week we shall have to move into our new Establishment. I insured our new house last Saturday for one month for 2000$ at ¼%—[68] This morning Ive received 700$ from N[ulsen] & M[ersman] Cincti balance due us.[69] We made our Expenses last Week most Satisfactory at present. Excepting my board & Washing I did not spend a dime—

Saint Louis Friday June 28th 1849.

We have had miserably wet and sickly Weather. Cholera has a very favorable auxilliary. There are from 120 to 140 deaths a day.[70] Since Monday I have written to Charles Underwood and Chas Herbst and addressed a paper to Chas Dexter. Business Continues very dull. it can hardly be Call'd a Business now. We have however made our expenses this Week. Sent Nulsen & Mersman 3 Hhds of Tobacco yesterday. were somewhat fortunate in Collecting our Money from a few Customers that are however very good. To day we have been actively engaged in Moving our Effects into our New Store.[71] it is not yet finished, but we had to get out of the old one. I have been troubled since last Sunday with dysentery, am now and then using "preventatives" and draughts to keep my Stomach in order. hope to Escape and also Sincerely trust that the Lord is willing. was somewhat freighten'd this Afternoon at a Fire which broke out in the immediate vicinity of our Store (old one) it would have been a Loss of 250 dollars[72] which we are ill prepared to Stand at present. The Lessee has the will to overthrow the bargain, but the Conditions at agreements are all in "black and white" and altho' he has Consulted Lawyers They could not detect any Error or omission to base a Suit upon. The Shelving we took to day, when I brot him the key. he was going to make that the ground of Contention. So to avoid dispute we agreed to have Them put in again for 12$ upon which he gave us a check dated July 3rd for 150$.[73]

Monday Evening July 2nd 1849.

Yesterday I addressed a letter [to] Christian Vefean. the forenoon I passed at home reading and writing. I did not feel well enough to go to breakfast. had my dinner at City Hotel. immediately afterwards I went to the Flora Garden per appointment with my french friend Dusushal. He was already There punctual as he promised.

After having enjoyed a glass of "Crab Cider"[74] we slowly walked to Mr Vandemal who was also Expecting us. We immidiately Commenced tip'ling and Continued to do so with Red Wine all The Afternoon until 6 o'clock. We were finely situated setting in a small harbour of Grape vines which Completely protected us from the sun. Wine tasted well under such Circumstances. I relish'd my Cigar unusually. Well had it been for us if we had stuck to the Wine, but about 6 we went to a Brewery near by and poured a gallon of beer in our Stomachs, and a good portion of cheese. I felt nearly dead for an hour afterwards and suspected it would do me hurt, but being Among Drinkers, I was Compelled to do as They did. the worst and most disagreable occurrance was that when we went home, the omnibuses had Ceased runing and we were Compelled to foot it. I was Completely worn out when I arrived home. it was ½ past 9.

I did not have the Satisfaction of Seeing *ma chère*[75] Fannie.[76] She kept out of my way purposely a sure token that I am not indifferent. O.K.[77]

Yesterday was also another great jubelee day for the Cholera. Among the important deaths, important to us, was that of our Builder D. Aufdenfelde. poor Fellow was Suddenly taken about 12 and 7 P.M. he was a corse.[78] the good luck so far attending us still Continues favourable. May the great Ruler and Disposer of distinies Continue to loock favourably on us, perhaps his most unworthy servants. Had Aufdenfelde died sooner, which easily [could] have been the case, as he has not been in good health for Some time, we would have been in trouble of the most vexatious kind. our House would have been delayed the Lord knows how long. This was a day set apart for Prayer and devotion, but was not observed by the Majority. The Cholera is indeed getting too fearful, is changing its primary symptomes, thus bafling the Skill of the Doctors, many of whom are also taken.[79] Every body is leaving the City.[80] I cannot however do, and would not do it. my God is heard in the City as well as in the Country. I was out to my Cistern maker this afternoon. the Rectifyers he has made wrong. still they Can be remedied. when I returned our August [Rittmeyer] was laid up with Cholera Symptomes. poor Boy! I sincerely hope he will recover. he had immediate medical aid, and this Evening he was in Sound Sleep and in gentle perspiration. I felt very well to day, somewhat surprising from the quantity I drank yesterday, but it seems that good wine does not hurt me. Henry,[81] My Partners Brother returned this Evening from Cincinnati, also my friend Wm Sleeth. They both draw a dark picture from the "Queen City."[82]

Saturday Evening July 7th 1849

Encore une Sémaine de passé, mais Elle ne nous a rien produit. notre Magasin n'étant pas en état pour y faire quelque chose, nous nous Sommes occupés toute la Semaine d'arranger, et de faire arranger les étagères. Elles ne Sont pas encore tout á fait finies, mais assez pour y mettre nos Cigars. ce que nous avons fait cette journée. cette après-midi nous avons aussi placé le "Counter" quoique je crains qu'il ne nous Conviendra pas, étant trop Court, et ayant tout à fait l'air d'appartenir á un Café de St. Louis. Mon Associé le pense bon, nous verrons—nous autres.

J'ai reçu une lettre de mon frère Henri. Sa femme à ce qu'il dit est très Malade. Mon père a été Malade aussi, mais il est, grace à Dieu! rétabli. Mr Dexter nous a écrit aussi. nous aurons tous ce que nous avons demandés. nous payerons pour le premier an comme il nous conviendra, ce tout que nous pouvions raisonnablement désiner. Il a quitté Cincinnati de peur peut-être que le Cholera lui attrapperait. à present il est Sans doute avec Charles son fils à Cambridge.

Mon Creutzbauer le Beau-Père de mon associé est parti pour Europe Mardi le 3 ième, par le lac jusqu'à Buffalo alors par batteau-à-vapeur à New York. il traversera la Mer sur un Steamer au Havre, de là directement à Carlsruhe. J'éspere que Ses ésperances réussiront de tout Mon Coeur. Mon associé et moi Manqions d'avoir un "fuss," il voulait tout à fait le contraire de moi, qui avais raison dans ce que je désinais. après une explanation nous nous Sommes bientôt arrangés. Je n'ai pas eu de dépens cette Semaine, n'ayant pas d'argent pour en dépenser.

[Another week has passed, however, it has produced nothing for us. Our store not being in proper shape, we kept ourselves busy for the week with moving in and having put up the shelves. They are not wholly finished yet, but enough to arrange our cigars on them, which we did today. This afternoon we also played the counter, although I am afraid that it won't do it for us, being too short, and looking as though it were straight out of a St. Louis bar. My associate thinks it looks fine. We shall see. We being the others.[83]

I received a letter from my brother Henry. According to him his wife is very ill. My father was sick too, but thank God, he is in good health now. Mr. Dexter wrote us as well. We will have everything that we requested. We can pay for the first year as we go, which we can reasonably map out. He left Cincinnati, in fear that perhaps he might be contaminated with cholera. At present he is certainly with his son Charles in Cambridge.[84]

Mr. Creuzbauer, my associate's father-in-law, left for Europe on Tuesday the 3rd, by lake to Buffalo, then by steamboat to New York. He will cross the ocean on a steamer to Le Havre, and from there, he is going to go directly to Karlsruhe.[85] I hope with all my heart that he will be successful in his ambitions. My associate and I almost had a "fuss" recently. He wanted completely the opposite of what I wanted, although I still think I am right. After an explanatory conversation, we came to a complete understanding. I had no expenses this week as a result of having no money to spend.]

Dimanche la 8ième de June[86] *1849 [Sunday the 8th of July 1849]*

Je Vais Commencer à écrire, mes actions et les événémens qui m'arrive en français. je n'ai pas beaucoup étudié la belle langue française depuis mon séjour ici. mais il faut Commencer de bon, et surtout écrire un peu tous les jours. je Serais toujours en état de comprendre ce que j'ai écrit. quand jamais j'aurais quelque chose de parti-culier à communiquer, je l'écrirais en Anglais. Mais pour ma propre satisfaction, j'écrirai pour la future en français. il ne faut pas que mes Parens ou mes Amis pourrions le comprendre. S'ils en auront de la Curiosité qu'ils le fassent traduire. Ce matin il fesait de la pluie de tems en tems. Mais, cette après-midi il fesait très beau. Je me suis proméné avec Mr. Block notre voisin au Prarie House une maison quatre mill de la Ville, très bien Situé pour y faire des affaires, mais le proprièTair à ce qui paraît ne sait pas comment les faire. Nous sommes aussi passé par the New Water Works qui sont très petit en les comparraisant avec ceux de Cincinnati. Mais que les rues sont dans une Condition déplorable. nous avions de la peine en y passant avec nos chevaux. j'avais un chevau qui marchait diablement mal. Que Diable l'emporte.

En révenant j'ai vu une demoiselle si jolie et bien fait, d'une taille tout à fait comme il faut, des yeux, mais je n'étais pas si heureux de pouvoir les voir de ce qu'elle les baissait. Oh! pour une femme aussi joli. Block m'a dit que son nom est Mademoiselle Block, que son Père était autrement Juif, mais qu'il ne l'est plus.

Mon Associé et moi ne sommes pas encore comme nous l'étions. J'ai dépensé aujourd'hui une piastre que j'ai emprunté de Mr Block qui m'a seduit à me promener.

[I am going to begin writing in French about my actions and events. I have not studied the beautiful language very much since my arrival here. But it certainly merits a good effort, and I have to write a little every day. I will always be able to understand whatever I write. If ever I would have something specific to share, I shall write in English. But for my own satisfaction, I will write for the future in French. It isn't essential that my family or my friends be able to understand it. If they were to be curious about it, they can have it translated. There was scattered rain this morning. But this afternoon the weather was beautiful. I went for a walk with Mr. Block, my neighbor, to the Prairie House, a place four miles from the city, very well situated for business. But the landlord seems not to know how to take advantage of it. We also went by the New Water Works, which are very small compared to those in Cincinnati.[87] The streets here are in awful condition. It was difficult getting around on them with our horses.[88] I had a horse that walked poorly and terribly slow. May the Devil take him!

Upon my return, I saw a young girl so beautiful and well shaped. And her eyes! Unfortunately I wasn't able to see them, since she kept her eyes lowered.

Oh, for a woman as pretty as she! Block told me that her name is Miss Block,[89] that her father used to be Jewish, but he no longer is.

My associate and I still have some tension between us. Today I spent the $1 that I borrowed from Mr. Block, who actually talked me into going for this promenade.]

Saint Louis July 9th 1849.

Ce le premier jour qu'il fesait beau toute la journée depuis deux Semaines, mais au même temps, il fesait très chaud. Nous avons vendu peutêtre pour dix écu entièrement, n'avons pas fait nos dépens. J'ai reçu une lettre de mon Ami Harry Brayley, qui fait aujourd' hui des affaires pour Soi-même. il parait être satisfait de Son Sort tel qu'il est. J'ai écrit à mon frère Henri, à Mr Vifean et à Mr McHugh. les deux derniers Sont Personnes dans l'emploi de Mr Dexter, et Je vais écrire ce Soir à Harry Brayley aussi. J'ai dépensé aujourd'hui dix Sous, essayant à faire des affaires.

[Today was the first day of nice weather in two weeks, but at the same time, it was very hot. Altogether we have sold probably ten dollars of merchandise, which is not even meeting our expenses. I received a letter from my friend Harry Brayley who is now in business for himself. He seems pleased with how things are going. I wrote to my friend Henry, to Mr Vifean, and to Mr McHugh. The last two are Mr. Dexter's employees. This evening I will also write to Harry Brayley. I spent ten cents today trying to get some business done.]

Saint Louis July 10th 1849.

Qu'il fesait chaud aujourd'hui plus que jamais. Le Cholera commence à descendre en bas de la Ville. Il est toujours Mortel à présent. Il y a de 100 jusqu'à 150 Persones de Morts par la jour. Nous n'avons rien fait dans le Commerce aujourd'hui. Si nous avions notre liquers nous pouvions en vendre beaucoup. Pas de dépens.

[Today it was so hot, hotter than ever! Cholera is spreading throughout the city. As always, it is very deadly. There are 100 to 150 people dying per day.[90] We did not earn anything with our business today. If we had liquor, we could have sold a vast quantity of it.[91] No expenses today.]

Saint Louis Wednesday 11th 1849.

Nous étions assez heureux de faire nos dépens aujourd'hui. Il fesait diablement chaud toute la journée, tout à fait trop chaud pour moi qui ne suis pas accoutumé à tant de chaleur. Je n'ai pas Courage de Mouvoir ou fair quelque chose. Au Soleil il la Chaleur est étouffant.

Nos charpentiers ouvrent bien lentement aussi. Je ne crois pas que tout soit fini avant de deux ou même trois Semaines. Mais s'il est possible je vais pousser les choses un peu plus aussitot qu'il fait un peu plus froid. J'ai dépensé 5 Sous.

[We were fairly happy to cash in on some of our expenses today. It was intolerably hot all day long, much too hot for me, since I am not used to such heat. I didn't even have the courage to move or do anything. In direct sunlight the heat is roasting.

Our carpenters work also quite slowly. I am not positive if everything will be done in two or three weeks. But if possible, I am going to push things along just a bit as soon as it is a little cooler. I spent 5 cents.]

Saint Louis Jeudi, July 12th 1849 [St. Louis, Thursday, July 12th 1849]

Il y avait plus de cent persones de mort du Cholera avant hier. C'est beaucoup à présent, quand nous n'avons plus de 45000 inhabitants dans La Ville. Tous Ceux qui sont pris n'en reviennent pas. C'est un temps de dou leur, mais pour moi et mon Associé, nous ne pouvons rien faire que de rester en ville. le Commencement de notre nou velle Affaires vent tous nos Soins et Menagement. eh bien! Je ne doute point que nous ne reussirons, si le plus Grand dans Son bien veillance nous donne la vie. Les affaires sont bien mal allés, nous n'avons plus vendu que pour 4 à 5 piastre toute la journée. Il n'y avait pas tout de chaleur qu'ordinairement, et nous avons plus travaillé. J'espère que nous serons en état de Commerce à rectifier la Semaine prochaine. Je n'ai pas les Mayens de dépenser quand les affaires ne se vont pas.

[More than one hundred people died of cholera two days ago. That is a lot these days, considering that there are 45,000 inhabitants in the city.[92] All those who come down with it never get well. This is a time of grief, but as for my associate and me, the only thing we can do is stay in the city. The establishment of our new business necessitates all our care and planning. So! I have no doubts that we shall thrive if the Great God will grant us life in his care. Business is going very poorly. we only made four or five dollars the whole day. It wasn't as hot as normal and we were able to work. I hope that we will be in good enough shape to begin rectifying next week. I have no means of spending money when the business is not producing any.]

Vendredi Juli le 13ième 1849 [Friday, July 13th 1849]

Je crois faire Mieux de ne pas écrire en avant aujourd'hui. On n'est pas Certain de Vivre le jour prochain. le jour avant hier il y avait 124 de Mort par le Cholera. C'est presque aussi Sevère qu'à l'ordinaire. Moi je demure toujours en bonne Santé, et tout Ceux dont nous Som mes interessés. Nous attendons journellément l'arrivée de nos liqueures. Nous Saurons bien vendre toute l'eau-de-vie à pré sent. Il n'y en a pas beaucoup de bon en Ville, et on en demande Surtout. [I think I am better off writing early today. One cannot be certain of staying alive for the next day. There were 124 dead of cholera two days ago. This has become the norm. I remain in good health, as do all who we care about. We wait daily for the arrival of our liquors. We could have easily sold out our *eau-de-vie*[94] by now. There isn't much of a supply in the city and it is needed everywhere.] About 4 o'clock who should enter our new Store but my dear Sister and her husband Billy Lake.[93] they are both in good health, especially William. I went out to *Vide Poch*, where the Company performed to a fair house. I staid all night on the boat. Mrs Nunn was sick. Expenses 90¢.

Saturday July 14th 1849

I got up this Morning about 6. did not Sleep of any Account all night. the Mosquitoes troubled me too much. I pitched about in agony, not all night for we did not go to bed until about 1 or half past. Wm Lake deposited fifty five dollars with me.[95] I sold my Gold Watch to Mrs Lake my sister for 50 dollars, leaving a balance in favour of Wm Lake of five dollars. Twenty Dollars of the 55 are Claimed by Agnes herself. I Cannot however keep a Seperate Account of it. They will have to make it out between themselves. Shortly after I got up the boat started. about 7 we had breakfast. I was setting opposite Ex-Mrs Gossin. She is still a handsome Woman, although sick, having received an injury in the Side. The poor Circus Women! how they do have to suffer through their profession. The Company is going up to Galena or even farther.[96] I should liked to have accompanied them, was earnestly invited to do so, but Our Rectefying apparatus would have had to stand still. So I denied myself the pleasure.

The performance last Evening was Cut Short, but it Could not be avoided. about ½ past 9 it Commenced to Storm in such a way that it was thought best to do so.

Poor Agnes has lost her little boy in New Orleans Through the Cholera when it was 12 days old. I have undertaken some business for Wm in New Orleans, which I shall attend to to Morrow. He has lost about 700$ by Rockwell last summer.[97] The Company he is now with[98] owes him nearly 300$.[99] I got home about 9 oclock. the Boat put me off, foot of Washon [Washington] Avenue. No Expense.

Sunday July 15th 1849

Je cragnais de ne pas pouvoir faire l'entrée précédente proprement en français. Voilà la raison pourquoi elle est en anglais. Je me suis habillé avant d'aller à mon dejeuner, quoiqu'il était 7 heures et demi quand je me suis levé. Se matin j'ai passé chez Mr Nulsen, ou chez moi, car je loge dans sa maison. je suis en Pension à City Hotel.

Dans l'après midi moi et mon Associé nous nous sommes promenés dessus un Omnibus jusqu'à Flora Garden. N'y trouvant pas Dusushal, nous sommes allés faire visite à Mr Vandemal. tout le monde là se trouvait en bonne santé. Dusushal nous accompag nait au Flora jardin. Mon Associé nous a traita à une bouteille de "Crab Cidre" (Sauterne) très ordinaire.

Le Soir je me suis Amusé à étudier le français jusqu'à dix heures alors je me suis Couché. Dépens 50¢.

[Fearing I would make too many errors in French, I wrote the previous entry in English. I dressed before going to breakfast, even though it was 4:30 when I got up. This morning I went over to Mr. Nulsen's, also known as where I live since I am currently residing with him. I board at the City Hotel.[101]

During the afternoon my associate and I went for a ride on the omnibus to Flora Garden. Not finding Dusushal there, we paid Mr. Vandemal a visit. Everyone there was in good health. Dusushal came with us to Flora Garden. My associate delighted us with a quite ordinary bottle of "Crab Cider" (sauterne).[102]

I amused myself in the evening by studying French until 10 o'clock and then I went to bed. Expenses 50 cents.]

[Margin note] I have written to Anselmo Schloss[100] concerning Wm. Lake's Claim against Rockwell & Co.

Lundi, July 16th [Monday, July 16th]

Toutes les liqueures que nous attendons depuis une Semaine sont arrivées hier. nous les aurons demain. Voila enfin le Commencement de notre Nouvelle Affaire. Eh bien! Nous Verrons si nous en ferrons beaucoup d'argent. Nous avons à présent plus de quatre Mille piastres de dettes. Mon Moulinier m'a écrit aussi, ma lettre envelloppé avec les austres lettres. Nous étions bien occupés toute la journée en préparant le magasin pour les liqueures et en plaçant les Cisterns and Rectefyers que nous avons fini. Le Magasin à present a l'air très propre et Commode pour notre Affaire. peut-être nous Commencerons encore cette Semaine à rectifier. Pas du dépense

[All the liquors we had been waiting for over a week arrived in town yesterday. We are supposed to receive them at our shop tomorrow. Finally our new business begins. So! We will see whether or not we make a lot of money. We have, at present, more than four thousand dollars of debt. Mr. Moulinier also replied to me, a letter bundled up with all the others. All day long, we were very busy preparing the store for the liquor supplies and arranging the cisterns and rectifiers, two tasks that we have completed. Now the store has a very clean and proper ambiance for our business. Perhaps we will begin rectifying this week. No expenses.]

Saint Louis Mardi Juli 17th 1849 [Saint Louis, Tuesday, July 17th 1849]

Nous avons reçu toutes nos liqueures aujourd'hui. Elles ne sont pas toutes en bonne Condition. Moulinier etait trop parresseux quand ils les envoyais. Les Affaires sont très mal allées. que le Diable emporte les Chalands. Il me semble qu'ils n'ont besoin de rien. Il y avait 61 de mort hier de Cholera. Dimanche il n'y avait que 58, mais aujourd'hui le Nombre est plus grand à cause de la dissipation par les Irlandais et les Allemands. Je n'ai rien dépensé aujourd'hui n'ayant pas de l'argent.

[We received all our liquors today. They are not all in good condition. Moulinier was lazy when he sent them. Business continues to be bad. may the devil take away the challenge! It seems to me that customers don't need anything. There were 61 dead of cholera yesterday. Sunday there were only 58, but today the number is greater because of dissipation by the Irish and the Germans.[103] I spent nothing today since I have no money.]

Mercredi Juli 18th [Wednesday July 18th]

Nous avons fait plus d'affaire qu'à l'ordinaire aujourd'hui. Mon Associé est parti cet après Midi pour Quincy, pour y arranger nos affaires avec Mr Daneke qui est Mort, il y a deux ou trois semaines. [Today we sold more than usual. My associate left today for Quincy, to settle our accounts with Mr. Daneke[104] who died two or three weeks ago.]

We have this day insured 8000 dollars in Home Mutual insurance Co on Store and Stock. had to pay 49$ down. I was very busy all day. No Expense whatever.

Jeudi Juli 19th [Thursday July 19th]

Oh! Les mauvaise affaires. nous n'avons pas même fait nos dépens aujourd'hui. Il fesait bien chaud. l'après midi il a fait de la pluie. J'ai écrit une lettre à mon mi Moulinier et j'ai Commencé une autre pour Charles Herbst mais je n 'ai pas pu la finir, étant un peu occupé vers le soir. Le Cholera ne Cause pas tant de destruction que la Semaine passée. il n'y avait hier que 50 de Morts. Notre Charpentiers sont un peu parresseux. il ne font pas beaucoup. Je n'ai rien dépensé. l'argent est trop rare.

[Oh! How terrible business is! We did not even meet our expenses today. It is really hot. In the afternoon, it rained. I wrote a letter to my friend Moulinier and began another one for Charles Herbst, but being a little busy toward evening, I couldn't finish it. Cholera is not causing as much damage as it did last week. Yesterday there were only 50 deaths. Our carpenters are a bit lazy. They don't do much. I spent nothing. Money is too scarce.]

Vendredi Juli 20th 1849 [Friday July 20th 1849]

Je voudrais bien que mon Associé était de rétour de Quincy et avait 2 ou 3 Cent gourdes dans la poche. Nous en saurions faire usage bientôt, nous autres misèrables. Ce qui nous faut le plus à présent, c'est l'argent. Mais, c'est la chase le plus rare, pas d'affaires ou de Communications avec les Marchandes dans le Contré, personne n'essaye pas à faire des Collections. Eh bien après l'orage il fait beau tems. Les soirées je passe toujours dans ma Chambre. je n'ai pas encore fait les connaissances, et je ne veux pas Courir les Cafés, bien que ceci sera necessaire après que nous serons établis avec nos liqueurs. Pas de dépense.

[I wish my associate were back from Quincy and had 2 or 3 hundred dollars in his pocket. We would soon put it to use, we poor ones. Cash is what we most badly need at this time. But it is the most rare thing, no business or dealings with the merchants in the area. No one bothers himself with collecting on bills. Oh well! After the storm comes good weather. I always spend the evenings in my room. I have not met anyone yet and I don't want to frequent the bars, even if it is necessary once we are settled in the liquor business. No expenses.]

Samedi Juli 21ième [Saturday July 21st]

Le Commerce ne s'est pas Montré aujourd'hui. nous n'avons rien Vendu.

Le Matin j'étais occupé se temoigner le Cas de J. Newburg vs. J. Mitchell. *Mr Newberg l'a perdu. Après avoir fait connaître le Cas Comme il S'est passé Le Juge prononçait jugement en faveur de Mitchell. Notre Ami N— était tout à fait abattu. il ne s'est pas attendu une pareille termination. Mr M. m'a Amené aux plusiers Cafés et m'a traité en homme bien aise d'avoir réussi. Quand nous Sommes arrivés à notre Magasin Newburg m'y attendait. il ne S'en est pas beaucoup fallu qu'ils ne Se Soient battus. Mais je ne saurais pas permettre cela dans le Magasin. Je les ai pacifiés Comme deuse enfans. Nous avons tous dinnés avec Mr M— dans Sa maison.*

Je suis revenue au Magasin à 3 heures, et j'y suis resté. Mon Associé revenait à Minuit et demi. je ne m'étais pas encore Couché. dépens 50c.

[Today there was no business. We sold nothing.

In the morning I served as witness in the *J. Newburg vs. J. Mitchell* trial.[105] Mr. Newburg lost. After presenting the case to the judge as it actually happened, he ruled in favor of Mitchell. Our friend N. was completely beaten. He wasn't really expecting that outcome. Mr. M. took me around to several bars and treated me with the delight of a man who had won. When we got back to our store, Newburg was waiting for me. They were on the verge of fighting. But I don't permit that kind of behavior in my shop. I calmed them down like two children. We all had lunch at Mr. M's house. I came back to the store at 3 o'clock and stayed there. My associate finally returned at half past midnight and I still hadn't gone to bed. Expenses 50 cents.]

Dimanche Juli 22ième 1849 [Sunday July 22nd 1849]

Il fesait un tems très Comfortable aujourd'hui. pas trop chaud, mais il avait toujours l'air de pleuvoir. ce qu'il fesait de tems en tems. Je me suis occupé toute la Matinée d'écrire une lettre à mon beau-frère. il a oublié de nous envoyer le charcoal pour Commencer à rectifier. Sa letter avait quatre pages. J'étais de retour bientôt après diner n'ayant rien autre chose à faire. je m'occupais de lire Le Théâtre Anglais par Mad^{e} Inchbald. Après Souper J'ai fini la tome. J'ai dépensé 10 sous.

[It was very comfortable out today. Not too hot, but it felt like it would rain, which indeed it did from time to time. I was busy all morning writing a letter to my brother-in-law.[106] He forgot to send us charcoal so that we could begin rectifying. The letter was four pages long. I came back in right after lunch since I had nothing else to do. I occupied my time by reading *The English Theatre* by Mme Inchbald.[107] After dinner I finished the volume. I spent 10 cents.]

Lundi Juli 23ième [Monday July 23rd 1849]

Les affaires sont assez bien allées pour payer les dépens, mais ce n'est pas encore grande chose. Il était 5 heures quand je suis monté avec Mr Dusushal chez Mr Vandermal où je suis resté toute la nuit. Je m'y suis très bien Amusé, et sans avoir mon Souper, on n'y pensait pas. mais au lieu de manger nous avons autant plus bus. Mr Vandermal avait un grand fracas avec Sa Vache qui ne voulait pas se laisser tirer le lait, mais il l'a bientôt rendu traitable, lui! J'ai dormi dans la Chambre avec Mr & Madame Vandermale. Il voulait absolument que je me Mettais àu lit avec sa femme. Mais elle ne voudrait pas y consentir si publiquement. La petite Fannie était habillée très ordinairement, puavre fille! Elle doit Menager toute la Cuisine. Elle n'est pas permis de se parer.

J'ai réussi à vendre ces Messers un baril de J. J. Cupery dont J'ai fait 16$ au dessus les dépens. Je n'avais pas occasion de dépenser de l'argent.

[Business is doing well enough to begin paying expenses, but it is still not much. It was 5 o'clock when I went up with Mr. Dusushal to see Mr. Vandemal where I spent the night. I had a very good time even though I had no dinner. Who would have thought? But then, instead of eating, we mostly drank. Mr. Vandemal had a great fight with his cow that wouldn't allow herself to be milked, but she was more cooperative soon afterwards! I slept in the bedroom with Mr. & Mrs Vandemale. He absolutely insisted that I sleep in the same bed with his wife. But she didn't wish to consent so publicly.[108] Little Fannie[109] was dressed quite ordinary, poor girl! She has to manage everything in the kitchen and is not allowed to adorn herself.

I was pretty successful in selling a barrel of J. J. Cupery[110] to some gentlemen on which I made 16 dollars above cost. I had no opportunity to spend money.]

Saint Louis Mardi Juli 24ième 1849 [St. Louis Tuesday July 24th 1849]

Pas d'affaires aujourd'hui. il a fait de la pluie de tems en tems pendant toute la journée. On était assez honnête de me donner à manger ce matin. J'avais grand faim moi. il était 8 heures et demi quand j'arrivais au Magasin.

Nos Mdses de Cincti sont arrivées. du Tabac, des Cigars, des grands barriques vides. et Mr. Dexter m'a aussi envoyé le Machine pour peser l'esprit &c. J'étais dans ma chambre à huit heures ce soir, bien aise de ne pas être chez Mr. V—e. Pas de dépense.

[No business today. It rained off and on all day long. They were nice enough to give me something to eat this morning. I was extremely hungry. It was 8:30 when I got to the store.

Our merchandise from Cincinnati arrived. Cigars, tobacco, great empty barrels and Mr. Dexter also sent me the machine for weighing spirits et cetera.[111] I was in my room by 8:30 this evening, quite happy not to be at Mr V—e. No expenses.]

St. Louis Juli 25ième [St. Louis July 25th]

Voilà un autre jour très désagréable, toujours de la pluie. Les affaires se sont très mal allées. aujourd'hui nous avons reçu tous les articles du S B Phoenix. Le Tabac que nos frères nous ont envoyé ne nous Convient du tout. il est trop Sec. Nous essayerons à le vendre àu prix Coutant. J'ai enfin dépensé dix sous, pas beaucoup.

[Another horrible day, still raining. Business is going very poorly. Today we received everything from the Steam Boat *Phoenix.*[112] The tobacco that our brothers sent us will not do at all.[113] It is too dry. Will try to sell it at cost. I finally spent six cents, not much.]

Jeudi Juli 26ième 1849 [Thursday July 26th 1849]

Il fesait très beau aujourd'hui, plus agrèable qu'il ne fesait depuis long-tems. Nous avons ordonnés pour quatre Cents plus de liqueurs de Mr. Dexter, mais nous n'en ordonnons plus, parce qu'il ne nous envoit pas les liqueurs tout à fait pûre. Pas de Dépens.

[It was very nice today, better than it has been in a long time. We ordered four hundred more bottles of liquor from Mr. Dexter, but we won't order any more because he sent us liquor that isn't completely pure. No expenses.

Vendredi Juli 27ième [Friday July 27th]

Les Affaires se sont allés un peu mieux que dernièrement. Nous avons dix écus cet heureuse jour. Il a fait de la pluie cette après Midi. Nous esperons forte-ment de reussir, nous autres. rien dépensé.

[Business is doing a little better than before. We made 10 dollars this happy day. It rained this afternoon. We hope so much to succeed, we being the others. No expenses.]

Tuesday Evening July 31st 1849.

Other occupations have prevented the usual entries in this Journal. it was not business for we have not done any thing of any account. our rectefying apparatus is Still unfinished, neither have we any Coal.

Last Sunday I was out to McHose Cave with Wm. Sleeth. we amused ourselves Capittally. In the forenoon I was busily Employed writing to Kattenhorn and his Daughter Louisa. the young Lady is progressing. I received a letter from her on Saturday, written Evidently under the influence of a Sunday Scool lecture, for Christianity predominated to an unusual extant.[114]

Last Saturday night another awful destruction of Steam Boat property took place. Five splendid N. O. Steamers fell a prey to the devouring Element.[115] It will be difficult to obtain Insurance in forreign offices on Steamers runing to this Port. it will have the Effect of making the Commodity too Scarce for the Business done there. Immediately after the fire the Firemen and a party of Common Irishers got in a Spree. at first the latter had the advantage but soon the Americans turned on them, licked them, and Mobed and destroyed some 6 or 7 Irish Hell's or Grog Holes.[116] the excitement lasted all day Sunday. would have broke out again Sunday Evening but for a Severe rain that Commenced to fall about 9 and Continued till past 11.

I was home every evening, not Caring to risk my precious body in the rowdy filled Streets. My Expenses during this time have not exceeded 50 cts

Saint Louis August 1st 1849.

Poor Clemens was suddenly taken sick yesterday. immediately after dinner he became cramps in the Stomach, which, in a short time became so violent that he had to send for the Doctor. all afternoon he was in bed up Stairs, Suffering a great deal. in the Evening had to be taken home in a Cab, being to feeble already to Walk. the Medecin he took Caused him to vomit Extensively, hence his Weekness.

Business was very dull all day, not Worth a damn'd. I was busy arranging the rectefying apparatus. this afternoon Especially I had my hands full. The Plumbers were busy fixing the hydrant pipes, which by the bye run the whole lenght of the house and into the third Story.[117] The Tinners were tinkering all afternoon with the piping for the Rectefyers. I made a most damnable fool of myself to day in signing A. H. Beans drafts or rather accepting them before having received the goods. I trust we shall have no difficulty, however I shall never do any thing of the kind again. During the afternoon I was also taken with a most violent pain and griping in the Stomach. although the Cholera has almost disappeared (the enterments for yesterday Amounting only to three) still the other deseases are gaining ascendency and destroy more human life than Father Time does without these aids.

Our Coal also arrived this Evening direct from Loder, Cincinnati. Kattenhorn does not write about the matter at all. This Evening I was very sick. Damn Ice water say I.[118] Went to bed about 10. No Expense.

Saint Louis August 2nd 1849. Thursday

This day has been the most miserable and painful I have passed in Saint Louis. I should have gone to bed, if Clemens had not been confined to it already. I have never had such an accurate Conception of accute pain in the Stomach as to day. the nervous and Cramp-like twitchings made me sometimes roar with pain. I did not however leave my Post. Kept the Men steady at work all [day]. we have a hydrant at present on first floor and in 3rd Story the rectefyers are all placed and fixed. So that as soon as the damn Copper Smith puts the handle and sucker to the pump we are ready to Commence opperations. I was Compelled to spend 20 cts for washing.

The Great St. Louis Fire, May 1849. The fire started Thursday night, May 17, and destroyed twenty-four steamboats, all the merchandise on the levee, and all the buildings in fifteen city blocks near the river. (Nathaniel Currier, Missouri Historical Society, St. Louis.)

NOTES

1. Hunter, 100–105.

2. See Lloyd for descriptions of steamboat disasters. Newspapers often reported fatal accidents, for example, the *Cincinnati Enquirer*, 23 November 1847, and the *Cincinnati Commercial*, on 25 April 1848 and 6 January 1849. From 1834 to 1852, twenty-seven boiler explosions killed 1,002 persons (Stevens, 1:343). 1849 was a particularly bad year because of the steamboats lost in the St. Louis fire (Review, 15).

3. Adler, 93.

4. Mallinckrodt, 245.

5. Primm, 154–55.

6. Earliest reports recognized that the illness traveled on riverboats (SLU, 27, 30 March 1849).

7. Fisher (1), 189–211.

8. Nativism directed negative feelings toward the Germans and the Irish in St. Louis (Mallinckrodt, 245–46).

9. Ms. Orderman's identity has not been determined, but she is another example of chain migration. Earlier arrivals helped newcomers settle in their new land by providing advice, encouragement, job contacts, and financial support (Kamphoefner [2], 53–70).

10. JJM's father, Frederick Mersman, was then living with his older son, Henry, who had recently moved to a new residence four blocks west of his previous home. It is unclear whether the change of address or some mental impairment caused Frederick's confusion.

11. Adeline (or Adelaide) Tebbelman Mersman, Henry Mersman's wife, had a sister named Margarethe Tebbelman.

12. The *Thomas Jefferson*, a 279-ton sidewheel packet with a wooden hull, was built in Cincinnati in 1846. The boat carried passengers and freight between Cincinnati and New Orleans, but sank at Waterloo, Louisiana, in 1849 (Way #5369, 451).

13. Philippina Nulsen Wagner corresponded with her brother JCN in St. Louis.

14. Skipper of the *Thomas Jefferson.*

15. William McHugh supervised the work of laborers who hauled barrels to and from the levee.

16. The *Memphis,* a 196-ton sidewheel packet with a wooden hull, was built in Cincinnati in 1848 and ran between Cincinnati and Memphis. A storm in 1849 tore off the officers' quarters and pilothouse, causing twelve deaths, but the boat returned to service until destroyed by fire at Cincinnati in 1853 (Way #3895, 319).

17. The *Pike No. 7,* a 480-ton sidewheel packet with a wooden hull, was constructed in Cincinnati in 1844. One of the largest boats of the decade, it carried James K. Polk to his inauguration in 1845. However, because of its great size, it ran aground often. Therefore, its owners dismantled it in 1849 (Way #4492, 371).

18. *Cinq-Mars or A Conspiracy under Louis XIII,* a popular novel by Alfred de Vigny (1797–1863), was first published in 1847.

19. *Deutsch* or German.

20. The Portland and Louisville Canal (Yater, 38–39).

21. James Sheridan Knowles (1784–1862) published the novel *Fortescue* in 1847.

22. Kenneth McKenzie, a wholesale grocer and commission merchant, became an agent for the Missouri Wine Company in 1858 (ERA, 1 August 1849; DUN Missouri, 36:99, 304; 38:18).

23. A paraphrase of the words attributed to U.S. naval hero James Lawrence (1781–1813): "Tell the men to fire faster and not to give up the ship; fight her till she sinks" (Bartletts, 449).

24. About $100,800 in 2005 dollars.

25. About $24,000 in 2005 dollars.

26. Albertine Nulsen gave birth to Caroline Nulsen, on 5 March 1849, just ten months after her wedding to JCN. Albertine's sister, Claudine Creuzbauer, was the godmother named at the baptism a year later (Holy Ghost Evangelical Church, St. Louis, Missouri, Baptism Records, 1833–54, 224, 19 March 1850, FHL Microfilm 1433232).

27. Friedrich Creuzbauer owned a twenty-acre farm in Carondelet, Missouri, although he had no experience in agriculture prior to immigration.

28. Catawba grapes, which flourished in Cincinnati after being introduced in the 1840s, were then brought to Missouri and propagated (Cist [3], 266).

29. Self-control, self-restraint, and discipline of will are all characteristics that conduct books promoted (Newton, 58–59).

30. Candles, made using molds, were a common source of light in the West, although whale-oil lamps and gas illumination were increasingly popular in East Coast cities.

31. The illness called "consumption" in the nineteenth century was renamed "tuberculosis" in the twentieth century. An infection by *Mycobacterium tuberculosis,* pulmonary tuberculosis was a leading cause of death throughout the nineteenth century (Dormandy, 76–82).

32. The Lakes were unemployed because Rockwell's Circus went out of business with the owner's death in the 1849 cholera epidemic (Slout, 258). Furthermore, Agnes and William lost wages that Rockwell had withheld.

33. No further information has been found about this partnership or Lampe's murder.

34. It appears from this description that N & M agreed to build overlapping the property line and to permit their neighbor to construct a building using their wall as a common wall.

35. For an enumeration of the deaths throughout the epidemic, see McPheeters, 97–120.

36. The City Hotel provided daily meals at stated times for regular customers. JJM ate there and lodged with the Nulsens.

37. Many people fled the city, fearing the disease-causing miasmas there (Fisher [1], 197–99).

38. Julia Dean, popular with St. Louis audiences, performed throughout the month of June, despite the epidemic (Boxed Playbills, St. Louis, Box 59, Harvard Theatre Collection).

39. The ten-mile trip to the farm in Carondelet likely took nearly two hours each way.

40. Store clerk.

41. The Astor Place Riot, on 10 May 1849 in New York City, occurred when a rivalry between the American actor Edwin Forrest and the English dramatist Charles Macready escalated into street vio-

lence. About two dozen lives were lost when the militia sought to quell the rioters (Brockett, 361, 369; Levine, 63–69; Kimmel, 40–42; MOR, 21–24 June 1849).

42. Macready retired from the stage in February 1851 and never returned to the United States (HAS, 228–29).

43. Contamination of the water supply in St. Louis probably caused the epidemic to be worse there than in any other American city (Fisher [1], 207–10; MDC, 22 May 1849). One effect of the epidemic was to reduce travel by rail as well as ship (MDC, 14 May 1849).

44. On 17 May 1849, the Great Fire of St. Louis began when the fire broke out on steamer *White Cloud* and subsequently ignited the other ships along the levee. Descriptions of the disaster may be found in Primm, 167–68, and van Ravenswaay (1), 383–88.

45. Fire damage included the destruction of four newspaper offices and other property valued at an estimated six million dollars. Newspaper publication was interrupted—the *Missouri Republican* for four days, the *New Era* for ten—but when they resumed, there was thorough coverage of the calamity that had occurred in St. Louis (MOR, 21–24 May 1849; MDC, 22 May 1849).

46. JJM and his partner thus profited from the fire, which destroyed fifteen blocks of commercial buildings, but spared theirs.

47. Erastus Wells (1823–93) began the first omnibus lines in St. Louis in the mid-1840s with regular trips along Broadway to the city limits. At five cents a ride, the horse-drawn "buses" soon were packed with passengers (van Ravenswaay [1], 335–36).

48. No record exists of Harry Brayley's business in Madison, Indiana.

49. A hogshead, a barrel used for transporting goods, contained up to 1,400 pounds of tobacco.

50. Frank Mersman had returned to Cincinnati.

51. Creuzbauer's farm in Carondelet was about ten miles from JJM's store in the city.

52. Albertine Creuzbauer Nulsen was still recovering from giving birth (see note 26).

53. Caroline (Mrs. Karl Friedrich) Creuzbauer.

54. Since a hogshead held 1,400 pounds of tobacco, when Nulsen & Mersman increased the price $1.30 per 100 pounds and sold it wholesale, they made about 18 dollars profit.

55. "Wrappers" are tobacco leaves suitable for the outer layer of cigars.

56. No positive identification of this man has been made. A Charles Sonntagg, a commercial merchant, was the proprietor of a store at 10 West Front Street in Cincinnati (CCD 1853, 367).

57. JJM, acutely aware of his own mortality, paraphrased a line from *Hamlet:* "But that the dread of something after death, / The undiscover'd country, from whose bourn / No Traveller returns, puzzles the will" (3.1.77–79).

58. An accommodation house provided temporary lodging or accommodation. In this case, the cheap hotel was actually a brothel (OED, s.v. "accommodation").

59. Because of the many funerals, buggies were in scarce supply (van Ravenswaay [1], 389–91).

60. "Set out" means started first. The argument JJM describes is over who would make the first play, and thus have the advantage in a game of dominos.

61. During the Mexican War, Lewis Herzer served in the same U.S. Army unit as Edmund Creuzbauer (RG 94, E516, Battery B, Clark's Battalion, Missouri Light Artillery, Records of Lewis Herzer, NA).

62. St. Louis, where men fought duels on Bloody Island, was far more violent than Cincinnati. JJM had already experienced one murder in his circle of business contacts. Crime of all types was rampant (JJM diary, 29 April 1849; van Ravenswaay [1] 388).

63. In the event of his death, JJM anticipated his brother Henry would take possession of the diary.

64. Any condition that caused loose bowel movements was called "dysentery" by nineteenth-century doctors and patients.

65. A severe loss of body fluids commonly causes a headache.

66. The circuit court suspended operations, St. Louis University cancelled classes, and the post office shortened its hours (MOR, 28 June 1849; City of St. Louis Circuit Court, Record Book, 1849–1850, 19:159).

67. A census enumeration on 26 December 1850 found twenty-eight-year-old, German-born Louis (Luis) Herzer in the city of Santa Fe, New Mexico Territory. His subsequent fate is unknown (USC 1850, M432, roll 468, page 357, line 26).

68. Thus, JJM paid $5 per month on building insurance.

69. See JJM diary, 18 February 1849.

70. St. Louisans calculated that at that rate, *no one* would be left alive by Christmas. A public meeting was held on 25 June 1849 to demand the city government take action to protect the inhabitants, and a volunteer Committee of Public Health took over the governance of the city for the following five weeks (MOR, 28 June 1849; Primm, 155–56).

71. The new store at 100 N. Third Street appears on map 9.

72. N & M would have been unable to collect rent on a burned-out commercial space.

73. N & M accepted a postdated check.

74. Fermented crab-apple cider was a popular beverage (Rorabaugh, 111).

75. [Fr.] my dear.

76. Louis Vandemale's daughter Stephanie was called "Fanny" or "Fannie" by family members (RG 15, Records of the Veterans Administration, Vandemale's Civil War Pension Records, Cert. # 822,313, NA).

77. "O.K." meaning "all correct" or "oll korrect," a jocular alteration, was first used during Van Buren's election campaign in 1839. His nickname was "Old Kinderhook" (OED, s.v. "OK").

78. Cholera killed by rapidly causing profound dehydration. About two-thirds of cholera deaths in 1849 St. Louis occurred within twenty-four hours of becoming ill (Fisher [1], 202).

79. During the epidemic, at least fourteen St. Louis physicians perished, including Doctors Hardage Lane, Bernard Farrar, Marcellus Edwards, James Wise Hart, and George McCullough (Primm, 156; ERA, 1 August 1849).

80. So many people fled St. Louis that the population fell from 70,000 (McPheeters, 105) to about 45,000 (JJM diary, 12 July 1849).

81. Henry Nuelsen, JCN's brother, a Methodist missionary in St. Louis, had likely visited his relatives in Cincinnati (Barclay, 985; WPO, 21 August 1911).

82. "Queen City of the West" was a sobriquet given to Cincinnati early in the nineteenth century and popularized by Henry Wadsworth Longfellow (1807–82) in his poem "Catawba Wine" (HOC, 81, 90; see Preface).

83. JJM apparently includes August Rittmeyer and perhaps other assistants.

84. Cambridge, Massachusetts, the residence of Harvard College student Charles Dexter, provided a safe haven for Edmund Dexter.

85. Karl Friedrich Creuzbauer, a native of Durlach, at that time a town near Karlsruhe in the Grand Duchy of Baden, was leaving to deal with family matters in Europe. He never returned to the United States, and died in Durlach on 17 September 1870 (TAG, 18 September 1870).

86. The correct month was July.

87. St. Louis had grown rapidly in the previous decade, so demand far outstripped the supply of public water (see Schworm, 1–4; and Pritchard, 18–40).

88. St. Louis had no storm sewers, so rainwater collected in city streets, making some impassable (Fisher [1], 192–93, Primm, 154; van Ravenswaay [1], 336–37).

89. Miss Block has not been further identified.

90. Newspapers provided daily tallies of deaths and burials. For a summary, see Godwin.

91. Alcoholic beverages were much sought after as treatments for cholera.

92. Thousands had fled to the countryside, where cholera was less prevalent. The city's population before the epidemic was nearly 70,000, and JJM marveled at how many had left (MOR, 5 February 1849; McPheeters, 98).

93. Traveling with Spencer Q. Stokes's South-Western Circus, the Lakes performed at Vide Poche on 13 July 1849 (MOR, 13 July 1849).

94. *Eau de vie,* literally "water of life," was a brandy with a high alcohol content, thought to be effective treatment for cholera (OED, s.v. "eau de vie").

95. William Lake secured his extra money with JJM.

96. That season Stokes's South-Western Circus played in river towns as far north as Prairie du Chien, Wisconsin (Thayer, 468–69).

97. Rockwell & Company had withheld a portion of the Lakes' wages until the end of the season, and then been unable to pay them.

98. I.e., Stokes's Circus (MOR, 3 October 1849).

99. Circus companies commonly kept part of a performer's wages until the end of the season.

100. Anselmo Schloss, a liquor merchant in New Orleans, may have given advice to JJM (DUN Louisiana, 10:397).

101. JJM ate meals at the City Hotel and slept at JCN's residence (SLD 1851, 83).

102. Crab-apple juice was fermented to make a white wine or sauterne (Rorabaugh, 110–13).

103. Popular belief held that recent immigrants were more susceptible to cholera than long-established residents: the Irish because they drank whiskey and ate cabbage and the Germans because they drank beer and ate sauerkraut (ERA, 28 July 1849; Fisher [1], 197; Primm, 156).

104. Originally from Bremen, Albert Daneke (1807–49) immigrated in 1837 to Quincy, Illinois, opened a grocery, and became a customer of N & M. When he died in the cholera epidemic, he owed $12.40 to Nulsen & Mersman. JCN lost no time in filing his claim with the estate (Adams County Probate Records, Case 294, Box C-18).

105. No record of this litigation has been found.

106. Arnd Kattenhorn aided JJM's start in the world of commerce.

107. Elizabeth Simpson Inchbald (1753–1821), a theater critic, actor, novelist, and playwright, wrote numerous books about the theater (DNB, 29:221–25).

108. Vandemale offered the most comfortable bed to his guest, which did not necessarily suggest that JJM should take sexual liberties with his wife. Strange bedfellows were typical of the period (Kasson, 14–15).

109. Fannie or Fanny was Ferdinand Vandemale's daughter (RG 15, Records of the Veterans Administration, Civil War Pension Records, Cert. #822,313, NA).

110. "J. J. Cupery" is actually the firm John de Kuyper & Son of Holland. The distiller, founded in 1695, produced fine spirits and exported them widely. Between 1846 and 1850, de Kuyper produced at least a million liters annually in Rotterdam and shipped the whiskey in casks, many to distant markets, such as the United States. The business continues today as de Kuyper Royal Distillers (Sluyterman, 17–22).

111. This was probably a hydrometer, a device that measures the weight of a liquid in relation to the weight of water, i.e., the specific gravity. It is an essential tool in making spirits.

112. The same vessel sued by Edmund Dexter (see JJM diary, 26 January 1849), the *Phoenix* was destroyed by fire in St. Louis just three days later, on 28 July 1849 (Lytle, 289).

113. N & M (Cincinnati) had sent to N & M (St. Louis) tobacco unsuitable for cigar-making.

114. Although Elizabeth Mersman Kattenhorn had been raised Roman Catholic, the Kattenhorn family attended a Protestant church in Cincinnati and were buried in the German Protestant Cemetery (now Walnut Hills) (see Battistone, 466).

115. Lost boats included the *Phoenix,* which JJM mentioned on 25 July 1849, the *Dubuque,* the *San Francisco,* the *Mary,* and the *Algoma* (MOR, 29 July 1849).

116. A hellhole is a place totally lacking in comfort, cleanliness or order; a grog shop is a saloon (OED, s.v. "grog"). Reports of the fire and riot appeared in St. Louis newspapers. The flames broke out at 3:00 a.m. on Sunday morning on the steamer *Algoma* and spread to four other boats. Seven fire companies responded and extinguished the fire by 8:00 a.m. However, a fight between a firefighter and an intoxicated Irishman, which started while flames still raged, escalated when the drinker returned with armed friends. Pistol shots aimed at the firefighters infuriated them, but caused no serious injuries. They responded by attacking O'Brien's Coffee House and destroying all the furniture. The firefighters then wrecked three other Irish saloons and armed themselves with muskets from the St. Louis Greys' Armory.

The mayor and the police attempted to restore order, but the firefighters scattered. Throughout the morning they continued to assault the Irish and destroy their property. At one point, the firefighters threatened the police with a six-pound howitzer, a small cannon. Although the mobs of firefighters reached four hundred, only a few of them were arrested while two dozen Irishmen ended up behind bars. The riot ended late in the evening.

The Irish fared much worse than the firefighters, but there were no deaths on either side. Losses from the fire were about ten deaths and property damage of $148,000, but no one bothered to estimate the damages from the rioting (MOR, 30 July 1849; ERA, 30 July 1849).

117. JJM indicates that the source of water for his business was the public supply, not a private well or spring. The public water supply, drawn directly from the Mississippi River, delivered water to hydrants, not faucets (Schworm, 3–4; Pritchard, 20–40).

118. Icewater, fresh fruit, and vegetables were all blamed at various times for causing cholera (ERA, 2 August 1849, Fisher [1], 197).

CHAPTER TEN

Seeking a Cure

7 August 1849—19 June 1850

After the cholera epidemic, JJM faced two additional challenges. His first problem was a cash-flow crisis common to young entrepreneurs. JJM negotiated with relatives who had loaned him money and sought to extend the terms of the agreements.

JJM's second problem caused him to use the French language to protect his privacy. He had contracted the "Great Pox," i.e., syphilis. Fearful of the harsh treatments used by some medical practitioners, JJM sought help from physicians who used botanical treatments, first in St. Louis and later in Cincinnati. Instead of noxious chemicals, their prescriptions called for herbal ingredients. As JJM spent his money on decoctions, his emotions evolved from denial to anger and depression.[1] *He tried therapeutic baths and avoided "excitements" that might worsen his condition.*

JJM maintained a facade of normalcy while visiting his family in Cincinnati for two weeks in June 1850, but worried constantly about his "confounded condition." He took two doctors and a pharmacist into his confidence, but did not disclose to his family the fears that plagued him. JJM had already established his next goal in life: marriage. That was out of the question until a doctor gave approval.

Meanwhile, the careers of Bill and Agnes Lake were bringing them acclaim. Their travels intersected with JJM's in Cincinnati. Anxious to be parents after losing several infants to death, the Lakes adopted an eight-year-old child and called him William. JJM left Cincinnati determined to have a family of his own—soon.

August the 7th being on Tuesday

Lazyness and other occupation made me even omit posting up my Journal on Sunday. during the forenoon I was occupied with writing a long letter in german to my brother Henry. during the afternoon I was home reading a Novel by Marryatt Called *The Fantom Ship.*[2] Madam Detharding was there also on which account I Could not have wrote. Otto left on Saturday for Peru with Mrs Nulsen my Partners Wife who intends to remain some time with her Sister.[3]

Business is dull. we are however making our Expenses and about Clerks Wages. this for the Capital we have invested is not enough. We ought to make now about 100$ a week Clear, and I hope we shall My Expenses have been very trifling—

St Louis August Tuesday 14th 1849

Confound my lazyness. here is nearly a week gone by again without my journal being honored with a single item. Our business during this time has been and is now very dull. 'tis true we are making more than Expenses but I am somewhat fearful of the heavy payments we have to pay in some months hence, and unless we sell pretty extensively for Cash we shall have to Call again on my brother in law Kattenhorn.

Yesterday I bot the first lot of Whiskey from Chouteau & Vallé, 12 barrels at 19¾ cts per gallon. to day I was quite occupied with the rectefying apparatus, as also yesterday. Last Sunday, I and Clemens were out to Kunz, and regaled ourselves with 4 bottles of Hermaner Catawaba,[4] on which we got most jovially tipsy. returned & were home at 8 oclock precisely did not go out again.

Our good debtor C. M. Sells who owes us two hundred and 12 dollars and who sold a lot of Cigars to O. Creutzbauer in Peru, has been sued for Embezzleing goods, a penetentiary Act, by S. Stein. the Trial Comes off to Morrow. if Sells looses it he will get a view of Penetentiary arrangements. if he wins Stein looses every thing. As we are deeply interested I am most anxious to know the result whatever it may be. we are however I presume by this time pretty safe. My Expenses have been larger than formerly say for the whole time 2$.

Thursday August 16th 1849

It has been very warm all day. I was occupied incessantly fixing my rectefying Machinery. The dam'd large Cistern leaked this Morning when I first Commenced runing Spt [spirits] into it, but with the assistance of August[5] I got it tight at last. The uper rectefyers are still leaking have been for two days. presume shall lose about Ten gallons by the dam things.[6] am however pretty Confident that no Establishment of this kind was ever Started without a great deal of inconvinience, loss and vexation.

Wrote a very sad letter yesterday to N[ulsen] & M[ersman].[7] requested them to send Money if they wanted Tobacco, that we had nothing to Spare. the Lord knows that in this I did not exagerate.

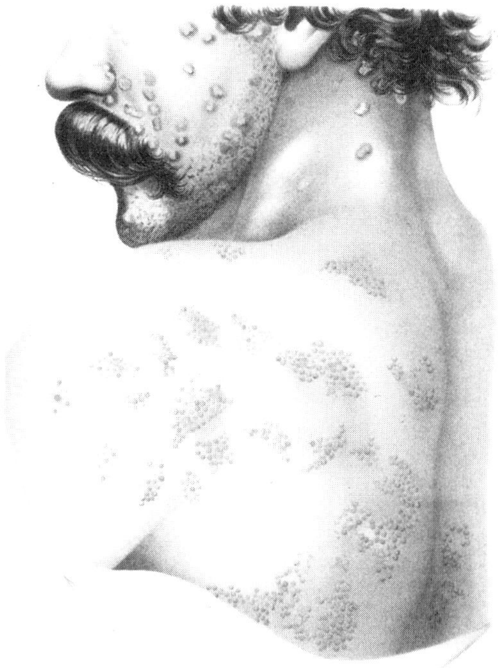

Syphilis rash. This illustration, from an 1889 medical text, shows the skin rash associated with syphilis. (Prince A. Morrow, *Atlas of Skin and Venereal Diseases*, plate XIV [1889].)

To day we had advice of some of our liquors on board the Steamer *Melodeon*[8] arrived this Morning. they were shipped on 18' June, now two months on the way. damn Nonsense to purchase in New York if it requires two months to receive goods.[9] Mr Dexter however will mix.[10] Can't help it, must try his hand on every pipe. think our domestic liquor will be by far the best. just now all the Trade togather is not worth a damned.

Monday, Tuesday and this evening until 10 I passed in Messers Thompson's and Cline's office. They are both young Buckeye Lawyers.[11] Very agreable Companions. was introduced by Billy Sleeth. next week I shall have some double rectefied ready. how it will turn out Can't be told at present. will be tho'. Sels Case was not Concluded to day. Continues to Morrow. Exp 25c

Friday August 17th 1849.

Business was very bad to day. I and august were most of the day occupied with our Whiskey matters. This [evening?] Otto Creutzbauer returned from Peru. altho' he was successful in getting hold and possession of the Merchandise, but unlucky not selling Ten Dollars worth of goods. damn the luck. old Dame Fortune is a fool. She bestows her favours with Damn'd bad judgment. Shall cut the old womans acquaintance. Not going to give the ship however. We received a part of our eastern Lot of Liquor to day. 7 Casks entirely, one partly Empty.[12] Very little Expense during the day, altogather 15¢

Sunday Evening August 19th 1849

I got up very late this morning. had to breakfast with my Partner. Shortly afterwards went to the Store to attend to the rectefyers. It was mot suffocatingly hot, or I should worked yet at my domestic Brandy flavouring. Bill and High Sleeth detained me at the Store until 10 oclock. I then returned home. did not go out again until the afternoon, when I and Clemens went only to the Store, from there again direct home. read all the afternoon. Otto went out yesterday to Big river for his Mother. intended [to return] to day but it is now near 10 and they are not likely to arrive any more this Evening.

Business yesterday was so so. we Sold about 50$ worth nearly all liquors. I thing we are bound to do a fair business after a Couple of years. Had no Expenses this day whatever, yesterday 15c.

Saint [Louis] August 23rd 1849 Thursday

Business has been very dull lately. the Consequence is that we are all very downhearted. I feel sometimes so exceedingly low spirited that I regret ever having left my old Employer, but as there are at present no prospects for me Except upon the prospect of our business we have to risk it and do all we Can. should we fail with our best exertions, we shall have the Consolation of having done our duty. Mrs Creuzbauer was this Evening discussing her prospects with her son. She would like to start a Candle factory, but unfortunately has not a Cent towards it, besides owing 500$ on her farm of 20 acres situated near Vide Poche. I Came very near to getting tipsy this Morning with old Kunz. the damn old Hunk did not buy any thing altho' he had things offered to him very low. C. M. Sels has settled with Stein. he has to pay him 200 dollars. Stein then gives Sels a receipt in full of all Claims. now the unfortunate part of the transaction is that we have to pay these two hundred dollars, or Sels would be taken as a Cheat and Swindler. we paid for his Lawyer 25$ Otto's trip to Peru about 25$ is 50$. 5$ we paid him Cash to day, and 213$ he was already indebted to us Amounts to 468$ which takes too much of our Cash. really I sometimes wonder that we keep so well afloat, as our payments are really too numerous and large. the fixing up of the Store and dwelling will Cost us over 300$ has already. day before yesterday I sold the first two barrels Whiskey. Expenses 50c

Sunday Morning September the 2nd 1849

Business, but principally other occupations have prevented me from devoting my customery attention to this journal. on last Friday the 24th ulto [ultimo] Wm Lake and my Sister returned from above.[13] their Company exhibited here 5 Nights to splendid houses. I was in the Canvas every evening. during the day of Course busy at the Store. Lake deposited with me or rather with us 120$ from which however some liquors that he took up with are to be deducted. the Company to which they are attached has been doing so far a very successful business. Lake is thus enabled to get his Money nearly as fast as he earns it. He expects to be able to deposit another 100$ with us this fall when returning from above. Wednesday Frank[14] Came from Cincti bringing Bernsdorf along with him. to Morrow Frank will go to work at Mosley's.[15] he is getting much more Manly and I should not be surprised if he were to become steady and make a little Money. time will show! I have not for months received any thing from Hal or Charles.[16] Chas Underwood has not replied to my last. Business Continues dull. we are however a little over expenses, and Consequently try to be satisfied. we made some few good little sales this ~~Evening~~ week. Friday Evening I was in Theatre with Lawyer Thompson. Mrs Farran performed Beatrice[17] and *Daughter of the Regiment.*

Yesterday Afternoon I and Bernsdorf were out on a selling excursion—made our Expenses—Exps small.

Monday September 10th 1849

Our Business last week was tolerbly fair. we cleared about 60$ over all expenses. our little business is steadily encreasing, a most pleasing fact. last Saturday we received about 600$ worth of Cigars from Otto Creutzbauer, actual proceeds of his and Sels transaction in Peru. We are at present amply indemnefied for our claim and all the trouble we have had with Sels. it is rather doubtful if ever he gets in our good graces again. Frank is employed with Mosley making Cigars. Can't say how he will make out, only hope he will avoid Contracting debts.

Last week I called on Eliza one of our Customers residing Almond Street.[18] the good woman took a fancy to my humble Self, while I took a fancy to one of her girls. had ample Satisfaction out of her at a Moderate rate only (| |) two gourdes.[19] *Ce n'est pas chère.*[20]

This Morning we received a little over 500$ worth of Cigars from Nulsen & Ficke. we have at present over 7000$[21] worth of Cigars in the house, we have.

Yesterday I and Clemens were working the Entire day in the Store painting the doors and Sash in the new rooms. we did not venture out any where else.

this Evening I ordered some more Catawba wine from Nulsen & Mersman,[22] having had a call for some to day. In making my domestic Liquors I am every day becoming more perfect. Expect in a short time to become perfect. My Expenses during last week were 5$

Wednesday October 10th 1849.

It is now just one month since I last Communed with myself, or put my Thoughts on paper. Business has prevented me from giving my Customary attention to my journal. Since my last Entry Commerce has gone well with us. we have Cleared upon average one hundred dollars a week Expenses deducted. Clemens now lives over the Store, & it is principally owing to his removal that I have forgot my Journal so long. we have lately Credited pretty Extensively, have at present over 800$ standing out on liquors. all however from present appearances good. in a few days we have to pay the first note for liquors of A. H. Bean. not more than half are Sold, in fact not half. My Brother in law Lake and Sister Agnes were here all last week.[23] They are still in Stokes' Circus Company. Lake deposited forty Dollars. I repaid him twenty five dolls. Our Books however show our indebtedness. our debts at present are numerous amounting over 5000 dollars, but I hope with the blessings of the Almighty on our Endeavours we Shall get along. If we do not, I am Confedent it will not be for want of trying. I had a letter from Charles Moulinier a few days ago, have not replied to it yet. on our house we still owe 600 dollars. the Account with the administratrix is Settled.[24] My Partners Ma' in Law has left us.[25] She is boarding out. I am still boarding in the City Hotel. Frank is working in the Same place. Lake's visit Cost me about 6$. my brother[26] is Expected here in a few days. Private Exps 20$=

Saint Louis Sunday October 21st 1849

My Journal I fear will for the future not have that regular attention that it has received hitherto. all our energies at present are required to promote the interests of our Business, and from this object even the Sundays are not held Sacred. for on this day we frequently have to Call on Customers and persons whose Custom we desire.

Last week Thursday Morning my Brother Henry arrived from Cincinnati. the old Boy has kept his word to Call and See me this fall. I am Sorry that I had no More time to attend to him. He was well pleased with St Louis and the Business done here. Last Sunday we were all out to old Kunz at the Camp Spring—we got most elegantly tipsy on Muscutella wine.[27] this week Thursday we went out

There again to a Wedding party. Clemens Could'nt go, being Sick from a Spree at the Cave.[28]

Henry transacted Some business here. he left on Friday about ½ past 1 on St Bt *Monroe.*[29] we shipped some 450 to 500$ worth of Tobacco and Cigars back with him. Shall do the same with Nulsen & Ficke. Last Evening I was again to a Ball out in Bremen at H. Greve's. he provided me with a Partner and every thing necessary for a Ball room. danced until ½ past 5 this Morning. at 9 I was dressed again went over to Ills town with Hinkin[30] to visit a Customer for Cigars. Shall write Louisa K[attenhorn] this afternoon yet.

Saint Louis December 9th 1849

The fears expressed in my previous entry are likely to be realized. I have Certainly had many evenings entirely unoccupied, but the weather has been too Cold to Sit down and write in our Parlour, in which we have until within week past not had a Stove. Still many Evenings are devoted to business purposes. frequently we [have] to work till 9 oclock. then again our principal Commercial Correspondence is carried on in the Evening. I shall for the future however endeavour to devote more attention to the Current Events of the times.

Week before last on Friday Evening my little Brother Frank left Saint Louis for Palmyra.[31] his Employer took another Assistant without giving Frank any previous [notice]. Murray of the firm of G[ranger] & M[urray] guaranteed Frank a Job by going to Palmyra.[32] I gave him Six Dollars along with him, so that in case his expectations of obtaining a Job should be disappointed, he has the Means to return. He has now been gone 10 days and must either shortly return or write to me which he promised to do.

Since my last entry I have been here to two Ball's, one in New Bremen by Greve, where I got half typldy. The other one was given by Erfort & Sickendick. amused myself Capittally, but did not drink any thing, because I had a sort *Poxum Secondarum,*[33] and my good *Docteur*[34] Petri recommended total abstinance of Liquors and Eatables.

Our Business during this time has Continually improved, in fact has been much better than I expected. Still our Supply of Cash is exhausted from week [to week], our Paymentz are so numerous and incessant that we are Continually short run.

Last week we remitted to Ficke 416.40 the balance due Estate of F. W. Ficke. Our Profits Since our first Commencement have averraged 100$ per week. our outstanding Claims amount to at least 1500$. Stock in Store is also pretty Complete. Still some 300$ of outstanding Claims may be lost. There is Certainly a great deal of risk Connected with the Crediting of Coffee Houses.

I have been lately more or less troubled with Colds & CC.[35] do not like this Climate as well as in Cincinnati. at present am entirely recovered from *all* my Complaints.

Yesterday we had the first Snow Storm of the Season and the first day that had really a wintry appearance. well it is time for winter to make his presense felt. Day before yesterday I had a letter from Sister Elizabeth and my little Niece Louisa Kattenhorn. a few weeks back had one from Wm and Agnes Lake,[36] directed an immediate answer to New Orleans to which so far I have not had a reply.

I shall for the future endeavour to make at least one entry a week. Shall also try to make my entries in french again. My Expenses have not been very Extravagant. JJM.

Christmas = 25th 1849

All alone . . . no relations to brighten the happiest day in the year. I made myself some pleasure in giving presents, altho' I did not receive any. I treated August Rittmeyer & Otto Creuzbauer to a fine Silk neck hand kercheif, Mrs Nulsen, a Spool Stand—the Baby sundry little nick-nacks.

To make Some amends by giving a Small Party, Consisting of ourselves, the Creuzbaur familly, the two Herzers and Mrs and Mr Helmering. We succeeded admirably in our endeavours to pass a happy time. about 10 Bill and Hiram Sleeth added themselves to our Party. We amused ourselves with drinking Catawba Wine, Punch and Playing Smut,[37] which agreable Smutty game was Successfully played until 12 oclock. Then Nulsen, who was a little tipsy wanted to black all the Lady's.[38] Mrs. H[elmering] was offended by him. This broke the game up, then I had to play and the good folks had a dance. of this they were soon tired also. it being one oclock and the Ladies Sleepy our good guests retired. Myself, Nulsen Herzer jr[39] the two Sleeths and O. Creuzbaur remaind up and Commenced playing Poker. I won about a Dollar, all lost more or less except myself.

Yesterday I had a letter from Agnes and Lake [in] N.O. to which I replied immediately. Business so far has been tolerbly fair. Christmass Expenses 8$.

Thursday January 16th 1850

I did intend to have made an Entry here the day after New Year but was prevented from doing so, thro' particularly disagreable feelings. Until dinner our Store was open. after it, I and Clemens went out with the intention of seeing and giving our Customers a call. our evil genius led us in Bremen to Pohlmyers.[40] there we met a Mrs Deobald who seems to have taken a fancy to my humble self. She invited us to Supper, after which we went to Greve's New Years Ball, with the firm intention of going home 10 oclock, but unfortunately stayed until 4 next Morning. O! What a Cloudy familly Meeting was ours the next Morning. all the blame was immediately thrown on myself, without any hearing. The Misunderstanding was however afterwards wrighted to my Satisfaction. the following Sunday I was out there again. went with Mrs D— to Greve's, Made her husband most outrageously jealous. Well if kissing ones wife is Sufficient reason for a Man to get Jealous, why the man was right. the next day I Called on them again. the poor hen pecked fool excused himself for getting Jealous. Pity I Could'nt follow up this Conquest, for Doctor Petri ordains that I shall keep my room for two weeks. there is no doubt I have the *Shankre Secondaire*[41] and must undergo a very disagreable cure. this is to drink every day a half gallon of Sarsaparilla decoction,[42] to keep quiet in my room and to eat very little, and nothing that Contains grease of any kind. the Cure is very disagreable, 12 glasses of a Mixture about as disagreable as any thing well can be. I commenced last Friday the 11th. the 14th finished the first 2 gallons of this *Decocque.*[43] yesterday I took a sort of intervening purgative,[44] and to day I commenced the 2nd 2 gallons. I do not so far experience the Effect of this treatment except getting very weak. If this Cure really Cures me I shall give vent to my joy in this faithfull journal.

During the last three days we have had a rather Melancholy time in our house. Last week, I beleive Wednesday Otto Creuzbaur Came from his work shop and Complained of his Eyes, unability of seeing with facility. he remained here with the intention of going to Work the following Monday. he was about every day, did not take any Medecin except a slight preparation from Doctor Gemp, a mere purgative. Sunday Evening he was playing Cards yet with the familly. About 3 oclock on Monday Morning he was Missed by his Mother who was Sleeping in the same room. She went into the kitchen and there the poor fellow lay on his face, the blood runing out of his Mouth. he lay all day suffering from a Congestion of the brain. the Evening at ½ past 10 he was released from his suffering. The Old Lady insisted upon his not being buried until decay Commenced.[45] yesterday he was buried at 2 oclock. in the Morning his Body Commenced Swelling to Such an extant that it was found necessary to Close the Coffin in which he was already placed [in] the evening. Poor Otto he is among those that have existed. he rendered us some timely assistance last summer, in helping us to arrange our Store when help was Scarce. Wrote to my Sister to day. received my Christmas presents from Cincinnati a few days ago.

Saint Louis January 18th 1850

To day I wrote a letter to Henry[46] of 6 pages *chuck full.* he requested a long letter some time ago, and now as I am still Confined to my room I embraced the opportunity of treating him to one. It is impossible for me to keep myself as I ought or as the Doctor requested. the damn Women[47] are Continually in the way, and as the Devil, of whom they are possessed will have they have just now taken a fancy to the parlour where they have not passed a half a day except on Sunday since we lived in this house. Day before yesterday I wrote to Elizabeth and Louisa [Kattenhorn]. So far I can not perceive any alteration for the better within me. hope, however, for an improvement.

Sunday feby 17th 1850

Il faut que j'écrive français, parce que je Veux raconter les Malheureuses Suites d'une maladie que j'ai eu il y a cinq ans. C'est la Shankre Secondaire, dont jétait affligé depuis les Cinq dernières Semaines. Un Doct. Petri m'a guèri d'un Thé de Sarsaparilla. j'en ai bu 6 gallons, une demie gallon les jour. Mais c'est une remède éffroyable. même à présent je ne crois pas en être tout à fait guèri parce qu'il y a encore une petite place qui est encore plus dure qu'elle ne doive l'être. mais je vais me Comporter pour le premier an ainsi que je n'aurai pas à crain un retour de cette Maladie.

Les Affaires Se Sont bien Mal allées dérnièrement. Je viens de recevoir une longue et agreable lettre de mon Ami Chas Herbst.

[I must write in French because I want to report the miserable consequences of a sickness I had first five years ago.[48] It is secondary chancre with which I have suffered in the last five weeks. A doctor named Petri healed me with tea made from Sarsaparilla. I had to drink 6 gallons, a half gallon a day. What a terrible medicine! But at present I don't feel fully recovered because there is still a place that is more painful than it ought to be.[49] But I have to carry on for the first year as though I had nothing to fear from a return of the illness.

Business has been very bad recently. I just received a very long and agreeable letter from my friend Chas Herbst.]

Sunday March 3rd 1850

Since my last Entry I have been confined over 3 weeks to "not my room" but to Mr Jägers room as my accommodations were too poor at home and I craved more substantial Society than our females. I accepted his offer to Share his room and keep him Company. We drank Sarsaparilla Tea togather for two weeks. Then I required another week to recover a little and to Strengthen myself. I had not yet entirely recovered when I foolishly went to a Ball at Werners were I caught a severe Cold and was laid on my back for another week. Yesterday a week ago I was again at a Ball at Werners but was more prudent Consequently escaped disagreable Consequences. The last Ball was a Sort of Maskerade which amused the Spectators more than the participators.

Our Commerce has been Tolerbly fair all winter. we have not had a week during which we did not realize [income] over expenses.

My back Correspondence (private) which had been quite neglected I have brot up to date. I have written twice to Charles Underwood, once to Chas Herbst, do Harry Brayley, do 3 Sister Agnes, once to Elizabeth. In fact more or less to all my acquaintances

This Week Monday Frank[50] returned from Quincy.[51] I also this week received a letter from the Proprietor of Quincy Hotel stating that Frank had left without settling for his board. Am at present Entirely recovered from *Shankre Secondaire,*[52] at least I thing so, tho' the Doctor thinks it is not certain and recommendeds very Careful diet every Spring and the anual repitition of Sarsaparilla Tea.[53]

Yesterday I witnessed a phenomena in Nature that I have never heard or read of. it was Snowing very hard when all at once a vivid flash of lightening and immediately a Stuning Clap of Thunder. The Clerk of the Weather evidently made a mistake. the oddity was repeated two or three times within an hour.[54]

Lake is at present in Cincinnati.[55] I have had 3 letters from Agnes within a few weeks past.

Henry[56] is friends again with Kattenhorns familly. They visit one another as relations should do.

Have no time to write any more.

Sunday Morning March 10th 1850

The Weather for past two weeks has been very Conducive to Colds. It rains snows, hails & thunders all in one day with the greatest ease, having no regard whatever for poor suffering humanity.

Yesterday however was a delightful day, excepting perhaps a too Strong north wind, making it very disagreable for a person to have his Phiz northward. now yesterday was an unusual eventful day, for a variety of reasons and incidents all going to have a detailed enumeration.

In the first place we received part of our Spring Stock from Steamer *Atlantic*[57] yesterday, and advise of the safe arrival of some Goods from Baltimore[58] which we had omitted to insure, and the loss of which we could have ill afforded. the Lord knows we have lost enough for the past year and by some persons that my Partner had every Confidence in. I presume we shall loose about 500 if not 600$ of course we can not tell precisely how much, as we have nearly 2000$ outstanding.

About 3 P M Self and Christian Miller rode out on top of an omnibus with the Strong North wind blowing Strong in our faces to New Bremen. We stoped first at Charley Krone's, but as he was detained an unusual long time trading of an old wagon, I, Miller and Sanders went to Grawe's. Coffee was just ready when we Came & we [were invited] to consume some which we did. we afterwards rolled 10 Pins as long as we Could see. The party with which I played won every game. I myself made the best roll during the afternoon, getting 45 Pins with 6 Balls.

Having ceased rolling, and having [nothing] to do, Charley Krone proposed that every one should Contribute towards paying the Musiciens and we would pass the Night with dansing. of Course no one objected. Grawe went on Deobalds (the Bakers) Horse and rode out to French Town to get the Music. until he came we danced to the Sound of a Flute in the hands of Sanders.

I was a little intimate[59] with Deobalds wife. She reproached me with having broke off my visits, and requested very earnestly a Continuance of the same. In the neighbourhood of one oclk [o'clock] we had supper. half an hour afterwards I, Miller and Stolteben[60] and his Wife left in an omnibus. I and Miller arrived about 2 at Werners.[61] The Company were just about Setting down to Supper. hardly had the Eatables disappeared when a fire broke out, which at first we supposed to be in our house, but which proved to be in the Planters Tobacco Wharehouse. and a great fire it was.[62] I, Henkel, Rose, his *Schwager,*[63] and Nulsen were up about the fire till 4, having taken the Ladies home previously. Exp 1$

Tuesday April 16th 1850

This has been the most disagreable Spring we have had for a long time, at least so all old inhabitants say. for instance last Sunday it snowed the entire day, Covering the Earth 4 to 5 inches.[64] yesterday it was nasty sloppy disagreable and to day it rained all the time. The regular Spring business has been very much retarded. our Country Trade this Spring has been quite limited so far. I am again troubled with that damned Complaint which has already given me so much trouble this winter. Doctor Petri has had the brazenfacedness to charge me 40$ and his Cure is still imperfect. it has lately shown itself again on my tongue and my lips.[65] the Doctor has given me a preparation to wash the Sore places with, and as soon as [it is] warm again I shall have to endure the damnable Cure again,[66] and hope to God I may get Cured for I am getting desperate, for unless I am Cured I shall never Marry, and as soon as I am Certain that I can not Marry I shall Care damn little about getting rich or making, or even remainging longer, an honest Man. were I to push matters now I doubt not but that I Could sleep every night with a good looking woman, but curse this affliction I dare not do it.

I feel like Courting a little now and then and have the acquaintance of a good loocking young Lady, but the excitement of feeling is forbidden by Medecin.[67]

The Theatre opened on 9th. I have seen Miss Logan twice, must acknowledge she is improving.

Six weeks elapsed before JJM wrote again in his journal—six long weeks filled with anxiety. His "cursed complaint" had persisted, so he decided to get a second opinion from a trusted German practitioner in Cincinnati, Dr. Franz Joseph Obendorf. JJM combined a business trip with his personal objectives and returned to the "Queen City" after an absence of fifteen months. He stayed at the home of his sister Elizabeth Kattenhorn and spent many hours visiting with his brother Henry Mersman.

Cincinnati Monday afternoon
June 3rd 1850

Once more in the old Place, the spot of my nativity, of my formation. I arrived here last Saturday about One o'clock, after a very pleasant trip of 3½ days having left St. Louis on Tuesday evening 28th May. the following day half past 11 we were in Cairo. Thursday at 11 in Louisville. until 3 P.M. the boat[68] was busy getting thro' the Locks and Canal and finally at 6 or perhaps 7 for it was evening we left there and arriv'd here as before said. during the leisure hours on board, I was usually one of a party of Whist or Euchre playing for the Cards [and] Liquor that was all, never thought of joining in a game of Poker.

Rosenfeld also Came with me, altho' he is a jew and already owes us two dollars. the poor Devil was without any Means at all on board. in Louisville I loaned him 25 cents to pay for the washing of a few shirts, not having a Clean shirt to put on. when afterwards the Clerk demanded the passage Money, he asked me to loan it to him so humbly that I Could not refuse him. he had fortuneately a 1000 Havana's on board which I took as Security, and of which I shall keep enough to Secure my 8 25/100 Dollars.

Yesterday I was out to Mount Pleasant[69] with Henry, Tony,[70] Grothouse and their Wifes and famillies. Henry and Tony intend to purchase some Lots there from a Man who is about 400$ in their good graces. I think they will buy them advised them to do so.

We returned part of the Way, and then struck off in a road that led in to a romantic piece of wood land, where we encamped and had our dinner. it was a lovely spot, well shaded and the green Carpet of Nature most downy and soft. Ex-Miss Bruning[71] excited my disgust in some degree. She Coquetted too much with me with her Eyes. Some time ago this would have amused and pleased me and I should no doubt have tried to turn her favor to advantage, but now that I have myself determed to Marry I have also made up mind to make myself as worthy of my future wife as I possibly Can and if I do not make as good a husband as any other it will be my wife's fault. we returned to town about 6 oclock. I and Kattenhorn visited Fortman's after Supper, drank a quart of beer and went home.

This Morning I visited my old Employer Dexter. the Old gentleman has not lost any of his rotundity, but looks well and enjoys good health. I had a long Conversation with him, in fact was there until it was high time to dinner. the afternoon I was at home. Kattenhorns house is my home during my Stay here. After supper I Called on my old friend Wagner at his Drug Store. After a long talk about old times which occupied us until past 9, I, Wagner and Toni went over the Canal to A. Moors Pleasure Garden. the arrangements there are very extensive, the beer verry good. the Garden itself has more right to that name than any other that has ever been in Cincinnati. I returned home Shortly after 10, but every one being in bed, I went down to Henry, but I Could not get in there. Went to Chas Kopp'. Saw Labarre there and Chas Sisters who are both Married.[72] had to pay 20 cts for Sleeping there.[73]

Cincinnati June 4th 1850.

I arose this Morning 6 oclock. paid for my Sleeping & went home to breakfast, which was already over.

Immediately after breakfast I went down to Henry's to see if any thing telegraphic had arrived—nothing—I noticed Corn has declined in Saint Louis, altho Whisky seems firm at 25 and one lot Sold at 26c I expect a decline there in a few days or I should buy now, as here it is only worth 22½c. If however Clemens[74] is in want, he will telegraph. About 9 I went out with Henry. Called on Chas Storch. also Saw Schrader there who is Storchs Partner. from there we went on some business for Henry. then Called on Meyer & Becker. both the young men look somewhat pale. Their Store is under my old friends the Misses Corbins house now.[75] I noticed Mrs Corbin still keeps boarding house there. I do not think I shall Call on her. We then Called on Beneke who has a most brilliant Cigar Store under the Burnet House.[76] the young man looked as handsome as ever. The Burnet is Certainly the Most Magnificent Establishment I have ever seen. I do not know what Stile it is, as to the Architecture, but it seems impossible to Surpass it in elegance grandeur and beaty. every thing appers in perfect taste. from there we Called on the Kochs. The Same old tune. had dinner with Henry. Slept afterwards till 4 oclock. Called on Loders and paid them balance of Acct 24$. After supper I called at Diek and Fahlbusch. Diek is the Daddy of a fine looking boy. from there I went to the *Liedertafel.* it was election eve. the Collection of old famillier faces reminded Strongly of old times. Went home ½ past 10—

Wednesday June 5th 1850 in Cincinnati

It is most Confounded hot at present. I do not thing St. Louis Climate surpasses this in heat. during the day I Called on some of my old acquaintances. part of the After noon I was employed writing to Clemens.

The Evening I went to the German Theatre with my brothers wife and her Sister Margaret.[77] The piece performed was passable containing a good deal of wit and humor. Rosenfeldt acted his part very creditably for the Short Time he had to study it. The female Characters were much better supported than the Male one's. altogather I was very well Amused. The Theatre presents pretty much the Same view as two years ago. Poor Frank[78] was unwell, so he and Henry[79] went home after the 2nd Act was over. I got to bed at 11 oclock. No Exp.

Thursday June 6th 1850

This Morning I had a letter from Clemens. it came too late to buy. I went down immediately to purchase but the Market was bare, nothing to be had. The bottom Whiskey all sold for 23c & at the Canal for 23¼ I shall buy to Morrow if I can ship reasonably. This Afternoon my Sister Mrs Kattenhorn gave a grand Coffee Party in honor of [my] presense. The most prominent of my Married female acquaintances were present. Mesdames Thiesing, Wagner, Nulsen, Ficke, Mersman, Evans, Tieman,[80] and a half dozen others who did not previously have the pleasure of my acquaintance. by the bye Mrs Wolf[81] was there also. altho' there was not a young Lady present I amused myself Capittally. My kind Sister offers to give me another party to which she intends to invite the most elegeable young unmarried females.

I have however for a very good reason declined her generous offer. *quand on est Malade, on ne doit pas penser à la Mariage, on quand on aime on ne peut pas bien S'amuser avec des autres.* [When one is sick, one should not think of marriage, or conversely, when one is in love, he cannot flirt with others.] The Married females of my acquaintance have preserved well. Mrs Wagner has not oldened any at all. Mrs Thiesing looks more juvenile than a few years back. She has Some 6 months ago become the Mother of a pretty little girl after a rest of eight years. Tonys wife looks also very good. Ficke's wife will in all probability live longer than he.

After supper I Called on my old Companions the Burkhardts. both young men look almost precisely as formerly, hardly any perceptible variation. we may do some business togather yet. from there I went to my old Christian.[82] the old boy was waiting for me. went in the new Museum Corner 5th and Walnut.[83] We were treated to Some very passable Hungarian and Messalenious Singing. The Collection of Curriosities is also tolerbly extensive. among others not bad is a group of Wax figures representing the trial of our Saviour which is really Sublime, the effects of intemperance &c. To Bed at ½ past 11—

Cincinnati Friday June 7th 1850.

This Morning I bot 30 bbls Whiskey 23¼c Shipped them at 50c per bbl on Steamer *Cambria.*[84]

The other day I saw my old Chum Companion Brown. he looks as dry as ever. invited me to come and dine with him. thus far I have not done so. Called on Grothouse and Tebelman. I think they will take the balance of our Cuba Tobacco, and pay in Seed Regalia[85] at 11$. Had dinner at Henry's. after dinner I went to Doctor Obendorf. he gave but a gloomy picture of my affliction, represented the difficulty of its cure. gave me however a recipe which he seemed confident would Effect a cure. The ingredients are as follows.

2. Parts Sour Dock or Sour halbergoul
1. Part Burdock, or Klettenwurzel
1. Part Brazilian Sarsaparilla[86]

Now I Shall have to Call on Wagner and get the bottanical names of these articles. I Shall to have it prepared every day, about a full handful put in a half gallon of water, which is to Simmer until one third has evaporated. this must be done in a Closed kettle so that none of the Strenght is lost. I intend to Commence as soon as I return.

The evening I passed at home playing Euchre with Kattenhorn, Sister and Frank. I was too tired to feel like going out. Paid 75 cents for telegraphic Notice.

Cincinnati Saturday June 8th 1850

I was busilly Employed to Day. During the forenoon I and Henry went to the Starch and Pearl Barley factory to arrange about Starch & barley.[87] Henry wanted to give in payment a Note on Osting[88] for 50$. we Could not arrange matters as one of the Partners was not there. Ficke returned to day. we [made] a dab at business already, but did not arrange any thing.[89] from there I and Henry went to the Starch factory. we finally arranged every thing. I bot 6 bbls Barley, 20 boxes Starch, 10 Wholes and 10 halfes. Shipped the whole on the *Cambria,* for Whiskey 55¢ and 20 cts per 100.[90]

The Evening, I, Henry, Frank and a young french workman of N & M's went to the german Theatre. *Die Reise auf gemeinschaftliche Kosten*[91] was the piece, Madam Vorraths benefit. She exerted herself very Creditably. I was better pleased than before. I should not have gone, but it being the last evening for this Summer and a benefit of a good looking Woman, I Considered it my duty to be *thar.* befor the performance commenced I and Rosenfeldt played a game at billiards. I beat him by about 10.[92]

I Shall not go to Ball Hill[93] to Morrow. feel too downhearted with my Confounded Complaint[94] and as I dare not indulge in dissipation of any kind, I can not of Course expect to amuse or be amused. Home about 11 oclock.

Cincinnati Sunday June 9th 1850

I arose about 7 oclock this Morning. After breakfast I Commenced a letter to Clemens. did not finish it. Henry and Frank Called about 9. we went to the Saloon in the german theatre building, played billiard until 12. I and Frank played 3 games, he gave me 60. I had the rubber in my favour. Henry Can not give me more than 50.[95]

After dinner I finished my letter to Clemens which I trust will Come to hand in time.

About ½ past 2 in Company with Kattenhorn and familly went to Henry's, where we passed a very pleasant afternoon. nobody present but the Members of the two families.[96]

The evening I passed at home. Henry and familly returned the afternoons visit. we played Euchre until 10 then retired to bed all of us.

Monday June 10th.

The Shower yesterday has had no other Effect than that of Making the Air a little Cooler. beautiful weather again. Immediately after breakfast I and Henry went out Walking. Called on Tappe. the old fellow is as lazy as ever. from there on my old friends the Menzels. they are doing a fine business and look about as well as ever.

The Afternoon I, Henry, Doctor Hudson and a young frenchman passed in a french Club room playing Euchre. had Supper at the N.Y. Dining rooms.[97] home 9—

Cincinnati June 11th 1850. Tuesday.

This forenoon I passed principally at Nulsen & Ficke's. Confound their Stingy and Mean Souls. they persisted very firmly in their demand of 10% interest on every Amount after 4 months had been given. When I found them deaf to reason and brotherly feeling, I flatly refused to give them 10% and at the Same time treated them to my private opinion on their proceedings. I got Nuilsen Slightly excited. he Said that if we did not Consider their having lent us Money in the Shape of Mdse, and only Charging us 10% as an especial favour, he would provided we paid the whole Amount with 10 days throw off the interest altogather. I promised to try, but fear shall not be able to get it. don't Care if I don't. we have used them as far as we need them, and Certainly have the advantage of them. It was a tough debate, but I had the advantage in determination and Coolness. The afternoon I passed with Wagner at his Store. poor fellow he is very much Confined. the assistant Can not Speak English.[98] Bugeleisen is in Louisville, Married to an Apothecary named Stein on upper Market,[99] is much prettier than formerly, has a fine boy &c. The Evening I and Christian[100] passed in the National Theatre. *Village Home* was performed, and *Ladder of Love.* the house was about half filled. I Saw my old acquaintance Kate and Julia Cobb. they are both married. I did not renew the acquaintance altho' Should like to have heard from Anne S. Rickey.[101] I Settled the tickets. Exp 1.00.

Cincinnati June 12th 1850 Wednesday

Weather Continues very warm. on going down to the river this Morning, I found the d—n *Cambria* still in port. She went however about 12 oclock.

Had a letter from Clemens to day. poor Devils they are evidently tired of working and out of humor with his unability to Supply the demand for Whiskey.

The Lord knows I suffer most with my Sickness. I am determined I will if possible get rid of this Sickness first, before I trouble myself about a future whose value is uncertain. poor Claudine,[102] I think she loves me. I certainly love and respect her much more than I have ever done any girl. but I shall never Marry her or any other one without her being made acquainted with my affliction, its Nature, the effect it may have on my Children &c. Even now I feel the necessity of avoiding all excitement, dare not See any of my former female friends, except married ones.

I do not yet know why I love Claudine, but the fact is pretty certain, and I am Confident she loves and will Never love another or I am much mistaken and have lived a long time without learning any thing. If after undergoing a few more Cures I think myself incureable I may perhaps either blow my brains out, or go traveling and Spend the Money I have made and then finish.

I felt very downhearted this evening. So I remained at home playing Euchre with Kattenhorn his wife and Frank. We played until 11 oclock. Frank staid all night with me, perhaps the last time in this world—

Cincinnati Thursday June 13th 1850

Weather Warm without any probability of any change. the forenoon I passed with my old friend Dexter. the old gentleman has acted and even now acts as generous with me as any of my relations. nobody Could possibly improve on his generousity. instead of wanting to charge interest, he offers himself to let the old amount Stand until it is entirely Convenient for us to pay it. I have bot 12 bbls old Whiskey from him at 42½ cts. freight to St Louis is 90 cts per bbl[103] so I shall not ship yet. leaving my old place I walked along lower Market St. saw many of my old acquaintances Still in business on the old Street. About 11 I went into N[ulsen] & M[ersman]'s Tobo factory.[104] After admiring every thing there, my evil genius tempted me to lift up a large iron Screw bar weighing about 200 lbs. having handled it enough, I was letting it down in one hand, when I felt it Slip in my hand. I was going to grab hold again with my other hand to prevent it falling on my feet, but it descended too rapidly, and as it touched the floor my unfortunate middle finger was caught, and Mashed so thouroughly that I Can not possibly make of my left hand in 10 days or so. Shall loose the Nail I think. Was home all afternoon reading some french operas of which I bot 10 for 200 cts this Morning.

The Evening I, Henry and Frank passed in a Concert given by Wallace, Strakosh and Madame Cassini.[105] Wallace is a Composer of Supr Merit, as well as a universal genius on every instrument. he is decidedly a good violinist and touches the Piano to admiration. Strakosh is known as a highly accomplished Pianist. he was rapturously applauded.

Madame Cassini's voice could not be well judged this evening. she was evidently very hoarse. her lower notes are weak without any ring in 'em but the upper she has a power and Command of her voice and such a Correct taste that renders her pleasing to every Musical ear. poor Henry had to Settle the damage for all three of us. To Bed 11 oclock.

Friday June 14th

The Morning I passed at N[uilsen] & F[icke] without accomplishing any thing diffinite. they persist in demanding interest at the rate of 6 pr ct to present time and from now on, 10% with our Notes at 6 and 12 months equally devided. Now in my opinion what ever the law will not allow is not right,[106] but I offered 6% from the maturity of every Amount to the time we Can pay it, or until present time no interest, and from now on 10%—We did not agree and fear I Shall not be able to Settle it. After dinner I amused myself at home until 4 then went down to Grothause and Tebelmann. Sold them the balance of our Cuba Tobo at 22 and 25¢ to be paid in Common Regalia at 11$.[107] The evening I passed at home talking to Kattenhorn. To Bed at 11.

Cincinnati Saturday June 15, 1850.

I called on N[uilsen] & F[icke] this Morning. having failed to make arrangements, the Conclude to Send their account with me made in Compliance with their last proposal.

About ½ past 10 being at N[ulsen] & M[ersman]'s my little sister Agnes and her little husband Wm Lake arrived upon us Suddenly both in apparent and actual good health.[108] They have taken a little boy in Portsmouth[109] whom they are going to adopt. till nearly 12 we were busy purchasing an outfit for the youngster. had dinner at Kattenhorns. about 2 we left per Omnibus for Sportsmens Hall. they have miserable Omnibuses here. the improvements all along in Fulton are not very extensive. The Hills Skirting all along the road and Protecting, as it were, the Continuous Chain of Houses Never seemed to me So grand, sublime and beautiful.

As there was no afternoon performance,[110] we—I, Bill, Henry and LeBrun—played Euchre on board the *Danl Boone*[111] until evening. we all had supper on board. I Stay'd all night. about dusk we went per "Buss" to the Canvass beyond Sportsmens Hall. at first the prospect for an Audience was poor, but as the performance progressed, the house filled very respectably. I caught a Cold going home which was about 11. Slept on board in Lake's double State room. before retiring we indulged in a Punch, then Smoked a Cigar. to bed at 12 oclock.

Sunday June 16th in Cincinnati.

I arose about ½ past 7 this Morning. had breakfast on board about 8. Read my *Police Gazette*[112] while William and Agnes were dressing. then Shaved myself and finally about ½ past we were ready and started for Kattenhorns. on Saturday I made William a present of my gold chain and this Morning in a Confectionary and fancy Store I added a patent *Porte-monnai*[113] for which I had to fork over a dollar, gave Agnes a breastpin for 75c and treated to refreshments to the Amount of 50 cents. I had just time to dress before dinner, it being ½ past 11 when we arrived.

After dinner I, Kattenhorn, Lake and Agnes played Euchre. I and Agnes won pretty extensively—about ½ past 2 Henry and his familly arrived. The whole familly was assembled under one roof, a reunion that may never take place again in this World. I enjoyed to the full the rarity of the occurrence. There was our venerable Father, his hair grey—but Still Stout, hale and hearty, Elizabeth the oldest of his Children, a good looking woman of 34 years, Henry the 2nd at no time particularly handsome—about the Same thing as of yore, only little more emaciated, Joseph (myself) No 3rd, if not for my unfortunate sickness the happiest and most Noble looking speciman in the Collection, Agnes, the 4th, a Still handsome woman, altho' I thing from her exposed life, She will soonest feel the hand of time rest heavily on her. the number finishes with Frank who always was and Continues to be the youngest in the familly. he commences only now to form his looks and appearance, altho' is still considerably childish. We five form the orriginal familly. now there are 3 auxillary Members, Kattenhorn, Lake and Henry's wife, persons that were taken in for the accomodation of Members of the old familly. if my next cure succeeds, I shall no doubt add another female auxillary within another year.

About ½ past 4 Helbusch with his wife (my old Sweetheart Mary P[uthoff]) arrived. Mary is yet a very pretty woman. She has not however suffered any from Marriage, having had No Children so far. poor Helbusch appears too weak for this purpose. I fear he is incapable of loving warm enough to reproduce. Mary appears to love her husband. I wish I was certain of her being happy, not that I have in reality any Cause for self reproach. she Could never expect to have done better, except by getting me. We Amused ourselves Capittally, Some of us were playing Cards. the junior Members were Amusing themselves with Music, the Ladies with talking Scandal as usual, and bothering their unfortunate husbands now and then. We all had Supper togather. I and Bill took a walk to the Burnet house to get some Cigars. Billy met a lot of old acquaintances at the American Theatre. About 8 the visiters went home. we played till 10. then Went to bed—

June 17th Monday in Cincinnati

It rained more or less the entire day. Agnes and Billy went about 11 oclock to the boat from there to the Tent. they gave no performance during the afternoon. The Evening Audience was also but indifferent. The Canvas was too far back from Civilization.[114]

I called on Loder. they promise to send us coal on Commission as soon as they are Clear of Catherwood.[115] part of the forenoon I was occupied writing to

Clemens. had dinner at home. took a nap afterwards and about 3 oclock I called on Mrs Wagner. we had a long Conversation togather which made time pass rapidly until 6 oclock, when I left. Supped at home. After it, I went to Henry's he would not go along with me to Forsters Varieties late American Theatre, so I went myself. Mrs Martine, Sister of Mrs Kent met with Considerable approbation. She possesses an extensive share of the libertinism ways of her sister, is however a very lively actress. Old Harry Chapman also appeared in a suitable Character. Harry bids fair to continue a favorite of the Cincinnati Public for a long time. He is in my opinion the best Comic Actor I have ever seen

The Theatre has undergone no perceptible alteration since my last visit to it in Company with my old friend Brown. I met my old chum Companion the other day. he invited me to dinner to see Brown No 2.[116] have not had time to do it. To Bed 10 oclock

Cincinnati June 18th 1850, thursday

The Weather was lovely, but rather too hot. after breakfast I went to Doctor Obendorf to Show him the Samples of Sour Dock and Burdock. he Confirm'd their being O.K. I went back to the old woman in the Market in 5th St and bot 4 lbs of first and two of the 2nd. from there went to Nulsen & Ficke got their statement of our account. then returned to Kattenhorn. Agnes, Lake and her adopted Boy's Mother were all there. I remained home all day. in the evening I went to the Circus. it was crowded which was disagreable for me as I had a Lady[117] with me. Lake as usual pleased the Audience very much.

Wednesday June 19th

This morning I and Bill went down to the river, Wm to engage passage for a Lady to Portsmouth I for myself to St. Louis. I made arrangements with the Clerk of *Ben West.*[118] from there went to Henrys arranged all my business. Called on Grothause & Tebelmann. made him ship 4 M[119] Common Regalia. Called on Burkhardt & Co. arranged some business with him. then went over to bid farewell to my friends there. Mrs Wagner old Mrs Nulsen,[120] Tony's familly, Wagner, Steinberg,[121] &c. Old Daddy wept as usual when I left. The boat finally pushed off at half past 5. farewell to Cincinnati.

NOTES

1. This progression of emotions in individuals with serious illness has been examined in modern times (Kübler-Ross, 38–137).

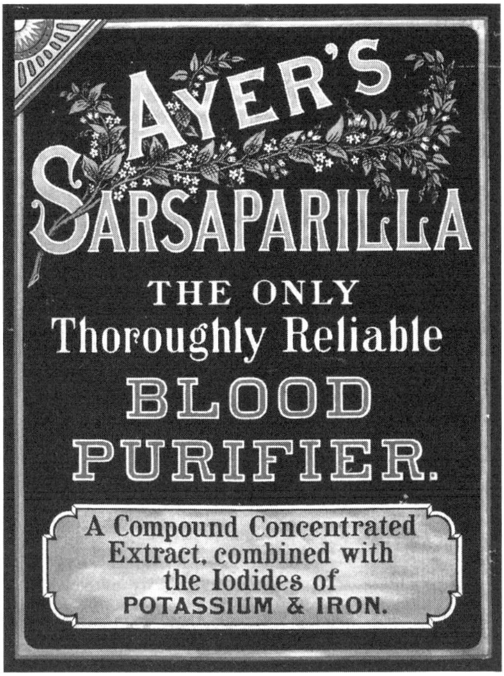

Ayers Sarsaparilla advertisement, c. 1880. Many products were marketed to cure a variety of ills. Some of the cures were worse than the disease. Sarsaparilla was touted as a "blood cleaner." Mersman used it as a cure for his syphilis, among other treatments. (The Detroit Historical Museum.)

2. Published in 1839, *The Phantom Ship* was written by Captain Frederick Marryat (1792–1848), a British naval officer who became a popular author.

3. Peru, Illinois, was the home of Otto Creuzbauer's and Albertine Nulsen's sister, Ottilia Creuzbauer Rhoades. The steamboat trip from St. Louis up the Illinois River took three days.

4. Wine made from Catawba grapes grown in Hermann, Missouri. German settlers produced the first wine there in 1846, and the community soon gained the title the "Wine City of America" (Shoemaker, 239–40). Catawba grapes, so profitable in the vineyards of Cincinnati, made a wine that improved with age, and so were introduced to Missouri (Muehl, 248).

5. August Rittmeyer.

6. Diagrams of distillation apparatus may be found in Monzert, 37–63.

7. Anthony Nulsen and Henry Mersman in Cincinnati.

8. The *Melodeon*, a 244-ton sidewheel packet with a wooden hull, was built in Cincinnati in 1849 and "fitted up in the most elegant style." The boat routinely plied the waters between Cincinnati and St. Louis, but was on a trip from New Orleans to Nashville in 1850 when it collided with the *G. W. Kendall* and sank near Plaquemine, Louisiana, with the loss of three lives (REV, 9, 10 March 1849; Way #3893, 318).

9. The liquors possibly traveled by wagon and packet boat from New York to Cincinnati, using the Miami and Erie Canal. Then steamboat transport on the Ohio and Mississippi Rivers could have brought them to St. Louis. Another possible route was from New York to New Orleans by an ocean-going vessel and then up the Mississippi River by steamboat.

10. JJM preferred to get his supplies from Cincinnati (only a four-day journey by steamboat). However, he knew Edmund Dexter's practice of adulterating liquors in an effort to improve their flavor and therefore ordered from New York rather than risk Dexter's tampering.

11. Ohio has been called the Buckeye State since the presidential campaign of 1840, because it was known for the tree, *Aesulus glabra*, also commonly called the horse chestnut. The large brown seeds resemble the eyes of a white-tailed deer (Cist [2], 97–100).

12. Whiskey manufacturers speak of an "angel's share" disappearing from barrels, but JJM hints that some person handling the cask siphoned a sample of the contents (personal communication, Jerry Dalton, master distiller, Jim Beam Products, 5 August 2002).

13. Spencer Q. Stokes's Circus had traveled on the Mississippi as far north as Prairie du Chien, Wisconsin, 450 miles above St. Louis, entertaining crowds in river towns (Thayer, 468).

14. Frank Mersman.

15. "Mosley" is possibly a misspelling. Charles F. Mosler (1814–54) was the name of a German tobacconist and cigar maker with a shop at 100 north Third Street, near N & M in St. Louis (St. Louis City Probate Court, Estate #4253; USC 1850, M432, roll 417, page 58, line 4; SLD 1848, 170).

16. Hal Brayley and Charles Herbst.

17. The St. Louis Theatre began its fall season on 8 August 1849 with a refurbished playhouse. Beatrice was a character in Shakespeare's play *Much Ado About Nothing*. Since that play has five acts and runs at least two hours, an abbreviated version of *Daughter of the Regiment* was performed (REV, 8 August 1849; Benefit of Mrs. Farren, 31 August 1849, Theater Programs Collection, MHS).

18. Almond Street, part of the red-light district of St. Louis, was called "hell's half acre" by the *Missouri Republican* (Carroll, 7; Dacus, 443; van Ravenswaay [2], 311).

19. French slang for money, in this case, two dollars.

20. [Fr.] it is not expensive.

21. The inventory was worth about $168,000 in 2005 dollars.

22. The Cincinnati firm had become a wholesaler of local wine.

23. Spencer Q. Stokes's South-Western Circus, in St. Louis for eight days beginning 1 October 1849, featured the Lakes. The clown's antics and Agnes's wire-walking won glowing reviews (MOR, 3 October 1849).

24. JCN's previous partner, Frederick W. Ficke, died in November 1847, and it took several years to settle the estate with the administrator (DDT, 16 November 1847).

25. Mrs. Creuzbauer had taken lodging separate from the JCN family.

26. Henry Mersman had promised to visit JJM.

27. Muscatella wine is a sweet wine made from Muscat grapes (OED, s.v. "muscadella").

28. McHose Cave.

29. The *Monroe*, a 183-ton sidewheel packet with a wooden hull, was built in New Albany, Indiana, in 1848. The boat carried passengers and freight on the Missouri and Mississippi Rivers, but sank above Natchez, Mississippi, in 1854 with thirty deaths (Way #4014, 329).

30. Hinkin has not been identified.

31. Palmyra, Missouri, eighty miles north of St. Louis, is on the west side of the Mississippi River.

32. How urban workers found jobs is described by Stott 90–96.

33. [Lat.] secondary pox or secondary syphilis.

34. [Fr.] doctor.

35. "CC" was JJM's abbreviation for his "cursed complaint" or "confounded complaint," syphilis.

36. William and Agnes Lake remained in New Orleans with Stokes's South-Western Circus from 12 November 1849 through January 1850.

37. Smut was most likely a word game in which the winners were permitted to put soot from the fireplace on the faces of losers. Players sat in a circle, with one of their number in the center. The leader would place a small object in the hand of the first player, who would ask, "What is this?" The leader would reply, and the object would be passed to the next player, who would ask the same question. The game went on until the object reached a player who was unable to name all the items in order, for example, "Six calves, five toads, four geese, three snakes, two ducks, and a fat hen." The fun of the game was in the penalty imposed on any player who failed to repeat correctly (OED, s.v. "smut"; O'Suilleabhain, 33–34).

38. The threat of soot on their faces caused the women to call a halt to the high jinks.

39. A younger Herzer, perhaps a brother.

40. Most likely the saloon in Bremen, Missouri, operated by Theodore Pohlmeyer, German immigrant.

41. [Fr.] secondary chancre or syphilis.

42. Sarsaparilla, widely believed to be a "great blood purifier," was promoted by physicians and newspaper advertisements for decades (CDG, 5 February 1874; Fisher [3], 18–19).

43. [Fr.] decoction, made by boiling a plant in water to extract a medicinal agent (OED, s.v. "decoction").

44. Laxatives were a common treatment for almost any ailment (Bethard, 16, 27).

45. The possibility of being buried alive concerned many people during the nineteenth century, especially because of reported instances of cholera victims' being entombed prematurely (NYC, 9 December 1865; HER, 11 June 1852; MDC, 16 August 1849).

46. Henry Mersman.

47. Albertine Nulsen and Claudine Creuzbauer shared lodging with JJM and JCN. Their mother, Mrs. Karl Friedrich Creuzbauer, visited frequently (USC 1850, M432, roll 417, page 46, line 19).

48. JJM likely had an episode of urethritis (manifested by painful urination) five years earlier, and concluded that was the first stage of the illness he experienced in 1849. Modern physicians know that urethritis may be caused by many infections, including chlamydia and gonorrhea. However, from the sixteenth century until the mid-nineteenth century, medical pundits taught that gonorrhea and syphilis were the same disease. Scottish physician John Hunter (1728–93) authoritatively stated in *Treatise on the Venereal Diseases* (1787) that gonorrhea was an early stage of syphilis, and JJM may have learned that incorrect concept. In 1838, Philippe Ricord (1800–89), a French physician, demonstrated that gonorrhea was a separate illness, but his discovery may not have been known to JJM (see PHS, 4–8).

49. Probably a reference to a genital lesion.

50. Frank Mersman.

51. Quincy, Illinois, ten miles north of Palmyra, Missouri, is on the east side of the Mississippi River.

52. [Fr.] secondary chancre, the secondary stage of syphilis.

53. See Fisher (3), 18–24 for a detailed discussion of the treatment JJM underwent.

54. Thunder snow, a rare winter weather phenomenon, occurs when the air closer to the ground is comparatively warmer than the air at higher altitudes, leading to the development of short-lived electrical storms during snow events (Cortinas, 298–300).

55. William and Agnes Lake wintered in Cincinnati with Burgess's American Circus, and opened the season on 18 April 1850 in Lafayette, Indiana (COR, 16 April 1850; Thayer, 475).

56. Henry Mersman.

57. The *Atlantic,* a 666-ton sidewheel packet, was built in 1848 in Cincinnati. Carrying passengers and up to one thousand tons of freight, it usually ran from St. Louis to New Orleans, but collided near Cairo, Illinois, in 1853 (REV, 10 March 1849; Way #381, 32).

58. Goods from Baltimore, Maryland, would likely have traveled by ship to New Orleans and then up the Mississippi River by steamboat, a voyage of nearly three thousand miles.

59. JJM describes flirtatious behavior, not necessarily adultery.

60. Possibly Mr. Stolteben, a German-born grocer in business with Martin Jurgens at 240 North Second Street (SLD 1851, 185).

61. Frederick Werner (c. 1801–51), a German immigrant, was the proprietor of the Frederick House, a hotel at 115 North Second Street in St. Louis (SLD 1851, 365; SLDR, B:9; USC 1850, M432, roll 417, page 53, line 22).

62. Planters's Tobacco Warehouse, on the corner of Washington Avenue and Second Street (near the Frederick House), contained commission merchants, a furniture business, and storage for tobacco. The flames destroyed that building, but did not spread to others. Losses from the fire, estimated at $120,000, were covered by insurance (MOR, 11 March 1850; INT, 11 March 1850).

63. [Ger.] brother-in-law.

64. A St. Louis newspaper, commenting on the unusual weather, reported that on 14 April 1850 the snow fell from early morning until 3 p.m., leaving "six or eight inches on the ground" and putting the fruit crop at risk (MOR, 15 April 1850).

65. Secondary syphilis typically results in lesions on the skin and mucous membranes.

66. See JJM diary, 3 March 1850.

67. Doctors believed that sexual arousal exacerbated the symptoms of syphilis.

68. JJM traveled on the *Mount Vernon,* a 77-ton sidewheeler built in 1847, which was bound from St. Louis to Pittsburgh (LJO, 31 May 1840; Way #4050, 333).

69. Currently, Mount Healthy, Ohio.

70. Henry Mersman and Anthony Nulsen.

71. The former Caroline D. Brüning had wed Wilhelm F. Grothaus on 23 December 1849 (Grothaus-Brüning Marriage, 23 December 1849, St. John's Unitarian Church, Cincinnati, Ohio, Church Records, unpaginated, Entry # 125 for 1849, FHL Microfilm 1510039).

72. The first names of the Kopf sisters have not been found.

73. JJM paid the usual fee for spending the night at the Farmers' & Traders' Tavern run by Charles Kopf.

74. JJM's partner JCN remained in St. Louis, minding the store.

75. The Corbins' house was on Third Street between Walnut and Vine streets (CCD 1848–49, 24).

76. The ground floor of the Burnet House featured retail space, perfect for a tobacco shop.

77. Margarethe (or Margaret) Tebbelman was the sister of Adelaide, Henry Mersman's wife.

78. Frank Mersman suffered from tuberculosis.

79. Henry Mersman.

80. The guests included the wives of Ernst Theising (Christina), Augustus Wagner (Philippina), Anthony Nulsen (Maria), Herman Ficke (Ottilia), Henry Mersman (Adelaide), Francis Evans (Hannah), and John Tieman (Elisabeth). See Annotated List of Persons, Places, and Businesses.

81. "Mrs. Wolf" may have been the wife of Samuel Wolff, who had a retail cigar and tobacco store at 38 Broadway (CCD 1853, 429).

82. Christian Vefean, Dexter's employee.

83. Wood's Cincinnati Museum, containing wax figures, was located in the Apollo Building on the corner of Walnut and Fifth streets. The museum was open daily from 8 a.m. until 10 p.m., and evening entertainments (vocalists and plays) began at 7:30 p.m. (COM, 7, 8 June 1850). From 1 June through 8 June 1850, a Hungarian Musical Festival was featured.

84. The *Cambria,* a sidewheel packet with a wooden hull, was built in Pittsburgh in 1845. The boat carried up to five hundred passengers and freight on the Ohio and Mississippi Rivers, but sank near Sainte Genevieve, Missouri, in 1851 (Way #0809, 69; REV, 14 April 1849).

85. A regalia is a type of cigar with a thick burning end and a pointed mouth end. A seed cigar is produced in the United States from domestic tobacco. Thus, N & M were trading Cuban cigars for domestic ones (Voges, 263, 282).

86. Sour dock or common sorrel is *Rumex acetosa;* burdock is *Arctium lappa;* and Brazilian sarsaparilla is *Smilax syphilitica* (Watts, 152, 302, 800; Clason, 46, 508, 574; for other therapeutic recipes, see Carson, 261–69, 436–37; Lost, 524–27; Smilax, 32–38).

87. Barley and starch were used in making whiskey. JJM purchased starch as a less expensive alternative to grain such as corn.

88. J. D. Osting, who operated the Ninth Ward Tavern on 468 Main Street, evidently owed money to Henry Mersman. Short of cash, Henry attempted to use Osting's promissory note as payment for a purchase from the starch factory (CCD 1850–51, 208).

89. JJM attempted to negotiate with Nulsen & Ficke, i.e., Anthony Nulsen and his partner, Herman Ficke, who had loaned money to N & M (St. Louis).

90. Shipping costs are expressed per barrel of whiskey and per 100 pounds of dry goods.

91. [Ger.] *The Journey on a Joint Account,* a comedy in five acts based on the French play by L. Augely, was performed (VOL, 6 June 1850).

92. In the previous nineteen months, JJM had learned to play well. See JJM diary, 27 November 1848.

93. Bald Hill, an elevation six miles east of Cincinnati, was a popular location for picnics.

94. JJM still suffered from syphilis.

95. JJM noted that his brothers were only a little better than he at billiards (Bartlett, 130–34).

96. The Kattenhorn family (Arnd, Elizabeth, Louisa, and Sophia) and the Henry Mersman family (Henry, Adelaide, and a daughter) plus JJM and Frank numbered at least nine individuals.

97. This location has not been identified.

98. The assistant was likely a recent immigrant and spoke only German.

99. Frederika Bugeleisen, JJM's childhood friend from Cincinnati, had married a man named Kessler. Widowed in 1848, she subsequently married in February 1849 a German druggist, Gustavus Charles Stein, who had a shop at 683 Market Street in Louisville, Kentucky (LAN, 18 April 1848; Louisville Marriage Register, 4:232, Filson Club; LCD 1851–52, 251).

100. Christian Vefean.

101. Anne S. Rickey has not been further identified.

102. JJM first mentions the name of Claudine Creuzbauer, the woman whom he eventually married.

103. Note the rate quoted; five days earlier, the freight to St. Louis was 55 cents per barrel.

104. The cigar factory was in their Main Street store.

105. The advertisement read, "William V. Wallace, Composer of the Imperial and Royal Theatres of Vienna and London, and Maurice Strakosch, Pianist to the Emperor of Russia" would appear with "Madame M. L'Cassini, the celebrated Prima Donna from the Opera in New Orleans." Tickets were 75 cents (COM, 13 June 1850).

106. Usury laws in Ohio and Missouri capped the loan interest rate at 6 percent (SLD 1848, xiii).

107. JJM describes a sale of Cuban tobacco (at $22.25 per one hundred pounds) paid for by bartering domestic cigars valued at $11.00 per hundred pounds. See note 85.

108. Agnes and William Lake, with Samuel B. Burgess's American Circus, played in Fulton, Ohio (15 June), Covington, Ohio (17 June), and Cincinnati (18–19 June 1850) (Thayer, 475).

109. When they passed through Portsmouth, Ohio, the Lakes, who had already lost two sons, found a child to adopt, whom they called William. Such adoptions were common among circus folk, who wished to recruit young talent, and sought by birth parents who hoped their children would learn marketable skills (personal communication, Stuart Thayer, 5 June 2005).

110. Because of the late arrival, the circus skipped the afternoon performance on 15 June 1850 (ENQ, 5–11 June 1850).

111. The *Daniel Boone,* a 169-ton sidewheel packet with a wooden hull, was built in Cincinnati in 1844. The boat mainly traveled between Cincinnati and Maysville, but it transported (1845) the bodies of Daniel Boone and his wife to Frankfort, Kentucky, and carried (1849) President-elect Zachary Taylor on part of his inaugural trip to Washington, DC. After it collided (1853) at College Point, Louisiana, it was replaced (Way #1441, 119).

112. The *Police Gazette,* published in New York from 1845 until 1931, was a sensational tabloid with lurid coverage of murders, prostitution, and boxing (Hoornstra, 151).

113. [Fr.] *Porte-monnaie* means moneybelt.

114. On 17 June 1850 the American circus played in Covington, Kentucky, across the Ohio River from Cincinnati. They gave only one performance in the evening (ENQ, 16 June 1850).

115. The Robert W. Catherwood Company, on the corner of Olive and Commercial streets in St. Louis, rectified whiskey. Loder & Company may have provided that firm with charcoal, and could not supply N & M, as well. Catherwood, "a poor businessman, extravagant and entirely unworthy of credit," likely had cash-flow problems that affected Loder (DUN Missouri, 36:32; SLD 1851, 79).

116. Since the time JJM had left Cincinnati, Charles Brown's wife had given birth. Brown prospered as a wholesale grocer and later bought a soap and candle factory (DUN Ohio, 78:124, 322, 323; 84:65, 93, 469).

117. JJM's companion was likely the mother of the child the Lakes planned to adopt.

118. The *Ben West,* a 241-ton sidewheel packet with a wooden hull, was built in Brownsville, Pennsylvania, in 1849. The boat carried passengers and freight mainly between Pittsburgh and St. Louis, but was fatally snagged in 1855 (Way # 0576, 49; LJO, 21 and 22 June 1850).

119. Four hundred pounds of tobacco.

120. JCN's mother, Philippina Holstein Nulsen (1786–1856), also bade farewell.

121. Wilhelm Steinberg, a clothier, lived on the west side of Main, between Canal and Twelfth (CCD 1850–51, 258).

CHAPTER ELEVEN

Courtship and Marriage

24 June 1850–11 April 1852

JJM wanted to "settle down," partly because many of his friends had already married,[1] but he needed to complete syphilis treatment before his doctors would approve of matrimony.[2]

St. Louis in 1850 contained nearly two adult men for each adult woman,[3] yet JJM found himself in the daily company of Claudine Creuzbauer, JCN's sister-in-law.[4] Her family had emigrated from Baden in 1838 and 1839.[5] Claudine's father, Captain Karl Friedrich Creuzbauer, a Napoleonic war hero, had become a "Latin farmer" in America.[6] Her mother, Caroline, the former Baroness Hornig von Hornburg, was from a distinguished military family. The Creuzbauer children, three boys and three girls, were now completely grown: Ottilie, the oldest daughter, wed Benjamin Rhoades of Jefferson County, Missouri, in 1842, at age seventeen;[7] Albertine, the youngest daughter, married JCN at age seventeen; and twenty-one-year-old Claudine was the only unmarried Creuzbauer still in St. Louis. The oldest son, Otto, had died (16 January 1850), and the two surviving sons, Robert and Edmund, had settled in Austin, Texas, after the Mexican War.[8] The Creuzbauer parents owned extensive real estate holdings: a forty-acre farm in Carondelet, 160 acres in Jefferson County, plus numerous lots in St. Louis and Carondelet.[9]

Meanwhile, Agnes and Bill Lake had financial problems. Several circus companies that hired them had major losses and ceased operations, leaving them stranded. The Lakes called on JJM for advice and assistance. He helped them as much as he could, and even included a bequest for Agnes in his 1851 will, in case he predeceased her.

Joseph J. Mersman (1824–93), c. 1850 (front facing). This photo was taken shortly before Mersman's marriage to Claudine Creuzbauer. The successful young businessman went on to operate a successful whiskey business, and later founded, and became the first president of, the Fourth National Bank of St. Louis. (Personal collection of Linda A. Fisher.)

St. Louis June 24th 1850

I arrived here after a pleasant but somewhat tedious passage of four and half days. we were delayed nearly 24 hours in Louisville. had an old acquaintance on Board Mr Lubbe[10] brother to the Manufacturer of Tobacco here. he is however a Confounded dull travelling Companion. fortunately, I had good books with me, which made time pass sufficiently pleasant. In my hurry to go, I forgot to bid *adieu* to my brothers wife and familly and quite a variety of acquaintances.

The next (if ever) time I visit Cincinnati it will be with my wife. I left the old Spot with much less regret than the first time. My good old Boss Dexter was also Swindled out of the parting handshake, not being in the Store when I left to go on the Boat.

When I arrived here every thing was as usual and friends all in good health. Sweet Claudine[11] appeared as handsome to me as formerly. Somehow she has occupied my thoughts much longer already than any young Lady I have ever known. T'is true I have paid my addresses to young Ladies for a longer period than I have thought of her as of a being that may one day be my wife, but I did not think of them except when I was with them. I think she loves me, and I certainly do not hate her. well I must wait until I am Cured before I Can think of Courting her. even this will not be an easy job unless I do it with the understanding of making her my wife.[12] Should like to know her first.

St Louis Septr 22nd 1850.

What a lovely Sunday Morning this is, and after such a night as the last. it seemed as if all the elements in Nature were warring with each other. poor Mortals! a most emphatic proof that after the severest Storm the most delightful Calm succeedes.

It is now nearly 3 months since I made the last entry. a most disagreable time have I had of it. the Summer has been the hottest known here for the last 10 years and I have taken every other Morning a Sulphur bath as hot as I Could bear it. at present I think I am Cured. there are Still some indications of its existance in my Mouth, but they are kept in existance through my Smoking. for over two months I followed Doctor Obendorfs Cure and Petri's at the Same time. am now very weak. I think in 3 or 4 weeks More I shall be through with Medecin and for fat and a good wife.[13]

I have and have not been Courting all this time. it depends with me to give my doings a name. I have been a good deal with Claudine, at home, riding out on Sundays, to Theatre with her, but to all appearance (including ourselves) we are as reserved as ever. Henry[14] has been paying us a visit. he arrived here on the 7th inst was here just 10 days left this week Tuesday in Company of Bill Lake and his wife, who were all this time boarding at the Walton House.[15] I sued Stokes for 150$. Won.[16] we have now 300$ of Bills Money for which we agreed to pay 6% as per Note. Jaeger is going to be married to day.[17] I and Swanz[18] are = invited—

St. Louis Septr 29th 1850. Sunday

Another week past, a Somewhat uninteresting [one] to me. not having done an overlarge business and passed every evening at home excepting the last night which was the first one of the season at Henry Graewa's. his first Ball was given last night. not only was I present, but my good *assoicié*[19] Clemens with his better half. I did not enjoy myself at all, knowing that the worst antidotes to my Medical habits are dansing and drinking. I endulged however in both to Some extant. drunk however very little and as for dansing I hardly got warm by the opperation being so accustomed to Hell thro' the frequency of my Baths. Another little circumstance also not a little detracted from the possibility of my being amused. from Conversation being led to Suppose that "Aunt" as Clemens Calls [Claudine][20] desired to go I very foolishly (thro' a mistaken Sense [of] gallantry) offered my Services to conduct and for my accommodation received a "ha—t"[21] a thing that wounded my Self-love not a little. I err much if She does not anticipate to Share Some fine Ball's this winter but things have to change Mightily if it takes place thro' an invitation thro' me. Sometimes I feel as tho' I lavish all my affections on her. then again she is so repelling in her behaviour that I am almoast disgusted with her. I am almost, in fact at present inclined to abandon her—if I can—[22] was at Doctor Petri's this Morning. He thinks I may now Slacken off in the Number of my Baths. when I am lazy I Shall do So.

Saint Louis Sunday Octr 13th 1850.

It is getting decidedly wintry. a Stove to day would have added much to indoor Comfort. as it was I was Cold the whole day. My Brother in law William Lake arrived last evening from Cincinnati to see if he can get a situation with Burgess, but as B— has sold out he will probably obtain one from Fred Hunt and Tryon present Proprietors of the American Circus.[23] we were in to see the performance last evening. it was very poor without any order or System. Afterwards went to Robbins. I & Bill treated ourselves to a Prairie-chicken[24] and when Hunt, Tryon and John Wing arrived, they treated to the oysters, Scotch Ale &c not to Mention the quantities of Brandies that were taken by all hands around except myself. The Gentlemen got quite jolly by twelve oclock. we did not go home until two, all pretty tipsy except Self and William. I was nearly freizing. any how I Caught a severe cold.

My Poor Brother Henry was taken sick on his return trip, and has been since quite dangerously ill at times. last Saturday he was not expected to recover.[25] Sunday pretty much in the Same Condition. Monday and Tuesday he recovered considerably. on tuesday at 2 oclock William left Cincinnati. to morrow I shall telegraph to Cincti concerning Henry. poor brother! I Should hate to loose him. This Morning I and Bill went early to the S. B. *Skuilkill*[26] to get his baggage, then dressed and went to Robbins to get our breakfast. I shall notice what William does here.

Sunday Morning October 20th 1850.

A most lovely morning. Abraham, Mrs A and Mrs C—[27] are to Mrs Henkels funeral. poor woman she departed this life night before last at ½ past 10.[28] poor Henkel is once more blessed with Single Missery. I am not cured yet of my damned Complaint. whether it is owing to my damned habit of Smoking or is not yet entirely eradicated from the System I Cannot Say. but during this week I have had two new Sores on the old places again.[29] true, I have been a little dissipating again, but if it was all gone it ought not to return so rapidly. I shall not Commence Courting in earnest until the Doctor tells me to go ahead.

Poor Bill! he is here still and in trouble. part of the Circus Stock is now attached. their Boat is on the other side of the river,[30] taken there by the precautionary Burgess. I have this week endorsed a note for the Concern for 150$ payable in 60 days from the 16th inst. John Wing intends to prosecute Sherwood[31] for Wms Claim, which by the bye has to be sued over again. their wise Lawyer [says] that an execution rendered in N.O. is not good here. to morrow will develop the plot further. Poor Agnes[32] she little thinks her worser half is loosing all his rhino[33] here and getting into debt besides.

Business was damn poor except some 5 Sales which with the smaller transactions net us for the week 175$ profit, a very good average. we are crediting again pretty extensively and must be prepared for losses or very good profits. I do wish I was entirely cured and a certain young Lady my wife. I should endeavour to be happy ~ [Margin note] was to Siekendicks Christening Party Tuesday evening. Caught Cold, hence my trouble, I think. my lips are enflamed from Cold. weather has been raw and disagreable also.

Sunday Evening November 10th 1850.

This has been a most disagreable day, so Confounded dark and gloomy that in a room having three large front windows one Could hardly see to read. the

Consequence has been that all of us have passed the entire day at home in extreeme *negligé.*[34] Last Sunday I was out with Wissman during the afternoon & Evening. we went to a dancing Party at Becker's.[35] I expected and in fact was told that we should meet some handsome girls there, but such was not the Case. I for my part was not disappointed however, in fact rather rejoiced than grieved because I might have been induced to dance which by the bye I had better lieve alone. In fact it seems to me that I am getting quite domesticated in my wishes. If my Dearest had been with me I should have taken more interest in the proceedings. also at Louis Horn's[36] Ball last week Tuesday I thought of her the whole evening altho' I had plenty of good dancers among my acquaintances there, Mrs Black, Miss Emma W—, Miss C who graced that graceless Scamp M—r.[37] I returned home half past 2 rather early for me.

Yesterday I had news from Bill Lake. they did a fine business in Memphis.[38] Carothers[39] informed me that John Winn has bought the Company from Hunt & Tryon and that Winn would not return unless he did a fine business so as to be able to Settle all his debts. Sweet C[laudine]— is absent I don't much like Can't however Say that I have a right to grumble. Business good. We are making and loosing money

[Margin note] my Dear Henry is Completely restored to health. I had a letter from himself last week.

St. Louis Sunday Evening Novr 24, 1850

A most beautiful day this has been. I did not however have leizure to enjoy it. the forenoon I was busy all the time making up Domestic Liquors. did not dress until past 2 oclock. went about 3 to Erforts for my lunchion the good Dutch Custom of taking Coffee after Dinner being no longer in existance with us. returned about 4. I and Abraham[40] then went out togather, gave Papa Frankson a call. the old chap is going to move next week and open a Coffee House on Broadway. we Spent for Oysters and wine 80 cents. My old friend Samuel Peebles arrived this morning from Cincinnati. poor Sam—says he has been considerably troubled in familly matters. Some of his relations have died. he asserts that 5 or 6 prominent failures have taken place in Cincinnati within the past two weeks, 3 for large amounts. Business with us has been very good during the past two weeks. we invested yesterday 550$ to buy a Note of Christian Miller which will net us over 100$ profit in 3 months from date, our first speculation of this kind. we paid out yesterday over 1100$ and have still over 200$ in Bank Henry B[ernsdorf] will want his money in the Course of next week nearly 200$ which will not however inconvinience us in the least.

I had a letter from William last week. Agnes is well, the Company is and has been doing so far a bad business.[41]

Claudine Creuzbauer Mersman (1829–90), c. 1850. Claudine married Joseph Mersman on January 30, 1851, in St. Louis. She bore him eight children. (Personal collection of JoAn Dreahn, a descendant of Edmund Creutzbauer.)

I shall have to write to him pretty soon. Agnes seems also to be discontented. I only fear we shall have to fork over the 150$ we endorsed for the Company. Sweet Sissy[42] returned last Monday.

Sunday, December 8th 1850.

Just two weeks elapsed since my last Entry. last Sunday I and Clemens walked out to [?] without however calling on anybody. Wissman had the honor to be with us. the evenings we always pass at home. This week may emphatically be termed the Commencement of winter. Very Cold since wednesday, the rivers above are closed, ice here runing very fast. fortunately I purchased yesterday evening 44 bbls whiskey at 21½ if this weather Continues it will advance perhaps to 25 cents.[43] Friday Self and dearest, Clemens and wife were to a Ball given by the Turner association[44] at Mochel and Horns. the Company was somewhat mixed altho' some passable specimens of Germania were present. I did not amuse myself as well as I should have done had I been alone, for with her I did not have one opportunity of speaking alone, or of enjoying myself with her. had I been alone, I Should have found other Sources of enjoyment. I do not feel at all inclined to be Coquettish like formerly, and sometimes it seems to me that under certain circumstances I could be jealous. to my taste there was no handsome female in the Ball room, no belleship, no rivalry among the women, not one having any great advantage as to beauty over another. of Course I can not but except some. there are females who become absolutely lovely when one knows them and all the beautiful traits in their character. thus at least it stands with me and what I have chosen for myself in the shape of a Wife. Oh Charles M[oulinier] & H[erbst] on first sight you would not perhaps acknowledge my former undoubted taste, but upon better acquaintance you would do justice to my choice. the affair cost Self and Abraham 15$ I am Satisfied with our business Speculations for past week. had a letter from Bill[45] and Winn. they are in N. O. and doing well. they were all well. wrote to Bill—
[Margin note] I did Some corresponding this week. wrote to Charles Moulinier and Herbst, Brother Henry.

Saint Louis Sunday Afternoon Decr 15th 1850

This week nothing of any interest has transpired, Except one thing which is very unusual. Gallagher the murderer of a woman on last 4th of July, under the most atrocious Circumstances was hung on Friday the 13th on the lower extremity of Duncans Island. the poor Devil died like a hero. he was attended by two Catholic Clergemen. Singular the Catholic Priests prepare their Sect much better for death than any other Sect. I did not see it. he had choice of between 12 and 4 oclock. thought he would not suffer himself to be strung before the last moment, but all those who thought so were disappointed. he was hung at 1 oclock. hung about 30 minutes, then his body delivered over to the Catholic Priests.[46]

Business was very good and advantageous for us this week. we sold tremendously of Whiskey. The Evenings I passed at home without exception. I shall take the first opportunity of concluding my life Contract with Sweet Claudine. I am now entirely cured and Can offer myself as an honest man. I should have courted the dear Girl more earnestly already last Summer, but could not do so as an honest man, not knowing if I should ever get well again. besides I was so Cast down all last Summer while undergoing this outrageous Cure.[47] however I am not certain yet that I shall be accepted. if not I doubt whether I shall ever offer myself again. but I think the little girl loves me and all will End as I wish. any how I shall know before long. had a letter from Elizabeth[48] this week have not replied to it yet. Shall do so that it will reach them about Christmas.
[Margin note] Yesterday I paid my Tailor Reinbold in full to date also Wesselhoeft for 3 Months Subscription to his library. JJM.

St Louis December 29th 1850

Business is getting most disagreably dull now. for the past [week?] we have hardly realized expenses. had a letter from Lake this week in which he communicates the disagreable fact that John Winn is broke and all his advances as well as our venture with Winn are a total loss.[49] we can stand it but poor William to be thus Swindled is rather hard on the poor Devil. I replied immediately offered him the balance of his Money in case he should need it.

The Christmas day I passed at home, the forenoon in church with my Sweetheart for I regarded her as such some time already. I presented the dear girl with a passable Dressing Case and a fine embroidered handkerchief, one of the same kind to Mrs Nulsen all my presents Cost me just 22.65$ I have spent more when I was less able.

Thursday evening we were all that is Self and Partner[50] with our better Halves to a Jäger Ball.[51] as I had good opportunity I availed myself of it to declare my Love to its dear object, which after some pretended or real doubts as to its reality was accepted. because my actions had not been those of a hydrophobical Lover it was presumed that it could not be very firm yet. to a being that wished me Cabable of exhonorating myself it was easy to do so with honest reasons, for whatever Coquettry may have existed in my previous Conduct to Ladies, it has been governed by the strictest honor towards my present Bride.

Karl Friedrich Creuzbauer (1793–1870), c. 1851. Claudine's father, a decorated military officer, served under Napoleon. He immigrated to St. Louis with his sons in 1838. (Personal collection of Linda A. Fisher.)

I have just finished a letter to Sister Elizabeth informing her of my present relationship with my Bride. my Ball Expenses were Small, as I passed my time with my Love. Joseph.

St. Louis January 16th 1851. Thursday afternoon

Business is and has been so far this year extreemly dull. even now I am writing this page in my Journal out of Sheer ennui, not having any thing to do and not knowing what to do with myself. I am at loggerheads with my Bride or I should go up and Court her.

The behaviour of my intended in one respect has been somewhat strange. altho' she would let me kiss her lately pretty freely, she has never kissed me herself. So far I have attributed this to her extreeme reserve and bashfulness, but night before last Clemens, being a little out of humor, said that Claudine had offered to bet him 50 dollars that she had never kissed me. I am now forced to beleive that her feelings can not be so very delicate on this subject or she would not have made it a matter of bet. were there a few grains more of Coquettry in the Composition of her Character I should be forced to beleive that altho' she had agreed to marry me, if she wished she could yet give the first kiss to him. as it is I am totally at a loss to devine what reason she had. if she said so without any object it was exceedingly foolish and thoughtles. I for myself must Confess that I have been over affectionate, and after her declaration and offered bet that she takes no part in all these exhibitions of affection that have taken place every evening I should Consider myself a fool and an Ass to Continue in Same Manner. So far I have felt too bad about it to seek any explanation. I should not be sufficiently Cool. I do hope this will be explained to my Satisfaction.[52]

St Louis Wednesday Evening January 29/51

To day I won a Trial against Steamer *Cambria*[53] for the recovery of one box of Mdse valued at 145.25. this value gives us 43$ profit. The Captain instead of paying put the Matter off to the Committee of Appeals of the Chamber of Commerce.

To Morrow is at last the eventful day of my Marriege[54] with Miss Claudine Creuzbaur, the day that will Seal my happiness or misery for with me there is no Medium. I consider the risk or chances however very trifling, for my Sweetheart says she is confident that she loves me fully as affectionately as I do her, and as I on my part intend to do every thing that any sensible Woman Can expect from a loving husband. as to being faithful that is a thing or a virtue that I owe to my self fully as much as to my trusting wife. the only Source from which I expect or can even immagine a possibility of discontent or misunderstanding is from the feminine humor that all Ladies will indulge in to some extant. however to give my intended credit for a fair Share of Common Sense is only doing her justice. Should my expectations be much disappointed, I shall as heretofore communicate my thoughts to this Journal. ~ " ~ I am now worth about 5000 Dollars. with my wife I receive nothing, consequently all my Property is honestly my own. I have not married for money or gain.[55]

I have corresponded considerably with all my Relations. none will be present at my wedding. Mrs Kattenhorn is going to give a Wedding Party to Morrow also for the benefit of my friends in Cincinnati. Joseph J. M.

St Louis February 6th 1851. Thursday Evening

It is now within an hour a week since self and wife were married Standing precisely where I am now setting.

I am entirely Satisfied with my Wife's person. she realizes my warmest expectation. even one inconvinience that I partly expected I found just situated where I feared it would be, i e, too far behind. it is somewhat difficult to Enter the haven of weded happiness. otherwise her person is well develloped, nay even with the exception of bubbies somewhat voluptuously.

I have also followed my Medical advise. Shall for the first three weeks take a sort of blood quieting preparation. in one respect however I have been sadly disobedient. instead of indulging in sexual enjoyment once a night I have been so incautous as to go it five times the first night, two the 2nd 3 the 3rd night and twice a night since, except yesterday morning when I was so warm that my tool would'nt stand. last evening I was in the same hobble. however during the night I made the Matter good.

My little wife is still backward and modest. however has been a little more Communicative since our Marriege. I flatter myself however that I will lead a very happy life with my little wife. She appears and pretends to love me dearly. will give a first Cause however for this love. however great many good wifes to husbands in Middling Condition would never have been caught by the best of men lower situated among the fortunate ones in this world. however I am truly happy so far. business very dull.

St Louis Sunday afternoon March 30th 1851

It is now two months since I married, and I can not but acknowledge that so far I prefer married to single life. it is true there are now and then little differences between self and wife. She has, unfortunately some of her good fathers quarelsome and unpleasing disposition, but with kindness mixed with that delicate firmness which every true woman must admire in her husband, except where she wants to rule and domineer over him, and this my wife can, I dare say, already discover that she can never hope to do with me. that she loves me devotedly I have no reason to doubt, and every one to beleive, and upon average I am as happy as I expected.

My Journal has been neglected some time, quite a variety of noteworthy items have occurred since my last entry. A few days after previous entry I wrote to my Brother in law[56] and proposed to pay him 655$ and leave the other Note Standing until next year. in due course had a reply that he had already put the Notes in Bank for Collection, that last year we had cheated him out of 5.50 by not giving him interest on interest and that it was his intention that it should not happen again this year. On the 22nd inst we collected two Notes, togather near 900$ I waited with my reply until these Notes were paid, for now we can pay his Notes with ease. last Sunday I replied to him and explained the Candid fact to him, that the reason of my not offering him interest on interest arose out of a feeling of delicacy, i e, I was fearful of offending him by making such an offer, and that so far from cheating we were very willing and glad to pay him all that he Considered himself entitled to. his notes amt to 1205 dollars. on 5$ we never allowed him interest and on one note due last 1st of May of 550$ we only allowed him 50$ for another year. we consequently owe him 6$. this gives him interest on interest. I have promised to send him this money with Henry.[57]

Until lately I have entertained the idea of going to Cincinnati with my wife. had already written my Relations to this Effect, but have now Changed my mind. I would not burthen my good Brother in law Kattenhorn to this Effect after his unbrotherly Conduct, and Henry I fear has no accommodations for us, and the Expenses are also a Serious hindrance, having to take so much Money out of the business. the best way to replace it is to save what we have and to use every exertion of making more.

My little Wife has this week written to her new relations. She would have done this sooner, but so far expected to go with me to See them all. I have also informed them of my new determination of Staying at home this year.

My health seems now entirely restored. in fact I am if any thing too healthy. beleive trouble my sweet little wife too much, have upon average rolled over her twice a Night since we are married.

Jenny Lind Concluded last week here her brilliant carrear.[58] She gave 5 Concerts. I was to none. Saved ten dollars at least. all of our benevolent Societies here enjoyed her bounty. the german *Frauen Verein*[59] of which by the bye my good mother in law is President, received 250 dollars. her total donations amt to about 5000 Dollars.[60]

Yesterday our friend Henry Bernsdorf returned from N. O. has now a Bar on a boat and is apparently doing well. he says he is going to patronize us for Liquors. just as lieve make money on him as on anybody else.

Business is improving the last two weeks considerably, although I fear we shall not have the Country trade we had last year. the Licence law[61] in Ills is knocked into a cocked hat.[62] Still we shall mighty hard to do very fair in town here.

My Expenses are modest. dare not indulge yet.

Next, JJM turned his efforts to achieving financial security. To him and his in-laws, real estate appeared to offer an excellent return on the investment. JJM had decided to start a family and knew that would take money.

St Louis June 20th 1851

Yesterday I and Clemens bot of Christopher Crone a house and lot on Chouteau's Pond for 710$ all to be paid in trade of such articles as we keep in Store for Sale. as the Rail road will come within a few squares of this place we consider it a favourable purchase.[63]

Caroline Hornig von Hornburg Creuzbauer (1794–1870), c. 1851. Claudine's mother, the daughter of a German baron, immigrated with the rest of the Creuzbauer family in 1839. (Personal collection of Linda A. Fisher.)

About ½ past 7 this afternoon my partners wife was delivered of a fine healthy boy. may he be the cause of happiness to his Parents.[64]

For the last 3 weeks all the Stores on the Levee have been under water.[65] quarantine Island is also covered. in Some places the distance of two Squares on the Mo side is covered. the Illinois bottoms are entirely Covered. the communication between there and here is cut off for Mdse, as the water on bottoms is not deep enough to let the Ferry run to the bluffs. Business has in a great Measure been Stopt. even now there is but a poor prospect for the next Month.

Business has been rather dull for past two weeks. upon the whole it has been rather fair for the entire Season. we have accumulated a few new Whiskey Customers.

Our Mother in law has Sold half of her Real Estate in Carondelet last Saturday for 3027.50 ⅓ Cash, ⅓ in two years ⅓ in four years with 6% per Ct interest on the Notes. to Morrow another attempt will be made to Sell the balance.[66]

My little Wife had her Coarses[67] yet day before yesterday. Consequently there is no hope yet for any Baby with us for the next 9 Months.

Cholera continued to plague St. Louis intermittently for the next four years. During one such summer outbreak, JJM paused in his work to record a will that reflects his sense of duty towards his wife, Claudine, and his great love for his sister, Agnes.

St. Louis, July 9th 1851. July ninth, fifty one[68]

As the Mortality rate of the City is and has been for the last Month altogather too large for a healthy state, and as some of my good friends and acquaintances have died very suddenly and in too short a time to prepare properly for their final departure from this world, I shall now proceed to make and detail my perhaps last wishes or will and unless a later will, than this bearing my signature is found or known to be in existence.

The books of the firm of Nulsen & Mersman will show my share or interest in the firm. of the articles now in use in the housekeeping of our two families the furniture in my bedroom as a matter of course is my private property, as also the Carpet in the parlour bot by me this spring. the small book case with Contents is also mine. The large book case and the two large rocking chairs in the parlor belong to the firm, consequently half to me. All the furniture and my personal Effects I wish and will to my Wife Excepting my Guitar which I give to my brother Henry, my flute and all my flute music to my brother Frank as also all my books of education. My Sisters Mrs Kattenhorns Children all my Novels and Piano Music. Should my wife at the time of my death have no children, I wish that my brother Henry, or in case of his death, my brother in law Kattenhorn will invest one half of my entire worth to the best advantage he can and faithfully pay over to my wife Claudine Mersman Semi-Anually the interest there of and this so long as she remains my widow. in case she marries again, and from that day this capital of which my wife has enjoyed the interest shall belong to my brother Frank and my Sister Agnes, now Mrs Lake, to be devided equally between them. Mrs Lake's share shall not however be paid over to her. A. Kattenhorn shall invest the money and Mrs Lake shall receive the interest thereof

The other half of my entire worth I will and wish to my dear old father so long as he lives. When he dies, it can and may with the balance of his Effects be equally devided among my dear brothers and sisters. I would strongly recommend to my brother Henry and Sister Elizabeth as they are both well off to give their share to the younger brother, and to the younger sister, as fortune so far has not been so kind to them as to themselves. You my dear brother and sister will beleive me when I say, that I would also with pleasure give over every thing either one of you might lieve me, in case of either of you dying before me. These in Short are my wishes, and altho' I am not certain if this will made privately and without witnesses is legal, Still my Hand writing is known to all my relations

Albertine Creuzbauer (1831–98), c. 1851. Albertine married John Clemens Nulsen in 1848. When Mersman married Claudine in 1851, the business partners became brothers-in-law. (Personal collection of JoAn Dreahn.)

and my brothers, Sisters, Father and my dear Wife will respect and Comply with them.

Joseph J. Mersman

Saint Louis April 11th 1852. Sunday

It seems nearly a year since my last entry. how time passes. Well! it has touched me but lightly thank God! I have since my last entry enjoyed uninterrupted good health. In looking over my last entry I find that then I had not even a prospect of becoming a Daddy, as my wife had just had her Courses. Now how different—I have now the pleasure of recording the birth of a healthy good looking Boy who weighed Nine pounds when born (fully).[69] On March 31st (Wednesday) at five oclock in the Afternoon the little Stranger first saw the light of this world. the pains he occasioned his poor Mother commenced at 10 oclock with Considerable violence. the midwife who arrived about this time thought the birth would take place yet before dinner, but there was much more difficulty than she anticipated. the baby was so large, and my wife who is now 22 years old was so firmly set that the bones and muscles would not yeald and give way so easily. at last however the thing was accomplished. the baby looked quite blue from squeesing it had undergone. fortunately the usual restoratives proved successful.

So far Mother and Child are well. at first there was some difficulty in making the little stranger take the breast but that is also nearly overcome. he sucks now like a good fellow.

Business so far has been better this year than last. we have also made improvements in our Rectefying apparatus. the baby is crying—must go up

NOTES

1. "Marriage was a mark of full manhood," a status to which JJM aspired (Rotundo, 115).

2. There were no laws requiring medical clearance, but JJM's personal ethics made him wish to comply with physician's directives. See the discussion of syphilis in the epilogue.

3. Adler, 95.

4. The 1850 federal census found JJM and Claudine residents in the same St. Louis boardinghouse, with JCN, Albertine Nulsen, their baby, and Karl Friedrich Creuzbauer (USC 1850, M432, roll 417, page 46, line 19).

5. The Creuzbauers came in two groups, first (June 1838), the father and three sons; then, eight months later, the mother and three daughters (Entry for Capt. Carl F. Crewsbaur and family; Ship *Kutusoff* Passenger Manifest, 22 June 1838, p. 1, lines 6–9, in *Passenger Lists of Vessels Arriving at New Orleans,* NA Microfilm M259, roll 16; entry for Creuzbauer family, Ship *Caroline* Passenger Manifest, 2 February 1839, p. 3, lines 28–32, NA Microfilm M259, roll 18).

6. So-called because their education in classical languages was often far better than their training in farming practices (Mallinckrodt, 163; Kamphoefner [3], 94–100).

7. Jefferson County Marriage Book, 1839–1849:109, Jefferson County Courthouse, Hillsboro, Missouri.

8. Travis County tax records provide documentation of Robert Creuzbauer's activities in Texas. In 1846, Robert Creuzbaur, as he then spelled his surname, settled in Austin, where he distinguished himself as a cartographer in the Government Land Office (Wheat 75–77, 341). He married and invested in Texas real estate (BDE, 26 October 1911; Texas, 2:404).

Edmund Creuzbauer marched all over Texas during 1846–47, when he served in the U.S. Army. He returned to St. Louis, became a citizen on 6 November 1849, and then joined his brother in Travis County, Texas. Edmund married Elizabeth Welhausen in 1853, then farmed in St. Clair County, Illinois, from the late 1850s until 1861 (Naturalization of Edmund Creuzbaur, City of St. Louis Court of Common Pleas, Naturalizations, Declarations of Common Intent, Microfilm Box C 25813, Missouri State Archives; Edmund Kreutzbauer, Private, Batt'y B, Clark's Battalion, Missouri Light Artillery, RG 94, Compiled Service Records of Volunteer Soldiers Who Served in the Mexican War, NA; Edmund Creuzbaur file no. 3219, Case files of Approved Pension Applications of Veterans Who Served in the Army in the Mexican War, RG 15, Records of the Veterans Administration, NA; USC 1860, M653, roll 225, page 894, line 26).

9. Extensive land records for this family include purchases by Otto, recorded as "Arthur." See Cash files for Arthur Creuzbauer, 6 January 1840, Final Patents 12,636 and 12,635; Cash files for Frederick Creuzbauer, 5 November 1840, Final Patent 13,157; Cash files for Friedrich Creuzbauer, 30 December 1845, Final Patent 15,503, Government Land Office, St. Louis, Missouri, Land Case Files, RG 49, Bureau of Land Management, NA. Numerous transactions involving Friedrich Creuzbauer are documented in other real estate records (St. Louis County Deed Books, U4:121, H5:120; W5: 400, 582; X5:578; Y5:300, 329, 375; A6:142; B6:63, 178, 605). Tax records indicate the real estate the Creuzbauers owned in Carondelet (Carondelet [MO] Tax Book, Real and Personal Property, Vol. 11, 1853, MHS).

10. No individual named "Lubbe" lived in St. Louis at that time, but a tobacconist named George W. Labby (c. 1825–?) resided in St. Louis in 1850 (SLD 1850, 93).

11. Claudine Creuzbauer.

12. Because Claudine Creuzbauer was JCN's sister-in-law, JJM could not trifle with her affections as he had with so many Cincinnati girls.

13. A "fat wife" was considered a complimentary term, because a stout spouse reflected well on a husband's ability to provide for his family.

14. Henry Mersman.

15. Bill and Agnes Lake had left Samuel B. Burgess's American Circus, which completely ceased operations by early October 1850. At the time of the 1850 federal census enumeration (7 September 1850), they were among the sixty guests at the Walton House hotel in St. Louis. A boy, identified as eight-year-old "William Lake" (perhaps the child they adopted from Portsmouth), was with them (USC 1850, M432, roll 417, page 121, lines 10–12).

16. Spencer Q. Stokes owed the Lakes back wages.

17. Adolph Julius Jäger underwent syphilis treatment with JJM. See JJM diary, 3 March 1850.

18. No one named "Swanz" has been located, but a single man named Abraham Swart who lived in a boardinghouse at 149 North Third Street (near the N & M store) was listed in the 1851 city directory (SLD 1851, 337). The individual was likely a friend or an employee of JJM's; either the city directory or JJM may have made an error in spelling.

19. [Fr.] associate.

20. Claudine Creuzbauer was, of course, the aunt and godmother of JCN's first child, Caroline.

21. Possibly Claudine Creuzbauer said, "Hang it," meaning, "Don't bother." She apparently was becoming frustrated with her suitor's inability to make a commitment to her.

22. JJM was uncertain if he could break off with Claudine without offending his business partner, JCN, who was married to Claudine's younger sister, Albertine.

23. The American circus survived only one season (1850) under the management of Samuel P. Burgess, who sold the show to Fred Hunt and John Tryon. They soon went out of business, too (Parkinson, 24).

24. A prairie chicken, also called a prairie grouse, is either of two North American birds, *Tympanuchus cupido* or *T. pallidicinctus,* having brown, black, and white plumage (OED, s.v. "prairie chicken").

25. Henry Mersman often consumed alcohol to excess; perhaps that played a roll in his illness (DUN Ohio, 78:181).

26. The steamboat *Schuylkill*, a 271-ton sidewheel packet with a wooden hull, was built in Shousetown, Pennsylvania, in 1846. It carried freight between Pittsburgh and Louisville, but sank after being struck by the *Buckeye State* at Pittsburgh in 1850 (Way #5052, 420).

27. This probably refers to N & M's employee Abraham Rosenfeld and the Creuzbauer sisters, Albertine and Claudine. JJM calls them "Mrs. A" and "Mrs. C," directly translating the honorific *Frau* that he would have used in German.

28. Rosanna Henkel (1818–50) died of "hypertrophic hepatitis" (SLDR, 1:40).

29. Lesions of secondary syphilis typically wax and wane, sometimes for months. See epilogue.

30. The boat was moored in Illinois, beyond the reach of Missouri law.

31. Charles E. Sherwood (1823–75) was a circus rider who appeared with Rockwell & Company in 1848. The details of Lake's claim against him are not known (Slout, 273–74).

32. Agnes Lake most likely remained in Cincinnati, near her family.

33. "Rhino" is slang for money (OED, s.v. "rhino").

34. [Fr.] dishevelment.

35. Matthias Becker was the proprietor of St. Louis Park, a beer garden west of Twelfth Street (SLD 1847, 28).

36. Charles Louis Horn was a tavern keeper in business with Louis Mochel (SLD 1848, 118).

37. None of the individuals mentioned have been identified.

38. It is not certain what dates the Lakes played in Memphis or what circus they may have joined.

39. Carothers has not been identified.

40. Abraham Rosenfeld, JJM's employee.

41. William and Agnes Lake, now traveling with the Olympic Circus, opened in New Orleans on 1 December 1850 and played there for several weeks (PIC, 5 December 1850).

42. Probably a reference to Claudine Creuzbauer, JCN's sister-in-law, whom JJM was courting.

43. Bad weather had the effect of increasing the price of whiskey in St. Louis, because it was difficult to transport loads to that destination via steamboat. See chapter 7, note 4.

44. The Turner Association was a German community organization dedicated to physical fitness through disciplined exercise (Primm 232). Nulsen and Mersman became established members in 1855 (St. Louis Turnverein Records, vol. 9, Membership Ledger 1855–63, MHS).

45. William Lake.

46. Hugh Gallagher was hanged for the murder by poison of Mary Crosby, but protested his innocence to the last. The execution was witnessed by about eight thousand people (MOR, 6 July 1850, 14 December 1850).

47. See JJM diary, 6 June 1850 and 22 September 1850.

48. Elizabeth Kattenhorn.

49. The details have not been found. The circus business was extremely risky, and many shows lasted only one season (see Parkinson).

50. JJM and JCN went with Claudine Creuzbauer and Albertine Creuzbauer Nulsen to the ball.

51. The Jäger Club may have been a sharpshooters' club or a philanthropic organization. Olsen (133–37) commented on the many organizations created by German immigrants: "Scores of *Vereine* or societies were formed to cover every interest; it seemed that anywhere there were at least three Germans they formed a society."

52. "Although women did have some power in courtship, it was largely the power to say no and thus to hurt or frustrate a suitor" (Rotundo, 112).

53. No further information on this case has been found. See chapter 10, note 84.

54. Etiquette books advised against long engagements. "Protracted courtship, or engagements, are if possible, to be avoided; they are universally embarrassing. Lovers are so apt to find out imperfections in each other—to grow exacting, jealous, and morose" (Ruth, 188).

55. Inspired by Scribe's play *Marrying for Money* (1828), JJM wrote an excerpt on the inside cover of his diary (see appendix). On the evening before his wedding, JJM wrote that his matrimonial choice did not reflect a financial calculation; that he was *not* marrying for money. However, the Creuzbauer family—Lutherans from the Grand Duchy of Baden (now part of Baden-Württemberg

in southern Germany)—enjoyed a higher social status than JJM, a Catholic from the Grand Duchy of Oldenburg (now Lower Saxony in northern Germany). Captain Karl Friedrich Creuzbauer, a doctor's son and decorated artillery officer, had wed Caroline, the Baroness Hornig von Hornburg. Their daughter Claudine Creuzbauer would be the wife of JJM, a man with no title, no education, and no family fortune. Although Claudine's marriage to JJM would probably not have taken place in Europe, America offered greater social mobility for an ambitious man. JJM apparently identified with Scribe's character Poligni. (For a discussion of German marriage in America, see also Mallinckrodt, 135–36).

56. Arnd Kattenhorn.

57. Henry Mersman visited St. Louis and could transport cash to Cincinnati.

58. Jenny Lind's one-year concert tour took her to major U.S. cities including New York, Philadelphia, Baltimore, Washington, Charleston, New Orleans, Cincinnati, and St. Louis (MOR, 12 November 1850; van Ravenswaay [2], 320).

59. [Ger.] Women's Benevolent Association.

60. Jenny Lind's concert tour included numerous benefit performances that stimulated ticket sales. In St. Louis, general admission was five dollars, but P. T. Barnum also auctioned premium tickets, so that some paid as much as fifty dollars for seats in Wyman's Hall, which had a capacity of 1,100. Receipts in St. Louis were $40,000 for five performances. Miss Lind and Mr. Barnum jointly donated two thousand dollars to charities (Barnum, 88–101; Stevens, 1:945–49; MOR, 27 March 1851).

61. In April 1851, the Illinois legislature passed the "Quart Law," which forbade the selling of liquor in quantities of less than one quart. This prevented local taverns from selling liquor by the glass. The Quart Law in effect replaced the licensing system or the "License Law." Thus, the "country trade," i.e., local taverns on the Illinois side of the Mississippi River near St. Louis, would no longer purchase from N & M (Stowell, 12).

62. "Knocked into a cocked hat" means totally defeated (OED, s.v. "cocked hat").

63. The Pacific Railroad, the first railroad west of the Mississippi River, broke ground on 4 July 1851 with a public celebration (Jennings, 296–97).

64. Edmund Nulsen died only two days later, on 22 June 1851.

65. The Mississippi River, created by the union of three great branches (the upper Mississippi, the Missouri, and the Ohio rivers), has a long history of devastating floods. Heavy rain in 1851 caused flooding in Iowa and set records that remained unsurpassed until 1993. In St. Louis, the river remained at flood stage for weeks, although it did not reach the elevation it had in 1844. The water flooded the Illinois shore for a distance of four miles and washed away Duncan's Island. The quarantine boat was permanently removed from Arsenal Island to the main shore (MOR, 2, 4, 6, 7, 9, 14, 21 June 1851).

66. The extensive real estate transactions appear in St. Louis County Deed Record Books, B6:63, 178, 605; Y5:300, 329, 372; WS: 400, 582; and others.

67. "Courses" is a term for menstrual period (OED, s.v. "course").

68. Originally located on the back pages of the source text, this document appears here in chronological order.

69. Joseph John Mersman Jr. (1852–1925), a healthy baby, was the first of eight children born to JJM and his wife, Claudine. He was baptized 14 October 1852, the same day (and at the same Evangelical church) as Anna Ottilie Nulsen, the third child of JCN and his wife, Albertine (Holy Ghost Evangelical Protestant Church, St. Louis, Missouri, Baptism Records, 1833–54, 393, FHL Microfilm 1433232).

CHAPTER TWELVE

Settling Down

18 July 1853–25 September 1864

The first part of this section was written entirely in German, presented here with translation. JJM used German so that his jealous wife, who could not read English, would not be able to check on his activities. At the time of the entries, St. Louis faced another cholera epidemic. Hundreds of people, including some of JJM's friends, died from the disease, which was spread primarily by contaminated water.

To escape the plague, many fled to the outlying countryside. JJM's wife, Claudine, and their seventeen-month-old child, Joseph Junior, traveled to the farm in Jefferson County owned by her parents (see map 7). Although JJM remained in the city to tend to business, he visited the Creuzbauers in Hillsboro for one week during the month that his wife and son vacationed there.

While a summer bachelor, JJM busied himself with activities in town. Earlier in the year, JJM had joined Erwin Lodge No. 121, a chapter of the Freemasons, and quickly advanced in the ranks. Chartered in 1851, the lodge, which conducted all business in German, was Missouri's only foreign-language chapter.[1] *While JJM devoted considerable time to Masonic activities, his partner, JCN, joined the Independent Order of Odd Fellows.*[2] *The fraternal orders helped Nulsen and Mersman promote their business and expand their social network outside the German-speaking community.*[3] *Because St. Louis had a score of Freemason lodges, JJM could be out of the house virtually every night of the week with an acceptable excuse to mollify his possessive wife.*

Claudine Creuzbauer Mersman, with her first son, Joseph Mersman Jr. (1852–1925), 1852. This portrait was made shortly after Joseph Jr.'s birth. He was the eldest of eight Mersman children. (Personal collection of Linda A. Fisher.)

St. Louis. Montag 18ten July 1853. [St. Louis. Monday 18th July 1853.]

Es ist über ein Jahr, zeit ich das letzte Mahl in meinem Tagebuche geschrieben habe, und würde jetzt nicht daran gedacht haben, wenn meine Frau nicht vereist wäre. Aber indem meine gute Claudine ungewöhnlich stark eifersüchtig ist, halte ich es für meine Pflicht hier zu notiren wie und auf was für eine Art ich meine müßige Zeit zugebracht habe. Ich werde deswegen jeden Abend notiren wo ich den

Abend gewesen bin, den wärend des Tages bin ich im Geschäfte. Und sollte ich wo anders gewesen, so wird es sich hier finden.

Diesen Morgen um halb drei ist Claudine mit unsern kleinen Joseph und ihre Mutter mit Stage oder Post nach Hillsborro abgefahren. Der kleine Junge der nicht ganß wohl ist schlief sanft und fest bei dem abfahren. Ich hoffe und wünsche von ganßen Herzen das Sie glücklich und ohne viele Mühe dort angekommen sind. Ich bin gleich wieder zu Bet, konte aber nicht schlafen—ich war zu aufgeregt, machte mich selbst so viele Gedanken über meinen Jungen, besonders ob er nicht durch die Eigenheiten der Mutter zu viel Durst leiden würde. Es war schon hel-Tag als ich einschlief. Den Tag hindurch war ich wie gewöhnlich im Geschäfte, hatten aber fast nichts zu thun.

Als ich von Abendessen zurück in unsern Parlor kam, fand ich alles so öde und einsam—alles stand noch wie Claudine es gelassen hatte, das es mir ganz unheimlich wurde um mich mal zu zerstreuen ging ich ins Theatre, bin aber gleich nach dem erstem Stück zu hause. 11 Uhr war ich im Bette.

[It has been over a year since I last wrote in my diary, and I would not have thought of it if my wife had not departed. But since my dear Claudine is extraordinarily jealous, I consider it my duty to note down here how and in what way I have passed my spare time. For that reason I will note down every evening where I have been for the evening, because during the day I am in the store. And should I be anywhere else, it will be found here.

This morning at half past two Claudine departed by the stage or postal coach for Hillsboro with our little Joseph and her mother. The little boy, not entirely well, slept softly and deeply on departure. I hope and desire with my whole heart that they have arrived there happy and without much trouble. I immediately went back to bed, but I could not sleep—I was too agitated, worrying so much about my boy, particularly that he might get too thirsty due to his mother's peculiar ways.[4] It was already broad daylight before I fell asleep. Throughout the day I was at the store as usual, but there was almost nothing to do.

When I came back to our parlor after supper, I found everything so empty and desolate—everything still stood as Claudine had left it—that I got quite an eerie feeling. In order to divert myself I went to the theater,[5] but came right back home after the first play. I was in bed by 11.]

Dienstag July 19ten 1853 [Tuesday July 19th 1853]

Heute war ich nicht den ganßen Tag im Geschäfte. Es ist nämlich zeit einigen Tage die erste Section der Pacific Rail Road fertig, und diese Begebenheit, wurde durch eine Frei-fahrt zum Ende der Linie, und ein prachtvolles Dinner gefeiert, wozu alle

Stockhalter eingeladen waren, und indem wir dazu gehören, und eine invitation hatten bin ich mitgegangen, und habe Brauckmann mitgenommen in Nülsens Platz. Ich möchte hier noch die Bemerkung machen für meine Frau das keine Damen mitwaren. Der Zug fuhr ab um 10 Minuten nach 11. Kurz nach der Abfahrt fing es an zu regnen, was das schnell-Fahren verhinderte. Die Aus-Fahrt dauerte 3 Stunden, 44 Meilen. Das Essen obschon kalt war herlich, das Trinken so gut als es nur sein konte. Um 8 Uhr Abends war bei Nülsens um den Schlüssel zu holen, habe dan auch gleich Supper gegessen, bin dan auch gleich zu hause, und 9 Uhr war ich im Bette.

[Today I was not in the store the whole day. That's because the first section of the Pacific Rail Road was completed several days ago, and this occasion was celebrated by a free trip to the end of the line and a splendid dinner, to which all stockholders were invited, and as we belong to them and had received an invitation, I went along, taking Brauckmann along in Nülsen's place. Here I wish to make the comment for my wife that no ladies came along.[6] The train left at 10 minutes past 11. Shortly after departure it began to rain, which prevented traveling fast. The trip out took 3 hours, 44 miles. The meal, though cold, was excellent, the drinks as good as they could possibly be. At 8 o'clock in the evening I was at Nulsen's to get the key.[7] I ate supper right away, then went home right away and by 9 o'clock I was in bed.]

Mitwoche July 20ten 1853 [Wednesday July 20th 1853]

Ich war heute wie gewöhnlich im Geschäfte, ausgenommen den Nachmittag war ich aus um collectionen zu machen für unsere Loge. Nach dem Supper bin ich noch zu Gehner um Geld zu collectiren, fand ihm aber nicht zu hause.

Von Gehner bin ich zu Meyer, habe ein Glass Beer getrunken, und zwei Partie Billiard gespielt. Um 10 Uhr war ich wieder zu hause, habe mich eine halbe Stunde mit meine Guitar amusirt und bin dan so um halb 11 zu Bett, nachdem ich dieses erst geschrieben hatte.

[Today I was in the store, as usual, except in the afternoon when I was out making collections for our lodge.[8] After supper I went to Gehner's to collect money, but I did not find him at home.

From Gehner's I went to Meyer's, drank a glass of beer, and played two games of billiards. At 10 o'clock I was back at home again, amused myself with my guitar for a half hour, and then around 10:30 went to bed after first writing this.

Donnerstag July 21ten 1853 [Thursday July 21st 1853]

Unsere Geschäfte gehen augeblicklich sehr schlecht. Den Vormittag war ich beschäftigt mit collectiren für unsere Loge. Diesen Nachmittag bekam ich per Post einen Brief

Nulsen & Mersman advertisement, 1863. The thriving whiskey business was located at 100 North Third Street, St. Louis. The site is now part of the Jefferson National Expansion Monument Park—the Gateway Arch in St. Louis. (Missouri Historical Society, St. Louis.)

von Mama der mich sehr viel erleichtert hat, nach den Brief zu urtheilen scheint es als wen meine gute Claudine doch ziemlich viel Mühe gehabt hat. Aber was mir besondere Freude macht, ist das Sie den nämlichen Tage glücklich noch angekommen sind, und das mein lieber Joseph sich dort zu Hause fühlt und vergnügt gesund ist, jetzt kan ich die nächste Woche mit Rühe abwarten.

Den Abend habe ich zugebracht in unsere Loge, ich war Richter zwischen zwei Brüder die nicht einig werden konten wegen einen Handel, jedoch war ich nicht den ganzen Abend dort, indem die eine Partie seine Zeugen nicht da hatte konte die Klage nicht vorgenommen werden, und bis Sontag-Morgen verschoben. Nachdem das wir vertagt hatten, bin ich, Erfort und Eggers noch hingegangen und haben ein Glass Beer getrunken. Von da bin ich und Erfort zu hause. Um ½ 11 war ich im bette.

[At the moment our business is going very badly. In the morning I was busy making collections for our lodge. This afternoon I received in the mail a letter from Mama[9] that relieved me very much. Judging from the letter it appears that my dear Claudine had quite a bit of trouble after all. But what gave me special joy was that they arrived safely that same day and that my dear Joseph is feeling at home there and is cheerful and healthy, so now I can wait out the next week with peace of mind.

I spent the evening in our lodge. I was the judge between two brothers who could not agree over a transaction. However, I was not there the entire evening as one of the parties did not have his witnesses there, so that the complaint could not be taken up and was postponed to Sunday morning. After we adjourned, I, Erfort and Eggers still went out and drank a glass of beer. From there I and Erfort went home. I was in bed by 10:30.]

Freitag 22ten July 1853 [Friday 22nd July 1853]

Ich war den Tag hindurch fortwärend zu hause, und habe an unsere Bücher geschrieben. Es ist eigentlich nicht nöthig zu notiren wo ich diesen Abend war, denn Claudine weiß das ich noch nie einen Abend die Loge verfehlt habe, ausgenommen einen Abend, und da bin ich ihr zu lieb zu Hause geblieben, weil es so stark donnerte, und ein Gewitter sie so viel Furcht verursacht. Von die Loge zu hause und um 11 Uhr im Bette. Joseph.

[I was at home all through the day, and I wrote in our books. Actually it is not necessary to note down where I was this evening, because Claudine knows I have never missed an evening at the lodge, save for one evening when I stayed home out of deference to her because it thundered so much and a thunderstorm causes her so much fear. I went home from the lodge and was in bed at 11. Joseph.]

St. Louis Samstag July 23ten 1853. [St. Louis Saturday July 23rd 1853.]

Geschäfte waren diese Woche sehr schlecht. Ich war wärend dem Tage fast nicht aus dem Hause, mit Ausnahme des Nachmittags eine Stunde bei Meyer um zwei Partien Billiard zu spielen. Den Abend habe ich in Begleitung von Klinkhardt im Peoples Theatre zugebracht. Wir waren unten im Parterre wo es nur 35 cts kostet und wo auch keine Damen sind. Die beiden Stücke waren ziemlich gut, und auch passabel gespielt, haben uns also gut amusirt. Es war aus um ½ 12. Um 12 Uhr war ich im Bette.

[Business was very poor this week. I hardly left the house during the day, except for one hour in the afternoon to play two games of billiards at Meyer's. I passed the evening with Klinkhardt[10] in the People's Theatre.[11] We were down on the ground level where it only costs 35 cents and where there were also no ladies. The two plays were rather good, and also reasonably well acted, so we had a good time. It was over at 11:30. At 12 o'clock I was in bed.]

Sontag July 24ten 1853. [Sunday July 24th 1853.]

Ich bin diesen Morgen um ½ 8 aufgestanden, gleich angekleidet, gefrühstückt, und bin dan gleich zu unsere Loge gegangen. Um ½ 9 ist das Verhör in die Klage angefangen, um ein Viertel vor 4 waren wir erst fertig, habe also heute kein Dinner gehabt, ich wurde in dieser Klage einstimmig als Richter ernannt, ich brauche aber über diese Ehre, und mein Vergnügen darüber, nichts zu schreiben, den meine Frau hätte auf diese Ehre geblasen (Ein Lieblings-Ausdruck von ihr) weil ich nicht zum Mittag Essen hätte kommen können. Von der Loge bin ich direckt zu Nülsens Hause gegangen, habe dort ziemlich viel Kaffee getrunken, weil ich nichts gegessen hatte. Um ½ 6 bin ich und Clemens noch ein wenig zu Forster (ein Kunde von uns) gegangen. Um ½ 8 waren wir wieder zurück, haben Supper gegessen, ich bin dan so um 9 Uhr zu Hause gegangen, habe noch ein wenig Guitarre gespielt, dieses geschrieben und indem es jetzt 10 Uhr ist will ich zu Bett gehen, und von meinem Lumps treumen.

[I got up this morning at 7:30, dressed immediately, had breakfast, and then went to our lodge right away. At 8:30 the hearing on the complaint began, and it was not until 3:45 that we finished, so I had no dinner today. I was unanimously named judge in this complaint, but I need not write about this honor and my pleasure at it, since my wife would have *blown* on this honor (a favorite expression of hers) because I could not come home to lunch. I went directly from the lodge to Nülsen's home, where I drank quite a lot of coffee because I hadn't eaten anything. At 5:30 I and Clemens went to Forster's (a customer of ours) for a while. By 7:30 we were back, ate supper, and then around 9 o'clock I went home, played a little guitar, wrote this, and as it is now 10 o'clock I will go to bed and dream of my Lumps.[12]]

St. Louis July 25ten 1853. Montag [St. Louis July 25th 1853. Monday]

Geschäfte ziemlich gut heute, ich war den ganzen Tag zu hause. Den Abend war ich in eine Amerikanische Loge, es dauerte bis 11 Uhr von da zu hause und Bett.

[Business was rather good today, I was at home all day. In the evening I was at an American lodge,[13] it lasted until 11 o'clock, and from there I went home and to bed.]

Dienstag July 26ten [Tuesday July 26th]

Geschäfte schlecht. Ich habe heute ein Lot gekauft das zu 3500 Thaler kommt. Ich bin aber bange das der Titel zu stark verwickelt ist um es mit sicherheit nehmen zu können. Diesen Abend war ich wieder mit einem von unsern Kunden im Theater. Mr. France hat auch diese Nacht bei mir geschlafen. Es war 12 Uhr als wir zu Bette gingen, zu spat für mich.

[Business bad. Today I bought a lot that comes to $3,500.[14] But I am afraid that the title is too clouded to be able to take it with confidence. This evening I was again in the theater[15] with one of our customers. Mr. France[16] also spent the night at my place. It was 12 o'clock when we went to bed, too late for me.

Mitwoche July 27ten [Wednesday July 27th]

Den ganzen Tag im Store, aber wenig Geschäfte. Den Abend habe ich bei Meyer Billiard gespielt bis 10 Uhr, bin gleich nach Hause und zu Bett gegangen.

[The whole day in the store, but little business. During the evening I played billiards at Meyer's until 10 o'clock, went straight home and to bed.]

Donnerstag July 28ten. halb 9 Uhr. [Thursday July 28th. half past 8 o'clock.]

Unsere Geschäfte waren sehr gut. Diesen Nachmittag habe alle nöthige Sachen eingekauft. Morgen um zwei bis 3 fahre ich mit die Post nach Hillsboro meine liebe Frau und Jungen zu sehen. Obgleich ich sehr viele recht unglückliche Tage mit meine Frau verlebt habe so wünsche ich dennoch als meinen letzten Willen (im fall ich sollte Verunglücken, es ist dieses möglich) das Claudine meine Frau so lange als Sie nicht wieder heirathet und mein Sohn lebt, Sie die Interesse von meinen ganßen Vermögen bezieht bis mein Sohn 21Jahr alt ist. Solte Sie heirathen, oder das Kind sterben dan nur was ihr das Gesetz zuerkennt. Meine Bücher und sonstige Sachen mögte ich gern unter die Familie Vertheilt haben.

Joseph J. Mersman

[Our business was very good. This afternoon I bought all the necessary things. Tomorrow between 2 and 3 I'll be going by mail coach to Hillsboro to see my dear wife and boy. Although I have spent many rather unhappy days with my wife, still I desire as my last will (in case I have an accident, which is possible) that Claudine, my wife, should draw the interest on my entire property, until my son is 21 years old, so long as she does not remarry and my son is alive. Should she marry, or the child die, then she is to get only what the law awards her. My books and other things I would like to have divided among the family. Joseph J. Mersman.]

Mitwochen Abend August 3ten 1853 [Wednesday Evening August 3rd 1853]

Ich bin, Gott sei Dank heute um 8 Uhr glücklich wieder hier angekommen nach einer Abwesenheit von 6 Tagen. Ich kam letzten Freitag glücklich bei meiner Frau an, nicht ohne etliche Mühe, aber doch ohne Unglück gehabt zu haben. Samstag zogen wir alle zu Richters 7 Meilen entfernt von Riedels. Da sind wir dann geblieben. Meine liebe Claudine nebst Kind war ziemlich wohl, mit eine Ausnahme die ich hier nicht nennen will. Wir haben uns gut amusirt mit Besuchen von Nachbaaren, alle alte Bekante von Claudine und Mama, so viel Corn brodt und Speck gegeßen als unsere Magen verdauen konten. Diesen Morgen um 8 Uhr habe ich meine Frau wieder lebe wohl gesagt und bin in begleitung einen gewissen Behrens zu Pferde nach den Franklin Depot geritten, wo wir nach eine drei-malig Verirrung den auchf glücklich um ½ 2 angekommen sind, also vollig 5 Stunden im

Sattel. Etwas auf 5 ging der Zug ab, um ¼ nach 7 waren wir in St. Louis, indem ich doch zu Nulsens mußte wegen den Schlüssel so habe da gleich Supper gegessen, und dan auch gleich zu hause gegangen. Jetzt will ich mich baden, reines Zeug anziehen und dan zu Bette gehen, bis dahin wird es halb 10 werden.

[Thank God, I returned here safe at 8 o'clock after an absence of 6 days. I arrived at my wife's safely last Friday, not without some trouble, but without having had any accident. Saturday we all went to Richter's, 7 miles from Riedel's.[17] That's where we stayed. My dear Claudine, with the child, were quite well, with one exception I will not name here.[18] We enjoyed ourselves visiting the neighbors, all old acquaintances of Claudine and Mama, ate as much corn-bread and bacon as our stomachs could digest. This morning at 8 o'clock I said farewell to my wife again and rode by horse accompanied by a certain Behrens[19] to the Franklin depot,[20] where we finally arrived safely at 1:30 after losing our way three times, thus a full five hours in the saddle. The train left a little before 5, we were in St. Louis about at quarter past 7. As I still had to go to Nülsen's on account of the key, I ate supper there at the same time, and then went straight home. Now I want to bathe, put on clean clothes and then go to bed, and by then it will be 9:30.]

Donnerstag 4ten August 1853 [Thursday 4th August 1853]

Ich war heute noch sehr lahm und angegriffen von der Reise, indem ich aber nichts zu thun hatte konnte ich ausruhen um 4 Uhr Nachmittags ging ich Nohl und Lackman zu unsern Kunden Musenfechtler, um halb 9 waren wir wieder zu hause. Den Abend war ich bei Nohl in seinem Boarding house, zu Bett 12 Uhr.

[Today I was still very sore and worn from the trip, but as I had nothing to do, I could rest. At 4 o'clock in the afternoon I, Nohl and Lackmann went to our customer Musenfechtler.[21] At 8:30 we were home again. I spent the evening with Nohl in his boarding house, to bed at 12 o'clock.]

Freitag August 5ten 1853 [Friday August 5th 1853]

Geschäfte gingen heute schlecht, was mich gar nicht ärgerte, den ich bin immer noch recht lahm zwischen die Beine. Es ist eigentlich unnöthig zu sagen wo ich diesen Abend war, den, Claudine kan leicht begreifen, das wen beinahe nie einen Abend fehle zu die Loge zu gehen wen Sie hier ist werde ich gewiß nicht fehlen jetzt da ich doch sonst nichts zu thun habe. Ich war um 11 Uhr im Bette zu hause.

[Business went badly today, which did not bother me, since I am still quite sore between the legs. It is actually unnecessary to say where I was this evening, since Claudine can easily comprehend that I hardly ever miss an evening going to the lodge when she is here, and I am certainly not going to be absent now that I have nothing else to do. I was home in bed by 11 o'clock.]

Samstag den 6ten August [Saturday 6th August]

Den Tag hindurch wie gewöhnlich im Geschäfte. Den Abend habe ich im Peoples Theatre zugebracht. Es wurden zwei gute Stücke gespielt, den ganzen Abend habe Claudine bei mir gewünscht. Sie würde sich so gut amusirt haben, wen Sie den kleinen Jungen abgewöhnt so wollen wir diesen Winter mehrmals zum Theatre gehen. Um ½ 12 war ich zu hause im Bette.

[All day as usual at the store. The evening I spent in the People's Theatre.[22] Two good plays were presented; the whole evening I wished Claudine was with me. She would have amused herself so much. Once she has weaned the little boy we will go to the theater several times this winter.[23] I was home in bed at 11:30.]

Sontag August 7ten [Sunday August 7th]

Um 7 Uhr habe ich Frühstück gegeßen, bin dan gleich zur Meridian Loge in Frenchtown gegangen. Ein gewißer Hr. Block erfüllt seinen 3ten. Grad in die Maurerei um ½ 10 war ich wieder zu Hause, hatte eine Stunde Arbeit mit die Rectifiers. Gestern hatten wir Kohlen gewechselt, um ½ 11 bin ich und Nülsen zum Beer Hause haben 2 Partien Billiard gespielt und ein Glas Bier getrunken, und sind dan zu Mittag, ich habe mein Dinner und Caffee mit Clemens gehabt. Nach Caffee sind wir zu Forster, haben da mit Herrn Forster drei Flaschen Wein getrunken. Wir erwarten viel zu verkaufen an ihn diese Woche. Supper bei Nulsen's, um 9 zu hause, 10 im Bette.

[At 7 o'clock I had breakfast and went at once to the Meridian Lodge[24] in Frenchtown. A certain Mr. Block completed his third degree in Masonry, I was back at home at 9:30, had an hour of work with the rectifiers. Yesterday we changed coal, at 10:30 Nülsen and I went to the beerhouse, played two games of billiards and drank a glass of beer, then at noon we left. I had my dinner and coffee with Clemens. After coffee we went to Forster's, drank three bottles of wine with Mr. Forster. We expect to sell a great deal to him this week. Supper at Nülsen's, home at 9, in bed at 10.]

Montag August 8ten 1853. [Monday August 8th 1853.]

Geschäfte öfneten heute ziemlich. Ich war den ganßen Tag zu Hause, und des Abends auch, den nach Supper hatte ich und Clemens etliche Fässer Brandy zurecht zu machen. Klinkhardt war heute bei uns, sein kleines 3 järiges Mädchen ist auf den Lande gestorben. Er hat es nicht lebendig mehr gesehen. Ich bin den ganßen Tag in großer Angst gewesen wegen meinen kleinen Joseph, ich wolte Claudine wäre wieder zurück mit dem Kinde. Ich bin um 9 zu Bett, habe aber noch eine Stunde gelesen.

[Business went well today. I was at home all day, and in the evening too, because after supper Clemens and I had to prepare some barrels of brandy. Klinkhardt was at our place. His little three-year-old girl died in the country. He did not see her alive again [after she left the city]. I worried the whole day over my little Joseph. I wished Claudine were back again with the child. I was in bed at 9, but still read for another hour.]

Dienstag 9ten August. [Thursday 9th August.]

Geschäfte gingen heute ziemlich gut. Es waren die- sen Tag hindurch mehrere plötzliche Todesfälle in Folge der unerträglichen Hitze. Kinder sterben auch sehr viel und schnell. Es freut mich das mein lieber Lumps jetzt bequem auf dem Lande ist, den Abend habe ich zugebracht in einer amerikanische Loge, Polar Star. Die Leute Arbeiten sehr schön und regelmäßig. Um 11 Uhr war ich im Bette.

[Business went rather well today. Throughout this day there were several sudden deaths as a result of the unbearable heat. Children also are dying, very many and fast. I am happy that my dear Lumps is now comfortable in the country. The evening I passed in an American lodge, Polar Star.[25] The people there work nicely and in keeping with the rules. I was in bed at 11 o'clock.]

Mitwochen 10ten August [Wednesday 10th August]

Den Tag hindurch wie immer im Geschäfte, die wieder ziemlich gut gingen. Nach dem Abend-Eßen bin ich und Erfort zu Meyer und haben Partien Billiard gespielt um 10 Uhr war ich zu hause, habe mich gebadet und bin dan zu Bett.

[All day as always at the store. Business went quite well again. After supper I and Erfort went to Meyer's and played games of billiards, at 10 o'clock I was back home, bathed and then to bed.]

Donnerstag August 11ten. [Thursday August 11th.]

Die Hitze ist jetzt unaustehlich, heute 103 grade im Schatten, und vier plötzliche Todesfälle durch Sonnenstich. Geschäfte langsam. Nach dem Essen bin ich, Erfort und Wissmann, ausgefahren, in Busch & W's Wagen und Erforts Pferd, nachdem das wir eine Stunde herumgefahren und uns abgekuhlt hatten sind wir bei Reicherts eingekehrt, haben 2 Glass Beer getrunken und sind dan um halb 10 zu hause, nach ein gutes Bad bin ich zu Bette 11 Uhr.

[The heat is now intolerable, today 103 degrees in the shade, and four sudden deaths through sunstroke. Business slow. After the meal, I, Erfort and Wissmann took a ride in Busch & W[issmann]'s wagon and Erfort's horse, and after we had traveled around for an hour and cooled ourselves off, we stopped at Reichert's, drank two glasses of beer and then went home at 9:30, and after a good bath I went to bed at 11 o'clock.]

Freitag August 12ten 1853. [Friday August 12th 1853.]

Unser Whiskey geschäft hebt sich diese Woche besonders hervor, im allgemeinem machen wir jetzt gut aus. Diesen Morgen erhielten wir Nachricht von unsern alten getreuen Freund und Kunden Christopher Crone das seine Frau Gestern Abend um 5 Uhr gestorben sei. Es war uns besonders auffallend weil sie noch vor einn paar Tage mit ihm hier in die Stadt war. Ich bin mit zum Begräbniß gewesen. Der arme Crone scheint seinen Verlust sehr zu fühlen, der Zufall wollte daß ich Zeuge eines sehr schmerzlichen Auftrittes oder Scene war. Als ich ins Leichenzimmer kam, war der Sarg eben zugeschroben, grade als man da mit fertig war, wachte das jüngste Kind (ein Knabe von zwei Jahr, der auch Krank war) auf, und verlangte weinend zu die Mama zu gehen. Dieses Verlangen, in diesen Augenblicke, machte so einen heftigen Eindruck auf das Gefühl des Vaters, daß er laut und heftig Weinte, ich konnte meine Thränen auch nicht zurück halten. Die andern beiden Kinder (Mädchen von 5 und 7 Jahr) standen neben ihren Vater und Weinten mit. Man kan kaum begreifen was ich diesen Nachmittag ausgestanden habe. Der Zug war sehr groß—ich war in einem von den letzten Buggies, der Staub war so dick das man kaum das Pferd sehen konte. Die Entfernung ist völlig 7 Meilen, wir waren über 2 Stunden auf den Wege, in einer Hitze von 100 bis 105 grade. Durch Schweiß und Staub war ich des Abends als ich zurück kam einen großen Haufen Dreck. Ich hatte kaum Zeit was zu Essen, mich zu Waschen, als es völlig Zeit war zu die Loge zu gehen, es scheint als wen man mich zum Sekretair oder Schreiber der Loge machen will, um halb 11 war ich im Bade, 11 Uhr im Bette.

[Our whiskey business is doing especially well this week, and in general we are now doing well. This morning we received news from our old faithful friend and customer Christopher Crone that his wife died yesterday evening at 5 o'clock. It was especially shocking to us because she was with him here in the city only a few days ago. I went to the funeral. Poor Crone appeared to feel his loss intensely. As it happened, I witnessed a very painful episode or scene. When I came into the room where the body was, the coffin had just been screwed tight. At that very moment, as they were finished with that, the youngest child (a boy of two who was also sick) woke up and crying, asked to go to his mama. This plea, at that instant, made such a strong impression on the feelings of the father that he wept loudly and intensely. I too was unable to restrain my tears. The two other children (girls of 5 and 7 years) stood next to their father and wept with him. One can hardly imagine what I endured this afternoon. The procession[26] was large—I was in one of the last buggies, the dust was so thick that one could hardly see the horse. The distance is a full 7 miles; we were on the road over 2 hours in a heat of 100 to 105 degrees. Because of the sweat and dust, I was a big heap of dirt when I returned in the evening. I hardly had time to eat something and wash up when it was time again to go to the lodge. It looks as if they want to make me secretary[27] or scribe of the lodge. I was in the bath at 10:30 and in bed at 11.]

Samstag August 13ten 1853. [Saturday August 13th 1853.]

Immer noch sehr heiß, obschon heute bisweilen etwas Bewegung in die Luft ist, etwas, was man Wind nennen würde, wen mehr davon da wäre. Heute wurde das Deutsche Publicum besonders in Erstaunen gesetzt durch den schnellen Tod von Chas. Crone, der Stadt-Marshal, er war bloß 5 Stunden Krank, Gestern war er noch hier, sehr Gesund. Nülsens Kleine Kind war die letzte Nacht auch krank, heute aber etwas ruhiger, unsern Heinrich seine Frau ist diesen Nachmittag auch auf ein mahl krank geworden, indem Er diesen Abend nicht zurück gekommen ist weis ich nicht ob Sie noch lebt oder nicht. Die Arbeiter von Block & Evers sind alle krank, mich selbst werde ich schon in Acht nehmen wen nur meine liebe Claudine und mein kleiner Joseph gesund bleiben. Es sind aber die letzte Woche über 1200 Menschen an das Gelbe Fieber gestorben in New Orleans. Diesen Abend war ich bis ½ 10 bei Meir und habe Billiard gespielt, bin von dort zu hause. Habe mich gebadet und um 11 Uhr zu Bette.

[Still very hot, although today there is at times some movement in the air, something that one would call wind if only there were more of it. Today the German public was quite astonished by the quick death of Chas. Crone, the city marshal, who was sick for only 5 hours. Yesterday he was still here, quite healthy. Nülsen's little child was also sick last night, but today somewhat calmer, our Heinrich's[28] wife also became sick all of a sudden this afternoon. As he did not return this evening, I do not know whether she is still alive or not. The workers of Block & Evers are all sick. I will surely take care of myself, I only wish my dear Claudine and my little Joseph remain healthy. But in the last week more than 1200 people died of yellow fever in New Orleans.[29] This evening I was at Meier's until 9:30 and played billiards, went home from there. I took a bath and was in bed at 11 o'clock.]

Sontag [Sunday] August 14th 1853.

Um 7 Uhr diesen Morgen war ich angezogen habe dan gleich mein Frühstück genommen und um halb 8 war ich in unsere Loge. Br. Eggers hat den 3ten Grad erhalten. Die Ceremony bei diesen Grad sind so schön das ich immer die Ertheilung desselben gerne mit beiwohne, um 10 waren wir damit fertig, etliche von uns, ich auch, sind dan zu Boernstein's gegangen und haben ein Glass Bier getrunken.

Dinner *habe ich heute in mein Boarding hause gehabt, von 2 bis 4 habe ich ruhig geschlafen auf den* Carpet *in unsern* Parlor, *bin dan zu Clemens. Caffee war gerade fertig wie ich erwartete, habe da gelesen &c bis* Supper, *eine halbe Stunde nachher war ich zu hause, und um 10 Uhr im Bette.*

[At 7 this morning I was dressed, had breakfast at once and at 7:30 I was in our lodge. Brother Eggers became a third degree Mason. The ceremony for this degree is so beautiful that I always enjoy participating in its bestowal. At 10 we were done, and some of us, including me, went to Boernstein's and drank a glass of beer.

I had dinner today in my boarding house, from 2 to 4 I slept quietly on the carpet in our parlor, then went to Clemens's. Coffee was just ready, as expected, and I read there until supper, a half-hour later I was at home and in bed at 10.]

Montag den 15ten August 1853. [Monday 15th August 1853.]

Geschäfte öffneten nicht besonders brilliant, obschon wir (ich und Clemens) heute sehr hart gearbeitet haben unsern Heinrich seine Frau war so krank das er den gan zen Tage zu hause war. Den Abend um mich ein wenig zu erholen habe ich mit Erfort und Wissman im Theatre zugebracht, nachher haben wir noch ein Glass Bier getrunken, und sind dan so um 12 Uhr zu hause.

[Business did not open in a particularly brilliant fashion, although we (Clemens and I) worked very hard today. Our Heinrich's wife was so ill that he was home all day. To relax a bit, I, Erfort and Wissman spent the evening in the theater,[30] afterwards we drank another glass of beer and then returned home around 12 o'clock.]

Dienstag 16ten August [Tuesday 16th August]

Geschäfte waren heute ziemlich gut. Heinrichs Frau ist heute auf der Besserung, er war meistens hier. Das Wetter ist immer noch sehr heiß. Diesen Nachmittag erhielt ich einen Brief von die Schwiegermutter, am 5ten geschrieben und am 16ten empfangen, also 11 Tage um eine Reise von 40 Meilen zu machen. Ich hätte gleich eine Antwort geschrieben, erwarte aber Claudine zurück eher als mein Brief ankommen würde. Diesen Abend habe ich und Erfort in St. Louis Loge zugebracht. Die Leute

Arbeiten sehr regelmäßig und schön, nachdem das die Loge haben wir noch ein Glas Bier getrunken, im Bette 11 Uhr.

[Business was quite good today. Heinrich's wife is improving today, and he was here most of the time. Weather is still hot. This afternoon I received a letter from my mother-in-law written on the 5th and received on the 16th, hence 11 days to make a journey of 40 miles. I would have written an answer at once, but I expect Claudine back before my letter would arrive. This evening I and Erfort spent in the St. Louis Lodge.[31] The people there work according to the rules and nicely. After the lodge, we drank a glass of beer, in bed at 11 o'clock.]

17ten August Mitwoche [17th August Wednesday]

Es war heute nicht so heiß als es die letzten 10 Tage gewesen ist, aber immer noch so warm das man nicht still sitzen kan ohne zu schwitzen. Es sind heute grade 14 Tage das ich meine Frau verlassen habe. Es würde mir sehr lieb gewesen sein wen sie heute mit unsern Kinde Gesund und wohl zurück gekommen wäre. Diesen Abend war ich im Theatre. Es wurde ein Neues und sehr schönes Stück gespielt, nach dem ersten bin ich zu Hause, habe dieses Geschrieben, und um 11 zu Bett.

[Today it was not as hot as it has been these last ten days, but still so warm that one could not sit still without sweating. It has now been exactly fourteen days since I left my wife. I would have been very happy if she had returned safe and sound with our child today. This evening I was in the theater.[32] A new and very beautiful play was presented, but after the first act I went home, wrote this and to bed at 11.]

Donnerstag August 18ten 1853. [Thursday August 18th 1853.]

Es ist heute gerade ein Monat zeitdem mein Lumps von Hause fort ist. Es scheint beinahe als wen sich mein Lumps gut amusirt zeitdem ich weg bin. Die einzige Ursache die ich mir denken kan ist, das Sie immer noch diesen Blut-Fluß hat, oder noch nicht ganß kurirt ist. Wen nur beide Gesund zurück kommen, so bin ich doch zufrieden, ob es nun eine Woche früher oder später ist. Geschäfte waren heute sehr schlecht, ich habe den ganßen Tag an unsern Bücher geschrieben. Nach Supper habe ich 4 Partien Billiard gespielt, bin um 10 Uhr zu haus gekommen habe dieses geschrieben, und dan um halb 11 zu Bette.

[Today it has been a month since my Lumps left the house. It appears almost as if my Lumps is enjoying herself well since I have been away. The only cause I can imagine is that she still has this flowing of blood, or that it is not yet entirely cured.[33] If only the two would return healthy, then I am satisfied, whether it is a week earlier or later. Business today was very poor, I spent the whole day on our books. After supper I played four games of billiards, came home at 10 o'clock, wrote this and then 10:30 to bed.]

Freitag August 19ten. [Friday August 19th.]

Es war heute ziemlich Kalt, wenigstens im Vergleich zu dem was es gewesen ist, wen es so bleibt, so wird das kalte Fieber auf dem Lande bald nicht mehr raar sein. Ich habe mich diesen Nachmittag amusirt mit dem Ausreinen von unsere Zimmer, ich war dabei von 4 bis 6 Uhr. Ich habe meinen Lumps heute gewiß erwartet, aber bin leider in meine Hoffnung geteuscht. Ich war den ganßen Tag zu Hause. Diesen Abend von 9 bis 10 war ich bei Meier, habe ein Glass Bier getrunken, und 2 Partien Billiard gespielt, bis 9 Uhr habe ich auf meinen Lumps gewartet, jetzt da es schon ½ 11 ist werde ich zu Bette gehen.

[It was rather cold today, at least in comparison to what it has been, and if it stays so the cold fever will soon no longer be a rarity in the countryside. I amused myself this afternoon cleaning our rooms, and I was busy with that from 4 to 6 o'clock. I expected my Lumps today for sure, but unfortunately my hopes were dashed. I was at home the whole day. This evening from 9 to 10 I was at Meier's, drank a glass of beer, and played two games of billiards. I waited for my Lumps until 9 o'clock, but since it is 10:30 already I will go to bed.]

Samstag August 20ten. [Saturday August 20th.]

Geschäfte waren heute schlecht, ich war den ganßen Tag zu hause. Es ist doch etwas sonderbar das meine Frau noch nicht da ist, ich fange an bange zu werden, das entweder Sie oder der kleine Junge krank ist, sollte etwas passirt sein so wäre es doch ihre Pflicht mich davon in Kenntniß zu setzen. Ich war den ganzen Abend zu hause und erwartete meinen Lumps, 10 zu Bett.

[Business was poor today, I was at home all day. It is rather strange that my wife is not here yet, I am beginning to worry that either she or the little boy is sick, but if anything happened, surely it would be her duty to let me know. I was at home the whole evening and expected my Lumps. To bed at 10.]

Mersman left his diary here for over a year and a half before resuming it with the following entry.

Sontag August 21ten 1853. [Sunday August 21st 1853.]
Sunday March 18th 1855.

The topmost date is the day on which my wife returned from the Country. She arrived here in a Country Waggon at about 8 oclock in the Evening.

As the previous Entries in german were solely written for her satisfaction, being memorandums through which I Can prove what I had been doing with myself during her absence, that in Case some damned Malicious old woman should attempt to spread lyes regarding my doings during her Absence I had the Means of proving facts. as my wife is known to be very Jealous, and we have had Quarrels enough without foreign interfereance I took this precaution of avoiding additional ones.

It is now a Year and a half since my last Entry in this my long neglected Journal. There are so many reason why I am Careless about making Entries, that it is hardly worth Commencing to Ennumerate them. Should the Course of my Life be an uninterrupted happy one, an occasional Entry stating this pleasing fact would be sufficient. but as I do not even enjoy my share of happiness, I do not find any pleasure in recording the Continual troubles and Quarrels that take place between my wife and myself. I shall however attempt a brief description of our mode of life and some prominent Events that have occurred since my last Entry in this Journal.

Tuesday March 20th 1855.

I could not continue last Sunday. being in the store without fire it was too cold. Yesterday, being Monday I was half Sick from having indulged too much in Catawba on Sunday Evening, Celebrating the birth of my Second Boy who was born last Tuesday Morning this day a week ago on the 13th day of March at a ¼ past 8 oclock in the Morning. The little Fellow was Estimated as weighing about 11 Pounds. he occasioned unusual severe Pains in forcing his Exit, and gaining Entrance into this world of troubles, cares and vexations. So far Everything has gone well, excepting some little inconviniences that take place at almost every birth. There was some trouble in making the little fellow take the breast, one of them being verry sore and the other no nipple for him to take hold of.[34] his Mother is and has been well, excepting perhaps unusual severe *Pains* and last Sunday night a touch of Chills or fever.

I have now two Children. the Eldest Joseph J. Mersman Jr was born March 31st 1852 at 5 in the afternoon. the Second who is not Christened yet, but who will most likely receive the name of Frederic after my wife's and my Fathers name is to day just a week old. The Eldest being born on 31 and Second on 13th March, both in the Same month and the Same figures used fore both only turned around 31. 13.

I and Nulsen are now living with our families each in fine house of 6 rooms on 5th St between Morgan and Franklin Av. we bought these houses on 1st of April 1854, had them repaired thoroughly and moved in the latter part of May 1854. the Property Costs us 7000$ repairs about 1250 dollars.

I did intend to give a brief Sketch of my domestic life, but this Sketch would contain so little that is pleasing that I dislike to note down here the troubles Caused in our household by the foolish, the senseless Jealousy of my wife. Suffice it that as long we Married we have not had 3 days uninterrupted peace, although she is perfectly Convinced of my honest behavior, and that so far from having any thing to do with any other woman, I have never for a moment thought of any such thing. This Jealousy is aroused by every female that ever Came in Contact with us, no matter how dirty, filthy or unnatural ugly the object may be. we are noted for having the ugliest Servant girls in the City, but we have not had one yet that was not honored with her Jealousy. her own Mother & Sister are not exempt from her Suspecions.

Last Sommer I, my wife and our Boy took a trip to Cincinnati per Rail Road.[35] we started from here on 24th of July and returned here August 17th. I amused myself finely, seeing all my old acquaintances. we stopped at Kattenhorns. while there my Sisters Eldest Daughter Louisa was married on August 4th to Charles (I disremember his name)—just thought of it = ~~Ahrens~~ Peters. my good wife had to be jealous of Louisa also. She was highly offended at my intimacy with Nulsens wife and Henry's wife.[36] To hear her one would Suppose that Cincinnati was one grand whore house, and no deecent woman living there. Our poor little boy suffered horribly on the return trip. having four large boyles on his back he had to stand leaning against me. I am done describing my happiness.

JJM put down his pen and did not take it up to write in his journal again for more than seven years. During that time he worked diligently to build his whiskey-rectifying business and purchased more land in St. Louis for investment purposes.[37] *He amassed capital and established an extensive network of friends throughout the German American community. His health appeared to be good.*

The start of the Civil War brought grievous losses, among them the death of Charles Rebstock, the Cincinnati tavern keeper who had relocated to St. Louis in 1860 with his wife and four children. With the help of JCN and JJM, Rebstock opened a similar business in St. Louis and developed a trade among the German Americans of the Gateway City. In street violence in May 1861, he was hit by a minié ball and subsequently died of a wound infection, leaving his family impoverished.[38] *JJM and JCN subsequently helped Rebstock's oldest son, also named Charles, establish a wholesale liquor business. Charles supported his mother and siblings, and ultimately became a wealthy man.*[39]

JJM's marriage was not happy, but he and Claudine proceeded to have three additional children. Their growing prosperity was indicated by their changing addresses, which moved westward with the growth of the city (see note 7).

St Louis September 28th 1862.
Sunday night near 12 oclock.

On referring to my last Entry, I find it was written just Seven years, Six months and Eight days ago, a long time. my Second boy was then just a week old. Now he can read and write, and in place of wasting my time on my Second boy So exclusively, I have to ecomeomise for three others that have arrived during this time. Since my last entry my hair has Commenced to turn white, although I am not so very old yet, having celebrated my 38th birthday on the 17th of July last. my wife however still thinks me Sufficiently handsome to be jealous of me yet. to assert that I am happy, would be Stretching truth rather unnaturally, but I can honnestly assert that "it don't annoy and bother me any more as much as formerly." When my last entry was written, we were living on 5th St in our own houses the first real property we owned. now we are living on Chouteau Avenue in fashionable houses built by ourselves for our own use.[40] then I and my partner were worth about 50,000. Now we are worth 150,000, but we are not a bit happier than then, if as happy. I have five children now, Joseph the eldest, Fritz the Second, Clara, 3rd Arthur, the 4th and the Baby not yet Christened,[41] but was born March 29th 1862 ¼ past one at noon. When I wrote my last Entry, this great and glorious Country was in its most prosperous period. no one dreamt of the possibility of Such a war as now desolates the whole Land. Should my next entry be again 7½ years removed from this, it will be interesting for me to [note] how I came to write this, and at this time of night too. Our poor *Männi,*[42] Arthur, is Sick. he has been very Sick. the last 5 nights we had to Set up with him. I am up until about ½ past two, And Claudine takes care of him till Morning. poor *Männi!* for 3 days he lay in a very hot fever Caused by the prickle heat turning in on him.[43] then one of his little testicles commenced swelling. during his sickness he also caught a Severe cold. Thank God! he is recovering.

Despite the national conflict, N & M prospered, partly because of lucrative contracts with the federal government to supply whiskey for the U.S. Army. In 1863, each of the partners netted $20,000, the 2005 equivalent of nearly a half million dollars.[44] *Both JCN and JJM signed loyalty oaths, pledging their allegiance to the Union cause.*[45] *JCN served briefly as a quartermaster in the Home Guard, a regiment of pro-Union soldiers that remained in St. Louis.*[46] *Meanwhile, their brothers-in-law, Edward and Robert Creuzbauer, loyal Texans, joined the Army of the Confederate States of America (C.S.A.).*[47]

To finance the Union's Civil War effort and create a national currency, the U.S. Congress passed legislation in 1863 permitting state banks to become national banks. By December that year, the federal government had issued charters to three national banks in St. Louis. Prominent citizens, including William Lemp, the "beer man," became involved in the effort to create new banks in the city.[48]

In February 1864, JJM and JCN joined 122 of their business contacts in establishing the Fourth National Bank of St. Louis. Capitalized with $160,000 (sixteen hundred shares at one hundred dollars), the bank's investors were mainly the German American businessmen whom JJM saw regularly on the streets of the city. Six founders (JJM, JCM, John Block, Christian Peper, Caspar Holthaus, and Frederick Schwieding) purchased one hundred shares or more; the majority of the others bought stock in lots of five or ten shares. JJM proudly assumed the position of first president of the institution.[49]

JJM appeared to be on a sure path to economic success. Nevertheless, he took time in the spring of 1864 to record a profound personal loss.

Saint Louis Sunday Evening April 24th 1864.

My last entry is not two years old. as we get old important events keep crowding on us. this unhappy Country is desolated by the great Rebellion. the Rebels are not conquered yet, although they are pushed back considerably from their own teretorial line.

My last entry was occasioned by the sickness of our *Männi* or Arthur. Death is the Cause of this one! my poor Father died= On Monday Morning the 11th of April I received a letter from Sister Elizabeth that Father was very Sick, and desired very much to see me once more. I started the same afternoon and was with him the following Morning at 7 oclock.[50] My presence Seemed to enliven the old man up again. I stayed with him the whole week until the following Monday Morning, when I left for home, being under the impression that Father might live some months yet, as he was not Sick with any particular desease, but simply very Weak from Confinement to his bed and old age. Friday, when I came to dinner there was a Dispatch home Since 11 oclock informing me of his Death and requesting my attendance at his funeral Saturday Morning. as it was too late to get ready and Start that evening, I could not possibly be there Saturday Morning to attend his Funeral.

To morrow or the day thereafter I expect a letter, giving me details of his last moments, death and funeral, which I will add here.

I had a letter from Elizabeth on Friday the 28th. She wrote on the 26th. She was with Father nearly Constantly the last two days, and the old man died in her arms. he had his full senses to within three hours before his death. he died on Thursday evening at 8 o'clock, being the 21st day of April. he was burried on Saturday Morning. the funeral Mass, and the Catholic Services for the dead,

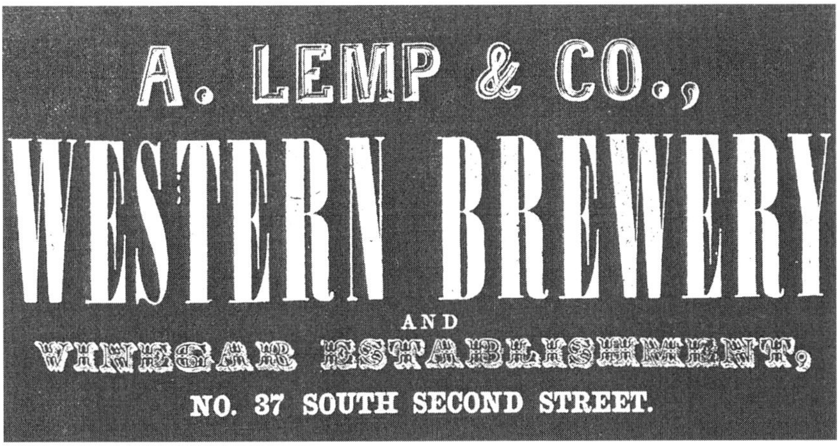

A. Lemp & Co. Western Brewery advertisement, 1850. The Lemp brewery operated into the middle of the twentieth century in St. Louis. Lemp also operated a vinegar factory in the city. (Missouri Historical Society, St. Louis.)

were given at the St. Mary's Church on 12th Street over the Canal. Father was about 85 to 87 Years old when he died.[51] He did his Duty while living.

Just five months later, JJM wrote his final diary entry. His pride at fathering a sixth child was nearly matched by his pride in having launched a bank, for he signed the entry with the title "President." Having come from Oldenburg with virtually nothing thirty years earlier, JJM had achieved material success, a thriving family, and a respected position in the community.

At home, in my house on Chouteau Avenue
Sunday morning September the 25th 1864.

The few entries in this my former daily Companion, while a young man, now always denote some important event. The last one was occasioned by the Death of Father this one by the birth of my Sixth Child, a boy, who was born just one week ago, on last Sunday Morning, September the 18th at a quarter before five oclock in the Morning— The little fellow Commenced fussing and kicking off the Water already the night before, but during Saturday remained pretty quiet. At 3 oclock on Sunday Morning I had to get up, dressed quickly, got Grand Mother and Mrs Nuelsen over and went for Mrs Carpentier. I returned with her in one hour and ten Minutes, but when we Came the Baby was there already. it came very quick, but was nevertheless a very hard birth. In the Course of Morning I weiged the little Man and found him to weigh 8 pounds, fully two more than he was Supposed to weigh. A week has now passed bye and every thing So far goes well. Mother and Baby are both in excellent health. the little boy has so far given less trouble than any of our other Children. he took the breast as easily, as though he was used to Sucking, and voided all his baby dirt[52] the first two days or so without any Syrups or tea being given him. he has every appearance of a Strong robust Child, with a Splendid Mouth for eating Water Melons— Jos. J. Mersman Prest[53]

NOTES

1. Membership records, Grand Lodge of Missouri.

2. MOR, 3 June 1906.

3. Relatively few Catholics belonged to fraternal orders, but both JJM and JCN began attending an evangelical church after they married the Creuzbauer sisters. The lodges met business needs for the whiskey merchants, who sought to expand their circle of contacts (Carnes, 4-14).

4. JJM's son was not yet weaned. Perhaps JJM feared that her extreme sense of modesty would interfere with Claudine's breast-feeding the child. See JJM diary, 6 August 1853.

5. The People's Theatre offered box seats and orchestra stalls at fifty cents. That evening, a drama entitled *The Jewess, or The Council of Constance* was performed (MOR, 18 July 1853).

6. The Pacific Railroad Company, incorporated 12 March 1849, celebrated the opening of thirty-seven miles of track on 19 July 1853. Six hundred guests—city officials, stockholders, and friends of the company—made an excursion to Franklin in just under two hours. Speeches, a banquet, and a band helped to mark the occasion. Changing locomotives in Kirkwood prolonged the actual journey, as JJM described. Although no ladies traveled in the Pacific Railroad cars, at the final destination an ample supply of local women contributed to the festive atmosphere of the banquet (Jennings; MOR, 20 July 1853; Mallinckrodt, 243–45).

7. The Nulsens and Mersmans lived close to each other for decades, even as the city grew larger and new neighborhoods, more distant from the river, became fashionable (Holt, 2:321–33). The families' growing prosperity was reflected in the addresses shown in the city directories:

Year	*Mersman's Residence*	*Nulsen's Residence*
1851	161 N. Third Street	161 N. Third Street
1857	119 N. Fifth Street	121 N. Fifth Street
1865	144 Chouteau Ave.	142 Chouteau Ave.
1867	1012 Chouteau Ave.	1016 Chouteau Ave.

They were next-door neighbors at four different addresses extending over two decades! (SLD 1851, 241 and 262; SLD 1057, 152 and 166; SLD 1865, 510 and 542; SLD 1867, 568 and 611.)

8. JJM was an enthusiastic member of the Erwin Lodge No. 121, a Freemason unit chartered 9 May 1851, which conducted all business in German, and held meetings on the second and fourth Fridays of every month (Records, Grand Lodge of Missouri).

9. JJM's mother-in-law Caroline Creuzbauer had a warm relationship with him. See also JJM diary, 2 February 1853 and 3 August 1853.

10. Possibly Anthony Klinkhart (also Klinkhardt) (c. 1825–60), an immigrant from Hanover who worked as a finish carpenter (USC 1860, Mortality Schedule, St. Louis, Ninth Ward, 334, line 1).

11. The performance included a tragedy, *Jane Shore,* and a farce, *Betsy Baker.* Charlotte Crampton played the leading roles (MOR, 23 July 1853).

12. "Lumps" is probably derived from the German *Lump,* "rascal."

13. Another chapter of the Masons, Missouri Lodge No. 1, chartered in 1816, held meetings on the second and fourth Monday of the month (SLD 1853, 127).

14. In addition to purchases of real estate in St. Louis, JJM later bought land in neighboring Illinois (St. Clair County Deed Book, E3:28; Montgomery County Deed Books 13:79, 4:266, 27:174, 40:338).

15. *Jack Sheppard* was the drama presented; a farce, *Irish Lion,* concluded the evening (MOR, 26 July 1853).

16. "Mr. France," JJM's customer, was possibly "Jacob Franc," a grocer and provision merchant on Morgan Street (SLD 1848, 90).

17. JJM describes a gathering of neighbors, who may have been two of the following families: Louis Riddle, a German-born farmer and his wife, Frederica, lived in Jefferson County, near two other German-born farmers with the surname of Richter. William Richter and his wife Isabel had five children; Louis Richter and his wife Charlotte had one child (USC 1850, M432, roll 402, page 432, line 12; USC 1850, M432, roll 402, page 419, line 21; USC 1850, M432, roll 402, page 425, line 18).

18. See JJM diary, 18 August 1853. Possibly Claudine Mersman had experienced a miscarriage and had vaginal bleeding, about which JJM avoids further comment.

19. Possibly Joseph Behrens, a tailor with a shop at 57 Plum Street (SLD 1851, 45).

20. The "Franklin Depot" is now called Pacific, Missouri, in Franklin County. JJM traveled five hours northwest by horse from Jefferson County and crossed the Merrimac River to catch the train for the thirty-seven-mile trip by rail to St. Louis. The fare was about three cents per mile. See map 7. (LOC Map Collection: Missouri Railroads, 1871, 1:1, 140, 480. R. P. Studley & Company; Jennings, 303).

21. John Liborius Müsenfechtler (1811–?) operated a grocery and later a saloon on Nineteenth Street (USC 1850, M432, roll 418, page 424, line 32; SLD 1854, 137).

22. The People's Theatre featured *The Naiad Queen* with Charlotte Crampton in the title role. A farce, *A Desperate Game,* and a solo dance completed the performance (MOR, 6 August 1853).

23. Joseph Jr. was nearly seventeen months old on this date, but in that era mothers commonly breast-fed their children up to age two (Clement, 50–51).

24. The Meridian Lodge No. 2, a Masonic chapter founded in 1852, held a special ceremony that Sunday morning to permit attendance by Masons from other lodges.

25. Polar Star Lodge No. 79, a chapter of the Masons chartered in 1846, had regular meetings on the second and fourth Thursday of each month (SLD 1853, 127).

26. St. Louisans went to great lengths to have elaborate funerals. A horse-drawn hearse with the coffin led the funeral cortege; family and friends followed in other wagons. The destination, a cemetery outside the city limits, has not been identified (van Ravenswaay [2], 319).

27. JJM was elected secretary of the Erwin Lodge in 1854 (Records, Grand Lodge of Missouri).

28. The surname of this employee is not known.

29. The yellow fever epidemic, spread by mosquitoes, raged in New Orleans during the summer of 1853, killing 7,848 and making it the worst outbreak in the city's history. From 1817 to 1905, more than 41,000 people died from the scourge (PIC, July and August, 1853; Augustin, 65).

30. The performance at the People's Theatre included the drama, *The Bottle Imp,* a farce, *Betsy Baker,* and a solo dance (MOR, 15 August 1853).

31. The Saint Louis Lodge No. 20, a chapter of the Masons, had regular meetings on the first and third Tuesdays of each month (SLD 1853, 127).

32. The People's Theatre offered *The Bottle Imp,* a farce, *Dumb Belle,* and a woman dancing the "Caledonian Fling" (MOR, 17 August 1853).

33. Possibly Claudine had miscarried a baby and was recovering with her mother's care.

34. Possibly Claudine Mersman had an inverted nipple, a condition that complicates nursing.

35. Railroad service between St. Louis and Cincinnati (via Chicago) became available in 1853; direct service began in 1859 (Flint, 83–84).

36. JJM refers to the wives of Anthony Nulsen (Maria) and Henry Mersman (Adelaide).

37. Land purchases are documented in St. Louis Deed Books B5:210, G6:66, V6:517, G6:66.

38. MOR, 23 May 1861.

39. Many years later, wholesale liquor dealer Charles L. Rebstock (1836–1928) donated a million dollars to Washington University and presented St. Louis University Medical School with a collection of microscopic slide studies of eye diseases (POD, 10 October 1928). After his death, a dozen charities, including three hospitals and several organizations that served the blind, received bequests from his estate (St. Louis City Probate Court, Estate #68,231).

40. JJM and Claudine resided at 144 Chouteau Avenue, while JCN and Albertine resided next door at 142 Chouteau Avenue (SLD 1865, 510, 542).

41. The baby was Emma C. Mersman (1862–1942) (Holy Ghost Evangelical Protestant Church, St. Louis, Missouri, Confirmation Lists, 1856–1905, unpaginated, arranged by date, 1876. FHL Microfilm 1503027).

42. A German nickname that translates as "little man."

43. Possibly this child had what modern physicians would diagnose as measles.

44. Undated news clip, Robert A. Barnes Papers, MHS.

45. Joseph J. Mersman Loyalty Oath, 1 April 1863, Box 65/folder 3; John Clemens Nulsen Loyalty Oath, 11 January 1864, B66/folder 1, Dexter P. Tiffany Collection, MHS.

46. 1890 U.S. Census, Special Schedule: Surviving Soldiers, Sailors, and Marines, and Widows, etc. Missouri, ED 331, 3, line 36, MHS.

47. An artillery captain, Edward Creuzbauer spent the entire war in Texas (RG 109, Records of the Confederate Army, 5th Texas Field Battery, Edward Creuzbauer, M323, roll 325, NA). A captain in the Army Engineer Corps of the C.S.A., Robert Creuzbauer invented an underwater cannon and a torpedo (RG 109, Records of the Confederate Army, Virginia Infantry Local Defense, Robert Creuzbauer, M324, roll 396, NA).

48. RG 101, Records of the Office of the Comptroller of the Currency, Records of the Division of Reports, List of National Banks, 1863–1934, vol. 1:23, 35, 43, 71; Records of the Organizational Division, Articles of Association, 1863–64, vol. 1:382, 582, NA.

49. Chartered on 26 February 1864, the Fourth National Bank merged with Mercantile-Commerce Bank on 15 January 1907 (RG 101, Records of the Organization Division, Organizational Files Relating to National Banks No Longer in Existence 1863–1944, Charters #283 and #4178, NA).

50. Transportation had improved so much that JJM made the trip by rail to Cincinnati in twelve hours, compared to the four days it took by steamboat in 1848.

51. Frederick Messman, born 3 March 1787 in Damme, the Grand Duchy of Oldenburg, was actually seventy-seven years old when he died on 21 April 1864 in Cincinnati (Kirchenbuch, 1650–1875, Taufen 1751–1787, 510, Katholische Kirche, Damme, FHL Microfilm 909910).

52. The passing of meconium, the first intestinal discharges of a newborn infant, indicates a healthy baby.

53. President of the Fourth National Bank of St. Louis, JJM used that title on Freemason records as well (Kargau, 160–62; Membership records, Grand Lodge of Missouri).

EPILOGUE

The Rest of the Story

Although JJM's diary ended on a positive note, the specter of his "confounded complaint" loomed over his future. Therefore, some background information about syphilis may help the reader interpret later events in JJM's life.

Medical practitioners have known for centuries that syphilis is a sexually transmitted disease with three stages. Primary syphilis, which appears as a painless sore or chancre at the site of infection, usually vanishes in weeks. Secondary syphilis, characterized by a rash on the skin and mucous membranes, may last many months, usually up to a year. Relapses of the secondary stage often occur, but even without treatment, the signs finally resolve, leading patients to think that they have been cured. Individuals with the infection are highly contagious during the first year or so, but after that time they can no longer spread it.[1]

The syphilis infection then becomes latent for a period that may last up to three decades. Finally, tertiary syphilis may cause irreversible damage to the neurological, cardiovascular, and musculoskeletal systems. In this advanced stage of the disease, patients may lose their vision, become demented, develop heart problems, or experience severe bone pain. Syphilitic lesions (gummas) may appear in internal organs, bones, eyes, and other parts of the body.[2] However, only one-third of untreated patients actually go on to develop tertiary syphilis, and the probability of dying as a result of untreated syphilis is less than twenty out of one hundred cases.[3]

When a woman has early syphilis and becomes pregnant, the illness can be transmitted to the fetus, causing a miscarriage or stillbirth. Babies with untreated congenital syphilis often die within the first few months; only half survive infancy. Later, such children may develop characteristic signs: notched teeth,

Joseph Mersman Jr. (1852–1925), c. 1875. The eldest son of Joseph and Claudine. (Personal collection of William Carlson.)

facial deformities, and deafness.[4] Today we seldom see the findings associated with congenital syphilis, but in Mersman's time they were common.[5]

In 1905, researchers identified the cause of syphilis, a spiral-shaped bacterium, *Treponema pallidum.* The next year, Wasserman developed a diagnostic blood test, and the modern age of treatment began.[6] Penicillin, available since 1945, provides a sure cure: a single injection eliminates primary or secondary syphilis, and a series spaced over several weeks treats tertiary syphilis. The screening of pregnant women and the treatment of newborns prevent the developmental abnormalities of congenital syphilis from occurring in children.

However, in the nineteenth century, syphilis was much like AIDS today: a deadly sexually transmitted disease that could be passed to the next generation.[7] Doctors advised treatments, but they only relieved symptoms and did not cure. Many physicians recommended mercury compounds, orally or topically, despite the toxic side effects. For example, calomel (mercurous chloride) caused anemia and renal failure. Some doctors prescribed potassium iodide in gargles, lotions, and tonics, although it caused gastrointestinal disturbances and skin reactions.[8] The ineffectiveness of treatments did not stop their widespread use.

Many practitioners prescribed opium for the pain of tertiary lesions. They recommended baths with "healing" potions added to the water. Some urged drinking decoctions (teas made from plants), often containing sarsaparilla,

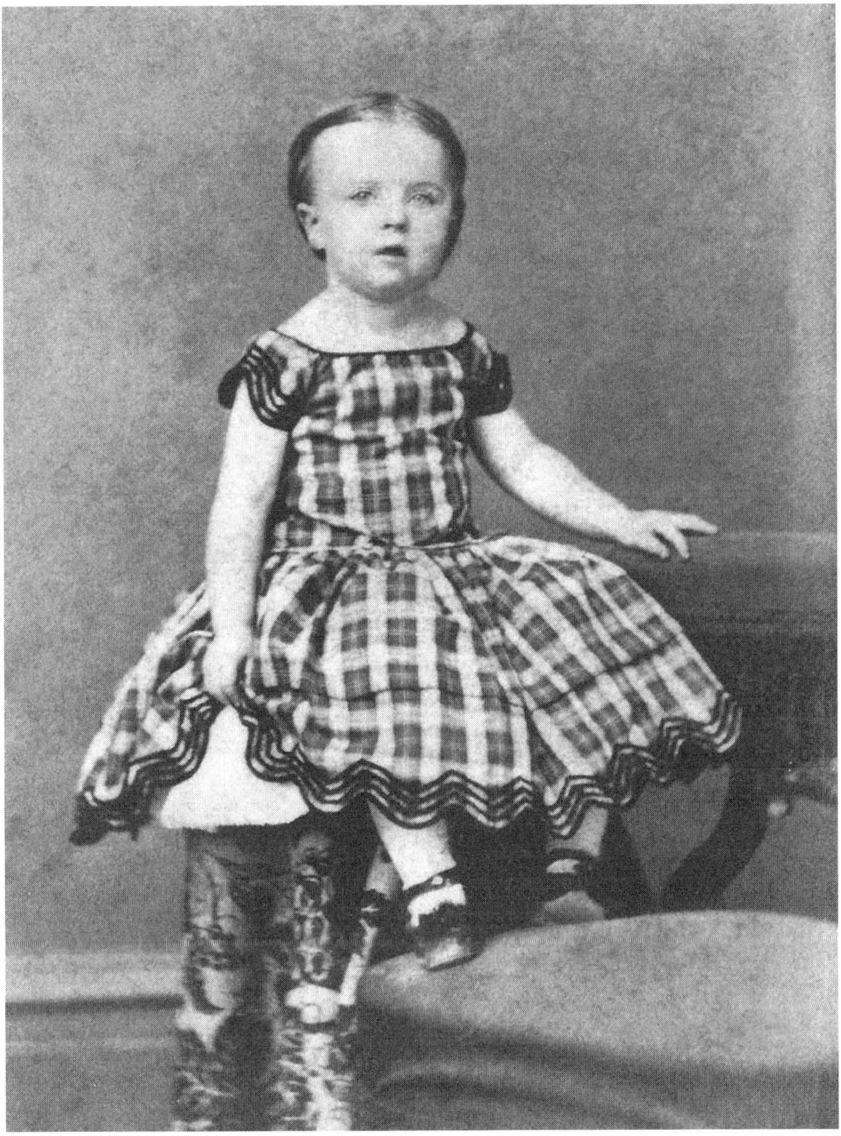

Clara Mersman (1857–1929), c.1860. Clara was the Mersmans' third child and the couple's eldest daughter. (Personal collection of Linda A. Fisher.)

considered a "blood purifier."[9] Sometimes they offered surgery or applied leeches to persistent sores. When treatments failed, doctors suggested a change of climate, a change of diet, or bed rest—or a combination of those measures.[10]

No matter which therapies they used, physicians routinely advised their patients to postpone marriage. Doctors debated, "When should syphilitics be allowed to marry?" Some believed that a patient could safely consummate a union three weeks after the disappearance of the last lesion; others recommended years of celibacy. They warned that "sexual excitement" might worsen a patient's condition.[11]

After JJM wrote his last diary entry, subsequent months brought unexpected sadness. His brother Henry became ill and died on 12 October 1864, in Cincinnati, at the age of forty-four, leaving a widow and five children ranging in age from eighteen to a few months.[12] Henry's will named Arnd Kattenhorn as executor of the estate, which included investment property and his tobacco business.

JJM's position as bank president made him take one step that he had long postponed. On 24 January 1865, JJM became a United States citizen in St. Louis.[13] William and Hiram Sleeth, his longstanding friends who had known him since his days in Cincinnati, were the witnesses. However, a new problem materialized soon after: JJM's vision began to fail. By the end of the year, JJM learned that his eye condition was progressive and incurable, and he resigned from his position as the president of the Fourth National Bank.[14] John C. H. D. Block, the vice president, took over as chief executive, and JCN became the new vice president.

Most likely, JJM's visual impairment was due to syphilis. He was just thirty-nine years old, too young for many other conditions that lead to blindness to be likely causes. However, chorioretinitis or optic atrophy, common manifestations of tertiary syphilis, are plausible explanations for his eye problem. His "confounded complaint" had not been cured by the botanical treatments recommended in 1850. Instead, his condition, which had been latent for about thirteen years, had silently progressed to the final stage. JJM would live for another twenty-seven years, but the relentless deterioration of his body finally caused his death.

Meanwhile, JJM's youngest brother, Frank, also was dying. On 11 January 1866, at the age of thirty-seven, Frank succumbed to "lung fever," probably tuberculosis.[15] During his last illness, Frank, a lifelong bachelor, lived at the home of their sister, Agnes Lake, at 10 West Ninth Street in Cincinnati. The residence of the Kattenhorns and the Lakes during the 1850s and 1860s, the three-story brick house currently stands in the middle of a commercial neighborhood, although urban development threatens it.[16]

In 1867, Nulsen & Mersman dissolved their business partnership, although their friendship remained lifelong and their destinies remained entwined.[17] Nulsen continued the whiskey business,[18] and JJM sought other uses for his capital and drive.

After JJM ceased reporting about them in his journal, Agnes and Bill Lake went on to great success in the circus business. First they starred as performers, and then, beginning in 1861, they became circus owners.[19] In the early days, their show was primarily a family affair featuring three of their children,[20] but by 1869, Lake's Hippo-Olympiad and Mammoth Circus had "two hundred forty men and horses,"[21] making it one of the largest tent shows in North America.

Unfortunately, circus life was frequently associated with senseless violence.[22] In August 1869, during a season of one-night stands, a bully shot and killed Bill Lake in southwest Missouri.[23] Agnes immediately began managing Lake's Circus, and thus became the first woman in the United States to own and operate a tent show. In subsequent years, her show traveled west to Wyoming and Utah, using the transcontinental railroad. Although she retired from the ring in 1874, Agnes lived until 1907 and married two other husbands. Her life was too long and too eventful to summarize here, but can be read elsewhere.[24] JJM could not have been more incorrect when he predicted that Agnes would be the first of his siblings to die.[25] In fact, she outlived all of her brothers and sisters by fifteen years!

JJM's older sister, Elizabeth Kattenhorn, raised three sons and a daughter in addition to her older girls, Louisa and Sophia, whom JJM mentioned.[26] When she died in Cincinnati at the age of sixty-eight on 10 December 1881, Elizabeth left numerous grandchildren among her survivors. Her husband, Arnd, died six years later, bequeathing an estate valued at $61,500 (the equivalent of approximately one and a half million dollars in 2005) to their surviving six children.[27]

Although he lost his eyesight, JJM found an opportunity to continue his mercantile interests. In 1870, he joined Charles F. Orthwein (1839–98) in a business styled as Orthwein & Mersman. Orthwein, an immigrant from Stuttgart, had married JCN's oldest daughter, Caroline Nulsen (1849–1908), in the autumn of 1866. Thus, Orthwein was JJM's nephew by marriage, and likely attended family gatherings that brought together the Nulsen and Mersman families.[28] A grain merchant in business since 1861, Orthwein found his best customers among the brewers and distillers of St. Louis. JJM offered much-needed capital for expansion, and with Orthwein's know-how, the firm prospered. Local companies such as the Lemp Brewery and the Anheuser-Busch Brewery purchased boatloads of grain. European markets opened to Orthwein & Mersman's exported corn and wheat. By the time fifty-five-year-old JJM completely retired in 1879, Orthwein had built an international business that he continued with his brother William, under the name Orthwein Brothers.

Orthwein & Mersman earned enough for the partners to build mansions in Lafayette Square, a stylish neighborhood in south St. Louis. JCN and Albertine picked 1641 Missouri Avenue (the west side of the square) as the site for a new home in 1873.[29] In 1878, JJM and Claudine constructed a red brick house at 1600

Otto Mersman (1864–1940), c. 1900. Otto, born in 1864, was the sixth child and the youngest son. (Sanders Engraving Co., after J. C Strauss, Missouri Historical Society Library RR Stl 920, C83, St. Louis.)

Mississippi Avenue (the east side of the square). By 1884, Caroline and Charles Orthwein had built one at 2035 Park Avenue (the north side of the square), and William D. Orthwein lived with his family at 2002 Lafayette Avenue (the south side of the square). The four households, united by business interests, blood ties, and marriage vows, remained neighbors for many years.

Claudine and JJM had two additional children after JJM's visual problems began: Alice Albertine, born in 1868, and Ella Claudine, born three years later. Altogether, the eight Mersman children—four boys and four girls—ranged in age a full twenty years from oldest to youngest. By 1882, when he was fifty-eight years old, JJM was totally blind and unable to write his signature. However, his mind remained clear throughout his last years, and he kept track of business matters. He purchased more bank stock, managed his income properties, and maintained his family in their Lafayette Square mansion.[30]

As they reached adulthood, JJM provided capital to launch the career of each of his sons.[31] Joseph Jr. (retail piano sales), Frederick (real estate sales), and Arthur (retail spice sales) had only limited accomplishments as businessmen, but the youngest boy, Otto Lewis Mersman, whose birth was the final event mentioned in JJM's diary, was more successful. A graduate of Washington University in St. Louis,[32] Otto began his career as the president of the Pacific Oil Company from 1886 until 1891, and subsequently became a real estate broker. In 1887, he

Alice Mersman (1868–1943), c. 1887. Alice was the seventh of the eight Mersman siblings. (Personal collection of Linda A. Fisher.)

married Mary Hord Scudder, the daughter of a prominent St. Louis family, and the couple resided at 71 Vandeventer Place, a fashionable address.[33] Like his famous aunt, Agnes Lake, Otto had an interest in horses, but his taste ran to polo rather than acrobatics.[34]

Claudine Mersman died on 21 February 1890 at the age of sixty. It appears that she did not die of syphilis. The St. Louis Death Register states the cause of death as "senile gangrene,"[35] a diagnosis which no longer has a clear meaning. The term may indicate that she had a type of peripheral vascular disease, something that can occur with diabetes mellitus or atherosclerosis. Because, as the diary documents, Claudine gave birth to at least two large babies (greater than ten pounds), it seems plausible to hypothesize that she developed diabetes mellitus in later life, which led to complications on her lower extremities, and eventually her death.[36]

JJM died two years after his wife, on 26 March 1892. Sixty-eight years old, he still lived in Lafayette Square with three of his unmarried children: thirty-seven-year-old Frederick (who had married in 1877, divorced in 1885, and then returned to the family home),[37] thirty-year-old Emma (who never married), and twenty-one-year-old Ella.

The cause of JJM's death, according to the St. Louis Death Register, was "paralysis."[38] Other records indicate that JJM had been ailing for several years before his death.[39] Although he was blind and required extensive care, his mind was intact. Perhaps anticipating some dispute over the terms of his lengthy last will and testament, JJM signed it in November 1890 in the presence of *five* witnesses, including William F. Orthwein (Charles D. Orthwein's brother).[40] Evidence suggests that JJM died from tertiary syphilis, for that disease would explain the blindness and central nervous system problems that preceded his death.

At probate, JJM's estate was valued at about a half million dollars, approximately twelve million dollars today, and included parcels of real estate in downtown St. Louis, stock in the Fourth National Bank of St. Louis, and the family home. JJM directed that several of the properties be kept in trust, so that the income could be divided among his children. However, he specified that his three unmarried children should be permitted to reside in the family home at 1600 Mississippi Avenue for as long as they wished. Additionally, he left a bequest for his only surviving sibling, twice-widowed Agnes Lake: eighteen shares in the Fourth National Bank of St. Louis, worth about $1,800 (or $43,000 in 2005).

Within a few months of JJM's death, his heirs were arguing. Some maintained that the mansion would lose its value and therefore should be sold so the proceeds could be shared. They reasoned that Emma, Ella, and Frederick could live together in equivalent housing, not the actual fifteen-room family home, because it was expensive to maintain. The dispute raged in St. Louis courts for years. Meanwhile, Ella married and left 1600 Mississippi Avenue. The Missouri Supreme Court ruled in 1896 that the Mersman family home, not any substitute, should be the residence for the offspring whom JJM had

Ella Mersman Hoblit Maccomas (1871–1952), c. 1876. Ella was the youngest of Joseph and Claudine's eight children. (Personal collection of Linda A. Fisher.)

named.[41] Emma moved out a few years later, but Frederick lived there until his death in 1918.[42]

Mersman family mansion, c. 1925. The Mersman mansion, located at 1600 Mississippi Avenue, St. Louis, was in Lafayette Square, a very fashionable part of the city. It was built in 1878 and demolished in 1970. Of all his possessions, only his diary survives. (Missouri Historical Society, St. Louis.)

Nevertheless, the Mersman siblings continued to fight over their father's estate and filed suits and countersuits in the ensuing years. When litigants died, their offspring replaced them as parties to the suits.[43] In the end, attorneys' fees claimed much of the estate. When the last checks were written in 1953, the recipients included twenty-five grandchildren, but many family members had stopped talking to each other. Descendents who moved away simply forgot they had relatives in St. Louis.[44]

John Clemens and Albertine Nulsen celebrated their fiftieth wedding anniversary together in May 1898. A dinner at the St. Nicholas Hotel included their eight surviving children and their spouses,[45] family members from Cincinnati, and friends from the German community of St. Louis.[46] The couple had more than forty-five grandchildren and had helped to establish many German American institutions. But less than two months later, Albertine hanged herself in her lovely home.[47] Grieving deeply, JCN lived another eight years. From observing the Mersman offspring (JCN's nieces and nephews) squabble over their father's complicated will, JCN learned a lesson that he applied to his own estate planning. When he died on 2 June 1906, JCN's two-page testament, written one month earlier, divided his assets into equal shares and bequeathed them to his children. Unlike JJM, he did not set up trusts in an attempt to control his heirs from the grave.[48]

Syphilis may have sickened JJM, but no evidence exists that his wife and children became infected. Claudine Mersman's obstetrical record does not suggest that she had any serious gynecologic problems after marriage: she did not have a series of miscarriages and neonatal deaths. The survival rate of Claudine's infants was far better than the mid-century average, and her children's birthdates do not include gaps that would suggest that she lost pregnancies.[49]

Research for this volume recovered the photographs of five of the eight Mersman children: Joseph Jr., Clara, Otto, Alice, and Ella. The portraits do not have facial abnormalities that suggest that any of them had congenital syphilis. Seven of the children (Joseph Jr., seventy-three years; Frederick, sixty-three years; Clara, seventy-two years; Emma, eighty years; Otto, seventy-six years; Alice, seventy-five years; Ella, eighty years) lived long lives. Only Arthur, who died at forty-five years of a kidney ailment, lived fewer years than was the average for his generation.[50]

Absent data prevent us from concluding definitively that all the Mersman children escaped congenital syphilis. First, a photograph of Frederick Mersman has not been found. Second, the health problem that affected Claudine Mersman in the summer of 1853 (the period between the births of Joseph Jr. and Frederick) is not known. One interpretation of the information uncovered to date is that she did have a miscarriage that summer, but it was not caused by a preexisting condition (i.e., syphilis). Another conjecture is that Claudine became infected after the birth of Joseph Jr. and that her second child, Frederick, was the only one born with congenital syphilis. Frederick's stormy personal life suggests a troubled individual, but whether his problems included an incurable, inherited infection is not known.[51]

Of JJM's St. Louis real estate, no building is left standing today. Dietrich Aufdenfeld's 1849 masterpiece, the first solid brick building on North Third Street,[52] was demolished in the early twentieth century. Mersman's downtown properties vanished to make way for the Jefferson National Expansion Memorial (including the Gateway Arch) and the interstate highways near the riverfront. Even JJM's mansion at 1600 Mississippi Avenue was torn down in 1970.[53] Of all his possessions, only JJM's diary survived. Years after JJM's death, it came into the hands of John Gundlach, a collector of historical manuscripts who was an acquaintance of Otto Mersman's. After Gundlach died in 1923, the diary came to the Missouri Historical Society, where it remained seldom read for decades, until good fortune brought it to my attention.

JJM's account of antebellum life in Cincinnati and St. Louis is perhaps the sole tangible evidence of his life that remains in existence. His words are his most valuable legacy, and this edition preserves them in a form that will make them available for many more generations.

NOTES

1. Holmes et al., 473–78; Isselbacher et al., 726–32; Johns, 1–5.

2. Holmes et al., 487–509; Johns, 1–5.

3. Danholt et al., 34:34; Holmes et al., 475–76.

4. Radolf et al., 1165–89; Stokes et al., 1068–1169.

5. Reliable statistics for antebellum America do not exist, but studies from later pre-penicillin years indicate widespread disease in the United States. For example, a 1917 estimate was that syphilis accounted for 20 percent of U.S. stillbirths; a 1922 study indicated that 8 percent of English schoolchildren had congenital syphilis; and a 1936 study indicated that 2 percent of U.S. children and 5.6 percent of U.S. infants were syphilitic (Holmes et al., 1166).

6. Pusey, 31; Holmes et al., 1166; PHS #1660, 9.

7. Many medical writers have compared these two diseases. See Arrizabalaga et al., 12, Johns, 220–41, and Quétel, 273–79.

8. Bumstead, 499–515.

9. Advertisements regularly promoted the use of sarsaparilla (CCD 1849–50, 144). To this day, the slang term "bad blood" can mean syphilis (Jones, 5–6, 71–73).

10. Hollick, 167–89, 213–28; Bostwick, 172–78, 341–48; Parker, 246–61.

11. Later in the century, medical pundits became more conservative in their recommendations concerning marriage, some prescribing up to five years of sexual abstinence for syphilis patients (Fournier; Schuster; Morrow; Hutchinson, 553–56).

12. Henry's alcohol consumption may have played a role in his early death (DUN Ohio, 78:181).

13. St. Louis Court of Common Pleas, Record Book G:123, St. Louis Civil Courts Building.

14. WPO, 27 March 1892.

15. Cincinnati Death Register, 1:13, record #536.

16. Cincinnati City Directory listings throughout the 1850s and 1860s confirm that address was the home of the Kattenhorn and Lake families.

17. The Nulsen & Mersman partnership appeared in the 1867 city directory, but was replaced by Peper, Rassfield & Company in the following edition (SLD 1867, 612; SLD 1868, 1011).

Evidence of the continued closeness between the two families comes from their many connections. Albertine Creuzbauer Nulsen served as the godmother for Alice Albertine Mersman, baptized in 1876 (see note 28 below). JJM had a business partnership with JCN's son-in-law from 1870 through 1879 (Cox, 415). JCN acted as JJM's attorney in 1882, when the two men signed documents to purchase additional shares in the Fourth National Bank of St. Louis (RG 101, Records of the Organization Division, Organizational Files Relating to National Banks No Longer in Existence 1863–1944, Charter 283, National Archives, College Park). August H. Schott, MD (1850–1922), husband of Emma Nulsen, JCN's niece (the daughter of Joseph Nulsen in Cincinnati), served as the physician for the Nulsen, Mersman, and Orthwein families in their later years (POD, 24 February 1922).

18. The wholesale liquor business continued as Peper, Rassfield & Company, with JCN providing capital until 1879. In 1879, his son, Anthony Joseph Nulsen, became a partner. In 1881, JCN established the Missouri Malleable Iron Company. One of the founders of the Fourth National Bank of St. Louis, he served as vice president (1865) and remained on the board of directors for many years (Leonard, 439; DUN Missouri, 40:265, 43:57, 46:250, 47:86; Kargau, 285–87).

19. Slout, 164–65.

20. The eight-year-old child, William, whom the Lakes adopted, disappeared after the 1850 census (USC 1850, M432, roll 417, page 121, lines 10–12). He may have returned to his birth mother in

Portsmouth, Ohio. However, the Lakes later adopted a girl they called Alice (c. 1850–67) and a second William (c. 1858–1932), called Willie, this one the orphaned son of William O. Dale, an equestrian who died in 1866. By birth or adoption (confusing records create some uncertainty), they had another daughter, Emma (c. 1855–1911). Eventually, those three Lake offspring—Alice, Willie, and Emma—became noted circus equestrians (Slout, 70, 164; ZAN, 25 April 1866).

21. CON, 8 April 1869.

22. Shootings, robberies, and brawls occurred at circus gatherings. For representative reports, see the NYC, 28 March 1868; 20 March 1869; 16 July 1870; 19, 26 November 1870.

23. TEL, 3 September 1869.

24. Fisher (2).

25. JJM diary, 16 June 1850.

26. Arnd Kattenhorn Jr. (1846–84) and William Kattenhorn (1854–?) became grocers like their father; Frank Kattenhorn (1849–?) went into the tin business with Charles Peters (Louisa's husband); and Henrietta married August Arnold and became a homemaker (DUN Ohio, 81:196).

27. Hamilton County, Ohio, Probate Court, Estate #32,672.

28. For example, on 30 January 1876, when Ella Claudine Mersman (JJM's seventh child, born 4 November 1871) was baptized, Charles and Caroline Orthwein's son, Ralph Hermann Orthwein (JCN's grandson, born 10 January 1876), was baptized as well (Holy Ghost Evangelical Protestant Church, St. Louis, Missouri, Baptisms, January 1873-December 1907, #2514. FHL Microfilm 1503027).

29. Addresses from the SLD, 1878, 693 and 634; and SLD 1884, 848.

30. RG 101, Records of the Organization Division, Organizational Files Relating to National Banks No Longer in Existence 1863–1944, Charter #283, NA.

31. At his death, Mersman forgave loans to each of his sons: approximately $37,000 to Joseph Jr.; $19,000 to Arthur; $28,000 to Frederick; and $66,000 to Otto. The credit ratings of Mersman's sons provide additional information about their father's involvement in their business dealings (DUN Missouri, 38:322, 46:89, 319).

32. Cox (1), 548; Leonard (1), 400.

33. Cox (1), 549.

34. Otto became a founding member of the St. Louis Country Club, a prestigious social group (Circular letter and meeting announcement of O. L. Mersman, St. Louis Country Club, William F. Pettus Papers, MHS).

35. Claudine Mersman entry SLDR, 53:358.

36. The size of Claudine's babies is mentioned by JJM in diary entries on 11 April 1852, 20 March 1855, and 25 September 1864. No record of the birth weights of the other children has been found.

37. St. Louis Circuit Court Case #67,146 (1885) documents Frederick C. Mersman's marriage and divorce; see also, Holy Ghost Evangelical Protestant Church, St. Louis, Missouri, Marriages, 5 July 1877, p. 145, FHL Microfilm 1433231).

38. Joseph Mersman entry, SLDR 54:71.

39. For a description of the physical condition of JJM during his last years, see Case #7269, *Mersman, et al. v. Mersman, et al.* (October Term, 1895) Supreme Court of Missouri; Statement of the Case, Abstract, Brief and Argument, Respondents and Appellants.

40. St. Louis City Probate Court, Estate #18,909.

41. *Mersman, et al. v. Mersman, et al.*, 37 *Southwestern Reporter* 909–13 (1896).

42. POD, 15 December 1918.

43. Documentation of the many cases may be found in the records of the St. Louis Circuit Court, for example, case #6504, *Hoblit, et al. v. Mersman, et al.*; case #12,628, *Lincoln Trust Company, et al. v. Nathan, et al.*; case #34,329, *Giraldin, et al. v. The Lincoln Trust Company, et al.*; case #64,585A, *Lincoln Trust Company, et al. v. Frederick C. Mersman, et al.*; case #94,665A, *Estate of Mersman v. Mersman and Mersman.*

44. Joseph Jr. moved to Michigan before JJM's death, and his descendents dispersed further; Ella moved to Illinois; and Otto retired to Florida. Of the five Mersman children who remained in St. Louis, only three (Clara, Arthur, and Alice) had offspring of their own, and several of them went to distant states (Joseph J. Mersman Death Certificate, 108,376 [1925], Michigan Department of Health, Lansing, Michigan; Ella MacComas Death Certificate, 74,435 [1952], Illinois Department of Public

Health, Chicago, Illinois; Otto L. Mersman Death Certificate, 22,633 [1940], State of Florida, Office of Vital Statistics, Tallahassee, Florida; Alice Mersman Giraldin Death Certificate, 1,600 [1943], Missouri Board of Health, Jefferson City, Missouri; Clara C. Roux Death Certificate, 31,935 [1929], Missouri State Board of Health, Jefferson City, Missouri; Frederick C. Mersman Death Certificate, 49,766 [1918], Missouri State Board of Health, Jefferson City, Missouri; Emma C. Mersman Death Certificate, 18,852 [1942], Missouri State Board of Health, Jefferson City, Missouri).

45. One son, Maximillian Nulsen (1858–97), had died eight months earlier, but his widow attended the celebration (WPO, 18 May 1898). Two other children, Albertine Amalia Nulsen (1854–57) and Edmund Nulsen (born 20 June 1851), had died in childhood (Holy Ghost Evangelical Protestant Church, St. Louis, Missouri, Burial Records, unpaginated, 21 February 1857, #6945, FHL Microfilm 1503029).

46. DEM, 18 May 1898; MOR, 18 May 1898; WPO, 18 May 1898.

47. An inquest determined that Albertine Nulsen had been suffering from "melancholia" (depression) for a long time. The Nulsens had moved out of their Lafayette Square residence in 1892, after JJM's death, and were living elsewhere in south St. Louis at the time of Albertine's demise. However, their former house at 1641 Missouri Avenue still stood as of 2005 (MOR, 8 July 1898; POD, 7 July 1898; DEM, 8 July 1898; WPO, 8 July 1898; City of St. Louis, Inquest Record, 7 July 1898).

48. DEM, 3 June 1906; St. Louis City Probate Court, Estate #32,826.

49. Before contraception was available in America, married women without medical problems commonly gave birth about every two years. (Schlumbohm [141] has documented that in the early and mid-nineteenth century married women of Mersman's homeland generally had a child every two and half years.) The interval between Claudine Mersman's marriage and the birth of her healthy first child, fourteen months, indicates that she most likely did not contract syphilis soon after she wed. The intervals between the births of Claudine's subsequent children (see Mersman Family Pedigree) were 1) thirty-six months, 2) thirty months, 3) twenty-six months, 4) twenty-nine months, and 5) thirty months; after the onset of JJM's eye problems, the intervals were 6) forty-five months and 7) forty-one months. In Claudine's case, only the long interval between her first and second children, Joseph Jr. and Frederick (thirty-six months, at a time when she could have had a recent infection with syphilis), raises the possibility of a miscarriage. By the time that Claudine conceived her seventh and eighth children, she was older (thirty-eight, and then forty-one, years old) and dealing with a disabled husband, two factors that may have impacted her fertility. JJM almost certainly was not infectious at that late date.

50. The SLDR, 53:273, lists Arthur's cause of death as "Bright's Disease, dropsy." No United States national life expectancy data for the nineteenth century exist, but information is available for the State of Massachusetts. A male born in 1855 could expect a lifetime of 38.7 years. If one survived to age 20, life expectancy was 39.8 more years, for a lifetime of 59.8 years (DoC, 1:56).

51. Frederick's marriage at age twenty-two ended in divorce years later. His wife testified about the domestic violence that she suffered at his hands.

Frederick's credit rating in 1879 noted that he had many debts "which [were] regarded as uncollectible." Significantly, Orthwein & Mersman were among his unpaid creditors (DUN Missouri, 46:89).

Following his divorce, Frederick remained in the family home until his death in 1918. Although he called himself a real estate broker, his earned income was small. Litigation in 1910 suggests that he and his brother Otto attempted to cheat their siblings out of their share of JJM's estate, because the court ordered them to pay $20,000 to their sisters.

52. JCN's obituary lauded him for building that structure (POD, 3 June 1906).

53. Wrecking permit E 8747, 2 April 1970, Department of Public Works, St. Louis City Hall.

ACKNOWLEDGMENTS

Many people and institutions have helped with the massive project of piecing together Joseph J. Mersman's life. Only one man lived it, but at least a hundred were required to decipher its meaning!

I sincerely appreciate all their help during the five years of work that were required to prepare the manuscript for this book. I also wish to thank the National Library of Medicine (NLM), the National Historical Publications and Records Commission (NHPRC), and the State Historical Society of Missouri (SHSMO) for providing funding that enabled me to finish the project. When I began, I had no idea that Joseph J. Mersman would lead me to archives in twenty-five states in the United States and across the ocean to Germany, but once I got started, there was no way that I could stop searching for information before I learned the full story of the diarist and his family. It took the help of dozens of people on both sides of the Atlantic Ocean to unravel the mysteries contained in Mersman's journal.

Reinhard Hennig provided translations of German sections of the diary, German publications, and other manuscripts found in various archives. He consistently gave sound advice concerning research initiatives. Darya Sultyana assisted by translating sections of the diary written in French, and Bonnie Fisher interpreted German church records written in Latin. Joel Cisne, my first research assistant, helped me plan the scope of my project. Dennis Northcott provided research support in St. Louis and provided comments on the entire manuscript. Ann Hambrecht conducted research in Cincinnati; Falk Liebezeit and Sylvia Möhle, in Germany; Jean Fisher, in New Jersey; Pat Fennerty, in New Orleans; and Eugene Zepp, in Boston. Stuart Thayer, William Slout, and Fred Dahlinger Jr. generously shared their insights concerning nineteenth-century American circuses. Jerry Dalton, master distiller of the Jim Beam Brands Company, provided information about American whiskey making, and Matthÿs Jansen of de Kuyper Royal Distillers told me of his firm's long history. Joseph Rosa and Robin Carmody offered information concerning the later life of Agnes Lake.

Several genealogists helped me trace the Mersman family from Oldenburg to the present: Ann Carter Fleming, Elizabeth Shown Mills, Roger Minert, and Marion Wolfert gave advice and assistance. Other people who aided the project included Rev. David Hoying and his mother, Rita Hoying, Allen W. Bernard, Anita Mallinckrodt, Simon Baatz, Christine Hughes, Don Heinrich Tolzmann, Jürgen Schlumbohm, Wolfgang Grams, Helmut Schmaul, Antonius Holtman, Rainer Schimpf, Charlotte Borst, William Roba, Stephen Rowan, Esther Katz, Daniel Stowell, Candace Falk, Marianne Wokeck, Faye Dudden, Jane Censer, and Allan Fisher. Members of the Victorian Dance Ensemble helped me understand the etiquette of the balls that Mersman attended. Michael Meier at the NHPRC, Susan Sparks and Valerie Florance at the NLM, and James W. Goodrich at the SHSMO provided assistance with funding applications.

Individuals at many libraries and archives helped me find significant primary and secondary source materials to further this project: Anne B. Shepherd (Cincinnati Historical Society Library); Paul Immel (State Library of Ohio); Kathy Connick (Lloyd Library and Museum); Sylvia Verdun Metzinger, Claire Smittle, and M'lissa Kesterman (the Public Library of Cincinnati and Hamilton County); Michael R. Veach (the Filson Club Historical Society); Juda Moyer (Troy Historical Society); Kathy Grillo and Melvina Conley (St. Louis Civil Courts Archives); Ronald Miller (Ancient Free and Accepted Masons of the Grand Lodge of Missouri); Mary Ellyn Hamilton (Oscar Getz Museum of Whiskey History); Erin Foley (Circus World Museum and Library); Mark Levine (Brooklyn Public Library); Joan Kilpatrick (Texas General Land Office); Lila Fourhman-Shaull and June Lloyd (York County Heritage Trust); Ernst Otto Bräunche (Stadt Karlsruhe, Institut für Stadtgeschichte); Gail Cassini (Historical Archives of the Chancery, Archdiocese of Cincinnati); Randy Blomquist and Emily Jaycox (Missouri Historical Society); Ruth Hager (St. Louis County Library); Sandra Bender (City of St. Louis, Recorder of Deeds Office); Lucas Dennis and Annette Fern (Harvard College Library); Charles Bean, David Kelly, Thomas Mann, and Travis Westly (Library of Congress).

A number of Mersman, Nulsen, Creuzbauer, and Orthwein descendents assisted with establishing family pedigrees and finding photographs of ancestors: Fred Althoff, Trish Blakely (Scudder Association genealogist), William Carlson, Agnes Cromack, John T. Dilschneider, JoAn Dreahn, William E. "Jerry" Giraldin, Nancy Lindquist, Leif E. Nulsen, George Petticrew, and Lori Steadman are among those who were especially helpful. The Johannes Pohlschneider family of Damme, Germany, gave me valuable insights concerning life in their community when Joseph J. Mersman was a child, and I enjoyed their warm hospitality.

Research assistants Veronica Fletcher, Kelly Jordan, Jason M. Beagle, Carolyn Bowers, James T. Garber, and Christopher Robertson aided the tedious process of manuscript preparation. Their research at the Library of Congress and the National Archives improved the annotation; their proofreading and computer skills made sure that the final document was an accurate reflection of the source text. Andrea Myles of Washington University Medical Photography, Illustration, and Computer Graphics prepared the maps; Jabr Dumit restored the vintage photographs.

Bertha Fisher and Tove Post-Roberts provided never-ending enthusiasm for this project; Cliff and Harriet Johnston provided housing during my expeditions to St. Louis. Christopher E. Byrne gave me technical assistance, unflagging encouragement, and much love.

APPENDIX

Recipes and Other Undated Diary Material

This is a complete transcription of the recipes located between the conclusion of diary entries and a page of financial notes in the source text. None of the recipes have been tested by the editor, so no warranties are made concerning them.

Cherry Brandy.

40 Gallons Whiskey. 2 wine bottles full of Lime Juice

6 Gall's Rum. 2 oz Spirite Sweet Nitre[1] to be put like oil. 3 or 4 lbs Raisins. Well broke or crushed and put in Whiskey. Color with extracts of Logwood.[2] Fine down and bung close.[3] to stand at least two weeks.

Muriatic Acid[4] has the property of precipitating the essential of Whiskey or any kind of Spirits in proportion of nearly a pint to the barrel.

French Brandy flavouring

To 4 Gallons Neutral Spirits.

½ Gallon pure Syrup

10. Cents worth arris root or *iris deflorentine*[5]

1. large bean Vanilla.

Bot this receipt for five dollars.[6]

Dom Brandy Old Plum

½ Pound Orris Root. ½ do Salt Petre.[7] ½ do bitter Almonds. bruise all togather in a bucket. then put on a half gallon Vinegar. Stir it well. let it Stand one day. the next it is fit to be put in 70 Gallons of Whiskey and 28 of Alcohol, or 98 of proof Whiskey. then color and put in 1 Gallon of Port Wine. If a ½ oz oil of Lavender[8] dissolved in a pint Alcohol is added it will make good improvement ¼ oz might do. Add 2 Gallons of the following preparation.

Preparation

Take 30 lbs Raisins. put them in 16 Gallons Whiskey. let them stand two days. This is enough for 400 Gallons Brandy.

Rule

To cut oil of Lemon, pour it on Loaf Sugar. Crush it.

To take must of any cask ¼ lbs in 2 gallon hot water.

To correct musty whiskey use oil of Cinnamon.[9]

Gin. American.

2½ oz oil Juniper. 4 oz oil Sweet almonds. Cut Serately in alcohol ½ Gallon to each to Stand 2 days. Stirring now and then. ½ lbs Angelica root.[10] put in ½ gallon hot water to dissolve. After two days preparation mix all in 60 Gallons Whiskey. to add 3 lbs of Capolerium[11] if necessary.

Rum. imitation Jamaica.

21 Gallons Whiskey. 6 do Alcohol

2 do Water 6 do Jam Rum, pure.

½ oz oil Jama Ginger. Color to suit.

Gin.

55. Gallons Whiskey 5 do Hollands Gin

1. oz oil Juniper[12] dissolved

Port Wine.

60 Gallons Sweet Cider. Put in Cask with a Faucett in. 3 lbs lean beef rolled in 1 lbs of dry Mustard. Put in the bung-hole. To remain for 2 or 3 days. Take 10 lbs Raisins, boil in 10 Gallons Water for 12 minutes. Strain it through Cloth. After having drawn off the Cider put the liquor of the raisins in it. then put 1 ½ lbs extract of Logwood to be dissolved in 1 gallon Common Whiskey. 4 Gallons Common Brandy, and ½ lbs Tincture of Rhatany[13] in the Brandy. then mix all togather. Sweeten slightly with Capolerium. then add 1 lbs ground Rice. bung up,[14] and fine as usual. in two weeks will be fit to use.

La Manière de préparer les différentes sortes de Liqueur.

[The manner of preparing different types of liquors]

Du Vinaigre [Vinegar]

50 Gallons Hard Cider. *On met dans le Cidre* 2 lbs Tartaric Acid. *Il faut mêler cela bien, et le laisser rester deux jours* [One puts in the cider 2 lbs tartaric acid.[15] Mix it well, and let it sit for two days]. At the same time that the acid is put in, Set 1½ pint of Sulphuric Acid[16] in ½ gallon ~~NL Spirits~~ Alcohol for Same lenght of time. then draw of the Cider Clean and Mix the Sulphuric Acid in the drawn Cider. Sulphuric Acid must be put gradually in Alcohol, and afterwards Corked down by fining[17] with white of Eggs. Will be fit for use in two weeks

Capolerium or Syrup

¼ gls Water 20 lbs loaf Sugar. to be boiled until it mixes with water clear. Say ½ hour or So.

Peppermint.

60 Gallons Water. 15 Gls Whiskey. 4 oz oil of Peppermint. to be dissolved in ½ Gallon Alcohol. 1 oz Essence of Jamaica Ginger. ¼ oz Salts Wormwood.[18] Sweeten the whole with 28 lbs Capolerium.

Un autre [an other].

23 Gallons Whiskey 10 below proof. 40 lbs Loaf Sugar, dissolve among 31 gallons hot water 1¼ oz oil pept [peppermint] in one pint Alcohol to cut it. mix of course all togather. a few Raisins will improve it.

This page is located in the source text between the recipes and a will dated 9 July 1851.

MONEY PAID TO MY FATHER

1848				
Janury	17	For Amount See old Journal	25. .	00
"	"	Paid Father	5. .	00
February	18	Paid to father~~~~~~~~~~~~~~~~~~~	10. .	00
May	11	Paid to father	13. .	00
"	"	Less Note for twenty Eight dollars }	53	00
		given to me by Father on F. Puthoff.}		
		which note Mr P. has accepted	28	00
		This amt of 25$ I agreed to pay	25	00
		Father From 1st of May 1847 to 1st May 1848		
		Joseph J. Mersman		
1848				
June	17	Paid to Father myself	5	00
July	5	Paid to Father "	3	00
August	18	Paid to Father "	7	===
Sepr	28	Paid to Father "	5	00
Octr	12	Paid to Father "	5	00

This undated transcription of a scene from a play by Eugéne Scribe was written by Mersman on the flyleaf of his journal.[19]

Un Morceau tirée du Mariage d'argent.[19]

Mad[e] de Brienne. *Et si je les Séparais, ils S'aimeraient davantage. (Vivement) Non, non, n'y pensons plus! Je ne suis plus telle que vous m'avez vue ce Matin, Sans énergie, Sans Force, Sans pouvoir et Sans Courage. Ma raison est revenue, et avec elle ma Fiérté et l'estime de Moi-Même.* (avec Fermeté.) *Je n'ai point Mérité mon Sort, je n'ai rien à me reprocher: je perds Celui que j'aime, mais je m'immole à Son bonheur, Mais je fais des Vœux pour lui, je le force à me plaindre, à m'estimer, à me regretter.* (Mettant la Main Sur Son Cœur) *Je Souffre encore, il est Vrai: Mais je suis Sans remords, et il en aura peut-être! . .*
Olivier. *Combien je Vous admire!*
Mad[e] de B_ *Vous restez à ce Contrat: moi, je ne puis. Mais je Vous Verrai demain, n'est-il pas Vrai? Vous avez Voulu Mon Amitié, elle Va Vous imposer bien des obligations, Vous être bien à charge.*

Olivier. *il faut rompre Ce Mariage. Mon cher Ami.*
Poligni. *Y pense-Tu? et dans quel Moment? Quand toute une famille est réunie pour Signer Ce Contrat, quand il y a dans ce Salon plus de deux Cents personnes qui Seraient témoins d'un pareil éclat! Et de quel droit déshonorer une jeune fille qui n'a d'autres fautes envers moi que de me Sauver moi-même du déshonneur, de faire ma fortune, et à qui je ne peux pas reprocher Ses défauts, Car je les Connais, je les accepte: C'est à moi au Contraire à la protéger, a la défendre, j'y suis engagé d'honneur, je suis lié par Ses bienfaits.* (à Voire basse) *Car j'ai déjà reçu Sa dot. elle est là, j'en ai disposé d'avance, je l'ai presque employée.*
[A piece from *Marrying for Money*
Madame de Brienne. And if I separate them, they will love each other more than ever. (*Vivaciously*). No, no, let's not think about it further! I am no longer the one you saw this morning: without energy, without strength, without courage. I've come to my senses and rediscovered my sense of pride and self-esteem. (*Determined.*) I've not deserved my destiny, I do not have anything to reproach myself for. I lose the one I love, but I sacrifice myself for his happiness. I wish him good fortune; I force him to feel sorry for me, to hold me in esteem, to regret losing me. (*Placing her hand over her heart*) I still suffer, it is true: But I have no regret, and he will likely have it!
Olivier. How I admire you!

Mme de B. You are staying for the contract signing; I cannot do it. But I'll see you tomorrow, isn't that so? You always wanted my friendship, and now you'll have the obligations and responsibilities that go with it.

Olivier. You have to call off everything, my dear friend.
Poligni. You think so? And when? When the entire family is assembled to sign the agreement, when there will be more than two hundred people to witness the event! By what right can we humiliate a young girl who has not committed any crime but saving me from dishonor, who enriches me, and whom I cannot reproach for any short-comings. Indeed I know them, and accept them. It's just the opposite; it's up to me to protect and defend her. Honor requires this. I'm bound to her by her good manners, (in a hushed voice) since I have already received her dowry. It is there. I received it in advance. I have basically used it up.] [*JJM added*] *Ces Sentimens Sont très noble de notre Ami Poligni!* [These sentiments of our friend Poligni are very noble!]

NOTES

1. Sweet spirits of nitre contains between 3.5 and 4.5 percent of ethyl nitrite (CH_3CH_2ONO) in 70% ethyl alcohol and is also known as spirit of nitre, spirit of nitrous ether, and ethyl nitrite spirit. It was used at one time as a diaphoretic to reduce fevers, its over-the-counter use was banned by the Food and Drug Administration in 1980 (*Federal Register* 45, no. 126, [27 June 1980]: 43400).

2. Logwood (*Haematoxylon campeachianum*) takes its name from the blood-red color of the heartwood. Imported from Jamaica, Santa Domingo, or Honduras, it is used as a coloring agent and produces red, violet, blue, grey, and black (Grieve, 2:496).

3. Clarify the mixture and close the cask with a stopper (OED, s.v. "fine," "bung").

4. Muriatic acid is hydrochloric acid (HCl): now only a commercial term.

5. Orris root consists of the peeled and dried rhizomes of *Iris florentina,* a plant with deep violet flowers, veined with brown, yellow, and white. The powdered rhizomes have the odor of violets and are used in perfumery (Bailey, 598–602; Grieve, 2:434–37).

6. Five dollars in 1850 is the equivalent of about one hundred dollars in 2005.

7. Saltpeter, named because it commonly encrusts stones, is a naturally occurring form of potassium nitrate, KNO_3.

8. Lavender, *Lavandula* species, a shrub indigenous to the Mediterranean lands, is also grown in France and England because of its aromatic flowers (Grieve, 2:467).

9. Musty whiskey, with a faint odor of mold, sometimes results from corn that spoiled before the spirit-making process began. Today, manufacturers comingle small amounts of musty whiskey with whiskey that is free from objectionable odors. Dilution minimizes the negative impact (Jerry Dalton, master distiller, Jim Beam Products, personal communication, 5 August 2002).

10. Angelica root (*Angelica archangelica*), a perennial herbaceous plant that grows abundantly in England and Spain, has medicinal qualities. The dried root has a strong, fragrant odor and a somewhat bitter taste (Bailey, 77; Grieve, 1:35–40).

11. The recipe for capolerium appears on the next page.

12. *Juniperus communis,* a small shrub widely distributed throughout the Northern Hemisphere, produces berries which are used to make a volatile oil which is a prime ingredient in gin (Grieve, 2:452–53; Bailey, 615–17).

13. Rhatany, *Krameria triandra,* a low shrub native to Peru, produces a root which is dried and used for its strongly astringent qualities (Grieve, 2:674–75).

14. "Bung up" means to close the cask tightly with a stopper (OED, s.v. "bung").

15. Tartaric acid, the organic compound $C_4H_6O_6$, is used in effervescent beverages and baking powders.

16. Sulfuric acid has the chemical abbreviation H_2SO_4.

17. "Fining" means clarifying the liquor and making it pure (OED, s.v. "fine").

18. Wormwood, of the genus *Artemisia,* is remarkable for the extreme bitterness of all parts of the plant. It grows in Europe, Great Britain, and the United States (Grieve, 2:858–61).

19. From Scribe (1792–1861), *Marrying for Money* (1828). JJM included stage directions, here italicized within parentheses, suggesting that he copied from a published script.

Scribe, a French dramatist and librettist, wrote numerous plays in which the protagonist's fortunes were reversed repeatedly. He endorsed the concept of a reasonable life over one surrendered to passion. Scribe promoted marriages based on esteem and sound finances over romantic love.

In this play, Madame de Brienne is a young widow who adores Poligni, who loved her when they were both teenagers. Economic obligations forced her to marry an older man. She now returns to her hometown to discover that Poligni is engaged to a wealthy young girl to whom he is not very attracted. De Brienne and Poligni declare their mutual affection, but Poligni nevertheless marries the heiress, for he considers it a matter of honor to proceed—and JJM apparently agrees with him. At the conclusion of the drama, the widow, who takes Olivier as her second husband, inherits unexpectedly and is thus rewarded with both love and money. Poligni receives only material gain while giving up his great love (Koon, 21, 64–66).

ANNOTATED LIST OF PERSONS, PLACES, AND BUSINESSES

This listing of individuals, places, and firms important to Joseph J. Mersman includes many unknown to modern readers: relatives and friends; taverns and hotels; villages and other locations. We used census enumerations, newspaper notices, death registers, and other records to identify individuals with reasonable certainty, but in about twenty cases we could not verify identities. City directories omitted women (unless they had businesses), overlooked boarding-house residents, and contained many errors. Therefore, we consulted books published before and after the time when Mersman resided in Cincinnati and St. Louis.

Anglicized names appear here; e.g., "Mersman" and "Hanover" instead of the German "Mersmann" and "Hannover." Entries include birth, death, marriage, and emigration dates, occupations, family relationships, and street addresses. "Circa" indicates calculated dates, and "fl." (flourished) indicates the years performing artists were active.

Birthplace information is as specific as possible. Prior to 1871, "Germany" was not a politically unified nation-state, although the term appeared in many records. We used "Germany" when a more precise location was unknown. Throughout the index, "Oldenburg" refers to the Grand Duchy of Oldenburg, "Hanover" indicates the Kingdom of Hanover, and "Baden" indicates the Grand Duchy of Baden. "Western U.S. cities" refers to places such as Louisville, St. Louis, Memphis, and New Orleans, so far from the East Coast in 1848.

Population statistics are from the United States Census of 1850. River distances, calculated using *The Ohio River Collection* and *Quimby's Harbor Guide,* provide only rough approximations of the constantly changing length of the channel.

KEY

C resident or place in Cincinnati or environs
S resident or place in St. Louis or environs

C Ablamowicz (also Ablamowics), Anna Maria (neé Rogers). fl. 1847–49. b. Ireland. Soprano and vocal coach; promoted as the "Nightingale of the West" in New York, Boston, and western U.S. cities; resided (1848–49) in Cincinnati; performed with Tosso, Sofge, and others (ANY, 5: 313–16, 319;

COM, 18, 21 October 1848; ENQ, 17 November 1847, 30 October 1848, 21 November 1848; REV, 18 November 1847, CCD 1849–50, 2).

Adams, Mrs. Augustus A. (Mary Duff). 1811–52. b. Dublin. Actor; debuted in Philadelphia (1831); later toured western U.S. cities (ANY, 5: 537; HAS, 106).

Adams, John Quincy. 1767–1848. b. Braintree, Massachusetts. Eldest son of the second president of the United States, John Adams (1735–1826); secretary of state (1817–25); sixth president of the United States (1825–29); defeated (1828) by Andrew Jackson; member of Congress (1831–48); participated (1842) in the cornerstone laying for the Cincinnati Observatory (DAB, 1:84–93).

Anderson, James Robertson. 1811–95. b. England. Actor; began his career in London (1834); debuted in New York (1844) as Othello; played American stages again in 1848, 1853, and 1856 (ANY, 5: 251, 341; DRA, 16 March 1895; HAS, 10).

C Andrews, Peter. c. 1813–? b. New York. Commission merchant; east Front Street, near the Railroad Depot (CCD 1848–49, 68; USC 1850, M432, roll 687, page 6, line 28).

C Annan, James. Bookstore proprietor (DUN Ohio, 78:95).

C Apollo Hall. Owner, J.P. Broadwell. Public hall used for concerts; northwest corner of Fifth and Walnut streets; main entrance was on Fifth Street (ENQ, 14 September 1848).

C Arcade Bath House. Proprietor, H. Jackson. Public bathing facility; west side of Sycamore Street between Third and Fourth streets (CCD 1848–49, 19).

C Arons, Mrs. William (Eliza). c. 1812–87. b. Virginia. Aunt of Charles Herbst; neighbor of Edmund Dexter; landlady of Joseph Tosso. Home address: 154 Broadway (CCD 1849–50, 23; USC 1850, M432, roll 687, page 49, line 32; HCDR, 1 1/2:184).

S Arsenal, St. Louis. At the city's southern border, three miles from the court house, the U.S. Army maintained a munitions storehouse that became a local landmark (Primm, 190).

C Assembly Rooms. Public hall; used for balls, social events, and performances; southeast corner of Pearl and Walnut streets (COM, 9 February 1848).

C Athenaeum (also called Rockwell's Amphitheater, Rockwell's New American Theatre, the American Theatre, and Foster's Varieties). Owner, Henry Rockwell. Three-story theater for stage productions; southeast corner of Sixth and Vine streets; main entrance on Vine Street (CCD 1848–49, 204; COM, 19 November 1847; ENQ, 27 April 1847, 10 October 1848; COM, 11 June 1850).

S Aufdenfeld (also Aufdenfelde), Herman Dietrich. c. 1821–49. b. Germany. Carpenter; constructed N & M's store on Third Street (1849), but perished in the cholera epidemic soon after finishing (Holy Ghost Evangelical Protestant Church, St. Louis, Missouri, Burial Records, 1849, #1071, FHL 1503029).

S Bach, Louis (also Lewis). 1811–65. b. Germany. Proprietor of a saloon (Western Brewery Depot) at 190 Fourth Street; investor in the Fourth National Bank of St. Louis. (MOR, 4 January 1865; SLD 1848, 23; USC 1850, M432, roll 417, page 200, line 20).

C Baker, Christian. Tobacconist; boarded (1843) with Henry Mersman (CCD 1843, 26).

C Bald Hill. Six miles east of downtown Cincinnati, the elevation was a popular picnic spot. It allegedly took its name because in early days Indians cleared away the trees in order to spy on settlers (WPA, 245).

Baltimore, Maryland. Population: 210,646. One hundred miles southwest of Philadelphia and forty miles north of Washington, DC, on the north side of the Patapsco River; the nation's third-largest city; integral to commerce because of water routes to New Orleans and overland routes to Pittsburgh (GAZ, 32).

C Bank Exchange Hotel and Restaurant. Proprietor, George Selves. Lodging and food service; south side of Third Street between Walnut and Main streets (CCD 1850–51, 241).

C Barber Shop. Proprietor, Judah Judah. Hair-cutting business; Main Street between Sixth and Seventh streets (CCD 1848–49, 18).

C Bartlett's Commercial College. Proprietor, Robert M. Bartlett (1807–92). Business school; offered courses in bookkeeping and management; one of at least five such academies in Cincinnati (1849); southeast corner of Fourth and Main streets (CCD 1846, 87; CCD 1848–49, 68; ENQ, 30 November 1847; USC 1850, M432, roll 685, page 78, line 18).

C Bavarian Brewery. Proprietor, Francis (or Franz) Fortman. Beer-making establishment and saloon; southwest corner of Twelfth and Main streets (CCD 1850–51, 100).

Bean, Aaron H. c. 1814–83. b. New Hampshire. Merchant; established (c. 1843) in New York City the firm of A. H. Bean & Company; imported liquors and teas (DUN New York, 268:523; USC 1850, M432, roll 552, page 117, line 2).

S Becker, Augustus. Grocer; in business with his brother Frederick; 167 Second Street between Poplar and Plum streets (SLD 1852, 18).

C Becker, A. F. Lithographer; east side of Walnut Street, between Third and Fourth streets (CCD 1848–49, 131).

C Becker, Christian F. c. 1821–? b. Germany. Tobacconist; partner of William C. Meyer (CCD 1849–50, 31; DUN Ohio, 80:112; USC 1850, M432, roll 688, page 363, line 21).

C Bellevue House. Proprietor, Louis (or Lewis) Drach. Hotel providing food and lodging; North Liberty Street at the head of Sycamore Street (CCD 1848–49, 118).

C Bender, Anthony. Hatmaker; had a shop at 131 Main Street, but closed it by September 1849 (CCD 1846, 91; CCD 1849–50, 33; DUN Ohio, 78:54; ENQ, 27 April 1847).

C Beneke & Wulkop. Proprietors, Casper Beneke (c. 1819–50) and Leopold Wulkop, Germans. Importers and dealers of cigars, wines, and liquors; located at 17 Broadway (CCD 1848–49, 56; ENQ, 31 March 1847; DUN Ohio, 78:78; USC 1850, M432, roll 687, page 250, line 42).

S Bennett, William. 1813–? b. Maryland. Wholesale grocer; partner of Samuel Russell (USC 1850, M432, roll 415, page 27, line 22).

S Bernsdorf, Henry. c. 1824–? b. Germany. Bartender and JJM's salesman; opened (1850) his own liquor business (USC 1850, M432, roll 690, page 961, line 30).

Big River, Missouri. Jefferson County. A rural township forty miles southwest of St. Louis; named for a waterway. The Creuzbauer family owned a farm there (GAZ, 44).

C Black Bear Tavern. Proprietor, Isaac Marchant. Hostler, August Schaffer. Food, lodging, and stable services; southeast corner of Sycamore and Ninth streets (CCD 1848–49, 120).

S Block, John Carl Henry Dietrich. 1816–91. b. Hanover. Merchant; emigrated (1836) to St. Louis; established (1840) Block & (John H.) Evers at 159 North Third Street; Erwin Lodge member; a founder of the Fourth National Bank of St. Louis and its second president (DUN Missouri, 36:123, 148, 185, 40:265; MOR, 21 December 1891; SLD 1850, 76; WPO, 21 December 1891).

S Bloody Island, Missouri. A sandbar one mile above St. Louis, near the Illinois shore; site for duels (beginning 1810); derived its ominous name from three fatal encounters (1817, 1823, 1831); became part of East St. Louis after nineteenth-century floods (Hyde, 1:179–81; Primm, 149, 174–175; Scharf, 2:1849–56; Stevens, 1:266).

S Boernstein, Henry. 1805–92. b. Hamburg. Immigrated (1849) to America; published (1850) *Anzeiger des Westens*, a German-language newspaper; owned (1853) a bar; served (1866) as U.S. consul in Bremen (DUN Missouri, 36:588; Rowan, 3–6).

C Bogen (also Bogan), George (1810–82) and Peter (1808–88). b. Bavaria. Butchers; brothers; emigrated (1826) to Ohio; owned G. & P. Bogen, a lard-oil factory near the Brighton House; produced Catawba wines (COM, 8 October 1882, 15 March 1888; CPP 415–16; DUN Ohio, 85:255; Dickoré, 218).

S Bolms, Gustav. c. 1827–85. b. Germany. Dry goods merchant; m. (1852) Stephanie Vandemale (see Vandemale); father of Philip (b. 1880) and Adolph (BEL, 1884–95, 44; MOR, 22 August 1885, 23 August 1885; RG 15, Civil War Pension Records).

Booth, Junius Brutus. 1796–1852. b. England. Actor; emigrated (1821) to the United States; settled in Maryland; performed widely; father of theater manager Junius Booth Jr. (1821–83), actor Edwin Booth (1833–93), and actor John Wilkes Booth (1838–65), Lincoln's assassin (ANY, 5:327, 362; HAS, 38–39; Matthews, 93–126).

C Boynton (also Boyenton), Rev. Charles B. c. 1806–83. b. Massachusetts. Public speaker and pastor of the Vine Street Congregational Church (CCD 1849–50, 41; COM, 28 April 1883; ENQ, 8 July 1847; 13 March 1848; 14 November 1848; 27 January 1849; USC 1850, M432, roll 691, page 251, line 29).

S Braukmann (also Brauckmann), George. c. 1811–80. b. Germany. Proprietor of a furniture store located at 157 North Third Street (SLD 1850, 75; SLDR, 10:360; DDT, 6 July 1849).

C Bradley (also Bradly and Brandly), John. Laborer; boarder with Jenkins (CCD 1849–50, 42).

C Brayley (also Braayley), W. H. "Harry" or "Hal." Resident of Mosher's and Ross's boardinghouses; relocated (1849) to Madison, Indiana, and opened a dry goods business.

S Bremen, Missouri. A village three miles north of Market Street; settled by Germans who named it after the European port; annexed (1855) by St. Louis (Primm, 145; Olson, 29).

C Brighton House. Proprietor, John Vance. A five-story brick hotel with verandas overlooking the Miami and Erie Canal; site of high-stakes card games; north Liberty Street at the junction of Colerain and Harrison Pikes (WPA, 242, 435).

C Brown, Charles F. c. 1826–? b. Ohio. Grocer; partner (1850) in (Charles E.) Spining, (William S.) Wilson & Brown at 380 Main Street. He went on to a long and prosperous career in the grocery business. JJM's roommate at Jenkins's Boarding House; m. (1848) Harriet; son, Charles (CCD 1849–50, 46, 268, 309; USC 1850, M432, roll 688, page 851, line 16; DUN Ohio, 78:102, 309; 84:65, 93, 469).

C Burckhardt (also Burkhard, Burkhart, and Burk), Leopold (also Leonard). c. 1820–? and Frederick, c. 1822–99. b. Germany. Merchants and amateur musicians; sold liquors and lard oil; firm styled as Burckhardt & Company at northeast corner of Sixth and Walnut streets. Residence: east side of Vine Street between Fifth and Sixth streets (CCD 1848–49, 128; COM, 10 January 1899; DUN Ohio, 78:206; USC 1850, M432, roll 687, page 153, lines 25–26).

Burgess, Sam. fl. 1850. Proprietor, Sam Burgess's American Circus (Slout, 37).

Burlington, Ohio. Population: 1,389. Seat of Lawrence County; 160 miles above Cincinnati on the Ohio River (GAZ, 58; Klein, 401, 409).

C Burnet House. Proprietor, A. B. Coleman. A grand hotel constructed in 1849; contained 340 rooms in six stories; provided views of the city; northwest corner of Third and Vine streets (ENQ, 9 September 1848, 3 May 1931; Cist [3], 164; Kenny, 27).

S Busch, Julius. c. 1822–93. b. Prussia. Wholesale liquor merchant; Busch & Wissmann (DUN Missouri, 36:243; SLDR, 29:228; USC 1850, M653, roll 655, page 35, line 1).

Cairo, Illinois. Population: 242. Alexander County. A village at the junction of the Mississippi and Ohio Rivers; two hundred twenty-five miles below St. Louis; five hundred miles below Cincinnati (DeBow [2], 344).

C Callison (also Collison), Cary. Female acquaintance; relocated to New Orleans (1849).

Cambridge, Massachusetts. Population: 15,213. Middlesex County. A town on the banks of the Charles River; the home of Harvard College (GAZ, 65).

S Camp Springs Garden. See Kunz, Joseph.

S Carondelet, Missouri. Population: 1,201. See also Vide Poche. A town five miles south of St. Louis, near the River Des Peres; settled (1767); incorporated (1832); annexed (1870) by St. Louis (DeBow [2], 345; Primm, 298–99; Scharf, 2:1863–66; Olson, 29–30).

S Carpentier, Mrs. August Joseph (Mary Elizabeth). 1816–99. b. Westphalia. Midwife; trained in Prussia; emigrated (1848) to St. Louis; established the St. Louis College of Midwifery; maintained a large practice among German immigrants (ANZ, 8 June 1850; DUN Missouri, 36:32; USC 1860, M653, roll 653, page 168, line 39).

C Carrman (also Currman). See Karrman.

S Catherwood, Robert B. c. 1800–74. b. Ireland. Whiskey rectifier; 41 South Main Street (DUN Missouri, 36:32; SLD 1850, 127; USC 1850, M432, roll 416, page 340, line 5).

Cassini, Mme. fl. 1850. Celebrated soprano who appeared with William Wallace and Maurice Strakosch in Cincinnati (ANY, 5:104; ENQ, 13 June 1850).

Chapman, Henry "Harry." 1822–65. b. England. Actor; immigrated to the United States; debuted in Philadelphia (1829); toured extensively; m. (1847) Julia Drake; managed Louisville theater (ANY, 5:222, 297; HAS, 66).

Chapman, Mrs. Harry (Julia Drake). 1824–1914. Actor; comedian; daughter of actors Alexander Drake (1798–1830) and Frances Ann Denny Drake (1797–1875); mother of actors Blanche and Ella (HAS, 66; DRA, 18 February 1914).

C Cheviot, Ohio. Hamilton County. A sparsely populated farming community seven miles northwest of downtown Cincinnati; platted (1800) by John Craig, who named the area after the Cheviot Hills of his native Scotland (WPA, 406, 445).

S Chouteau, Henry. 1805–55. b. St. Louis. Wholesale grocer; partnership styled as Chouteau & (Nevé) Vallé at 58 Water Street; died on an excursion train when the Pacific Railroad's Gasconade Bridge collapsed (DUN Missouri, 36:135; SLD 1850, 69; Hyde, 1:362).

S Chouteau's Pond. A lake in the middle of St. Louis created in the late eighteenth century by damming Mill Creek; used for recreation; became polluted with refuse; drained (1851) as a public health measure (Primm, 145–46; Hyde, 1:366–67).

C Cincinnati, Ohio. Population: 115,435. Hamilton County. A city on the Ohio River, six hundred miles above confluence of Ohio and Mississippi rivers.

C Cincinnati Brewery. Proprietor, Peter Nohl (or Noll). Beer garden; west side of Vine Street between Thirteenth and Fourteenth streets (CCD 1851–52, 193).

C City Hall (Cincinnati). Eighth Street between Plum Street and Western Row.

C City Hotel (Cincinnati). Proprietors, D. Tuttle and Sons. Popular inn; south side of Fourth Street between Main and Walnut streets (CCD 1848–49, 122).

S City Hotel (St. Louis). Proprietor, Theron Barnum, cousin of P. T. Barnum. Provided lodging and meals; frequented by army officers; northeast corner of Third and Vine streets. (MOR, 24 November 1853; Scharf, 2:1442, 1443; SLD 1851, 83).

S Cline, George W. 1823–1910. b. Ohio. Attorney; came (1849) to St. Louis; began a practice styled as Cline & Thompson (GLO, 4 March 1910; St. Louis Circuit Court, Attorney Roll Book, 1:21; USC 1850, M432, roll 417, page 5, line 18).

C Cobb, Kate, b. 1826, and Julia, b. 1834. Ohio. Daughters of Samuel Cobb (b. c. 1798, England), undertaker, and his wife, Mosiette (b. circa 1799, Ireland). Residence: west side of Sycamore Street between Fourth and Fifth streets (CCD 1849–50, 63; DUN Ohio, 81:196; USC 1850, M432, roll 687, page 71, lines 29, 35).

C Cole & Stall (Merchants Exchange). Proprietors Frederick Cole (b. 1817, Germany) and George B. Stall (b. 1820, Oldenburg). Saloon located on the north side of Fifth Street between Main and Sycamore streets (CCD 1848–49, 63; CCD 1849–50, 196; USC 1860, M653, roll 976, page 375, line 42).

Connor, Edmund Sheppard. 1809–91. b. Philadelphia. Actor; debuted in Philadelphia (1829); performed in major U.S. cities; m. (1847) Charlotte Barnes (ANY, V:358, 592; HAS, 78).

Connor, Mrs. Edmund Sheppard (Charlotte Mary Sanford Barnes). 1818–63. Actor; debuted in Philadelphia (1834) as Juliet; performed in London, New York, and western U.S. cities (ANY, 5:179, 592; HAS, 78).

C Cook, Sarah. Dressmaker; resided with her sister on the west side of Vine Street between Fifth and Center streets; neighbor of the Burckhardt brothers (CCD 1848–49, 80).

C Corbin's Boarding House. Proprietor, Mrs. Elizabeth Corbin (b. 1801, Vermont). South side of Third Street between Walnut and Vine streets (CCD 1848–49, 24).

C Corbin (also Corben), Julia and Mary (c. 1830–?). b. Vermont. Daughters of Elizabeth Corbin (USC 1850, M432, roll 688, page 363, lines 32–36).

C Corr, David. 1822–50. b. Ireland. Wholesale grocer and commission merchant; firm styled as Corr & (Patrick) Poland; located at 38 and 40 Sycamore Street, across the street from Edmund Dexter's store (CCD 1848–49, 113; DUN Ohio, 78:115; USC 1850, M432, roll 690, page 1060, line 9).

Covington, Kentucky. Population: 9,408. Seat of Kenton County; south of Cincinnati, across the Ohio River; settled (1812); reached by boat until a bridge was built (1867); a center for tobacco, whiskey, and furniture making (Andriot, 304; Goss, 529; HOC, 105).

Crampton, Charlotte. b. 1816. Actor; played leading roles at the National Theatre (HAS, 85).

S Creuzbauer (also Creuzbaur), Albertine. 1831–98. b. Durlach, Baden. Immigrated (1839) to St. Louis with her parents and siblings; m. (1848) John Clemens Nulsen; mother of ten children, eight survived to adulthood. See also Nulsen, John Clemens.

S Creuzbauer (also Creuzbaur), Caroline (Baroness Hornig von Hornburg). 1794–1870. b. Durlach, Baden. Daughter of Johann Jacob Ludwig, Baron Hornig von Hornburg (1765–1844); m. (1820) Karl Friedrich Creuzbauer; mother of six children, including JJM's wife; came (1839) to St. Louis with her husband and children (see below); returned to Baden 1867–70; d. in St. Louis (SLDR, 4:44).

S Creuzbauer (also Creuzbaur), Claudine. 1829–90. b. Durlach, Baden. Immigrated to St. Louis (1839); m. (1851) JJM; mother of eight children: Joseph Jr. (1852–1925), Frederick (1855–1918), Clara (1857–1929), Arthur (1859–1904), Emma (1862–1942), Otto (1864–1940), Alice (1868–1943), and Ella (1872–1952).

S Creuzbauer (also Creuzbaur), Karl Friedrich. 1793–1870. b. Kirchberg, Baden (now Kirchberg-Hunsrück in the State of Rhineland-Palatinate). Artillery captain; son of public health physician George Adam Creuzbaur (1762–1808); decorated for his service to Napoleon; m. (1820) Caroline, Baroness Hornig von Hornburg; father of Otto (1821–50), Robert (1823–1911),

Ottilie (1825–1916), Edmund (1826–71), Claudine (1829–90), and Albertine (1831–98); retired from the Army of Baden (1831); immigrated to St. Louis (1838) with his sons; d. in Karlsruhe after returning to Baden in the mid-1850s.

S Creuzbauer, Otto. 1821–50. b. Baden. The oldest of the Creuzbauer offspring; helped his father manage the family's real estate interests.

S Crone (also Krone), Charles (also Charley and Chas.) W. c. 1815–53. b. Hanover. Merchant; no relation to Christopher Crone; elected (1852) as city marshal (USC 1850, M432, roll 417, page 201, line 34).

S Crone, Christopher. 1816–77. b. Hanover. Merchant; came to St. Louis (1849); opened a grocery; organized an omnibus line (1860s); served as city park commissioner (1870s); m. (1842) Marilla Magdalena Meyer (d. 1853); m. (1854) Eliza Mueller (d. 1876); m. (1876) Sophie Herbkesmann (d. 1895); father of Sophie, Eliza, and Charles C. Crone (Hyde, 1:528–29; GLO, 6 March 1877; SLDR, 7:175, 296, 32:479).

C Cumminsville, Ohio (also Cuminsville). Hamilton County. A village five miles north of the Ohio River; annexed (1872) by Cincinnati (GAZ, 98; HOC, 413–14).

C Darling, Dr. Emerick G. c. 1808–58. b. Massachusetts. Dentist; resident of Jenkins's Boarding House; advertised (1848) "painless extractions" by using chloroform; m. Mary (1813–77); office located on Sixth Street, between Main and Walnut streets (CCD 1848–49, 79; COM, 13 January 1877; USC 1850, M432, roll 688, page 810, line 6).

C Daum, Valentine. d. 1849. Proprietor of the Napoleon Tavern on Second Street between Broadway and Ludlow streets (CCD 1848–49, 118; CCD 1849–50, 76).

C Day and Brother. Proprietors, Alexander M. and Timothy C. Day. Confectionary; west side of Walnut Street between Sixth and Seventh streets (CCD 1848–49, 72).

Dayton, Ohio. Population: 10,977. Seat of Montgomery County. A town fifty miles north of Cincinnati, at the convergence of the Great Miami River, the Mad River, and Wolf Creek (Andriot, 619; GAZ, 101; Roseboom, 219).

Dean, Julia. 1830–68. New York. Actor; daughter of actor Julia Drake Fosdick Dean (1800–32) and Edwin Dean, theater manager; debuted (1841) in Louisville; played leading roles in major U.S. cities; retired in 1867 (ANY, 5:190, 269, 574; HAS, 97).

C Delamater (also Delamaitre, Delamettre, Delamatter, DeLaMaître, De'lamaître, Delmattre, Delametre, and abbreviated Delr, Del'r, Del—r, Delar, Del—e, and Del—re), Chandler B. d. 1856. b. Syracuse, New York. Clerk; JJM's roommate (1848) at Jenkins's Boarding House (CCD 1843, 95; Hamilton County Probate Book 14, page 346).

C Dellinger, Julia. See Dillinger.

C Derby, Henry W. c. 1820–? b. New York. Publisher and bookseller; business at 145 Main Street styled as Derby & Co. (CCD 1848–49, 162; DUN Ohio, 79:293; USC 1850, M432, roll 687, page 179, line 40).

S Deobald, Frederick. A baker; married to a flirtatious woman (JJM diary, 10 March 1850).

S Detharding, George A. c. 1807–? b. Germany. Bookseller; friend of the Creuzbauer family; wife Elizabeth (née Kravel, c. 1808–?) (SLD 1851, 102; USC 1850, M432, roll 415, page 85, line 12).

C Dexter, Charles. 1830–93. b. Cincinnati. Businessman and poet; son of Edmund Dexter; received an A.B. degree (1851) from Harvard University (Harvard University Archives; USC 1850, M432, roll 687, page 49, line 17; Dexter [1]; Dexter [2]).

C Dexter, Edmund. 1801–62. b. Leicester, England. Merchant; emigrated to Cincinnati (by 1829); wholesale liquor supplier and whiskey rectifier; m. Mary Ann Dillinger (1805–75); father of Charles (1830–93), Julia (1832–66), Edmund (1835–79), George (1838–83), Julius (1842–98), and Adolphus (1844–70); hosted Charles Dickens (1842) at his home, 128 Broadway, corner of Fourth Street. Business: (1847) Lower Market Street between Main and Sycamore streets; (1848) 49 and 51 Sycamore Street between Second and Market streets (CCD 1840, 160; CCD 1842, 29; CCD 1848–49, 180; DUN Ohio, 78:98, 79:252, 84:106; USC 1850, M432, roll 687, page 49, line 15).

C Dieck (also Diek), Louis. c. 1831–83. b. Germany. Cigar manufacturer; firm styled as Dieck & Fahlbush, east side of Walnut Street between Fourth and Fifth streets; *Liedertafel* member (CCD 1848–49, 57; HOC, 250; USC 1850, M432, roll 691, page 216, line 31).

C Dillinger (also Dellenger, Dellinger and Dillenger), Julia. c. 1815. Sister of Edmund Dexter's wife; resided (1850) in the Dexter household with another unmarried sister, Sarah Dillinger (USC 1850, M432, roll 687, page 100, line 22).

C Diserens (also Deserins), Frederick. c. 1805–65. b. Switzerland. Tavern keeper (William Tell Exchange), on the south side of Fifth Street, between Main and Walnut streets (CCD 1848–49, 63; USC 1850, M432, roll 687, page 172, line 42).

C Douglass, Mr. Instrument maker associated with Joseph Tosso (HOC, 249).

C Dow, Mr. Resident of Mrs. Jenkins's Boarding House (1848).

C Drach, Louis (or Lewis). c. 1810–69. b. Germany. Confectioner and tavern keeper (Bellevue House); Sycamore Street north of Burgoyne Street (CCD 1844, 35; CCD 1846, 149; CCD 1848–49, 118; USC 1850, M432, roll 691, page 216, line 31).

C Drake, Mrs. Alexander (Frances Ann Denny). 1797–1875. b. New York. Actor; first American female star of the West (1815); mother of Julia Drake; Harry Chapman's mother-in-law (DAB, 5:428–29; Hill [2], 111–17).

C Dugan, Thomas S. c.1816–? Wholesale grocer; partnered (1842) with his brother, John A. Dugan (c. 1821–?) in Thomas S. Dugan & Co., Main and Water streets (CCD 1846, 151; DUN Ohio, 78:115, 79:3).

C Duhme, Herman. 1814–74. b. Hanover. Merchant; emigrated (1834) with his family; established (1842–61) a wholesale jewelry and fancy store on Fifth Street near Lodge Street; brother of H. H. Duhme (c. 1810) (CCD 1848–49, 87; CPP, 326–28; DUN Ohio, 81:49, 78:82; USC 1850, M432, roll 687, page 154, line 36; Dickoré, 219).

S Duncan's Island. A sandbar that extended from Market Street to the southern edge of St. Louis; named for Robert Duncan, who built a cabin there; the local landmark disappeared with nineteenth-century flooding; portions were absorbed into Illinois (Hyde, 1:617).

S Dushushal (also Dusushal and Dusuchal), Charles. c. 1811–63. b. France. Confectioner with a shop on Third Street (SLDR, K:199).

C Dwelle, Frank. Not identified.

C Eagle Bath House. Public bathing facility; west side of Court Street near Main Street (COM, 4 April 1848).

C Eckert (also Ekert), Thomas F. 1809–78. b. Ohio. Steamboat engineer and captain; began (1828) working on riverboats; residence fronted Mill Creek Bottom (CPP, 138–142).

S Edgar, Joseph C. 1810–93. b. New Jersey. Architect and builder; settled in St. Louis (1834); designed many structures there; residence: 278 North Fifth Street (USC 1850, M432, roll 687, page 87, line 40; SLD 1851, 114).

C Eggers & Wulkop. Proprietors August Eggers and Leopold Wulkop. Stationery and German bookstore; Wulkop left the business in late 1848 (CCD 1849–50, 90; DUN Ohio, 78:49).

S Eggers, H. H. c. 1812–71. b. Germany. Wholesale grocer; Erwin Lodge member (Membership records, Grand Lodge of Missouri).

C Ellis & Morton. Proprietors, Rowland (also Roland) Ellis (1804–91, b. Massachusetts) and John R. Morton. Bank; Third Street between Main and Walnut streets (CCD 1849–50, 92; DUN Ohio, 78:177; ENQ, 10 April 1847; USC 1850, M432, roll 687, page 87, line 40).

S Erfort, August C. 1816–96. b. Westphalia. Wholesale grocer; immigrated to St. Louis (1832); partner in Erfort & (Henry) Petring and Erfort & Sickendick; Erwin Lodge member (SLDR, 34:329; WPO, 4 July 1864).

C Ernest (also Ernst), Charles. c. 1813–74. b. France. Dancing instructor; classes in the Melodeon Building (1847) and the Masonic Hall (1848), assisted by his wife, Eliza (1830–?) (CCD 1846, 157; CCD 1849–50, 93; ENQ, 18 February 1848; USC 1850, M653, roll 970, page 128, line 18).

C Evans (also Evens), Francis L. 1818–79. Hardware merchant; partner (1849–53) in Evans & Theising; husband of Hannah (CCD 1849–50, 95; DUN Ohio, 78:70).

C Evans, Mrs. Francis L. (Hannah). c. 1821–79. Friend of Elizabeth Kattenhorn. See above (COM, 1 May 1879; 8 October 1879).

C Fahlbush (also Fahlbusch), Charles. c. 1817–65. b. Hanover. Cigar maker; established Dieck & Fahlbush. Residence: north side of Twelfth Street between Jackson and Vine streets (CCD 1849–50, 95; DUN Ohio, 78:163, 254; USC 1850, M432, roll 691, page 60, line 34; VOL, 30 April 1865).

Falls of the Ohio. A series of rapids in the Ohio River with a drop of twenty-six feet over two miles, located at Louisville, Kentucky. When the water level was low, the falls impeded steamboat travel; goods had to be portaged. The Louisville and Portland Canal, constructed 1830, permitted riverboats to bypass the dangerous area (Holmberg, 20–21).

C Farmers & Traders Tavern. Proprietors, Jacob and Charles Kopf. South side of Ninth Street between Main and Sycamore streets (CCD 1850–51, 159).

Farren, Mrs. George Percy (Mary Ann Russell). 1818–94. Actor; began career at age six in New York; popular with St. Louis audiences (ANY, 5: 338–39, 521–22; HAS, 121).

C Fenno, Augustus William. 1814–73. b. Boston. Actor, playwright, and lecturer; stage manager (1847–48) of the Athenaeum (ANY, 5: 243, 244; ENQ, 19 July 1847).

C Fessenden, Benjamin B. 1818–51. Attorney with Fessenden, (Robert B.) Warden & (F. C.) Becking, who represented coffeehouse owners in a suit against the City of Cincinnati (CCD 1849–50, 31, 98, 296; ENQ, 1 August 1848; CDT, 7 May 1851).

S Ficke, Frederick W. c. 1797–1847. b. Hanover. Tobacconist; partner (1845–47) of JCN in the business styled as Nulsen & Ficke; probably the brother of Herman Ficke of Cincinnati (DUN Missouri, 36:24; SLD 1847, 34; St. Louis Circuit Court Record Book, S:42).

C Ficke, Hermann. c. 1815–88. b. Hanover. Tobacconist; partner (1843–53) with Francis Nuilsen in Nuilsen & Ficke; continued the business alone until 1865 (CCD 1849–50, 99; DUN Ohio, 78:157, 80:212; USC 1850, M432, roll 691, page 12, line 5; Dickoré, 278).

S Flora Garden. Proprietor, Gerhard Goebel. Florist and confectionary, with hothouses, outdoor gardens, and an ice-cream bar that served nonspirituous refreshments; south side of Lafayette Avenue, west of Seventh Street (SLD 1851, 128; Western, 146).

Forrest (also Forest), Edwin. 1806–72. b. Philadelphia. Shakespearean actor; debuted (1820) in Philadelphia; appeared throughout the United States and England (ANY, V:418, 420, 426–27, 482–84; HAS, 129–33).

S Forster, C. Marquard. 1821–1901. b. Germany. Merchant; emigrated (1848) to St. Louis; began a grocery business; manufactured vinegar; established (1876) the Hyde, Park Brewery (DUN Missouri, 40:268; SLD 1854–55, 61).

C Fortman, Francis. c. 1807–67. b. Germany. Proprietor of the Bavarian Brewery, southwest corner of Main and Twelfth streets (CCD 1849–50, 103; VOL, 8 August 1867; USC 1850, M432, roll 685, page 241, line 26).

C Fountain Saloon. A coffeehouse that served nonalcoholic beverages and went out of business in February 1848 (ENQ, 19 February 1848).

S Franksen (also Frankson), Franke "Papa." 1808–53. b. Germany. Tavern keeper; m. (1838) Caroline Louise Wesselhoeft (1810–88) and joined her brother's effort to establish Hermann, Missouri (Bek [1], 24; HER, 18 January 1888; USC 1850, M432, roll 414, page 326, line 20).

S French Town. A neighborhood south of Chouteau Avenue and west of Columbus Street, primarily populated by French and German immigrants; entertainment district with many taverns; "The streets were usually [so] quiet one could hear at some distance when a new keg of beer was opened" (Rodabough, 9–75; Tolzmann, 124–25; Olson, 23–26).

Fulton, Ohio. Population: 3,224. Hamilton County. Platted 1826; extended two miles east of Cincinnati along the Ohio River; annexed 1854 (DeBow [2], 355; HOC, 408; WPA, 242).

Galena, Illinois. Population: 6,004. Seat of Jo Daviess County; 340 miles above St. Louis on the Mississippi River (DeBow [2], 355).

C Galt House. Proprietor, William E. Marsh. Hotel; southwest corner of Sycamore and Sixth streets (CCD 1848–49, 120).

C Ganter, John B. c. 1815–50. b. Germany. Tavern keeper (Sportsman's Hall); located on Front Street at the Fulton and Columbia Township Line (CCD 1848–49, 118; USC 1850 M432, roll 686, page 250, line 10).

S Gehner, John F. W. c. 1813–78. b. Hanover. Dry goods merchant at 133 Morgan Street; Erwin Lodge member; investor in Fourth National Bank of St. Louis (DDT, 4 July 1851; DUN Missouri, 36:109, 525, 550; GLO, 5 March 1878; WPO, 13 November 1870).

S Gempp (also Gemp), Heinrich Wilhelm. 1798–1851. b. Germany. Physician; immigrated (1836) to St. Louis; built a large practice; established a newspaper, *The German-American;* purchased (1850) with Henry Boernstein the

Anzeiger des Westens (ANZ, 1 and 3 June 1851; St. Louis City Probate Court, Estate #3486; USC 1850, M432, roll 415, page 47, line 34).

C German Theatre. Playhouse; on the north side of the canal between Main and Sycamore streets, near the Bavarian Brewery (CVB, 22 November 1848; CCD 1848–49, 204).

Giamboni (or Jamboni), Natali. fl. 1848. Vocal performer from Havana, Cuba, who appeared (1848) in Cincinnati (ENQ, 14 September 1848).

Gossin, Mrs. John (Lucinda). Circus equestrian; m. Gossin, the clown; divorced him; m. (1847) Thomas Nunn; performed then as "Mrs. Nunn" (ANY, 5:142, 247; Slout, 114, 223).

C Granger, Mr. Merchant; traveled to Mexico and New Orleans; established a firm in Palmyra, Missouri, styled as Granger & Murray.

C Granger, Mrs. Resident of Mrs. Jenkins's Boarding House; see above.

C Grener (also Greener), Miss. A young woman courted by Joseph Marsh.

S Greve, John F. 1826–72. b. Hanover. Tobacconist; owned a cigar store on Third Street, near N & M; m. (1848) Catherine M. Nelson (DEM, 14 May 1872; SLDR, 5:63).

S Grewe (also Grawe and Graewa), Henry Joseph. Proprietor of the Bremen Exchange, a site of public balls (ANZ, 1 January 1850).

C Groenlandt (also Groenland and Groenladt), Herman M. c. 1814. b. Itzehoe, Schleswig-Holstein. Portrait artist; active in the *Liedertafel* (CCD 1849–50, 120; USC 1850, M432, roll 687, page 157, line 14; Dickoré, 278).

C Grothouse, Miss. Probably sister of the tobacconist below.

C Grothaus (also Grothouse and Grothause), William F. c. 1824–? b. Germany. Tobacconist; business styled as Grothaus & Tebbelman (CCD 1850–51, 117; USC 1850 M432, roll 687, page 113, line 15).

Hackett, James. 1800–71. b. New York. Actor and comedian; appeared widely in the United States and England; introduced the Yankee character to the stage; imitated the voice and mannerisms of other famous people (ANY, 5: 324, 386, 426, 482, 516; HAS, 153).

Hamilton, Ohio. Population: 3,210. Seat of Butler County; twenty-five miles north of Cincinnati (Andriot, 620).

Harrison, William Henry. 1773–1841. b. Virginia. First presidential candidate from Ohio; governor of Indiana Territory (1801–13); congressman (1816–19) and senator (1825–28) representing Ohio; ninth president of the United States (1841) (DAB, 8:348–51).

C Harrington, John Quincy Adams. 1821–1908. b. Franklin, Ohio. Actor and drama critic who wrote under the name of "John Carboy"; appeared (1840s) with theatrical companies traveling on the Ohio and Mississippi rivers; went to New York (1850) and began a newspaper career (NYC, 24 October 1908).

C Heberhart, Charles. Not identified.

S Heinrich (no surname). Employee of N & M.

C Hellebusch (also Helbusch), Frank. c. 1824–? b. Damme, Oldenburg. Schoolteacher; immigrated to Cincinnati (1844); m. (1848) Mary Puthoff (see entry), from the same village in Oldenburg; resided in Covington, Kentucky (Ostendorf, 257).

S Helmering, Christian. 1820–1912. b. Osnabrück. Jeweler; emigrated (1824); came to St. Louis (1844); served in the Mexican War; went (1849) to California, but returned (1851) to St. Louis; m. (1849) Anna Koklmann (DUN Missouri, 36:222; SLD 1850, 133).

S Henkel, Otto. 1818–? b. Germany. Tailor; proprietor of a shop at 40 Chestnut Street; m. (1841) Rosette Kamper (1818–50) (DUN Missouri, 36:321; SLD 1848, 111; USC 1850, M432, roll 416, page 392, line 17).

C Henni, Rev. John Martin. 1805–81. b. Switzerland. Roman Catholic clergyman; ordained (1829) in Cincinnati; founded (1836) the *Wahrheitsfreund*, the first German Catholic newspaper in the United States; assisted Bishop Purcell; appointed first bishop (1844) and first archbishop (1875) of Milwaukee (Lamott, 352; Marty, 185).

C Herbst (also Erbest), Charles (or Chas.). b. Germany. JJM's roommate (1848–49) at Mosher's and Ross's boardinghouses; subsequently went to Philadelphia.

Heron Family (Agnes, Fannie, and an older sister). fl. 1848–60. Actors in musical productions; debuted (1848) in Philadelphia; two of them launched (1858) singing careers as Agnes and Fanny Natoli (ANY, 5:326; HAS, 261).

S Herzer, Louis William. c. 1822–? Friend of Edmund Creuzbauer; served (June 1846–October 1848) in artillery and cavalry units during the Mexican War; returned to St. Louis; later went to New Mexico (RG 94, Records of Mexican War Soldiers).

Hill, George Handel "Yankee" (also Yankey). 1779–1849. b. Boston. Actor; debuted in Boston (1799); played Yankee characters to acclaim; appeared in New York, Philadelphia, and London (ANY, 5:194, 477, 506; HAS, 176).

Hillsboro, Missouri (also Hillsborough). Seat of Jefferson County; forty miles southwest of St. Louis, near Big River (GAZ, 157, 229).

C Holy Trinity Church. Roman Catholic church; served a German-speaking congregation; south side of Fifth Street between Smith and Park streets (Cist [3], 77; Lamott, 134).

C Honkomp (also Hunkum), Frederick. c. 1812–? Tavern keeper (Second Ward House), south side of Fifth Street, between Race and Elm streets (CCD 1848–49, 119).

C Howe, Mary and children. Residents of Jenkins's Boarding House; moved (1849) to Burlington, Ohio.

C Hudson, Dr. Issac c. 1810–65. b. Virginia. Apothecary (CDT 19 June 1865; USC 1860, M653, roll 973, page 376, line 25).

Hunt, Fred. fl. 1848–69. b. Bath, England. Owner of the American Circus (1850) with his partner, John Tryon (Slout, 138).

Hunt, Henry B. ?–1854. b. England. Actor, singer; debuted (1828) in New York (HAS, 190).

S Illinois Town. The early name of East St. Louis, Illinois (Primm, 207).

Jackson, Andrew. 1767–1845. b. South Carolina. Seventh president (1829–37) of the United States; hero of the Battle of New Orleans (8 January 1815) during the War of 1812; expanded the power of the presidency and the Democratic Party (DAB, 9:526–34).

C Jacobus, Theodore Dwight. c. 1823–? b. New Jersey. Bookkeeper; lived in Mosher's Boarding House; m. (18 June 1848) Hannah F. Mosher (CCD 1849–50, 152; USC 1850, M432, roll 687, page 125, line 16).

C Jacobus, Hannah Frances (née Mosher). c. 1832–? b. New York. Daughter of Elizabeth Mosher and resident of her boardinghouse (1848); m. (1848) Theodore Dwight Jacobus (USC 1850, M432, roll 687, page 125, line 12).

S Jäger (also Jaeger), Adolph Julius. c. 1809–52. b. Germany. Grocer; m. (1850) Caroline Frank; died of "nervous fever" (possibly syphilis) in October 1852 (SLDR, B:165; SLCM 5:76; SLD 1851, 180).

C Jenkins's Boarding House. Proprietor, Mrs. Azubah Jenkins (b. circa 1794, Vermont), mother of Fanny (b. 1830) and Mary Jane (b. 1833). Rooming house on Third Street between Western Row and John Street (CCD 1843, 181; CCD 1849–50, 153; USC 1850, M432, roll 688, page 149, lines 41, 42).

C Johnson, Mr. Resident of Jenkins's Boarding House (1848); possibly a tobacconist who partnered (1844–46) with Clemens Nulsen in Cincinnati; relocated (1849) to Chicago (CCD 1846, 200).

C Judah, Judah. 1809–95. b. Hesse. Barber shop proprietor; Main Street between Sixth and Seventh streets (USC 1850, M432, roll 690, page 1004, line 37; Marks, 99; CDG, 21 November 1895).

C Karrman, Dorothea (also Karmann, Carrman and Currman). A friend of JJM; m. Otto Onken (Onken-Karrmann Marriage, 3 February 1848, St. Matthaeus German Evangelical Church, Cincinnati, Ohio, Marriage Records, 75, FHL Microfilm 1548046).

C Karrman, William. Drugstore proprietor; southeast corner of Fifth and Smith streets (CCD 1848–49, 84).

C Kattenhorn (abbreviated Katn and Katten), Arnd. 1810–87. b. Bremen. Wholesale grocer; emigrated (1830) to America and to Cincinnati (1832);

married (c. 1834) JJM's sister, Elizabeth; father of Louisa (b. 1834), Sophia (b. 1836), Henrietta (b. 1842), Arnd Jr. (1846–83), Frank (b. 1849), and William (b. 1854). Business: (1848) 381 Main Street. Residence: (1848–50) north side of Seventh Street between Main and Walnut streets; (1851) 10 West Ninth Street (CCD 1849–50, 159; CCD 1851–52, 138; CPP, 181–82; DUN Ohio, 80:132, 148, 341; 78:116; USC 1850, M432, roll 688, page 892, lines 32–38).

C Kattenhorn, Mrs. Arnd (Elizabeth Mersman). 1816–81. b. Damme, Oldenburg. JJM's sister; full-time homemaker. See above (USC 1850, M432, roll 688, page 892, line 13).

Kent, Mrs. William (Elizabeth Eberle). d. 1850. b. Philadelphia. Actor and singer; debuted (1824) in Philadelphia (COM, 9, 11 September 1848; Wemyss, 51).

C Koch (also Kock), John Heinrich (or Henry), c. 1827–84, and John D., 1829–97. b. Fürstenau, Hanover. Merchant tailors in business together; brothers; shop on Walnut Street between Fourth and Fifth streets; lived above the store (CCD 1846, 234; CCD 1849–50; DUN Ohio, 86:321; USC 1850, M432, roll 687, page 161, line 39).

C Koch, Miss. Sister of the Koch brothers (see above); first name unknown.

C Kolb, Charles M. Druggist; business partner of Louis Rehfuss.

C Kopf (also Kopp), Charles (or Charley). c. 1825–? b. Germany. Tavern keeper (Farmer's & Trader's Tavern); Ninth Street between Sycamore and Main; returned to Germany (1854) (CCD 1849–50, 167; DUN Ohio, 78:418; USC 1850, M432, roll 690, page 960, line 18).

S Krone, Charley. See Crone, Charles.

S Kunz, Joseph. 1799–1850. b. Germany. Proprietor of Camp Springs Garden, a beer garden in western St. Louis (Eighteenth and Market streets); his widow, Catherine, sold the business to J. Uhrig (DDT, 16 June 1850; St. Louis City Probate Court, Estate #3202; USC 1850, M432, roll 414, page 326, line 11; SLD 1850, 67).

C La Belle Restaurant. Eatery; 126 Broadway (CCD 1850–51, 161).

C Labarre, George. c. 1816–? b. Germany. Schoolteacher; musical conductor of the *Liedertafel* singing society (HOC, 250; USC 1850, M432, roll 690, page 961, line 2).

S Lackmann, Diederich H. c. 1820–? b. Germany. Proprietor of a variety store at 151 North Third Street, near N & M, styled as Wolff, Hoppe & Lackmann (DUN Missouri, 36:71, 331; SLD 1848, 251; USC 1850, M432, roll 417, page 25, line 29).

C Lacy, William (or Bill). c. 1821–67. b. Ohio. Clerk (CCD 1849–50, 170; USC 1850, M432, roll 688, page 896, line 18).

Lake, Agnes (also Agness) (née Mersman). 1826–1907. b. Damme, Oldenburg. Circus equestrian, rope walker and lion tamer; JJM's younger sister; m.

(1846) William Lake Thatcher and used the stage name Agnes Lake throughout her life; widowed (1869); she became the first woman tent show owner in America (Lake's Hippo-Olympiad and Mammoth Circus); retired in 1874; m. (5 March 1876) James Butler "Wild Bill" Hickok; widowed again (2 August 1876); m. (1877) "Texas George" Carson; mother of equestrians Emma Lake (c. 1855–1911), and Alice Lake (c. 1850–67) (Slout, 164).

Lake, William "Bill." 1817–69. b. New Jersey. Circus clown and ringmaster; actually named William Lake Thatcher; derived his stage name from his mother's maiden name (Slout, 164–165).

C Lange, Christian. 1812–76. b. Hanover. Maker of boots and shoes; shop on corner of Vine and Twelfth streets; *Liedertafel* member (CCD 1848–49, 34; DUN Ohio, 85:81; HOC, 250; USC 1850, M432, roll 688, page 433, line 20; VOL, 21 March 1876; Dickoré, 279).

C Larkin, D. Mayle. Clerk at a business on Main Street; boarder (1848) at Corbin's Boarding House (CCD 1849–50, 171).

Lawrenceburg, Indiana. Population: 2,651. Dearborn County. A town twenty-five miles below Cincinnati, on the Ohio River (DeBow [2], 363; ORC, 408–11).

Lebanon, Ohio. Population: 2,088. Seat of Warren County; twenty-seven miles northeast of downtown Cincinnati (GAZ, 186).

Lebrun, W. C. fl. 1850. Circus strongman (Slout, 170).

C Lemaire, Louis. c. 1803–54. b. France. Music dealer, pianist, oboe player; sold pianos at his shop on Fourth Street, between Walnut and Main streets (CCD 1848–49, 141; CDG, 5 October, 1854; DUN Ohio, 78:148; USC 1850, M432, roll 687, page 326, line 12).

S Lemp (also Lempe), Johann Adam. 1798–1862. b. Eschwege, Hesse. First brewer in St. Louis to make lager; emigrated to St. Louis (1838); established (1840) the Western Brewery and Vinegar Factory on Second Street between Walnut and Elm streets; father of William (1836–1904), also a prominent brewer (DUN Missouri, 36:271; Hyde, 3:1255–1256; SLD 1850, 11; Walker, 1–7).

Lewis, Mrs. Henry (Bertha Harvey). d. 1854. b. London, England. Actor; debuted (1835) in the United States; performed in western U.S. cities; m. (1830) Henry Lewis (1802–92); divorced (1849); mother of actor Bertha Lewis (ANY, 5:54, 550; HAS, 218).

C *Liedertafel*. 1839–55. Organized by Fritz Tappe; Cincinnati's first amateur singing society; provided opportunities for Germans to socialize; met in the Rising Sun Saloon at the corner of Thirteenth and Main streets (ENQ, 31 December 1848; Wimberg, 8).

Lind, Jenny. 1820–87. b. Sweden. Coloratura soprano; toured the United States (1850–52); billed by P. T. Barnum as the "Swedish Nightingale" (ANY, 5:553, 564; HAS, 218).

S Lindell, Peter. 1776–1861. b. Maryland. Merchant; settled in St. Louis (1811) and amassed a portfolio of real estate (ENG, 1287–1288).

S Linkenmeyer (or Linkemeyer), Henry. c. 1807–58. b. Hanover. Proprietor of a livery stable and tavern (Walnut Street House), corner of Walnut and Third streets (ANZ, 12 June 1850; SLD 1848, 145; USC 1850, M432, roll 415, page 217, line 5).

Lockland, Ohio. Hamilton County. Platted (1828); incorporated (1865); thirteen miles north of Cincinnati; named for the canal locks, which constituted a landmark (Goss, 530).

C Loder, Benjamin. d. 1883. Merchant in business with his brother William (1812–90); sold liquors and charcoal to rectifiers at 270 East Main Street, between Sixth and Seventh streets (COM, 23 October 1883; CDT, 27 January 1869, 19 January 1890; DUN Ohio, 78:334; USC 1850, M432, roll 690, page 1003, line 40; USC 1850, M432, roll 688, page 413, line 22; CCD 1849–50, 178).

C Lodge's Boarding House. Proprietor, Ann M. Lodge (c. 1793–1869, Ohio), mother of Louisa (c. 1824), Eveline (c. 1826), John (c. 1830), and Julian (c. 1834). Living quarters of Charles Moulinier (1850), the Lodge family, and others; 77 West Fourth Street between Walnut and Vine streets (CCD 1849–50, 178; COM, 28 January 1869; USC 1850, M432, roll 687, page 300, line 21).

C Lodge, Miss. Boarder at Mrs. Mosher's Boarding House; possibly a daughter of Ann Lodge (USC 1850, M432, roll 687, page 300, line 23).

C Logan, Cornelius Ambrosius. 1806–53. b. Baltimore. Playwright, comedian, and theater manager; debuted in Philadelphia (1825); specialized in Yankee roles; father of actors Eliza, Celia, and Olive (CCD 1849–50, 178; HAS, 222).

C Logan, Eliza. 1830–72. b. New York. Actor; debuted in Philadelphia (1841); performed in New York, Cincinnati, and western U.S. cities; retired in 1859 (ANY, 5:443; HAS, 222).

C Louisiana House. Hotel; 22 Sycamore Street between Front and Columbia streets (CCD 1846, 535).

Louisville, Kentucky. Population: 43,194. Jefferson County. Tenth-largest city in the United States; at the Falls of the Ohio River; 140 miles below Cincinnati on the Ohio River (Andriot, 304; Klein, 409, 415).

C Louisville and Portland Canal. Constructed 1830; enabled river craft to bypass the Falls of the Ohio (Yater, 39).

C Lyon & Smith. Proprietors, Joseph W. Lyon (b. 1812, Massachusetts) and John H. Smith. Hardware dealers; store at 218 Main Street between Fifth and Sixth streets (CCD 1848–49, 114; CCD 1849–50, 182, 264; USC 1850, M432, roll 688, page 414, line 6).

Macready, William Charles. 1793–1873. b. London. Actor; debuted in 1809; played Othello, Romeo, King John, Shylock, and Virginius on both sides of the Atlantic; retired in 1851 (HAS, 228–29; Matthews, 4:1–32).

Madison, Indiana. Population: 8,012. Seat of Jefferson County. One hundred miles below Cincinnati and fifty miles above Louisville on the Ohio River; settled 1806; largest city in the state by 1850 (Andriot, 225).

C Marsh, Joseph. Not identified.

Martine, Mrs. fl. 1849. Actor; sister of Mrs. Kent.

C Masonic Hall. A three-story building with six business suites on the first level, a public hall on the second, and meeting rooms for lodge members on the third; northeast corner of Third and Walnut streets (CCD 1853, 66; Cist [3], 159–160).

Mathews, Miss. fl. 1849. Actor (ANY, 5:214, 234, 331).

Maysville, Kentucky. Population: 4,256. Mason County. A town seventy miles above Cincinnati on the Ohio River (DeBow [2], 367).

C McGurk (also Magurk and McGurke), James. c. 1821–? b. Maryland. Clerk; resided with his mother and sister (CCD 1849–50, 190; USC 1850, M432, roll 689, page 321, line 12).

C McGurk (also Magurk and McGurke), Miss. Milliner; lived with her mother and brother (above) on Court between Plum and Western Row (CCD 1849–50, 190).

S McHose Cave. A natural limestone formation used by the St. Louis Brewery (McHose & English); opened as a recreation center at 306 South Second Street (SLD 1851, 228).

C McHugh, William. Laborer; employed by Edmund Dexter.

S McKenzie (also MacKenzie), Kenneth. c. 1795–? b. Scotland. Wholesale grocer and commission merchant; sold wines and liquors; burned out (1849) from store on First Street (DUN Missouri, 36:99, 304; 38:18; USC 1850, M432, roll 460, page 340, line 1; SLD 1848, 153).

C Mehner, Louis. c. 1822–76. b. Germany. Proprietor of a grocery at 7 Lower Market Street (CCD 1848–49, 131; CFP, 24 January 1876; USC 1850, M432, roll 687, page 261, line 4).

S Meier (also Meyer), Henry. 1819–1900. b. Hanover. Grocer; styled (1846–61) firm as Meier & (John G.) Kaiser; Erwin Lodge member; investor in Fourth National Bank of St. Louis (Membership records, Grand Lodge of Missouri; Stevens, 2:258–60).

C Melodeon Building. Three-story building constructed in 1846: the lower floors provided space for businesses, and the top level featured a hall suitable for public events; northwest corner of Fourth and Walnut streets (CCD 1850–51, 187).

Memphis, Tennessee. Population: 8,841. Seat of Shelby County; five hundred miles below Cincinnati and approximately 450 miles below St. Louis on the Mississippi River (Andriot, 747).

C Menzel (also Mensel), Gustav Adolphus. 1815–1905. b. Prussia. Lithographer; business styled as Klauprecht & Menzel, southwest corner of Fifth and Vine streets; active in the *Liedertafel* (CCD 1848–49, 131; DUN Ohio, 81:37; HOC, 250; USC 1850, M432, roll 691, page 80, line 16; Dickoré, 279).

C Menzel (also Mensel), Jacob. c. 1819–? b. Germany. Cigar maker; referred to as "Menzel Junior" by JJM, but a relationship to Gustav Adolphus Menzel has not been established (USC 1850, M432, roll 691, page 33, line 41).

C Mersman, Frank. 1830–66. b. Damme, Oldenburg. Tobacconist, retail clerk, and circus roustabout; youngest brother of JJM; son of Frederick Mersman (1782–1864); emigrated (1833) to Ohio with family; worked in St. Louis, Cincinnati, and Louisville; never married; died of tuberculosis in Cincinnati (HCDR, 1:13).

C Mersman, Frederick (also Friedrich Messmann and Friedrich Polschneider). 1782–1864. b. Damme, Oldenburg. Farmer and tobacconist; m. (1811) Maria Catharina Pohlschneider and used her surname for twenty-two years; father of Elizabeth (1813–81), Frederick (1815–33?), Henry (1820–64), Joseph (1824–93), Maria Agnes (1826–1907), and Frank (1828–66); emigrated (1833) to America; settled (1840) in Cincinnati.

C Mersman (also Mersmann), Henry. 1820–64. b. Damme, Oldenburg. Tobacconist; son of Frederick Mersman; JJM's brother; emigrated (1833) with family; came to Cincinnati (by 1840); conducted (1842–61) a retail tobacco business, (Anthony) Nulsen & Mersman, then continued alone; m. (1842) Maria Imsicke, from Damme; m. (1845) Adelaide Tebbelman (1828–81), from Bremen; father of Josephine (1846–91), Ferdinand (b. 1852), Charles (1856–82), John Henry (1858–62), Augusta (b. 1861), and Henry (b. 1864). Residence: (1847) Center Street between Race and Elm streets; (1848) Main Street between Sixth and Seventh streets (CCD 1840, 284; CCD 1849–50, 197; DUN Ohio, 78:181; HCMR, A9:411, A14:75; USC 1850, M432, roll 687, page 134, line 10).

C Metropolitan Bath House. Proprietors, Jackson and Ophof. Public bathing facility; west side of Sycamore Street between Fourth and Fifth streets (Cist [3], 167).

C Meyer & Becker. Proprietors, William C. Meyer (b. circa 1824, Germany) and Charles F. Becker. Tobacco and cigars; corner of Third and Walnut streets (CCD 1848–49, 57; USC 1850, M432, roll 688, page 363, line 26).

C Miami and Erie Canal. Built 1825–45; connected the Ohio River to Lake Erie, cutting Cincinnati in half and defining distinct communities; remained operational until drained (1919), creating Central Parkway (Cist [3], 131–32; Wimberg, 70).

Mill Creek, Ohio. Population: 6,287. Hamilton County. A town immediately west of Cincinnati which took its name from a small river (COM, 20 March 1848; GAZ, 223).

Minster, Ohio. Population: 428. Auglaize County. Founded in 1832 by Oldenburg immigrants, who called it Stallotown; one hundred miles north of Cincinnati (GAZ, 226; DeBow [2], 820).

S Missouri Hotel. Proprietor, A. C. Peckham. Large hotel; southwest corner of Main and Morgan (SLD 1852, 177).

S Mitchell, Mr. Defendant in *Newburg v. Mitchell* (1849). No records have been found.

S Miller (or Mueller) Christian. b. Germany. Partner of Julius Busch in a liquor business (1850); dissolved by 1852 (DUN Missouri, 36:234).

Mobile, Alabama. Population: 20,515. Seat of Mobile County; 1,600 miles from Cincinnati via water using the Ohio River, the Mississippi River, and the Gulf of Mexico (Andriot, 9).

S Mochel, Louis. c. 1820–56. b. France. Barkeeper (St. Louis Hall); corner of Broadway and Biddle Street; business partner of Charles Louis Horn (St. Louis City Probate Court, Estate #4789; SLD 1852, 178; USC 1850, M432, roll 418, page 352, line 11).

C Moffitt, Rev. John. c. 1812–? b. Pennsylvania. Methodist minister (USC 1850, M432, roll 693, page 371, line 42).

C Monfort (also Monfred and Monfrod), Mr. Medical student who left Cincinnati (c. 1848) after becoming a physician.

S Montezano (also Montesano) House. Proprietor, John H. Corl. Hotel, six miles south of St. Louis, on a bluff 115 feet above the Mississippi River; featured a tower, gardens, and orchards; burned November 1849 (REV, 10 June 1849, 24 August 1849).

Monplaisir (also Montplaisir), Hyppolyte. 1821–77. b. France. Dancer, choreographer, and founder (with his wife, Adéle) of the Monplaisir Troupe; toured (1847–53) the United States (ANY, V:412, 428–29, 560).

C Moor, Augustus. 1814–83. b. Leipzig. Proprietor of Moor's Pleasure Garden, corner of Main and Liberty streets; immigrated to America (1831); arrived in Cincinnati (1838); opened (1845) a combination beer garden, bathhouse, restaurant, and billiard parlor (USC 1850, M432, roll 691, page 174, line 38; Wimberg, 60).

C Mosher's Boarding House. Proprietor, Elizabeth Mosher (also Mozier, Mosser, Mosier, and Moser) (1804–80, b. New York), widow of Stephen Mosher, apothecary; mother of Mary, Libby, and Hannah. Roominghouse on Third Street between Walnut and Vine streets (CCD 1843, 252; CCD 1856, 195; USC 1850, M432, roll 687, page 125, line 10).

C Moulinier, Charles (or Charley) P. c. 1823–? b. Italy. Language teacher and merchant; emigrated to Cincinnati (by 1840); clerked (1849) for Edmund Dexter; opened (by 1855) a grocery business styled as Moulinier & (Charles W.) Rowland; married (c. 1850) Helen; father of Josephine, William, Helen, and Charles. Residence: (1848) east side of Elm Street between Third and Fourth streets (CCD 1840, 296; CCD 1842, 26; CCD 1849–50, 207; DUN Ohio, 78:219, 220; HOC, 254; USC 1850, M432, roll 687, page 300, line 29; USC 1860, M653, roll 973, page 295, line 27).

C Moulinier, Josephine. 1800–? b. Italy. Mother of Charles Moulinier (USC 1860, M653, roll 973, page 295, line 32).

C Mount Adams. A hill east of downtown, originally called Mount Ida; renamed (1843) for John Quincy Adams, who attended the dedication of the Cincinnati Observatory.

C Mount Auburn. A hill two miles north of downtown; established as a village (1792), annexed (1849) to Cincinnati (Goss, 531; WPA, 355).

C Mount Pleasant, Ohio. Population: 755. Hamilton County. A town ten miles north of downtown; settled (1817); provided refuge from cholera; renamed (1893) Mount Healthy; incorporated (early 1900s) (Goss, 533; DeBow [2], 370; www.mthealthy.org; www.ohiohistorycentral.org).

Mowatt, Anna Cora (née Ogden). 1819–70. b. France. Actor, novelist, and playwright; immigrated (1825) to America; m. (1834) James Mowatt; debuted (1845) in New York; performed in the U.S. and England; retired in 1854 (ANY, 5: 249–50, 323–24; ENQ, 27 April 1847; HAS, 253–54).

C Mulholland, Robert. c. 1810–? b. Ireland. Coffeehouse proprietor (Drayman's Hall); corner of Sycamore and Eighth streets (CCD 1849–50, 208; CCD 1850, 144;USC 1850, M432, roll 690, page 968, line 5).

S Mullen (also Mullan), Thomas. c. 1816–67. b. Ireland. Tobacconist; shop near N & M; 21 Washington Avenue between Main and Second streets (MOR, 4 March 1867; SLDR, 3:253; SLD 1850, 28; USC 1850, M432, roll 417, page 100, line 20).

Murdoch, James Edward. 1811–93. b. Philadelphia. Actor and elocutionist; performed throughout the United States; debuted (1856) in London (ANY, 5: 273; HAS, 254–55).

S Murray, Mr. Tobacconist; partner (1849) in Granger & Murray in Palmyra, Missouri.

C Napoleon Tavern. Proprietor, Valentine Daum. Boardinghouse and coffeehouse; south side of Second Street between Broadway and Ludlow streets (CCD 1848, 118).

C National Theatre. Proprietor, J. Bates. Manager, D. A. Sarzedas. Promoted (1837–71) as the "queen" of theaters in Cincinnati; featured touring actors and a resident company in popular productions; Sycamore Street between Third and Fourth streets (CCD 1848–49, 204; Green and Bennett, 36; HOC, 374).

New Albany, Indiana. Population: 8,180. Seat of Floyd County (Andriot, 225).

New Bremen, Missouri. See Bremen.

New Orleans, Louisiana. Population: 119,460. Seat of Orleans Parish. A city on the north bank of the Mississippi River, one hundred miles above the Gulf of Mexico and 1,185 miles below the mouth of the Missouri River (Andriot, 318).

S Newburg, Mr. Plaintiff in *Newburg v. Mitchell*, lost the case (1849). No records have been found.

Newport, Kentucky. Population: 5,895. Seat of Campbell County; directly south of Cincinnati and east of Covington, Kentucky (Andriot, 304; Goss, 529; DeBow [2], 371).

S Nohl, Charles F. c. 1826–95. b. Prussia. Clerk with Block & Evers; bought (1871) the business; founder of the Fourth National Bank of St. Louis (DUN Missouri, 3:123, 324; USC 1850, M432, roll 417, page 77, line 16).

C Nuilsen & Ficke. Proprietors, Francis Nuilsen and Herman Ficke. Cigars and tobacco. 233 Main Street (CVB, 13 June 1850; CCD 1848, 180).

C Nuilsen (or Nuelsen or Nulsen), Francis. 1809–63. b. Nörten, Hanover. Tobacconist; oldest son of Franz Christian Nulsen (1778–1843); brother of JCN; emigrated to Cincinnati (c. 1837); spelled his surname differently from other family members; established (1839) Nuilsen & Ficke; m. (1839) Dorothea Tice; father of Amelia (b. 1840), Dorothy (b. 1843), Francis (b. 1847), Augustus (b. 1848), and Emma (1853–54). Home (1849): Franklin Street between Main and Sycamore streets (CCD 1848–49, 180; CCD 1849–50, 216; DUN Ohio, 78:157, 80:114; HCMR, A8:90; USC 1850, M432, roll 690, page 834, lines 21–28).

C Nulsen (also Nuilsen), Anthony (also Tony, Toni, or Toney). 1821–1910. b. Nörten, Hanover. Tobacconist; third son of Franz Christian Nulsen (1778–1843); brother of JCN; immigrated to Cincinnati (1839); conducted a tobacco business (1842–61) with Henry Mersman styled as N & M; represented the Liggett-Meyers Co; *Liedertafel* member; m. (1844) Maria Risch; father of Anton Clemens (1845–94), Albert (1847–1903), Christopher (1849–52), Amelia (1851–58), Emma (1853–54), August (1855–56), Maria (1857–?), Bertha (1860–1926), Eugenia (1862–1953), and Alice (1864–1904). Home: (1848) 50 Milton Street; (1849) corner of Sycamore and Franklin streets (CCD 1849–50, 216; DUN Ohio, 78:142, 163, 194; USC 1850, M432, roll

690, page 833, line 4; HCMR, 13:368; Anthony Nulsen Family Bible in possession of Leif Nulsen, Indianapolis).

S Nuelsen, Henry. 1826–1911. b. Nörten, Hanover. Methodist clergyman; youngest brother of JCN; emigrated to America (1842); converted from Catholicism in Cincinnati (as his siblings—Francis, Amelia, and Philippina—had done); came to St. Louis (1844) as a preacher; returned to Germany (1851–89) as a missionary; father of Bishop John Louis Nuelsen (1867–1946) (Barclay, 985; Box 3–68, Folder 22, Nippert Collection).

S Nulsen, John Clemens. 1824–1906. b. Nörten, Hanover. Tobacconist; emigrated to Cincinnati (1842); worked for his brothers, Anthony and Francis; relocated to St. Louis, started (1845–47) Nulsen & (Frederick W.) Ficke; partnered (1849–64) with JJM in N & M; m. (1848) Albertine Creuzbauer; father of Caroline (1849–1908), Edmund (1851–51), Ottilia (1852–99), Albertina (1854–57), Anthony (1856–1938), Maximillian (1858–97), Estella (1860–1924), Alice (1862–1936), Julia (1865–1957), Francis (1867–1934), and Albert (1870–1942) (DUN Missouri, 36:24, 216; MOR, 3 June 1906; Stevens, 3:238–41; SLD 1848, 176).

C Nulsen & Mersman (Cincinnati). Proprietors, Anthony Nulsen and Henry Mersman. Cigars and tobacco; 210 Main Street between Fifth and Sixth streets (CCD 1848–49, 57).

S Nulsen & Mersman (St. Louis). Proprietors, JCN and JJM. Wholesale whiskey and tobacco merchants; 161 North Third Street between Washington and Green streets (SLD 1851, 262).

Nunn, Mrs. Thomas (Lucinda). Circus equestrian; appeared with Rockwell & Company (1848) and Stokes's Circus (1849); m. (1847) Thomas Nunn, a rider and equestrian director. See also Gossin, Mrs. (REV, 18 November 1847).

C O'Connor, Tim. Not identified.

C Oberdorf (also Obendorf), Franz Joseph Constantin. 1776–1860. b. Heidelberg. Botanical physician (used plant extracts to treat patients); came to America (1816); established (1833) a medical practice in Cincinnati, m. (1844) Jane Whitehouse. Office: Longworth Street, between Plum Street and Western Row (CCD 1849–50, 216; Klauprecht, 156; Juettner, 97–98).

C Observatory Hill. See Mount Auburn.

C Over-the-Rhine (also "Over-the-Canal"). A section of the city north of the Miami and Erie Canal where many German immigrants settled. The waterway was nicknamed the Rhine, and bridges connected the neighborhood to the rest of Cincinnati (Kenny, 129–36; Wimberg, 4).

Palmyra, Missouri. Population: 1,284. Seat of Marion County; eighty miles above St. Louis on the Mississippi River (GAZ, 280).

C Pantheon. Saloon; Fifth and Walnut streets (JJM diary, 12 March 1848).

C Pauck (or Pauk), Henry. Tobacconist and cigar maker; the father of several daughters (CCD 1849–50, 223).

C Pearl Street House. Proprietors, Noble and Duble. An older hotel located near the landing and railroad depots; site of a dinner (1849) for President-elect Zachary Taylor; northeast corner of Pearl and Walnut streets (CCD 1848–49, 121; Cist [3], 6).

S Peebles, Sam. Tobacco manufacturer (DUN Missouri, 41:145, 42:311).

S Peoples Theatre. A playhouse on the southeast corner of Third and Olive streets (SLD 1848, 316).

Peru, Illinois. Population: 4,500. La Salle County. A town 250 miles north of St. Louis on the Illinois River; the home (1849) of Ottilie Creuzbauer Rhodes, the sister of Albertine Creuzbauer Nulsen and Claudine Creuzbauer Mersman (DeBow [2], 375).

C Peters, William C. c. 1800–? Music publisher; retired in 1860 (CDT, 20 April 1866; DUN Ohio, 78:133, 169; USC 1850, M432, roll 687, page 176, line 5).

C Peters & Sons. Proprietors, William C. (father), William M., and Alfred C. Peters. Piano and sheet music stores; 50 West Fourth Street and 161 Walnut Street (CCD 1848–49, 141).

S Petri, Ignatius Antonius. c. 1811–73. b. Saxony. Physician who used botanical treatments; m. (1851) Leontine Herckenrath; father of Eugenia, Frederick, Arthur, and Theophile (City of St. Louis Probate Records, Estate #10696; MOR, 20 April 1873; SLD 1850, 89; USC 1860, M653, roll 652, page 234, line 26; WPO, 20 April 1873).

Piqua, Ohio. Population: 3,277. Miami County. A town eighty miles north of Cincinnati; platted (1807); boomed (1837) when the Miami and Erie Canal extended from Dayton (PIQ, 15 April 1848; Andriot, 621; GAZ, 292).

Piqua Hotel (or House). Provided lodging in Piqua, Ohio.

Pitt, Charles Dibdin. 1818–66. b. England. Actor; debuted (1847) in Philadelphia; performed Shakespeare in England and the United States (HAS, 291).

Pittsburgh, Pennsylvania. Population: 46,601. Allegheny County. A city three hundred miles west of Philadelphia and 470 miles above Cincinnati, at the head of the Ohio River, which is formed by the confluence of the Allegheny and Monongahela rivers (GAZ, 294; Klein, 409).

Placide, Henry (Harry). 1799–1870. b. Charleston, South Carolina. Actor; debuted (1823) in New York; played comic roles (ANY, 5:385, 424, 531, 561; HAS, 291).

C Planters House (or Hotel). Proprietor, J. A. Kline. Boardinghouse; southeast corner of Walnut and Court streets (CCD 1848–49, 120).

C Pöppelman, Henry. 1808–95. b. Prussia. High school teacher; *Liedertafel* member (HOC, 250; USC 1850, M432, roll 690, page 961, line 11; Dickoré, 280).

Polk, James Knox. 1795–1849. b. North Carolina. Governor of Tennessee (1839–41) before becoming the Democratic candidate for national office (1844); elected the eleventh United States president (1845–49) on a platform of territorial expansion; added over five thousand square miles to the country (DAB, 15:34–39).

Pope, Mrs. Coleman. 1809–80. b. Yorkshire, England. Actor; debuted in New York (1846); performed in major U.S. cities; played Lady Macbeth at the Astor Street Opera House (1849) opposite Macready (ANY, 5:270–271, 276, 482; HAS, 293).

Portland Canal. See Louisville and Portland Canal.

Portsmouth, Ohio. Population: 4,011. Seat of Scioto County, at the confluence of the Scioto and Ohio rivers; 115 miles above Cincinnati on the Ohio River (Andriot, 621; GAZ, 299).

C Post Office (Cincinnati). (1831–48) Third Street, between Main and Sycamore streets; relocated (1849) to the northwest corner of Fourth and Sycamore streets (Goss, 184).

S Post Office (St. Louis). 87 Chestnut Street (SLD 1848, vi).

C Potter, Dr. Joseph F. c. 1810–68. b. Massachusetts. Allopathic physician; office located on Sixth Street, between Main and Walnut streets (CCD 1849–50, 229; COM, 13 October 1868; USC 1850, M432, roll 687, page 75, line 19).

S Prairie House. Tavern with a racetrack; four miles west of downtown (Field, 164).

C Price, Mary. c. 1832–? Resident of Mrs. Jenkins's Boarding House.

C Pullan, Joseph. c. 1820–64. b. England. Grocer and commercial merchant; began partnership with George Hatfield, Thomas Brown, and his brother Richard Pullan, styled as Pullan, Hatfield & Brown; resident of Lodge's Boarding House (CCD 1846, 308; COM, 13 October 1864; USC 1850, M432, roll 687, page 300, line 27).

C Pullan, Mrs. Joseph (Elizabeth also Eliza). 1830–? b. Maine. Resident of Lodge's Boarding House (USC 1850, M432, roll 687, page 300, line 28).

C Purcell, Rev. John Baptist. 1800–83. b. Ireland. Roman Catholic clergyman; emigrated to America (1818); ordained (1826) in Paris; returned (1828) to the United States; appointed bishop (1833) and archbishop (1851) of Cincinnati; oversaw the construction of St. Peter in Chains Cathedral (CPP, 240–42; DAB, 15:266–68; HAS, 73, 84, 85).

Puthoff (also Putthoff), Francis Heinrich. b. Oldenburg. Tailor; emigrated to America (c. 1839); settled in Covington, Kentucky; borrowed money from JJM (Ostendorf 265, 266, 272; Kenton County Deed Records 3:290; 11:124).

C Puthoff (also Putthoff), Mary. 1829–60. b. Oldenburg. Daughter of Francis and Mary Puthoff (above entry), who emigrated c. 1839; m. (1848) Frank Hellebush; died following childbirth (VOL, 22 February 1860).

C Puthoff (also Putthoff), Frank (also Franck). 1820–1910. b. Oldenburg. Tailor; shop on Main Street (CFP, 24 April 1910; DUN Ohio, 79:74; Ostendorf, 273; USC 1850, M432, roll 690, page 926, line 7).

S Quarantine Island. A large sandbar south of St. Louis; used (1849) as an inspection site for incoming steamboats during the cholera epidemic. Physicians examined passengers and crew; ill ones were detained on the moored steamboat, *St. Louis.* By 1856, floods had washed the island south into Illinois (Primm, 155, 156).

Quincy, Illinois. Population: 6,902. County seat of Adams County. A town one hundred miles above St. Louis on the Mississippi River (Andriot, 193; GAZ, 304).

C Rebstock's Coffee House. Proprietor, Charles (or Carl) Rebstock (1817–61, b. Germany). Provided food, drink, and lodging in the Over-the-Rhine neighborhood; northwest corner of Fifteenth and Vine streets (CCD 1848–49, 121; DUN Missouri, 37:455, DUN Ohio, 78:189; USC 1850, M432, roll 691, page 94, line 23).

C Rehfus & Kolb. Proprietors, Germans Louis Rehfus (also Rohfuss and Rehfus) (1806–55) and Charles M. Kolb. Wholesale drug business (1838–54); southwest corner of Fifth and Vine streets (CCD 1848–49, 84; DUN Ohio, 78:132; Leonard 684–685; HOC, 137; USC 1850, M432, roll 689, page 235, line 6).

S Reichert, Mr. Proprietor of a bar (1853).

S Reinbold, Andrew. c. 1816–? b. Germany. Tailor; specialized in regalia (principally Masonic and Odd Fellows); lost his shop at 65 Olive Street to fire (1856); closed business (1860) (DUN Missouri, 36:268; USC 1850, M432, roll 417, page 10, line 12).

Reinhardt, Mr. Proprietor of a liquor store in Madison, Indiana; Edmund Dexter's customer.

C Richards, W. T. "Uncle Dick." c. 1774–? b. New York. Dancing teacher and bandleader who organized public balls; known widely as "Uncle Dick" (COM, 17 April 1848; ENQ, 18 October 1847, 22 February 1848; USC 1850, M432, roll 687, page 170, line 15).

C Rittmeyer, August. 1824–? b. Nörten, Hanover. Laborer and store clerk; worked at N & M (Cincinnati) and N & M (St. Louis) (USC 1850, M 432, roll 417, page 23, line 21).

S Robbins's Restaurant. Proprietor, Elihu H. Robbins (1807–54). Fashionable eating place; 45 Fourth Street between Chestnut and Pine; opposite Planters House (SLD 1851, 388; DUN Missouri, 36:297; SLDR, C:195; USC 1850, M432, roll 416, page 390, line 18).

S Rose, William. ?–1876. Copper, brass, tin, and sheet-iron worker; made distillery equipment; Second Street between Almond and Poplar streets (SLD 1851, 295; St. Louis City Probate Court, Estate #12,248; DDT, 11 September 1847).

S Rosenfeld, Abraham. Clerk in N & M's store.

C Rosenfeld (also Rosenfeldt), Henry. c. 1820–? b. Germany. Actor at the German Theatre (USC 1850, M432, roll 690, page 961, line 5).

C Ross's Boarding House. Proprietor, Abner L. Ross (b. 1810, Ohio). Boardinghouse where JJM resided for eight weeks; south side of Third Street between Sycamore and Broadway streets (CCD 1849–50, 244; USC 1850, M432, roll 687, page 444, line 1).

C Runge, William. fl. 1848. b. Germany. Vocalist; director of the *Liedertafel* (ENQ, 4 April 1848).

C Ruhl (also Rule), Peter. *Liedertafel* member (CVB, 23 December 1848).

Runnels, Burnell R. 1826–1908. b. Georgia. Acrobat and equestrian; performed (1837–76) with Rockwell & Company's Circus and other shows (Slout, 262).

C Runnels, Mrs. Burnell R. Homemaker; wife of performer (see above).

S Russell, Samuel. c. 1802–59. b. Pennsylvania. Wholesale grocer and commission merchant; partnership (1837–?) styled as Russell & (William) Bennett (DUN Missouri, 36:178, 441; USC 1850, M432, roll 415, page 217, line 14; SLD 1851, 297; St. Louis City Probate Court, Estate #5600).

S Sanders, Rufus K. Attorney; office southwest corner Third and Pine streets (SLD 1852, 223).

C Sarcedas (or Sarzedas), David Augustus. fl. 1827–47. Actor and stage manager; debuted (1827) in New York; managed the National Theatre (1847) and a New Orleans theater (ENQ, 18 September 1847; HAS, 324).

C Scheidler (also Sheidler), George Valentine. c. 1810–49. b. Germany. Vocalist; first director of the *Liedertafel* (CCD 1846, 331).

C Scheidler (also Sheidler), Mrs. George (Bertha). fl. 1847–48. b. Germany. Vocalist.

C Schrader, Herman. Partner of Charles Storch; importer of French, German, and English fancy goods; 66 Main Street (CCD 1853, 343).

C Scott, E. c. 1808–71. b. Virginia. Farmer in Columbia Township, Hamilton County; father of five (CDT, 7 July 1871; USC 1850, M432, roll 685, page 150, lines 13–19).

Scott, John Randolph. 1808–56. b. Philadelphia. Actor; appeared in England and many U.S. cities (ANY, 5:455, 458, 537; HAS, 327).

C Second Ward House. Proprietor, Frederick Honkomp. Tavern; south side of Fifth Street between Race and Elm streets (CCD 1848–49, 119).

S Sells (also Sels), Charles M. Tobacconist; shop at 10½ Green Street; arrested for grand larceny in August 1849 (REV, 20 August 1849; SLD 1848, 208).

C Selves, George. c. 1814–62. b. England. Tavern keeper (St. Charles Exchange and Restaurant); south side of Third Street between Main and Walnut streets (COM, 7 October 1862; CCD 1848–49, 65).

S Senden, John D. 1829–73. b. Hanover. Merchant; immigrated to America (1846) with his parents; came to St. Louis (1849); clerked for Busch & Wissman; opened (1857) a liquor and tobacco business styled as (Henry W.) Wissman & Senden; father of eight children (ANZ, 10 June 1873; DUN Missouri, 36:243; GLO, 10 June 1873).

C Shires Garden and Theatre. Entertainment center; northwest corner of Third and Vine streets; destroyed (1848) by fire (CCD 1846, 330; HOC, 374).

C Shotwell, Theodore. c. 1826–? b. Ohio. Dry goods salesman with Winston & Co. (DUN Ohio, 79:14; USC 1850, M432, roll 687, page 896, line 36).

S Sickendick (also Siekendick), John Henry. d. 1854. b. Germany. Confectioner; business styled as Erfort & Sickendick, corner of Broadway and Morgan (DUN Missouri, 36:347; SLD 1853, 101).

S Sleeth, Hiram H. "High." c. 1829–? and William "Billy." c. 1827–? b. Indiana. Merchant tailors; brothers; specialized in gentleman's clothing; migrated (1849) from Cincinnati to St. Louis; witnessed (1865) JJM's naturalization (DUN Missouri, 38:257; USC 1850, M432, roll 417, page 278, lines 6–7).

C Sofge (also Softge), Professor Henry E. 1815–95. b. Germany. Flutist and music teacher; established the Cincinnati Academy of Music; performed with Ablamowicz, Tosso, and others (COM, 5 January 1895; USC 1850, M432, roll 687, page 49, line 37).

C Sportsman's Hall. Proprietor, John B. Ganter. Popular tavern and hotel; south side of Front Street between Fulton Street and the Columbia Township Line (CCD 1849–50, 109).

C St. Charles Exchange Hotel. Proprietors, George Selves and John Roth. Third Street between Main and Sycamore streets (CCD 1849–50, 248).

C St. Joseph Church. Roman Catholic. Built in 1846; the congregation grew rapidly, and a new church was built in 1848; corner of Linn and Laurel streets (Lamott, 141).

St. Louis, Missouri. Population: 77,860. St. Louis County. A city seven hundred miles from Cincinnati, via the Ohio and Mississippi rivers.

C St. Peter in Chains Cathedral. Roman Catholic; completed (1845) under the direction of Archbishop Purcell; the church derived its name from a painting by the artist Murillo; southeast corner of Plum and Eighth streets (National Register of Historic Places Inventory Nomination Form, Cincinnati Preservation Association, 1960).

C St. Philomena Church. Roman Catholic. Cornerstone laid (1846); served a German-speaking congregation; north side of Congress Street between Pike and Butler streets (Lamott, 335; CCD 1853, 920).

C Stallo, John Bernhard. 1823–1900. b. Damme, Oldenburg. Attorney; nephew of Franz Stallo (1798–1833), the founder of Stallotown (now Minster, OH); emigrated (1839) to Cincinnati; served as lawyer (1849–85), judge (1853–55), and U.S. ambassador (1885) to Italy (HOC, 143–146; USC 1850, M432, roll 691, page 57, line 20).

S Stein, S. Importer of cigars and tobacco; store at 99 North First Street (DUN Missouri, 36:159; SLD 1848, 220).

Stokes, Spencer Q. 1819–88. b. Cincinnati, Ohio. Horse trainer and showman; managed (1848) Rockwell & Company's Circus; then owned shows of his own (Slout, 292).

Strakosch, Maurice. 1825–87. b. Butschowitz, Moravia. Pianist and composer; debuted (1848) in America; performed in major cities; managed soprano Adelina Patti (HAS, 352).

Stratton, Charles Sherwood (General Tom Thumb). 1838–83. b. Connecticut. A celebrated small person (3 feet 4 inches) promoted by P. T. Barnum (1810–91) beginning in 1842 (ANY, 5:421, 507; Barnum, 48–57; DAB, 18:126–127; HAS, 361; Slout, 302).

C Storch, Charles. c. 1821–89. b. Germany. Importer of French, German, and English fancy goods; shop on Main Street (CCD 1849–50, 275; COM, 18 October 1889; DUN Ohio, 78:158; USC 1850, M432, roll 690, page 1002, line 22).

C Sycamore Hill. At the north end of Sycamore Street in Cincinnati, the road had a steep grade, so locals referred to the elevation in this manner.

C Tappe, Fritz. 1811–59. b. Germany. Clock- and watchmaker; made musical instruments; *Liedertafel* founder (CCD 1849–50, 279; Goss, 465; HOC, 450; Wimberg, 8; USC 1850, M432, roll 689, page 67, line 34; VOL, 9 August 1859).

Taylor, Zachary. 1784–1850. b. Virginia. Commander during the Mexican War (1845–47); national hero because of his military campaigns; elected the twelfth United States president (1849–50) as a Whig candidate; died in office (DAB, 18:349–50).

C Tebbelman, Albert. Cigar maker (CCD 1850–51, 117, 267).

C Tebbelman (also Tebelmann), John. 1826–85. b. Hanover. Tobacconist; firm styled as Grothaus & Tebbelman (CFP, 3 November 1885; USC 1850, M432, roll 688, page 321, line 6; Dickoré, 281).

C Tebbelman, Margaret (or Margarethe). b. Germany. Sister of Adelaide Tebbelman Mersman, Henry Mersman's wife. Probably a sister of John and Albert Tebbelman.

C Theising (also Tiesing), Ernst. b. Germany. Merchant; hardware business styled (1848–53) as Theising & (Francis L.) Evans; divorced (1853) by his wife (CCD 1849–50, 281; DUN Ohio, 78:70, 80:18).

S Thompson, Alexander M. c. 1823–54. b. Ohio. Attorney; firm of Thompson & Cline at 92 Chestnut Street (St. Louis Circuit Court Attorney Roll Book, 1:133; SLD 1851, 343; USC 1850, M432, roll 416, page 387, line 2).

C Thompson, Jacob. c. 1813–? b. Denmark. Hotel proprietor (Louisiana House); inn at 22 Sycamore Street catered to boatmen (USC 1850, M432, roll 687, page 242, line 11).

C Thompson, Peter. c. 1799–? b. Scotland. Tavern proprietor (Thompson's Coffee House); southwest corner of Third and Walnut streets (CCD 1848–49, 66; USC 1850, M432, roll 688, page 364, line 21).

C Töppelman, Albert. Merchant; partner of Mr. Grothaus in Chicago, Illinois. Possibly the same person as Albert Tebbelman.

C Tosso, Joseph. 1803–87. b. Mexico. Musical instrument maker; violinist trained in Italy and France; music professor at the Cincinnati Female Academy (1829); conductor of a community orchestra (1835–40); proprietor of a shop on Longworth between Plum and Western Row (CCD 1848–49, 141; COM, 7 January 1887; Goss, 453–465).

Troisgross & Lampré. Proprietors, Eugene Troisgross (d. 1888) and François Lampré (c. 1801–60). Wholesale grocers; French immigrants; had an extensive trade with Cuba; located at 26 Old Levee in New Orleans; retired (1852) (DUN Louisiana, 9:296).

Troy, Ohio. Population: 1,956. Seat of Miami County; founded (1807) near the Great Miami River; seventy miles north of Cincinnati (Andriot, 622; GAZ, 359).

Tryon, John. c. 1800–76. b. New York, New York. Showman, agent, and writer; proprietor (1843–47) of Tryon's Circus (Parkinson, 396; Slout, 306).

C Ulrich, August. c. 1821–94. b. Germany. Clerk, then proprietor, of a dry goods store; immigrated to U.S. (1837); failed (1856); began a coffeehouse (DUN Ohio, 79:109).

C "Uncle Dick." See Richards, W. T.

Underwood, Charles. Friend with whom JJM corresponded (1848–49).

c United States Hotel. Proprietors, Albert Wetherbee and Sweney. Hotel with 150 rooms and an attractive bar; southwest corner of Walnut and Sixth streets (CCD 1848–49, 122).

c United States Tavern. Proprietor, John A. Kreis. Saloon. South side of Fifth Street between Walnut and Vine streets (CCD 1848–49, 120).

Van Buren, John. 1810–66. b. New York. Lawyer, politician, and son of Martin Van Buren; helped organize the Free-Soil Party and persuaded his father to accept their nomination for president in 1848; tireless campaigner (DAB, 19:151).

Van Buren, Martin. 1782–1862. b. New York. United States senator (1821–29), then governor of New York (1829–37); became the eighth United States president (1837–41); defeated by William Henry Harrison in 1840; lost the Democratic nomination to James K. Polk in 1844; ran as the Free-Soil presidential candidate in 1848, but lost the election to Zachary Taylor (DAB, 19:152–57).

Vandalia, Ohio. Population: 228. Montgomery County. A village sixty miles north of Cincinnati and ten miles north of Dayton (GAZ, 366; DeBow [2], 388).

s Vandemale (also Vandemal and V—e), Ferdinand. 1815–? b. France. Merchant; wholesale wines and liquors; emigrated (1849) with his wife, Marie Josephine, and children, Victor (1839–1909), Hortense (c. 1833–?), and Stephanie ("Fanny") (1835–?). Business: southwest corner of Third and Olive streets (DUN Missouri, 36:356; USC 1850, M432, roll 416, page 378, line 35).

c Vefean (also Vifean), Christian. Foreman for Edmund Dexter (CCD 1850–51, 277).

Vicksburg, Mississippi. Population: 3,678. Seat of Warren County. A town 480 miles below St. Louis on the Mississippi River (Andriot, 429; GAZ, 369).

s Vide Poche, Missouri. An early name for Carondelet, translated as "empty pockets." Early French settlers from this area often came to St. Louis without money, and the city folk looked on their poverty with scorn (Primm, 42; Tolzmann, 124; Stevens, 1:807).

c Vorrath, Madam. c. 1820–? b. Germany. Actor; performed German-language roles (USC 1850, M432, roll 691, page 25, line 5; VOL, 6 June 1850; COM, 11 June 1850).

c Waddle, James. Boarder at Ross's Boarding House (1849).

c Wagner (also Waggoner), Augustus. 1818–86. b. Hanover. Apothecary; immigrated (1842) with the Nulsen family; m. Philippina Nulsen two months later, thus became JCN's brother-in-law; father of Carl, George, Emma, Julia, Amelia, and Alfred. Business: corner of Main and Thirteenth streets. Residence: west side of Sycamore Street north of Thirteenth Street (CCD 1848–49, 85; DUN Ohio, 79:183; HCMR, A10:53; USC 1850, M432, roll 690, page 832, line 41).

C Wagner, Philippina (née Nulsen). 1818–1908. b. Nörten, Hanover. Sister of JCN; m. (1842) Augustus Wagner (see above).

C Walker, Timothy. 1806–56. b. Wilmington, Massachusetts. Prominent attorney, law professor, and judge of the Hamilton County Court of Common Pleas (CCD 1846, 380; http://virtualology.com/aptimothywalker1; USC 1850, M432, roll 685, page 71, line 14).

C Wardner, Mr. Resident of Mrs. Jenkins's Boarding House.

C Walnut Hills, Ohio. Small settlement three miles east of downtown; annexed 1850 (Goss, 530; WPA, 283).

S Walton House. Proprietor, Charles D. Walton (1815–55). Hotel and livery stable; Third Street between Olive and Locust streets (DEM, 31 August 1855; SLD 1847, 96; St. Louis City Probate Court, Estate #4609).

Warren, Mrs. fl. 1848. Actor; appeared at the National Theatre (COM, 23 March 1848).

C Water Works Office. Northeast corner Third and Vine streets; works on Front Street east of railroad depot (CCD 1849–50, 296).

C Watson's Bath House. A public bathing facility on the north side of Third Street between Main and Walnut streets (CCD 1848–49, 19).

C Wellman's Coffee House. Proprietor, Herman Wellman (1789–1860, b. Damme, Oldenburg). Tavern; Main Street between Thirteenth and Allison streets (CCD 1848–49, 66; COM, 23 January 1860).

C Werner, Mr. b. Germany. Pianist; performed with Germans (ENQ, 21 November 1848).

C Werner, Mrs. fl. 1848. b. Germany. Amateur vocalist.

S Wesselhoeft, Johann George. 1805–58. b. Germany. Proprietor of a German bookstore (1843–54); immigrated (1832) to America; helped establish Hermann, Missouri (DUN Missouri, 36:204; USC 1850, M432, roll 415, page 245, line 35; DDT, 6 July 1849).

Whareham (also Wharam), William (or Billiam). d. 1849. Actor (ANY, 5:36; HAS, 387).

C Wilkins, Mr. and Mrs. Residents of Jenkins's Boarding House (1848).

Wilkinson, Mrs. fl. 1848. Actor; performed in many tragedies (ANY, 5:273, 360).

C William Tell Restaurant. Proprietor, Frederick Diserens. An eatery named for a Swiss hero, on the south side of Fifth Street between Main and Walnut streets (CCD 1848–49, 63).

Wing and/or Winn, John. Not identified. May be one person or two.

S Wissman (also Wisemann), Henry W. c. 1820–? b. Baden-Baden. Merchant; wholesale liquor and tobacco; firm styled as Busch & Wissmann, 180 North Fourth Street (DUN Missouri, 36:243; SLD 1854–55, 208; USC 1850, M432, roll 415, page 200, line 1).

C Wood, Rev. James Frederick. 1813–83. b. Philadelphia. Roman Catholic priest; ordained (1844) bishop (1860) and archbishop (1875) of Philadelphia (Lamott, 352).

C Wulkop (also Woolkup), Leopold. c. 1825–? b. Germany. Tobacconist; partner of Casper Beneke (CCD 1849–50, 314; DUN Ohio, 78:78; USC 1850 M432, roll 686, page 250, line 35).

C Young Men's Mercantile Library Association. College Hall. A private library organized in 1835 and still active to this day; 1,100 members (1848); reading rooms, on Walnut Street between Fourth and Fifth streets, open six days, 8:00 a.m. to 10:00 p.m.; 10,000 volumes and numerous periodicals; sponsored lectures (CCD 1849–50, 316; COM, 1 February 1848; ENQ, 7 December 1847, 5 February 1848; Cist [3], 117).

SOURCES CITED

NATIONAL ARCHIVES (NA), WASHINGTON, DC

Textual Records

RECORD GROUP (RG) 15, RECORDS OF THE VETERANS ADMINISTRATION.

Mexican War Pension Records.
Civil War Pension Records.

RG 49, BUREAU OF LAND MANAGEMENT.

Government Land Office, St. Louis, Missouri, Land Case Files.
Government Land Office, Lima, Ohio, Land Case Files.

RG 94, RECORDS OF THE ADJUTANT GENERAL'S OFFICE, 1780–1917.

Records of Volunteer Soldiers who served during the Mexican War.

NATIONAL ARCHIVES (NA), COLLEGE PARK, MARYLAND

Textual Records

RG 101, Records of the Office of the Comptroller of the Currency, 1863–1981.
RG 241, Records of the Patent and Trademark Office.

NA MICROFILM PUBLICATIONS

RG 29, Records of the Bureau of the Census.

M704, 1840 Census (USC 1840), roll 399.
M432, 1850 Census (USC 1850), rolls 115, 415-418, 460, 552, 665, 685–91, 693, 711, 713.
M653, 1860 Census (USC 1860), rolls 225, 655, 976, 1306.
M593, 1870 Census (USC 1870), rolls 813, 1210, 1212, 1585.
T9, 1880 Census (USC 1880), rolls 237, 722, 1025, 1329.
T623, 1900 Census (USC 1900), rolls 894, 1339.
T624, 1910 Census (USC 1910), rolls 975, 979.

RG 36, Records of the United States Customs Service, 1820–c. 1891.

M255, *Passenger Lists of Vessels Arriving at Baltimore, 1820–91,* roll 3.
M596, *Quarterly Abstracts of Passenger Lists of Vessels Arriving at Baltimore, 1820–69,* rolls 2, 4.
M259, *Quarterly Abstracts of Passenger Lists of Vessels Arriving at New Orleans, 1820–1902,* rolls 16, 18.

RG 109, War Department Collection of Confederate Records.

M323, *Records of Confederate Soldiers Who Served in the State of Texas,* roll 235.
M324, *Records of Confederate Soldiers Who Served in the State of Virginia,* roll 396.

LIBRARY OF CONGRESS (LOC), WASHINGTON, DC

American Memory Homepage (http://memory.loc.gov/ammem). An American Ballroom Companion: Dance Instruction Manuals, ca. 1490–1920. Video Directory.
Map Collection.
Prints and Photographs Collection.

UNPUBLISHED PRIMARY RECORDS

Germany

Bistumsarchiv (Hildesheim). Baptism records, marriage records, death records.
Catholic Church Archives (Vechta). Baptism records, marriage records, death records.
Evangelisches Archiv (Karlsruhe). Baptism records, marriage records, death records.
Evangelische Archivstelle (Boppard). Baptism records, marriage records, death records.
Generallandesarchiv (Karlsruhe). Military records, death records, marriage records.
Landeshauptarchiv Koblenz. Tax records, marriage records, census records.
Rheinische Missions-Gesellschaft (Wuppertal). Manuscript documents, student records.
Staatsarchiv Oldenburg. Tax records, census reports, court records.
Staatsarchiv Osnabrück. Notary documents of Justus Graff.
Stadtarchiv Karlsruhe. City directories, public records.

California

San Diego Probate Court. Probate records.

Florida

Private collection of Alice Cromack (Holiday).

Illinois

Adams County Courthouse (Quincy). Probate records.
Illinois State University, Milner Library. Circus Collection.
LaSalle County Courthouse (Ottawa). Deed records.
Montgomery County Courthouse (Hillsboro). Deed records, marriage records.

Private collection of Bernice Seaverns Berth (Lake Forest).
St. Clair County Courthouse (Belleville). Deed records.
Oak Woods Cemetery (Chicago). Interment records.

Indiana

Indiana Historical Society. Vertical files.
Private collection of Leif E. Nulsen (Indianapolis).

Kansas

Kansas State Historical Society. Photograph collection.

Kentucky

Jim Beam Distillery (Clermont). Interview with Jerry Dalton, master distiller.
Kenton County Courthouse (Covington). Deed records, marriage records.
Kenton County Courthouse (Independence). Deed records, marriage records.
Kentucky Department for Libraries and Archives (Frankfurt). Deed records, marriage records.
The Filson Club Historical Society. (Louisville). Vertical files.

Louisiana

Jefferson Parish Archives. Marriage records.

Massachusetts

American Antiquarian Society. Handbill collection.
Harvard Business School, Baker Library. R. G. Dun & Company Collection (DUN).
Harvard University, Houghton Library. Theatre Collection.
Harvard University Archives. Manuscripts.

Missouri

Ancient Free and Accepted Masons, Grand Lodge of Missouri (Columbia). Membership records, annual reports.
Bellefontaine Cemetery (St. Louis). Interment records.
Calvary Cemetery (St. Louis). Interment records.
City of St. Louis Court Archives. Circuit Court records.
City of St. Louis Department of Health. Birth records.
City of St. Louis Public Library. J. C. Strauss Portrait Collection.
Gasconade County Archives and Record Center (Hermann). Probate records.
Jefferson County Courthouse (Hillsboro). Deed records, marriage records.
Missouri Historical Society (MHS).
Business Letterheads Collection.
City of St. Louis Committee of Public Health, Minutes, 1849.
Dexter P. Tiffany Collection.
Joseph Nuelsen's Tagebuch, 1833-1839.

Joseph J. Mersman Diary, 1847-1864.
Ludwig Jacoby File. Vertical files.
Minutes of the Missouri Historical Society.
Robert A. Barnes Papers.
St. Louis Clippings Scrapbook, vol. 5.
St. Louis Turnverein Records, vol. 9.
Theater Programs Collection.
William G. Pettus Papers.
Missouri State Archives (Jefferson City). Deed records.
St. Louis Civil Courts Building.
Circuit Court record books.
Court of Common Pleas record books.
Probate records.
St. Louis City Hall. Real estate tax records, deed records, marriage records.
St. Louis County Court Archives (Clayton). Probate records.
St. Louis County Library (SLCL).
St. Louis Death Register (SLDR).
St. Louis City Inquest Records.
Private collection of William E. Giraldin.

New Jersey

Atlantic County Courthouse (Mays Landing). Deed records.
Methodist Center, Drew University (Madison). Manuscripts.
New Jersey Division of Archives and Records Management (Trenton). Birth records, marriage records, death records.

New York

Green-Wood Cemetery (Brooklyn). Interment records.
Kings County Surrogate's Court (Brooklyn). Probate records.
New York Historical Society (Manhattan). Photograph collection.
New York Public Library for the Performing Arts (Manhattan). Vertical files.
Somers Historical Society (Somers). Broadside collection, photograph collection.

Ohio

Archives, St. Augustine Parish (Minster). Transcriptions by Rita and David Hoying.
Auglaize County Courthouse (Wapakoneta). Deed records, probate records.
Cincinnati Museum Center, Cincinnati Historical Society Library.
Collection of Joseph Donnelly, compiler.
Nippert Collection of German Methodism.
Hamilton County Courthouse (Cincinnati). Deed records, court records.
Hamilton County Government, William Howard Taft Center (Cincinnati). Marriage records, probate records, register of ministers' licenses, wills.
Historical Archives of the Chancery, Roman Catholic Archdiocese of Cincinnati (HAC). Baptism records, marriage records, death records.
St. John Cemetery (St. Bernard). Interment records.

Mercer County Courthouse (Celina). Deed records.
Miami County Courthouse (Troy). Deed records.
Montgomery County Courthouse (Dayton). Deed records.
Public Library of Cincinnati and Hamilton County.
Cincinnati Panorama of 1848.
Vertical files.
Zion Evangelical Church records.
Shelby County Courthouse (Sidney). Deed records.
Spring Grove Cemetery (Cincinnati). Interment records.

Pennsylvania

York County Heritage Trust (York). James W. Shettle Collection of Photographs.

Texas

Austin Public Library. Annals of Travis County, Annals of the City of Austin, Travis County deed records, tax records.
Private collection of JoAn Dreahn (Schulenberg).
Texas General Land Office (Austin). Land records, personnel records, map collection.
Texas Historical Commission (Austin). Vertical files.

Utah

Family History Library (FHL) (Salt Lake City).
Campbell County (Kentucky), Clerk of the County Court. Deeds 1795–1912. Microfilms 523792, 523793, 523795, 523799.
Evangelische Kirche, Durlach, Germany. Kirchenbuch, 1685–1761. Microfilms 1189374, 1189389.
Evangelische Kirche, Stadtkirche Giessen, Germany. Kirchenbuch, 1575–1875. Microfilm 1193406.
Evangelische Kirche, Militärgemeinde Karlsruhe, Germany. Kirchenbuch, 1754–1945. Microfilm 1189368.
First Presbyterian Church, Nokomis, Illinois. Session records, 1862–1920. Microfilm 1313849.
Holy Ghost Evangelical Protestant Church, St. Louis, Missouri. Church records, 1833–1961. Microfilms 1433231–1433236 and 1503026–1503029.
Katholische Kirche, Damme (AG Vechta), Germany. Kirchenbuch, 1650–1875. Microfilms 909909–909913.
Katholische Kirche, Nörten (Kr. Northeim), Germany. Kirchenbuch, 1645–1886. Microfilms 1258473–1258475.
Österreichische Armee. Feldsuperiorat Budapest (Pest), Hungary. Kirchenbuch, 1774–1916. Microfilm 1442890.
St. John's Unitarian Church, Cincinnati, Ohio. Church Records, 1822–1935. Microfilm 1510039.
St. Matthaeus German Evangelical Church, Cincinnati, Ohio. Church Records, 1843–1918. Microfilm 1548046.

Wisconsin

Circus World Museum and Library (Baraboo). Manuscripts, posters.

Wyoming

Buffalo Bill Cody Historical Center (Cody). Manuscripts.
Laramie County Clerk's Office (Cheyenne). Marriage records.
Wyoming State Archives (Cheyenne). Photograph collection.

NEWSPAPERS

ANZ	*Anzeiger des Westens*, St. Louis, Missouri
BDE	*Brooklyn Daily Eagle*, Brooklyn, New York
CDG	*Cincinnati Daily Gazette*, Cincinnati, Ohio
CDT	*Cincinnati Daily Times*, Cincinnati, Ohio
COM	*Cincinnati Daily Commercial*, Cincinnati, Ohio
CON	*Atlanta Constitution*, Atlanta, Georgia
COR	*Daily Courier*, Lafayette, Indiana
CVB	*Cincinnati Volksblatt*, Cincinnati, Ohio
DDT	*Die Deutsche Tribüne*, St. Louis, Missouri
DEM	*Missouri Democrat*, St. Louis, Missouri
DRA	*New York Dramatic Mirror*, New York, New York
ENQ	*Cincinnati Enquirer*, Cincinnati, Ohio
ERA	*St. Louis Daily New Era*, St. Louis, Missouri
FRE	*The Free Press Gazette*, Nokomis, Illinois
GLO	*Globe-Democrat*, St. Louis, Missouri
HAD	*Hermann Advertiser Courier*, Hermann, Missouri
HER	*Weekly Herald*, Welsburg, Virginia
INT	*The Intelligencer*, St. Louis, Missouri
LAN	*Louisville Anzeiger*, Louisville, Kentucky
LDC	*Morning Courier*, Louisville, Kentucky
LJO	*Louisville Journal*, Louisville, Kentucky
MAY	*Maysville Eagle Tri-Weekly*, Maysville, Kentucky
MDB	*Madison Daily Banner*, Madison, Indiana
MDC	*Madison Daily Courier*, Madison, Indiana
MOR	*Missouri Republican*, St. Louis, Missouri
MOR	*St. Louis Republican*, St. Louis, Missouri
MOR	*St. Louis Republic*, St. Louis, Missouri
NAD	*New Albany Democrat*, New Albany, Indiana
NAS	*Nashville Union*, Nashville, Tennessee
NDP	*Nashville Daily Press*, Nashville, Tennessee
NYC	*New York Clipper*, New York, New York
PIC	*Daily Picayune*, New Orleans, Louisiana
PIQ	*Piqua Register*, Piqua, Ohio
POD	*St. Louis Post-Dispatch*, St. Louis, Missouri
QUW	*Quincy Whig*, Quincy, Illinois
REV	*The Daily Reveille*, St. Louis, Missouri

SLU	*Daily Union*, St. Louis, Missouri
TAG	*Karlsruher Tageblatt*, Karlsruhe, Germany
TEL	*Missouri Telegraph*, Jefferson City, Missouri
VOL	*Volksfreund*, Cincinnati, Ohio
WAS	*Washington Post*, Washington, D. C.
WPO	*Die Westliche Post*, St. Louis, Missouri
ZAN	*Zanesville Courier*, Zanesville, Ohio

PUBLISHED SOURCES

Adler Adler, Jeffrey S. *Yankee Merchants and the Making of the Urban West: The Rise and Fall of Antebellum St. Louis.* New York: Cambridge University Press, 1991.

Anbinder Anbinder, Tyler. *Five Points: The 19th-Century New York City Neighborhood That Invented Tap Dance, Stole Elections, and Became the World's Most Notorious Slum.* New York: Plume, 2002.

Andriot Andriot, John L., ed. *Population Abstract of the United States.* Vol. 1, *Tables.* McLean, VA: Andriot, 1983.

ANY Odell, George Clinton Densmore. *Annals of the New York Stage.* 15 vols. New York: AMS Press, 1970.

Arksey Arksey, Laura, Nancy Pries, and Marcia Reed. *American Diaries: An Annotated Bibliography of Published American Diaries and Journals.* 2 vols. Detroit: Gale Research, 1983.

Arrizabalaga Arrizabalaga, John, John Henderson, and Roger French. *The Great Pox: The French Disease in Renaissance Europe.* New Haven: Yale University Press, 1997.

Asche (1) Asche, Susanne, and Olivia Hochstrasser. *Durlach: Staufergründung, Fürstenresidenz, Bürgerstadt.* Karlsruhe: Badenia Verlag, 1996.

Asche (2) Asche, Susanne, Ernst Otto Bräunche, Manfred Kock, Heinz Schmitt, and Christina Wagner. *Karlsruhe: Die Stadtgeschichte.* Karlsruhe: Badenia Verlag, 1998.

Ashendel Ashendel, Anita. "Notorious Home of Harlotry: Regulating Prostitution in the Ohio Valley, 1850–1860." *Ohio Valley History* 3, no. 1 (2003): 17–30.

Augst Augst, Thomas. *The Clerk's Tale: Young Men and Moral Life in Nineteenth-Century America.* Chicago: University of Chicago Press, 2003.

Augustin Augustin, George. *History of Yellow Fever.* New Orleans: Searcy & Pfaff, 1909.

Bailey Bailey, Liberty H., and Ethel Zoe Bailey. *Hortus Third: A Concise Dictionary of Plants Cultivated in the United States and Canada.* New York: Macmillan, 1976.

Ballard Ballard, Edward, and Alfred Baring Garrod. *Elements of Materia Medica and Therapeutics.* London: Taylor and Walton, 1845.

Barclay Barclay, Wade Crawford. *History of Methodist Missions.* 6 vols. New York: Board of Missions and Church Extension of the Methodist Church, 1950.

Barnum Kunhardt, Philip B. Jr., Philip B. Kunhardt III, and Peter W. Kunhardt. *P. T. Barnum: America's Greatest Showman.* New York: Knopf, 1995.

Bartlett Bartlett, Vernon. *The Past of Pastimes.* London: Chatto & Windus, 1969.

Battistone Battistone, Betty Heis. *Hamilton County, Ohio, Burial Records.* Vol. 16, *Walnut Hills, 1843–1993.* Milford, OH: Little Miami, 2004.

Beach Beach, Wooster. *Beach's Family Physician and Home Guide for the Treatment of the Diseases of Men, Women, and Children, on Reform Principles.* Cincinnati: Moore, Wilstach, Keys, 1861.

Beadle Beadle. *Beadle's Dime Ballroom Companion and Guide to Dancing.* New York: Beadle, 1868.

Beaver (1) Beaver, Patrick. *Victorian Parlor Games.* Nashville: Nelson, 1974.

Beaver (2) Beaver, Patrick. *Victorian Parlour Games for Today.* London: Davies, 1974.

Bek (1) Bek, William G. *The German Settlement Society of Philadelphia and Its Colony, Hermann, Missouri.* Philadelphia: Americana Germanica, 1907.

Bek (2) Bek, William G. "The Followers of Duden." *Missouri Historical Review* 14, no. 1 (October 1919): 29–73; 14, no. 2 (January 1920): 217–32; 14, nos. 3–4 (April–July 1920): 436–58; 15, no. 3 (April 1921): 519–44; 15, no. 4 (July 1921): 660–99; 16, no. 1 (October 1921): 119–45; 16, no. 2 (January 1922): 289–307; 16, no. 3 (April 1922): 343–83; 16, no. 4 (July 1922): 523–50; 17, no. 1 (October 1922): 28–56; 17, no. 3 (April 1923): 331–47; 17, no. 4 (July 1923): 479–504; 18, no. 1 (October 1923): 36–54; 18, no. 2 (January 1924): 212–49; 18, no. 3 (April 1924): 415–37; 18, no. 4 (July 1924): 562–84; 19, no. 1 (October 1924): 114–29; 19, no. 2 (January 1925): 338–52.

Bethard Bethard, Wayne. *Lotions, Potions, and Deadly Elixirs: Frontier Medicine in America.* New York: Taylor Trade, 2004.

Boernstein Boernstein, Henry. *Memoirs of a Nobody: The Missouri Years of an Austrian Radical, 1849-1866.* Translated by Steven Rowan. St. Louis: Missouri Historical Society Press, 1997.

Borchers Borchers, Perry E., et al. *"The finest thing of its kind in America!": The Story of The Old Court House, Dayton, Ohio.* Dayton: Montgomery County Historical Society, n.d.

Bostwick Bostwick, Homer. *A Complete Practical Work on the Nature and Treatment of Venereal Diseases, and Other Affections of the Genito-Urinary Organs of the Male and Female.* New York: Burgess, Stringer, 1848.

Brewer Brewer, Ebenezer Cobham. *Brewer's Dictionary of Phrase and Fable.* London: Cassell, 1981.

Brockett Brockett, Oscar G. *History of the Theatre.* 8th ed. Boston: Allyn & Bacon, 1999.

Bucke Bucke, Emory Stevens, ed. *The History of American Methodism.* 3 vols. New York: Abingdon, 1964.

Bumstead Bumstead, Freeman. *The Pathology and Treatment of Venereal Diseases.* Philadelphia: Lea, 1874.

Burke Burke, Thomas Aquinas. *Ohio Lands: A Short History.* 8th ed. Columbus, OH: Auditor of State, 1996.

Burnett Burnett, Robyn and Ken Luebbering. *German Settlement in Missouri: New Land, Old Ways.* Columbia: University of Missouri Press, 1996.

Burnham Burnham, John C. *Bad Habits: Drinking, Smoking, Taking Drugs, Gambling, Sexual Misbehavior, and Swearing in American History.* New York: New York University Press, 1993.

Carnes Carnes, Mark C. *Secret Ritual and Manhood in Victorian America.* New Haven: Yale University Press, 1989.

Carroll Carroll, William F. "The Days of Wicked Jenny." *Westward* 10, no. 2 (May 1981): 7–11.

Carson Carson, Gerald. *The Social History of Bourbon: An Unhurried Account of Our Star-Spangled American Drink.* New York: Dodd, Mead, 1963.

CCD 1836-37 Williams. *The Cincinnati Directory for 1836–1837.* Cincinnati: Woodruff, Pugh, 1836.

CCD 1840 Schaffer, David Henry. *The Cincinnati, Covington, Newport, and Fulton Directory for 1840.* Cincinnati: Donogh, 1840.

CCD 1842 Cist, Charles. *The Cincinnati Directory for 1842.* Cincinnati: Morgan, 1842.

CCD 1843 ———. *The Cincinnati Directory for 1843.* Cincinnati: Brooks, 1843.

CCD 1846 Jones and Robinson. *Robinson & Jones' Cincinnati Directory for 1846*. 1st issue. Cincinnati: Robinson & Jones, 1846.
CCD 1848–49 Williams. *Williams' Cincinnati Directory and General Business Directory*. Cincinnati: Williams & Son, 1848.
CCD 1849–50 ———. Williams' Cincinnati Directory and General Business Directory. Cincinnati: Williams & Son, 1849.
CCD 1850 ———. *Williams' Cincinnati Almanac, Business Guide and Annual Advertiser*. 1st issue. Cincinnati: Williams, 1850.
CCD 1850–51 ———. *Williams' Cincinnati Directory and Business Advertiser for 1850–1851*. 2nd issue. Cincinnati: Williams, 1850.
CCD 1851–52 ———. *Williams' Cincinnati Directory and Business Advertiser for 1851–1852*. 3rd issue. Cincinnati: Williams, 1851.
CCD 1853 ———. *Williams' Cincinnati Directory, City Guide, and Business Mirror*. 4th issue. Cincinnati: Williams, 1853.
CHC Greve, Charles T. *Centennial History of Cincinnati and Representative Citizens*. Chicago: Biographical, 1904.
Chudacoff Chudacoff, Howard P. *The Age of the Bachelor: Creating an American Subculture*. Princeton: Princeton University Press, 1999.
Cist (1) Cist, Charles. *Cincinnati in 1841: Its Early Annals and Future Prospects*. Cincinnati: Morgan, 1841.
Cist (2) ———. *The Cincinnati Miscellany*. 2 vols. Cincinnati: Robinson & Jones, 1846.
Cist (3) ———. *Sketches and Statistics of Cincinnati in 1851*. Cincinnati: Moore, 1851.
Clark Clark, C. M., ed. *The Picturesque Ohio*. Clark's Guide-Books of the States Cities, and Picturesque Water-ways and Railroad Routes of the United States, 3rd Series, no. 1. Cincinnati: Cranston & Stowe, 1888.
Clason Clason, W. E. *Elsevier's Dictionary of Wild and Cultivated Plants in Latin, English, French, Spanish, Italian, Dutch, and German*. New York: Elsevier, 1989.
Clement Clement, Priscilla Ferguson. *Growing Pains: Children in the Industrial Age, 1850–1890*. New York: Twayne, 1997.
Coe Coe, Lewis. *The Telegraph: A History of Morse's Invention and Its Predecessors in the United States*. Jefferson, NC: McFarland, 1993.
Cohen Cohen, Patricia Cline. *The Murder of Helen Jewett*. New York: Vintage, 1999.
Cohen-Stratyner Cohen-Stratyner, Barbara Naomi. *Biographical Dictionary of Dance*. New York: Schirmer, 1982.
Cortinas Cortinas, J. V., Jr., and C. C. Robbins. "Winter Thunderstorms in the United States." Preprints, Sixteenth Conference on Weather Analysis and Forecasting, Phoenix, American Meteorological Society, 1997.
Cox (1) Cox, James. *Old and New St. Louis*. St. Louis: 1894.
Cox (2) ———, ed. *Notable St. Louisans in 1900: A Portrait Gallery of Men Whose Energy and Ability Have Contributed Largely Towards Making St. Louis the Commercial and Financial Metropolis of the West, Southwest and South*. St. Louis: Benesch Art, 1900.
CPP Joblin, M. *Cincinnati Past and Present: Its Industrial History as Exhibited in the Life-Labors of its Leading Men*. Cincinnati: Elm Street Printing, 1872.
Crowgey Crowgey, Henry G. *Kentucky Bourbon: The Early Years of Whiskeymaking*. Lexington: University Press of Kentucky, 1971.
CSIR Council of Scientific and Industrial Research. *The Wealth of India: A Dictionary of Indian Raw Materials and Industrial Products*, vol. 5. New Delhi: Council of Scientific and Industrial Research, 1959.

DAB Johnson, Allen, and Dumas Malone, eds. *Dictionary of American Biography.* 20 vols. New York: Scribner's Sons, 1928–36.

Dacus Dacus, J. A., and James W. Bell. *A Tour of St. Louis or the Inside Life of a Great City.* St. Louis: Western Pub., 1878.

Danholt Danholt, N., et al. "The Oslo Study of Untreated Syphilis: A Restudy of the Boeck-Brunsgaard Material Concerning the Fate of Syphilitics Who Receive No Specific Treatment." *Acta Dermato-Venereologica* 34 (1954): 34.

DeBow (1) DeBow, J. D. B. *The Seventh Census of the United States, 1850.* Washington, DC: Armstrong, 1853.

DeBow (2) ———. *Statistical View of the United States: Compendium of the Seventh Census.* Washington, DC: Senate Printer, 1854.

Dexter (1) Dexter, Charles. *In Memoriam.* 2nd ed. Cincinnati: Robert Clark & Co., 1891.

Dexter (2) Dexter, Charles. *Versions and Verses.* Cambridge: Sever & Francis, 1865.

Dexter (3) Dexter, & Sons. *The Newfoundland Bitter.* Cincinnati: Gibson & Co., 1869.

Diagram Diagram Group. *The Official World Encyclopedia of Sports and Games.* New York: Paddington, 1979.

Dickoré Dickoré, Marie. "Der Deutsche Pionier Verein von Cincinnati: Membership." Pts. 1 and 2. *Bulletin of the Historical and Philosophical Society of Ohio* 21, no. 3 (July 1963): 217–19; 21, no. 4 (October 1963): 278–82.

DNB *Oxford Dictionary of National Biography.* 60 vols. New York: Oxford University Press, 2004.

DoC U.S. Department of Commerce, Bureau of the Census. *Historical Statistics of the United States: Colonial Times to 1970.* 2 vols. Washington, DC: 1975.

Doctrines *The Doctrines and Discipline of the Methodist Episcopal Church.* New York: Lane, 1840.

Dormandy Dormandy, Thomas. *The White Death: A History of Tuberculosis.* New York: New York University Press, 1999.

Douglass Douglass, Paul F. *The Story of German Methodism: Biography of an Immigrant Soul.* Cincinnati: Methodist Book Concern, 1939.

Drake Drake, B., and E. D. Mansfield. *Cincinnati in 1826.* Cincinnati: Morgan, Lodge, & Fisher, 1827.

DTZ *Von Baltimore nach Bünde.* Bünde, Germany: Deutsches Tabak- und Zigarrenmuseum, n.d.

Dulles Dulles, Foster Rhea. *A History of Recreation: America Learns to Play.* 2nd ed. New York: Appleton-Century-Crofts, 1965.

Durang Durang, Charles. *The Fashionable Dancer's Casket, or, the Ball-Room Instructor: A New and Splendid Work on Dancing, Etiquette, Deportment, and the Toilet.* 1856. Bedford, MA: Applewood, 1997.

EAPH Finkelman, Paul, and Peter Wallenstein, eds. *The Encyclopedia of American Political History.* Washington, DC: C.Q. Press, 2001.

Earl Earl of Suffolk and Berkshire [Henry Charles Howard], Hedley Peek, and Frederick G. Alflalo, eds. *Encyclopaedia of Sport and Games.* Philadelphia: Lippincott, 1911.

Faust Faust, Albert Bernhardt. *The German Element in the United States.* Vol. 1. New York: Steuben Society of America, 1927.

FDS *Auf Auswandererseglern: Berichte von Zwischendecks und Kajütenpassagieren.* Führer des Deutschen Schiffahrtsmuseums no. 5. Bremerhaven: 1976.

Field Carson, W. G., ed. "The Diary of Mat Field." *Missouri Historical Society Bulletin* 5, no. 3 (April 1949): 157–65.

Fisher (1) Fisher, Linda A. "A Summer of Terror: The Cholera Epidemic of 1849." *Missouri Historical Review* 99, no. 3 (April 2005): 189–211.

Fisher (2) Fisher, Linda A., and Carolyn M. Bowers. *Agnes Lake Hickok: Queen of the Circus, Wife of a Legend.* Norman, OK: University of Oklahoma Press, forthcoming.

Fisher (3) Fisher, Linda A. "A Patient's Point of View: Nineteenth-Century Syphilis Treatment." *Documentary Editing* 25, no. 1 (Spring 2003): 15–32.

Flint Flint, Henry M. *The Railroads of the United States: Their History and Statistics.* 1867. New York: Arno, 1976.

Fournier Fournier, Alfred. *Syphilis and Marriage.* New York: Appleton, 1881.

Fox Fox, Charles, et al. *The Explosion of the Moselle.* Cincinnati: Flash, 1838.

Frost Frost, S. A. *Frost's Laws and By-Laws of American Society: A Condensed but Thorough Treatise on Etiquette and Its Usages in America, Containing Plain and Reliable Directions for Deportment in Every Situation in Life.* New York: Dick & Fitzgerald, 1869.

Gastright Gastright, Joseph. "Latonia Springs." In *Papers of the Kenton County Historical Society* 1:26–28. Covington, KY: 1990.

GAZ *Fanning's Illustrated Gazetteer of the United States.* New York: Phelps, Fanning, 1853.

Getz Getz, Oscar. *Pictorial History of Whiskey: From Colonial Times to the Civil War.* Chicago: Barton Distilling Associates, 1975.

Gilfoyle Gilfoyle, Timothy J. *City of Eros: New York City, Prostitution and the Commercialization of Sex, 1790–1920.* New York: Norton, 1992.

Godwin Godwin, Bette. "The Saint Louis Cholera Epidemic of 1849 as It Appeared in the Newspapers." MA thesis, St. Louis University, 1951.

Golder Golder, C., John H. Horst, and J. G. Schaal. *Geschichte der Zentral-Deutschen Konferenz.* Cincinnati: Jennings & Graham, 1906.

Goss Goss, Charles Frederic. *Cincinnati, The Queen City, 1788–1912.* 2 vols. Cincinnati: Clarke, 1912.

Grieve Grieve, Maud. *A Modern Herbal: The Medicinal, Culinary, Cosmetic, and Economic Properties, Cultivation, and Folk-Lore of Herbs, Grasses, Fungi, Shrubs, and Trees with All Their Modern Scientific Uses.* 2 vols. 1931. Reprint, New York: Dover, 1971.

Hall Hall, James. *The West: Its Commerce and Navigation.* Cincinnati: H. W. Derby, 1848.

Halttunen Halttunen, Karen. *Confidence Men and Painted Women: A Study of Middle-Class Culture in America, 1830–1870.* New Haven: Yale University Press, 1982.

Hansen Hansen, Marcus Lee. *The Atlantic Migration, 1607–1860.* Edited by Arthur M. Schlesinger. New York: Harper & Row, 1961.

HAS Brown, T. Allston. *History of the American Stage: Containing Biographical Sketches of Nearly Every Member of the Profession That Has Appeared on the American Stage, from 1733 to 1870.* New York: Blom, 1969.

Hemphill Hemphill, C. Dallett. *Bowing to Necessities: A History of Manners in America, 1620–1860.* Oxford: Oxford University Press, 1999.

Herbert Herbert, Jeffrey G. *Restored Hamilton County, Ohio, Marriages, 1808–1849.* 2 vols. Bowie, MD: Heritage Books, 1998.

Herz Herz, Walter. "Such a Glaring Inconsistency: The Unitarian Laity and Anti-Slavery in Antebellum Cincinnati." Cincinnati: First Unitarian Church, 2002.

Hill (1) Hill, Marilynn Wood. *Prostitution in New York City, 1830–1870*. Berkeley: University of California Press, 1993.

Hill (2) Hill, West T. *The Theatre in Early Kentucky*. Lexington: University Press of Kentucky, 1971.

Hinrichs Hinrichs, Ernst, and Christoph Reinders. "Zur Bevölkerungsgeschichte des Oldenburger Landes." In *Geschichte des Landes Oldenburg: Ein Handbuch*, edited by Albrecht Eckhard, 661–708. Oldenburg: Holzberg Verlag, 1987.

Hogan Hogan, John. *Thoughts about the City of St. Louis, Her Commerce and Manufactures, Railroads, etc.* St. Louis: Republican Steam Press, 1854.

Hollick Hollick, Frederick. *A Popular Treatise on Venereal Diseases*. New York: Strong, 1852.

Holmes Holmes, King K., et al., eds. *Sexually Transmitted Diseases*. 3rd ed. New York: McGraw-Hill, 1999.

Hoornstra Hoornstra, Jean, and Trudy Heath, eds. *American Periodicals, 1741–1900: An Index*. Ann Arbor, MI: University Microfilms International, 1979.

Holt Holt, Glen E. "The Shaping of St. Louis, 1763–1860." 2 vols. PhD dissertation, University of Chicago, 1975.

Hoying Hoying, Louis A., Rita M. Hoying, and David A. Hoying. *Pilgrims All: A History of Saint Augustine Parish, Minster, Ohio, 1832–1982*. Minster: St. Augustine Parish, 1982.

Hoyle Moorehead, Albert H., Richard L. Frey, and Geoffrey Mott-Smith. *The New Complete Hoyle*. New York: Doubleday, 1991.

Hulbert Hulbert, Archer Butler. *The Ohio River: A Course of Empire*. New York: Knickerbocker, 1906.

Hunter Hunter, Louis. *Steamboats on the Western Rivers*. Cambridge: Harvard University Press, 1949.

Hutchinson Hutchinson, Jonathan. *Syphilis*. New York: Funk & Wagnalls, 1913.

Hyde Hyde, William, and Howard L. Conard, eds. *Encyclopedia of the History of St. Louis*. New York: Southern History, 1899.

Isselbacher Isselbacher, Kurt, et al., eds. *Harrison's Principles of Internal Medicine*. 13th ed. New York: McGraw-Hill, 1994.

Jahn Jahn, Raymond. *Tobacco Dictionary*. New York: Philosophical Library, 1954.

Jennings Jennings, Dorothy. "The Pacific Railroad Company." *Missouri Historical Society Collections* 6, no. 3 (1931): 288–314.

Johns Johns, James H. *Bad Blood: The Tuskegee Syphilis Experiment*. New York: Free Press, 1993.

Johnson Johnson, Hugh. *The World Atlas of Wine: A Complete Guide to the Wines and Spirits of the World*. New York: Simon & Schuster, 1971.

Jones Jones, Robert Leslie. *History of Agriculture in Ohio to 1880*. Kent, OH: Kent State University Press, 1983.

Juettner Juettner, Otto. *Daniel Drake and His Followers: Historical and Biographical Sketches*. Cincinnati: Harvey, 1909.

Kamphoefner (1) Kamphoefner, Walter D., Wolfgang Helbich, and Ulrike Sommer, eds. *News From the Land of Freedom: German Immigrants Write Home*. Ithaca: Cornell University Press, 1991.

Kamphoefner (2) Kamphoefner, Walter D., Peter Marschalck, and Birgit Nolte-Schuster. *Von Heuerleuten und Farmern*. Bramsche: Landschaftsverband Osnabrücker Land e.V., 1999.

Kamphoefner (3) Kamphoefner, Walter D. *The Westfalians: From Germany to Missouri.* Princeton: Princeton University Press, 1987.

Kargau Kargau, Ernst D. *Mercantile, Industrial, and Professional St. Louis.* St. Louis: Nixon-Jones, 1902.

Kasson Kasson, John F. *Rudeness and Civility: Manners in Nineteenth-Century Urban America.* New York: Hill & Wang, 1990.

Kenny Kenny, Daniel J. *Illustrated Cincinnati.* Cincinnati: Clarke, 1875.

Kimmel Kimmel, Michael. *Manhood in America: A Cultural History.* New York: Free Press, 1996.

Klauprecht Klauprecht, Emile. *German Chronicle in the History of the Ohio Valley and Its Capital City Cincinnati in Particular.* Edited by Don Heinrich Tolzmann. Translated by Dale V. Lally Jr. 1864. Bowie, MD: Heritage, 1992.

Köllmann Köllmann, Wolfgang, and Peter Marschalck. "German Emigration to the United States." In *Dislocation and Emigration: The Social Background of American Immigration.* Vol. 7 of *Perspectives in American History,* edited by Donald Fleming and Bernard Bailyn. Cambridge: Harvard University Press, 1973.

Koon Koon, Helene, and Richard Switzer. *Eugène Scribe.* Boston: Twayne, 1980.

Kost Kost, John. *Elements of Materia Medica and Therapeutics: Adapted to the New Physiological System of Practice.* Cincinnati: Kost & Pool, 1849.

Kroll Kroll, Harry Harrison. *Bluegrass, Belles, and Bourbon: A Pictorial History of Whiskey in Kentucky.* South Brunswick, NJ: Barnes, 1967.

Kübler-Ross Kübler-Ross, Elisabeth. *On Death and Dying.* New York: Macmillan, 1970.

Kutler Kutler, Stanley I., ed. *Dictionary of American History.* New York: Scribner's Sons, 2003.

Lachs Lachs, Johannes. *Schiffe aus Bremen: Bilder und Modelle im Focke Museum.* Bremen: 1994.

Lammers Lammers, Robert J., ed. *Remembering . . . A Commemorative Look at Minster, Ohio, 1832–1982.* Minster: Midmark, 1982.

Lamott Lamott, John H. *A History of the Archdiocese of Cincinnati, 1821–1921.* New York: Pustet, 1921.

LCD 1848–49 Jegli, John B. *Directory for 1848–1849 in the City of Louisville.* Louisville, KY: John C. Noble, 1848.

LCD 1851–52 ———. *Directory for 1851–1852 in the City of Louisville.* Louisville, KY: Brennan, 1851.

Lemp Walker, Stephen P. *Lemp: The Haunting History.* St. Louis: Lemp Preservation Soc., 1988.

Leonard (1) Leonard, John W., ed. *The Book of St. Louisans.* St. Louis: St. Louis Republic, 1906.

Leonard (2) Leonard, Lewis Alexander, ed. *Greater Cincinnati and Its People: A History.* New York: Lewis Historical, 1927.

Levine Levine, Lawrence W. *Highbrow/Lowbrow: The Emergence of Cultural Hierarchy in America.* Cambridge: Harvard University Press, 1988.

Lloyd Lloyd, James T. *Lloyd's Steamboat Directory, and Disasters on the Western Waters.* Cincinnati: Lloyd, 1856.

Longfellow Longfellow, Henry Wadsworth. *Birds of Passage: The Courtship of Miles Standish, and Other Poems.* London: W. Kent, 1858.

Longstreet Longstreet, Abby Buchanan. *Cards: Their Significance and Proper Uses as Governed by the Usages of New York Society.* New York: Stokes, 1889.

Loomis Loomis, Linn. *Here and Now—Ohio's Canals: The Background of Ohio's Canal System.* Sugarcreek, OH: Schlabach, 2000.

Luebke Luebke, Frederick C. *Germans in the New World: Essays in the History of Immigration.* Chicago: University of Illinois Press, 1990.

Lytle Lytle, William M. *Merchant Steam Vessels of the United States, 1790–1868: "The Lytle-Holdcamper List," Initially Compiled from Official Merchant Marine Documents of the United States and Other Sources.* Baltimore: University of Baltimore Press, 1975.

Mallinckrodt Mallinckrodt, Anita M. *From Knights to Pioneers: One German Family in Westphalia and Missouri.* Carbondale: Southern Illinois University Press, 1994.

Manual *A Manual of Politeness, Comprising the Principles of Etiquette, and Rules of Behaviour in Genteel Society, for Persons of Both Sexes.* Philadelphia: Lippincott, Grambo, 1851.

Marks Marks, Anita S., and Mary H, Remler, eds. *Walnut Hills United Jewish Cemetery, 1850–2002.* Vol. 15 of *Hamilton County, Ohio Burial Records.* Milford, OH: Little Miami, 2003.

Marty Marty, Martin. *Dr. Johann Martin Henni, Erster Bischof und Erzbischof von Milwaukee.* New York: Benzinger Brothers, 1888.

Matthews Matthews, Brander, and Laurence Hutton, eds. *Actors and Actresses of Great Britain and the United States.* New York: Cassell, 1886.

McCusker McCusker, John J. *How Much Is That in Real Money? A Historical Commodity Price Index for Use as a Deflator of Money Values in the Economy of the United States.* Worcester, MA: American Antiquarian Society, 2001.

McPheeters McPheeters, William. "History of Epidemic Cholera in St. Louis in 1849." *St. Louis Medical and Surgical Journal* 7 (March 1850): 97–120.

Minnigerode Minnigerode, Meade. *The Fabulous Forties: 1840–1850.* Garden City, NY: Garden City, 1928.

Moltmann Moltmann, Günter, ed. *Germans to America: 300 Years of Immigration, 1683 to 1983.* Stuttgart: Institute for Foreign Cultural Relations, 1982.

Monzert Monzert, Leonard. *Monzert's Practical Distiller: An Exhaustive Treatise on the Art of Distilling and Rectifying Spirituous Liquors and Alcohol.* Bradley, IL: Lindsay, 1987.

Morris Morris, William W., and E. B. Krieger, eds. *The Bench and Bar of Cincinnati: Commemorating the Building of the New Court House.* Cincinnati: New Court House, 1921.

Morrow (1) Morrow, Prince A. *Atlas of Skin and Venereal Diseases.* New York: Wood, 1889.

Morrow (2) ———. *Social Diseases and Marriage: Social Prophylaxis.* New York: Lea Brothers, 1904.

Muehl Muehl, Siegmor. "Winegrowing in the Hermann Area: Early Year's Chronicle." *Missouri Historical Review* 87, no. 3 (April 1993): 233–52.

Natta Natta, Larry. *Canal Town: Ottawa and the Building of the Illinois and Michigan Canal.* Ottawa, IL: Ottawa Visitors Center, 2000.

Nelligan Nelligan, Moore. *Medicines, Their Uses and Mode of Administration.* 3rd ed. New York: Harper & Brothers, 1848.

Newton Newton, Sarah E. *Learning to Behave: A Guide to American Conduct Books before 1900.* Westport, CT: Greenwood Press, 1994.

Norris Norris, James D. *R. G. Dun & Co., 1841–1900: The Development of Credit-Reporting in the Nineteenth Century.* Westport, CT: Greenwood, 1978.

Oda Oda, James C., and Linda Grimes. *Piqua and Miami County: A Primer of Community History.* Piqua, OH: Miami Printery, 1991.

O'Conner O'Conner, Richard. *The German-Americans: An Informal History.* Boston: Little, Brown, 1968.

Olson Olson, Audrey L. *St. Louis Germans, 1850–1920.* New York: Arno, 1980.

Ostendorf Ostendorf, Johannes. *Zur Geschichte der Auswanderung aus dem alten Amt Damme (Oldb.), insbesondere nach Nordamerika, in den Jahren 1830–1880.* In *Oldenburger Jahrbuch,* vols. 46–47 (1942–43).

O'Suilleabhain O'Suilleabhain, Sean. *Irish Wake Amusements.* 1967. Cork, Ireland: Mercier, 1969.

Parker Parker, Langston. *The Modern Treatment of Syphilitic Diseases.* Philadelphia: Blanchard & Lea, 1854.

Parkinson Parkinson, Robert L. *Directory of American Circuses, 1793–2000.* Baraboo, WI: Circus World Museum, 2002.

Parlett Parlett, David. *The Oxford Guide to Card Games.* New York: Oxford University Press, 1990.

Peters Peters, Harry. *America on Stone.* New York: Doubleday, Doran, 1931.

PHS *Syphilis: A Synopsis.* U.S. Department of Health, Education, and Welfare. Public Health Service Pub. No. 1660. Washington, DC: USGPO, 1967.

Primm Primm, James Neal. *Lion of the Valley.* 3rd ed. St. Louis: Missouri Historical Society, 1998.

Pritchard Pritchard, John C. *The St. Louis Water Works: A History of a Century of Service.* St. Louis, 1933.

Pusey Pusey, William, "Syphilis as a Modern Problem." Journal of the American Medical Association Monograph. Chicago: AMA, 1915.

Quétel Quétel, Claude. *History of Syphilis.* Baltimore: Johns Hopkins University Press, 1990.

Quimby Quimby, Mildred. *Quimby's Harbor Guide.* St. Louis: Waterways Journal, 1984.

Randel Randel, Don Michael, ed. *The Harvard Biographical Dictionary of Music.* Cambridge: Belknap Press of Harvard University Press, 1996.

Rayner Rayner, John A. *The First Century of Piqua, Ohio.* 2nd ed. Piqua: Magee Brothers, 1967.

Reemelin Reemelin, Robert E. *Mad River Township (Dayton).* Vol. 1 of *Montgomery County, Ohio, Cemetery Burial Records.* Dayton: Ohio Genealogical Society, 2001.

Regan Regan, Gary, and Mardee Haidin Regan. *The Book of Bourbon and Other Fine American Whiskeys.* Shelburne, VT: Chapters, 1995.

Rippley Rippley, LaVern. *Of German Ways.* New York: Gramercy, 1986.

Roberts Roberts, Robert B. *Encyclopedia of Historic Forts: The Military, Pioneer, and Trading Posts of the United States.* New York: Macmillan, 1988.

Robins Robins, William, ed. *A Plot Against the People: A History of the Audacious Attempt by Certain Kentucky "Straight Whisky" Interests to Pervert the Pure Food Law in Order to Create a Monopoly for Their Fusel Oil Whiskies and to Outlaw All Refined Whiskies.* 3rd ed. New York: Hiram Walker & Sons, 1911.

Robinson Robinson, Gilbert. *Old Wagon Show Days.* Cincinnati: Brockwell, 1925.

Rodabough Rodabough, John. *Frenchtown.* St. Louis: Sunrise, 1980.

Roller Roller, Otto Konrad. *Die Einwohnerschaft der Stadt Durlach im 18. Jahrhundert.* Karlsruhe: Braunschen, 1907.

Rombauer Rombauer, Irma S., and Marian Rombauer Becker. *Joy of Cooking.* Indianapolis: Bobbs-Merrill, 1964.

Ronald Ronald, Bruce W., and Virginia Ronald. *Dayton: The Gem City.* Tulsa, OK: Continental Heritage, 1981.

Rorabaugh Rorabaugh, W. J. *The Alcoholic Republic: An American Tradition.* New York: Oxford University Press, 1979.

Roseboom Roseboom, Eugene H., and Francis P. Weisenburger. *A History of Ohio.* 2nd ed. Columbus: Ohio Historical Society, 1996.

Rotundo Rotundo, E. Anthony. *American Manhood: Transformations in Masculinity from the Revolution to the Modern Era.* New York: BasicBooks, 1993.

Ruth Ruth, John A. *Decorum: A Practical Treatise on Etiquette and Dress of the Best American Society.* Chicago: J. A. Ruth, 1877.

Ryan Ryan, Mary P. *Cradle of the Middle Class: The Family in Oneida County, New York, 1790–1865.* New York: Cambridge University Press, 1981.

Scarne Scarne, John. *Scarne's Encyclopedia of Games.* New York: Harper & Row, 1973.

Scharf Scharf, J. Thomas. *History of St. Louis City and County, from the Earliest Periods to the Present Day Including Biographical Sketches of Representative Men.* 2 vols. Philadelphia: Everts, 1883.

Scheiber Scheiber, Harry N. *Ohio Canal Era: A Case Study of Government and the Economy, 1820–1861.* Athens: Ohio University Press, 1989.

Schlumbohm Schlumbohm, Jürgen. *Lebensläufe, Familien, Höfe: Die Bauern und Heuerleute des Osnabrückischen Kirchspiels Belm in proto-industrieller Zeit, 1650–1860.* Göttingen: Vandenhoeck & Ruprecht, 1997.

Schmaul Schmaul, Helmut. *Verpflanzt, aber nicht entwurzelt: Die Auswanderung aus Hessen-Darmstadt (Provinz Rheinhessen) nach Wisconsin im 19. Jahrhundert.* Frankfurt: Peter Lang, 2000.

Schuster Schuster, Ludwig. *Wann dürfen Syphilistische heiraten?* Berlin: Schoetz, 1893.

Schworm Schworm, William B. *History of Water Supply in the St. Louis Area: St. Louis Water Works.* St. Louis, 1968.

Scribe Scribe, Eugène. *Le Marriage D'argent, Comedie en Cinq Actes et en Prose.* Paris: Bezou, 1828.

Shakespeare Shakespeare, William. *The Riverside Shakespeare.* Edited by G. Blakemore Evans. Boston: Houghton Mifflin, 1974.

Shoemaker Shoemaker, Floyd C. "Hermann: A Bit of the Old World in the Heart of the New." *Missouri Historical Review* 60, no. 3 (April 1957): 235–44.

Siepmann Siepmann, Katherine Baker, ed. *Benét's Reader's Encyclopedia.* 3rd ed. New York: Harper & Row, 1987.

Simmons Simmons, Amelia. *American Cookery.* 1796. Bedford, MA: Applewood, 1996.

Simpson Simpson, Matthew, ed. *Cyclopaedia of Methodism.* Philadelphia: Everts & Stewart, 1878.

SLD 1847 *St. Louis Business Directory for 1847.* St. Louis: 1847.

SLD 1848 Sloss, J. H. *St. Louis Directory for 1848.* St. Louis: Charles & Hammond, 1848.

SLD 1850 Taylor, J. N. *St. Louis Business Directory for 1850.* St. Louis: St. Louis Union Office, 1850.

SLD 1851 *Green's St. Louis Directory for 1851.* St. Louis: Charles & Hammond, 1850.

SLD 1852 *Morrison's St. Louis Directory for 1852.* St. Louis: Morrison, 1852.

SLD 1853-54 *St. Louis Directory for 1853.* St. Louis: Montague, 1853.

SLD 1854-55 *St. Louis Directory for 1854–1855.* St. Louis: Chambers & Knapp, 1854.

Slout Slout, William. *Olympians of the Sawdust Circle: A Biographical Dictionary of the Nineteenth-Century American Circus.* San Bernardino, CA: Borgo, 1998.

Sluyterman Sluyterman, Keetie E. and Huib H. Vleesenbeek. *Three Centuries of De Kuyper: A History of Geneva and Liqueurs, 1695–1995.* Schiedam: De Kuyper, 1995.

Smilax Smilax, Linnaeus. *Sarsaparilla, and Sarsaparilla So-Called: A Popular Analysis of a Popular Medicine.* London: Aylott, 1854.

Smith Smith, Cliff Neal. *Early Nineteenth Century German Settlers in Ohio.* McNeal, AZ: Westland, 1984.

Steele Steele, Robert W. and Mary Davies Steele. *Early Dayton.* Dayton, OH: Shuey, 1896.

Stevens (1) Stevens, Walter B. *St. Louis: The Fourth City, 1764–1909.* 3 vols. St. Louis: Clarke, 1909.

Stevens (2) ———, ed. *St. Louis: One Hundred Years in a Week.* St. Louis: St. Louis Centennial Association, 1909.

Stockman Stockman, R. L. *North Germany to North America: Nineteenth Century Migration.* Alto, MI: PlattDüütsch, 2003.

Stokes Stokes, John, Herman Beerman, and Norman Ingraham Jr. *Modern Clinical Syphilology.* 3rd ed. New York: Saunders, 1944.

Stott Stott, Richard B. *Workers in the Metropolis: Class, Ethnicity, and Youth in Antebellum New York City.* Ithaca: Cornell University Press, 1990.

Stowell Stowell, Daniel W. "Staggering Toward Reform: Temperance and Prohibition in Antebellum Illinois." Paper presented at the Illinois History Symposium, Springfield, IL, 1998.

Texas *The New Handbook of Texas.* 6 vols. Austin: Texas State Historical Association, 1996.

Thayer (1) Thayer, Stuart. *Traveling Showmen: The American Circus before the Civil War.* Detroit: Astley & Ricketts, 1997.

Thayer (2) ———. *Annals of the American Circus, 1793–1860.* Seattle: Dauven & Thayer, 2000.

Tolzmann (1) Tolzmann, Don Heinrich, ed. *The German Element in St. Louis: A Translation from German of Ernst D. Kargau's St. Louis in Former Years: A Commemorative History of the German Element.* Translated by William G. Bek. 1893. Baltimore: Genealogical, 2001.

Tolzmann (2) ———. *The German Immigrant in America: F. W. Bogen's Guidebook.* 1851. Bowie, MD: Heritage Books, 1992.

Trevorrow Trevorrow, Frank W. *Ohio's Canals: The Miami and Erie Canal.* Oberlin, OH: Frank W. Trevorrow, 1973.

Troy *Troy: The Nineteenth Century.* Troy, OH: Troy Historical Society, 1970.

Tucker Tucker, Frank C. *The Methodist Church in Missouri, 1798–1939.* Joint Committee of Historical Societies of Missouri East and the Missouri West Annual Conferences, 1996.

Tuttle Tuttle, Sam. *Manners and Morals of Yesterday.* Scotia, NY: Americana Review, 1994.

Tyrrell Tyrrell, Ian R. *Sobering Up: From Temperance to Prohibition in Antebellum America, 1800–1860.* Westport, CT: Greenwood, 1979.

Universal *Universal-Lexikon vom Großherzogthum Baden.* Karlsruhe: 1844.

van Ravenswaay (1) van Ravenswaay, Charles. *Saint Louis: An Informal History of the City and its People, 1764–1865.* Edited by Candace O'Connor. St. Louis: Missouri Historical Society, 1991.

van Ravenswaay (2) van Ravenswaay, Charles. "Years of Turmoil, Years of Growth: St. Louis in the 1850s," *Bulletin of the Missouri Historical Society* 23, no. 4, pt. 1 (July 1967): 303–24.

Voges Voges, Ernst, ed. *Tobacco Encyclopedia.* Mainz, Germany: Tobacco Journal International, 1984.

Walker (1) Walker, Mack. *Germany and the Emigration, 1816–1885.* Cambridge: Harvard University Press, 1964.

Walker (2) ———. *German Home Towns: Community, State, and General Estate 1648–1871.* Ithaca, NY: Cornell University Press, 1971.

Washington Washington, George, and Marvin Kitman. *George Washington's Expense Account.* New York: Simon & Schuster, 1970.

Watts Watts, Donald. *Elsevier's Dictionary of Plant Names and Their Origin.* New York: Elsevier, 2000.

Way Way, Frederick Jr. *Way's Packet Directory, 1848–1983.* Athens: Ohio University Press, 1983.

Webster Webster, Noah. *Webster's Dictionary: An American Dictionary of the English Language.* New York: Harper Brothers, 1844.

Weisert Weisert, John Jacob. *A large and fashionable audience: a checklist of performances at the Louisville Theatre, 1846 to 1866.* Louisville, KY: 1955.

Western *The Western Journal and Civilian* 7, no. 2 (November 1851), 146.

Wemyss Wemyss, Francis C. *Wemyss' Chronology of the American Stage, from 1752 to 1852.* 1852. New York: Blom, 1968.

Wheat Wheat, Carl I. *From the Mexican War to the Boundary Surveys, 1846–1854.* Vol. 3 of *Mapping the Transmississippi West.* 5 vols. San Francisco: Institute of Historical Cartography, 1959.

Wilcox Wilcox, Walter F., ed. *International Migrations.* 2 vols. New York: Gordon & Breach Science, 1969.

Williamson Williamson, C. W. *History of Western Ohio and Auglaize County.* Columbus, OH: Linn & Sons, 1905.

Wimberg Wimberg, Robert J. *Cincinnati: Over-The-Rhine.* 2nd ed. Cincinnati: Ohio Book Store, 1988.

Wittke Wittke, Carl. *William Nast: Patriarch of German Methodism.* Detroit: Wayne State University Press, 1959.

Wortley Wortley, Lady Emmeline Stuart. *Travels in the United States, etc. During 1849–1850.* London: Bentley, 1851.

WPA (1) Writer's Program of the Works Projects Administration (Missouri). *Missouri: A Guide to the "Show Me" State.* New York: Duell, Sloan & Pearce, 1941.

WPA (2) ——— (Ohio). *The WPA Guide to Cincinnati: A Guide to the Queen City and Its Neighbors.* 1943. Cincinnati: Scripps-Howard, 1987.

Wyman Wyman, Mark. *Immigrants in the Valley: Irish, Germans, and Americans in the Upper Mississippi Country, 1830–1860.* Chicago: Nelson-Hall, 1984.

Yater Yater, George H. *Two Hundred Years at the Falls of the Ohio: A History of Louisville and Jefferson County.* Louisville, KY: Filson Club, 1987.

Zaslaw Zaslaw, Neal. *The Compleat Mozart: A Guide to the Musical Works of Wolfgang Amadeus Mozart.* New York: Norton, 1990.

INDEX

Page numbers in italics refer to illustrations.

Dr. Linda A. Fisher, a Board-certified internal medicine physician, was researching historical documents for an article on the mid-nineteenth-century epidemic when she happened upon the diary of Joseph J. Mersman, stored in the files of the Missouri Historical Society. She was fascinated by the entries, and so began a nearly ten-year journey to learn about Joseph and about his life in the 1840s and 1850s. The end of her trek is this book, an edition of the Mersman diary with full references and commentary.

Sadly, Linda Fisher succumbed to a long-term heart disease and, following transplant surgery, passed away in January 2006, shortly after the completed manuscript was sent to the Ohio University Press. Her greatest work in life was as a physician and healer. Her greatest literary accomplishment is the volume you hold in your hand.

We miss her . . .